THE MAN IN THE WATER

THE
MAN
IN THE
WATER

Essays and Stories

Roger Rosenblatt

RANDOM HOUSE

NEW YORK

Library of Congress Cataloging-in-Publication Data

Rosenblatt, Roger.
The man in the water: essays and stories/by Roger Rosenblatt.
p.   cm.
Includes index.
ISBN 0-679-42693-0
I. Title.
PN4874.R595A5   1994   814'.54—dc20   93-5006

Manufactured in the United States of America on acid-free paper

24689753

FIRST EDITION

Book design by Carole Lowenstein

For Ginny

Acknowledgments

I would like to thank the following editors with whom I have worked:
Peter Osnos of Random House, who guided this collection; Maud
Wilcox of Harvard University Press; Martin Peretz, Leon Wieseltier,
Ann Hulbert, Michael Kinsley, and Hendrik Hertzberg of *The New
Republic*; Peter Gay of *The American Scholar*; George Core of the
Sewanee Review; Ben Bradlee, Meg Greenfield, Stephen Rosenfeld,
and Philip Geyelin of *The Washington Post*; Ray Cave, Henry Grun-
wald, Ralph Graves, Edward Jamieson, and Otto Friedrich of *Time*;
Robert MacNeil, Jim Lehrer, Michael Saltz, Lester Crystal, and
Linda Winslow of *The MacNeil/Lehrer NewsHour*; Philip Pochoda
of Anchor Press/Doubleday; Frederick Morgan and Paula Dietz of
the *Hudson Review*; Jack Rosenthal, Rebecca Sinkler, Walter Good-
man, Mitchel Levitas, Warren Hogue, Connie Rosenblum, Harvey
Shapiro, James Atlas, Alan Burdick, and Robert Vare of *The New
York Times*; Jim Silberman and Fredrica S. Friedman of Little,
Brown; Kai Erikson, the late Michael Cooke, and Penelope Fitzgerald
of the *Yale Review*; Lisa Grunwald and Lee Eisenberg of *Esquire*; Jim
Gaines, Jay Lovinger, and Paula Glatzer of *Life*; Jacqueline Leo and
Nancy Clark of *Family Circle*; Edward Kosner and Richard Babcock
of *New York* magazine; Wynn Handman of the American Place

Theatre; Mort Zuckerman, Michael Ruby, Merrill McLoughlin, and Lee Rainie of *U.S. News & World Report;* Jann Wenner and John Rasmus of *Men's Journal;* Karen Reyes and Tom Dworetzky of *Modern Maturity;* and Graydon Carter and Michael Caruso of *Vanity Fair.* Special thanks to my lifelong and most exciting editor, Ginny Rosenblatt, and to her associates, Carl, Amy, John, and Joannie.

Introduction

In the winter of 1975 my father died, and in the spring of that year I became a journalist. For two years I had been out of Harvard, where I had been teaching writing and modern literature. At the time of my father's death I was working as a director of the National Endowment for the Humanities in Washington. My "work" was to give away approximately $31 million a year to colleges and universities. As a result, no idea I had was deemed anything but brilliant, no joke I cracked anything but hilarious. These gifts suddenly deserted me when I left the endowment.

At Martin Peretz's invitation, I joined *The New Republic* as literary editor. Marty brought me into journalism. For that, and for a deep, abiding friendship, I am gladly in his debt.

My father died just about the time Marty hired me. I had assumed that after the endowment job was done I would return to university teaching, even though I always had wanted to write but lacked the nerve. Marty saw that wish in me, I think. He may also have intuited that my father's death had, in an oblique way, freed me to become a writer.

My father, a physician, was a hardened and lonely man. He had always wanted to be a journalist himself but had chosen what he saw as the safer, more conventional life, and he sought the same thing for me. By turning to journalism at his death, I was at once defying him and realizing his lifelong ambition. The mystery of our relationship thus continued beyond his death.

To explore that mystery, I wrote my first piece as a professional journalist about my father. It was called "Introduction to the Reader," as it marked my first appearance as literary editor before the readers of *The New Republic*. I place that piece last in this collection because, upon rereading it, I find that I understand no more about the relationship between my father and me now than I did nineteen years ago. It was the mystery that drew me to write the piece in the first place, and the mystery remains unsolved. My end is in my beginning.

In putting this collection together, I discovered that the expression of mystery characterizes most of my work. At least it characterizes those pieces I am least ashamed of, the ones I have included here. It is dismaying to see how much junk one produces over the course of a career, while, in the process, deluding oneself that a piece of the moment "works" or "is fine" or some equivalent lie. The fact that out of nearly 1,000 stories and essays I have written in the past nineteen years I have selected fewer than sixty speaks for itself.

By "mystery," I mean that I did not understand what I was dealing with when I confronted a particular subject, and the exercise of writing was my way of stating, and perhaps celebrating, that fact. Looking again at these selections, I feel the same helplessness before the subjects that I felt originally, the same unsatisfied yearning to know what it was, what it really was, that I saw and heard at a particular time or in a particular place. I see that my language, while sometimes definite, still shows a writer overwhelmed by the person or the event before him. When I was overwhelmed, I was also, strangely, most self-assured.

In the past few years I have been giving occasional classes at Columbia's Graduate School of Journalism and School of the Arts. My main objective has been to tell the students how to enjoy journalism; so I made up a number of perverse-sounding "rules" for them to try.

One rule is "Write dead stories." Over the years I have grown convinced that stories only begin to reveal themselves when they appear to be over. You may recall the murder in the Midwest in the early 1980s of a town bully. After a career of terrorizing his fellow citizens, the bully was shot to death in the middle of the town's main street in the middle of the day. The police investigated, but no one in the town claimed to have seen the killer. The F.B.I. stepped in, stating that the bully had been denied his civil rights by being shot to death—an incontestable rationale. Still, no one talked. To this day, not one of the citizens has said a thing publicly about the murder in the town. Yet they have lived with the murder for over a decade and are morally complicit in it. Technically the story of the murder is over. Yet the town's present state of mind is the story, if one would dare to get it.

The commemorative piece on Hiroshima in this collection is a dead story, as are the essay on the Loud family, of the public television documentary series *An American Family,* and the essays on the columnist Joseph Kraft, Professor Douglas Bush, a mercy killing in Florida, the *desaparecidos* in Argentina, and, of course, my father. It was interesting for me to note, as I reviewed my material, that the pieces I wrote on what were urgent and sensational news items of a particular moment lie dead on the page—which is why I did not include them—whereas most of the "dead" stories have life in them still.

"Betray your sources." That is another rule I made up. I did not mean that one should betray sources of privileged information but that the mere act of the interview involves a necessary betrayal. The journalist smiles and nods, and his subjects open up, innocent as flowers. Often the subjects show themselves to be awful people, and the journalist eggs them on.

For the Hiroshima story I interviewed Richard Nixon on nuclear diplomacy. He was wonderfully informative. Indeed, he broke news in that interview by stating that the United States had definitely considered using nuclear weapons both in Vietnam and in the Indo-Pak War. Nixon felt that my interview was accurate, and, because it mentioned nothing of his darker side, nothing of his character at all, I think he came to regard me as one of the journalists on whom he could count as he attempted to improve his station in the public mind. When I asked him if I could write a profile of him for *Time,* therefore, also included here, he readily agreed. The profile, however, was harshly condemning of Nixon. He hated it and swore never again to grant an interview to any medium with which I was associated.

Nixon thought I had betrayed him, and I had. Similar betrayals occur in other pieces. I betrayed an ignorant and abusive father in "A Christmas Story" by actively encouraging him to reveal his ignorance and abusiveness, as well as his own sexual brutalization when he was a boy. In "Portrait of a Prisoner," I betrayed an inmate in Attica by encouraging him to reveal his helplessness before his own menacing nature. I betrayed a Latvian fisherman into betraying his anti-Communist thoughts in "Enter This House and Let the Ice Melt," a story that accompanied the photographs in *A Day in the Life of the Soviet Union.* I betrayed Lewis Thomas, for whom I have great affection and respect, into focusing on his dying, which he was loath to do. I betrayed Ed Koch, whom I grew to like immensely in the course of writing about him, into describing his mother's death by cancer. I betrayed Candice Bergen, whom I also liked, into talking about her fears and isolation. I even betrayed the children I interviewed for "Children of War" by urging them to revisit hellish experiences they would have preferred to bury.

This is how it must be, I believe, if a journalist is to get into the lives of his subjects for the benefit of his readers (no other motive will wash). One must do everything possible to encourage one's subjects to be who and what they are, or, to put it more accurately, to be who and what one believes they are, though they resist. The process also requires a vanishing act on the part of the writer; the subject must appear to be exposing his soul to the reader directly, with no middleman intervening. The only two reasons for including oneself in a story are to make oneself into an Everybody, or into a character who enhances the person who is the true center of attention. Otherwise, one ought to be as small as possible. Older journalists like Joseph Mitchell of *The New Yorker* understood this art of self-diminution better than those of my generation, who have grown up thinking that journalists are important and are part of every story they write, perhaps the main part. But journalism, if it is to approach art, must use the ways of art, one of which is that the writer stays out of the picture.

To keep one's face or biography out of the picture, however, does not mean to stifle one's own imagination. Journalists cannot make up facts, but they can build surmises based on fact; they can intuit. Shelley put it right: "We need the power to imagine what we know." Journalists must learn to see invisibilities along with the things in front of their noses, and to feel their validity as strongly as any sound, sight, or motion.

Rule number three, then: "Make guesses." As long as the line is made clear to the reader between what one has actually seen and what one has felt, the imagination has a place in journalism, I believe, often the commanding place. The imagination is part of reality, too, after all. Inevitably a writer not only thinks his way into a subject; he dreams his way into it—in those dead quiet, expressionless moments when he or she unconsciously receives all the various little signals shocking the air. Somerset Maugham said, "A state of reverie does not avoid reality; it accedes to reality." I have learned to trust a dull ache in the area behind my back teeth to tell me secrets about a story—to tell me what else, besides the information of my five senses, is happening in a story. I have disregarded messages from that area to my peril.

The story "Do You Know This Woman?" is about a homeless woman named Betty, a woman in her late sixties whom I met in a project for the mentally ill homeless in my neighborhood in New York. Some friends and I do volunteer work there, producing a journal for the project's clients. We interview them and write their stories; it sometimes pleases them to see their names and their lives certified in print.

When I asked Betty if I could write her story, she told me that she would give me as much time as she could spare, but that CBS was coming over to talk with her about her life as a Latin Quarter show girl and a former Miss America, and about her Hollywood screen test and, of course, her dates with Joe DiMaggio. I asked the people who run the project if there was any harm in publishing Betty's fantasies, and they said no, not if Betty believed they were true. I should have listened to my back teeth.

"Look away from the ball." That's another so-called rule. The point guard of a college basketball team, who was playing poorly, once asked his coach what he was doing wrong. The coach asked him what he did in practice. "Pass, dribble, and shoot," said the player, indicating that he kept the ball in his control. The coach told him to have someone clock how much time he actually spent handling the ball in a regulation game. The player did so, and, very surprised, told his coach that he had his hands on the basketball less than three total minutes out of a forty-minute game.

"What do you learn from that?" asked his coach.

"Beats me," said the player.

"You learn," said the coach, "that most of the game is played away from the ball."

The journalism I most admire of my colleagues is that which deliberately does not turn its head toward the noise of a moment but instead focuses on a steady condition or continuing process. If one wants to learn about America's poor, one ought not to look at some spectacular event like a city street riot or a march on Washington. The poor are poor all the time. To write about the poor, to write about most enduring and significant things, really, one has to look away from the ball.

"Take it personally." All I mean by that rule is that in the writing of every story, no matter how small or apparently ordinary, one will inevitably find something private, even secret in himself or in herself, that is deeply affected. Instead of disowning that personal connection, I believe one should play to its strength. The personal element, lying unconscious in the mind, is probably the reason one was attracted to a story in the first place.

In the pieces here I see a recurrent attraction to children in danger or trouble. "Children of War" was the first story, as distinguished from a reported essay, that I wrote for a magazine, for *Time.* "A Christmas Story" is largely about imperiled children in a poor area of Brooklyn. One of the stories on Hiroshima tells of a boy's escape on the day of the bombing. And a recent piece is "The Last Place on Earth," written for *Vanity Fair,* on the "lost boys" of the Sudan. These boys, victims of civil war, starvation, and disease, escaped from villages where they saw their families murdered by the Muslim fundamentalist government troops—"theocratic" as opposed to "ethnic" cleansing. At least 100,000 boys set out on hundred-mile treks that lasted months to find places of safety in a country where an entire civilization is disintegrating. They have nothing in the world save immense and innate dignity, yet I never felt more at home than when I was with them.

The pieces also seem to show a recurrent attraction to the lonely— from Nixon and Ronald Reagan to the poor, homeless, and imprisoned. When I have done justice to these people, it is because I have brought them into the place of my own loneliness and studied them there.

"Be out of it." That is almost an unnatural rule for journalists to follow because journalists strive to be frantically "in it," that is, on top of the world's events. Yet I believe it is more useful to one's work to be out of it, aggressively out of it, when it comes to the news. Instead of urging students to read ten accounts of a story, I urge them to read one account and to do nine other unrelated things while brooding about the story. Read history, fiction, poetry—especially poetry, as the similarities of structure, voice, and intent between poetry and journalism can be striking. Instead of busying oneself with the daily papers, journey into the past. Or take a long, meandering walk, or see a movie, or do anything that keeps the mind dealing with other knowledge.

One of the more rewarding ways to be out of it is to make a connection with nature. In our century, people have lost this connection, and we are paying a penalty for that. Since we are part of nature, keeping away from it is a form of self-denial. I believe that the environmental movement was started not by people's concern over the ozone layer, but by the desire—the need—to reestablish a comforting proximity to the natural world.

Farmers in France staged a protest against the E.C. in Paris several years ago by bringing sheep, cattle, and slabs of wheat fields to the center of the Champs-Élysées. Police braced themselves for the outbreak of fights between the Parisians and the farmers. But when people saw the sudden farms arisen in the middle of the city, their reaction was to stroll in the fields—lovers, farmers, policemen, all. No one said so, but I am sure that reaction was a result of the citizens rediscovering the companionability of the countryside. Then everyone was gloriously out of it.

The main rule I came up with is "Do not understand it," which brings me back to the subject of mystery. Do not understand it—whatever the "it" may be. Dwell in a state of puzzlement. When I offer this most important rule to students, some of them think I'm kidding or being cutely inventive to make a point. Some think I mean *pretend* you do not understand it, so as to create an *impression* of mystery. But I mean the rule as stated. Somewhere in the experience of writing a story, a journalist realizes that he will never get it. The facts, the chronology, the motives may all be there for the telling, yet the story eludes him.

The only times I have written well are when I have embraced the mystery and have walked around inside it. My sketch of Mario Cuomo is about a man with whom I felt a deep and admiring kinship, yet do not understand. I do not understand the three elderly women who read aloud to me as a child, and my piece about them shows it, flaunts it. I do not understand my dog in "Dogstoevsky," or my mother in "The Aged Mother," or the inanities of fashionable chitchat with which I play in the monologue "Ashley Montana Goes Ashore in the Caicos," or myself in any of these pieces—that goes without saying. The review of Russell Banks's novel *The Sweet Hereafter* is about the futility of pinning blame on things we will never understand.

Often I will wait to write till the last possible minute before deadline, hoping not to solve a particular mystery, but to feel it more deeply. "The Man in the Water," my title essay, was written in forty-five minutes, but I brooded about it for many days. The subject was the Air Florida plane crash in the Potomac River in Washington, D.C., in January 1982, specifically the unidentified man who remained in the river and rescued his fellow passengers before he succumbed to the cold. Three full days that air crash led the evening news. I came to believe that the man in the water was the reason, yet no one had said so because he had done something people could not understand.

In too many ways the piece shows that it was written in forty-five minutes, but it resonated with readers at the time because it dwelt on the mystery of an act that people did not understand, or want to understand. Certain stories people do not want to understand. The mystery makes them feel closer to one another than would any solution.

You will not be surprised to learn that the order in which these pieces are arranged depends on the mysterious as well. In establishing a sequence here, I was making a guess as to how the reader's mind would move, where it would wish to travel after having read one story and before it went on to another. So I set up a sort of cadence of inner reaction. Of course, the success of the strategy depends on one's reading the collection from start to finish rather than skipping around, which is the normal practice. If you are good enough to read this book, do it any way you choose. Should the order you create suit you better than the one I have imagined for you, it only means that your instincts are more creative than mine.

After all my professions of faith in mystery, I must admit that I find most wonders in facts, the deepest mysteries in facts. The journalist does not exist who has not thought while interviewing a subject, "Oh, please say what I want you to say," or, when observing an event, "God, let this or that happen now." The thing desired never occurs, but something better usually takes its place.

I keep a quotation from the Sherlock Holmes stories in my office at home. Holmes tells Watson:

My dear fellow, life is infinitely stranger than anything which the mind of man could invent. We would not dare to conceive the things which are really mere commonplaces of existence. If we could fly out of that window hand in hand, hover over this great city, gently remove the roofs, and peep in at the queer things which are going on, the strange coincidences, the plannings, the cross-purposes, the wonderful chains of events, working through generations, and leading to the most outré results, it would make all fiction with its conventionalities and foreseen conclusions most stale and unprofitable.

The journalist who takes that to heart can be surprisingly happy in his work.

Also pinned up in my office is a poem by Robert Francis called "Pitcher." In high school I was a pitcher, a lousy one, but I claimed the position because it occupied the center of the field, thus being both essential and alone, and because of what Francis wrote about it:

> His art is eccentricity, his aim
> How not to hit the mark he seems to aim at,
>
> His passion how to avoid the obvious,
> His technique how to vary the avoidance.
>
> The others throw to be comprehended. He
> Throws to be a moment misunderstood.
>
> Yet not too much. Not errant, arrant, wild,
> But every seeming aberration willed.
>
> Not to, yet still, still to communicate
> Making the batter understand too late.

The journalism I have practiced strives to create a misunderstanding at both ends of the relationship of writer and reader. At the conclusion of an especially sweet inning, the batter walks away from the plate, and I walk off the mound, neither of us knowing exactly what happened.

When I was not playing sports in high school, I liked to go to the theater (studying was out of the question), and I often went to the theater with my father. One night he took me to *Inherit the Wind*. It starred Paul Muni as the Clarence Darrow character and Ed Begley as the William Jennings Bryan character. Tony Randall, a newcomer, played a wiseass reporter, a character based on H. L. Mencken. The subject was the Scopes "monkey trial" in Tennessee, and before going I boned up on the trial: how the teacher Scopes had been fired for teaching evolutionary biology, how Darrow had defended him, how Bryan had stood up for creationism, how finally Darrow lost the verdict but won the day.

At a crucial point in the play the Bryan character, though desperate to believe in his position, is overwhelmed with its illogic; his brain bursts; he has a stroke and dies. This is taken as a sign of Darrow's moral victory by the Mencken character, the journalist, who, standing onstage with Darrow, bellows his congratulations on humiliating "that Barnum-bunkum Bible-beating bastard!"

Darrow, of course, has been in the right all along while Bryan has been in the wrong. And Darrow has been fighting Bryan with all the irrefutable reason at his disposal. Yet he explodes at the reporter: "You smart-aleck! You have no more right to spit on his religion than you have a right to spit on *my* religion! Or my lack of it!" Then he adds, speaking of Bryan: "There was much greatness in this man." In effect, he was asking the reporter: "What could a man like you possibly know about a man like that?"

Sitting with my father in the dark, I did not hear that question as rhetorical.

Contents

THE MAN IN THE WATER

Lewis Thomas
on the
Art of Dying

❧❦❧

L ᴇ ᴡ ɪ s Tʜᴏᴍᴀs, the physician and biologist, is widely known as the author of *The Lives of a Cell, The Medusa and the Snail, The Fragile Species,* and *Late Night Thoughts on Listening to Mahler's Ninth Symphony.* On one level, these books are treatises on biology as philosophy, the works of a scrupulously observant, appreciative, self-deprecating, and dryly funny mind. On another level, the one that has earned the author the grateful affection of hundreds of thousands of readers, they are unsentimental, informed testimonies to the value of life.

Now he is dying. His wheelchair stands collapsed behind the purplish wing chair he sits in much of the day, his feet propped up on a stool with a floral-pattern cushion. Within his reach are his unfiltered Camels (he is not quite a chain-smoker), an ashtray with a built-in fan to dissipate the smoke, a cellular phone, a remote for the TV, and two dictionaries on the floor under the table beside his chair. Dictionaries are essential to one of Dr. Thomas's three principal interests—the study of etymology. The others, of course, are cells and people.

His Manhattan apartment, into which he moved for convenience to be near his doctor, is located in the Sixties, about a block from the East River. Besides himself, the household consists of Beryl, his wife of fifty-two years, a nurse, and a Yorkshire terrier puppy named Emma, a gift of his three daughters. The apartment he regards as pleasant enough—a typically efficient, clean and cold place built in the early 1950s; the gray-white walls feel like steel to the touch. Everything turns into something else: A living room becomes a dining alcove becomes a kitchen and a hall and a bedroom. At the far end of the living room, opposite the end where Dr. Thomas has his wing chair, is a wall-size window, from which the river is visible, and which allows the room the various lights of the day.

"There's really no such thing as the agony of dying," he says. He speaks in a high-pitched whisper that fades in and out like an old radio, depending on his strength. When he runs out of steam, his voice makes the breathy music of a recorder. "I'm quite sure that pain is shut off at the moment of death.

"I first noticed this in field mice caught by our cat in the country—how, at the end, they would hang languidly in the cat's jaws. They'd given themselves over. Certainly, death doesn't involve any aggravation of the pain of a disease. A lot of people fear death because they think that so overwhelming an experience has to be painful, but I've seen quite a few deaths, and, with one exception, I've never known anyone to undergo anything like agony. That's amazing when you think about it. I mean, how complicated the mechanism is that's being taken apart."

He pauses and watches Emma mysteriously select a place to sit on the rug.

"When I was in the Army in Okinawa, two M.P.s driving a jeep crashed into a troop carrier. The jeep was crushed flat, and the M.P.s were pinned in the wreckage. While we all worked like mad to pry them free, the two of them went along chatting calmly with us, apologizing for the accident, asking if anyone was hurt. Then they both died.

"You see, something happens when the body knows it's about to go. Like the field mice with the cat. Peptide hormones are released by cells in the hypothalamus and pituitary gland. Endorphins. They attach themselves to the cells responsible for feeling pain.

"The exception was a patient in a charity hospital in New Orleans, when I was much younger. I saw him on rounds in the morning. He'd been bitten by a rabid squirrel, and he kept repeating, raving, that he was dying. He couldn't stop talking about his symptoms. And he was heaving in pain. People thought he'd gone crazy. He died that afternoon. I wondered if the rabies hadn't knocked out some center in his brain stem designed to prevent that kind of thing. On the whole, though, I believe in the kindness of nature at the time of death."

These days, Dr. Thomas himself feels not pain but "lousy" frequently, weak and increasingly tired. He is both frustrated by and interested in the fact that, for the moment, his mind has misplaced the identification of his illness. "I've forgotten the name of my own disease!" His condition, which resembles lymphoma, a class of tumor of the lymphoid tissue, was detected in 1988. Within a year he had dropped from his normally steady weight of 170 down to 110; he had no appetite. Today, weighing about 130, he looks as thin as a man can look without looking gaunt. His shirt billows in a breeze, and his khaki pants flap like a scarecrow's. Depending on the light, his skin is translucent like an old man's—he turns eighty on November 25— or creamy like a boy's. His hair is very much like a boy's—sand-colored and neatly brushed with a straight part on the side, as if just cut by the town barber. Again, depending on the light, his face can show cachexia, that wasted look cancer patients often get, or it can appear vibrant. Without his glasses his eyes look hollow, with dark smudges underneath; but when he wears his glasses, he looks quite keen, as if he is about to study some new phenomenon.

He has great difficulty moving forward on his walker, which he treats as less of a transportation aid than an obstacle to push out of the way. The walker—and the wheelchair—became necessary three years ago after he fell and broke his left hip.

"I had an operation to get the joint removed, and I was going to get a brand-new joint, but the trouble was I bled so much that my heart stopped. And that seems to have done so much damage to my hearing, and my nerves and muscles, that I'll never get the joint back at all. So I've been hobbling about. Occasionally I feel a little *old*."

That the hip has never healed has led Dr. Thomas to suspect that the cancer, which appears to be quiescent elsewhere in his body, may be lodged in the bone marrow. He notes this as would any diagnostician, looking off into the middle distance, having pondered the evidence.

"Waldenström's disease! That's it!" He is amused at his forgetting the name, because Waldenström, a Swede, was a friend of his. The disease named for his friend identifies an abnormal proliferation of T cells, or lymphocytes, that produces a flawed kind of gamma globulin—the class of immune proteins. These lymphocytes give rise to plasma cells that produce an excess of IgM—a form of circulating immune proteins—which is sticky and in turn produces viscosity in the blood. All this leads to a deep, invading weakness. "That's what I felt first. Then the weight loss."

I usually arrive at the apartment around eleven in the morning, the hour he has a glass of sherry with Beryl. When Dr. Thomas and I talk, Beryl, a serene and handsome woman with relentlessly inquisitive eyes, sits reading a book at the window end of the living room. She once defined their marriage for their oldest daughter, Abby: "Your father believes that he is personally responsible for the sunrise. What he doesn't know is that he couldn't do it if I weren't up to make the coffee and open the curtains."

Because he is forced to maintain a sedentary state these days, Dr. Thomas's mind takes on a special prominence, like the Wizard of Oz's disembodied head—though, in fact, Dr. Thomas seems to have lived in his mind most of his life. It is thus sad, though not as sad as it might be with a less intellectual man, to see him so confined.

"Maybe I should have taken better care of myself," he says. "I don't know. These people do all that jogging today. I don't know that it does much good. But it can't do much harm. My doctor keeps an eye on me. Takes blood once a week. We've never had a conversation about smoking."

"That's just his tact," I muttered with disapproval.

"Yeah." He smiles.

"When did you know that you wanted to be a doctor yourself?" I ask him.

"My father was a doctor, and I admired him and got along well with him. He took me with him on house calls. We were living in Flushing, which was then a sleepy village of twenty-five thousand— before the subway got there. I've been *sure* I wanted to be a doctor since I was about twelve. In summer camp, in the Poconos, I served time in the infirmary, helping out the camp doctor. By the time I got to Princeton [at the age of fifteen], I gave the idea up, and I decided I wanted to be a writer. Only I couldn't figure out what I'd be writing about. So I changed my mind again."

He graduated in 1933, after a so-so academic career. He did better at Harvard Medical School, graduating *cum laude* in 1937; then he went on to Boston City Hospital for his internship. He took his residency in neurobiology at Columbia College of Physicians and Surgeons. He was twenty-seven when he married Beryl Dawson. There was, after that, a succession of jobs: at Harvard, up to Nova Scotia, back to Harvard. Then came the war and his experiences in Okinawa. Then the children. When the war was over, he practiced and held professorships and research posts at Johns Hopkins, Tulane, and Minnesota.

At some point in midcareer, Dr. Thomas stopped being a general practitioner and worked solely as a researcher and an administrator. His last administrative post, after he was dean of the medical schools at N.Y.U. and Yale, and chancellor of the Sloan-Kettering Cancer Center, was as scholar-in-residence at Cornell Medical School, where he studied and attacked cancer cells—until cancer struck back.

"I tell you, I don't fear dying, really, but it is very hard to think that this is the end. Hard for everybody. Always has been. I doubt that any important topic has been given such imaginative attention as death. Where do we go? Are we on our way back to dust, or is there something else in store? Sometimes I think I've had enough. I want to give it up. Other times I want to hang around to see what happens next to the world. I don't want to be reincarnated, that's for sure. When you've had rewarding experiences in your life—a loving family, friends—you don't need additional reassurances that you're going to do something with a new cast of characters. I'd just as soon pass."

I put it to him: "What if you came back as a sexy actress?"

"Too difficult an assignment," he says.

"How about a professional athlete?"

"I'd break my hip."

I ask, "Is there any point to people thinking about death, since no one can know?"

He says, "It seems to do valuable things for those who are convinced that the stories told in childhood are true—that we'll all be judged and go somewhere like heaven."

"But you don't believe that."

"Nope. I'm not sure that we'll come to a flat end, but I don't believe in heaven either. There may be some other plan in progress, though."

This is the way he likes to think about nature—as a suspicion of coherence. Everything connects; he suspects this. He also suspects that human beings reflect nature as a whole. Sir Thomas Browne (1605–82), the first great humanist-physician writing in English, whom Dr. Thomas has quoted in his books, wrote in *Religio Medici* (the religion, or faith, of a doctor): "There is no man alone because every man is a Microcosm, and carries the whole World about him." John Donne expressed the same idea—"I am a little World made cunningly"—which was, among the more forward-looking, and spiritually troubled, writers and thinkers of the seventeenth century, a way of seeing God in science, and vice versa. When Dr. Thomas speaks of a thinking universe, he too envisions a comprehensive and intelligently planned structure.

Yet unlike Browne and the metaphysical poets, he does not mention God in his universe. For him it is wonder enough that there are observable fundamental mysteries in nature that are also benign.

"In the building of a termite hill," he says, "there comes a point when most, if not all, of the uprights are in place. And the word gets around among the termites that it's time to turn the arch. And they all begin to turn the arch. And at just about the same time. And it turns out to be architecturally just the right time to do it, if you're going to have the right kind of ventilation and air-conditioning in the hill. But I don't think there's anybody calling the shots from some central platform, and saying: 'Turn the arch.' "

He comes as close as he will to admitting the existence of the soul: "I think it's the property of the mind that we call consciousness—and conscience—that we will never find a satisfactory mechanistic explanation for." But he does not think that the soul outlives the body. To believe that, he says, "You have to dress death up with the notions of rewards and penalties. I don't think that's reasonable. Then I have this other, I suppose, professional biologist's notion about crowding. How are you ever going to cope with the numbers in heaven? You'd have to have another universe next door, where everybody could go." It is hard to tell how seriously he takes this. "Not only that, there is a certain kind of discrimination implicit in the idea of heaven. Only humans go to this place. No frogs or dragonflies. No [he looks across the room] Yorkshire terriers."

"You said in *Lives of a Cell* that nothing in matter disappears."

"When we get better at living together, I think the question of an afterlife will not seem so important, because there will be so many opportunities for us to experience in our own lifetimes the effects of enlightened, good behavior, on the part of all of us, or most of us, in a better world. And once we acquire that as a habit of living in our dense populations—the habit of peacemaking—I don't think that we'll feel the need for ideas like immortality."

"Won't that put religions out of business?" I ask.

"That *aspect* of religions. I think there are plenty of other aspects of religious thought that we'll find necessary to have at hand, and to observe. I don't think that the existence of the permanent life of the individual human soul is an indispensable part of religious thought."

"But the soul can be identified?" I try once more.

"Yeah," he says.

"So who put it there?"

"I guess evolution put it there. That's a very unsatisfactory answer. But biology put it there."

"God did *not* put it there?"

"Could be. Put it there, and then left it alone, and let it emerge over its own billions of years. Maybe even *planned* it that way. But I don't know whether something like that could have happened, or ever *did* happen. And I think I could cook up explanations that would rely more on what we already know about the evolutionary development of the nervous system, or the creatures on the planet."

The reference to "peacemaking" goes deep into his ideas about the evolution of human beings. Dr. Thomas's mind is an odd mixture of perpetual curiosity and perpetual optimism; what he cannot understand he still thinks will be good when revealed. Even when he is at his most cautionary, as when he is warning the species against hubris—a theme of his writings—he imagines us eventually fitting into a benign scheme of things. In *The Fragile Species,* he wrote: "All the other parts of the earth's life seem to get along, to fit in with each other, to accommodate, even to concede when the stakes are high. We can see no evidence of meanness or vandalism in nature. [The earth] is, on balance, an equable, generally amiable place, good-natured, as we say."

"If nature were not kind," he tells me, "you wouldn't have a built-in mechanism for friendship, or something like friendship. What we think of as a predatory relationship—if we could observe it long enough—gradually shifts to parties who had agreed to get along. The final stage is when they can't get along *without* each other."

"You've written that there is an evolutionary tendency on the part of species to live longer."

"To be *useful,*" he corrects me. "One nice example of that is the relationship that has always existed in the environs of Houston, Texas, between the mimosa tree and the beetle. A particular species of mimosa tree around Houston is infested with a particular species of beetle. The female beetle becomes pregnant and has to lay her eggs. She goes out on one of the older branches of the mimosa tree, partway to the end, and makes an incision in the bark longitudinally, and deep, down into the living tissue of the branch lays her eggs in that deep slit, then goes somewhere else." He looks off for a second as if trying to picture where the female beetle has gone. "The eggs eventually develop and crowd out the branch's tissues around it. The branch then dies and falls to the ground. Then—and only then—the eggs hatch, and a new generation of beetles goes off to new trees that are available to it. And the mimosa trees are said to be healthier—and to live longer because of the pruning that continually goes on—than any other trees in Texas.

"But we humans are the anomalies for the moment in evolution," he says. "I guess it makes sense that we should be. We've only been here a short time—at least as compared with other, more familiar species, like cockroaches and horseshoe crabs. But we simply haven't learned to get along in large groups. People come together at a soccer game, and something goes haywire. When clusters are too dense, we lose our minds. We fill ourselves up with hate and death wishes. I don't understand it."

"What about the group or mass of the family?" I ask.

"That's different, because with a family we feel affection. We don't merely imitate affection. As a species, we're really *good* at feeling affection. I think a family is a biological necessity, a good higher organism for people. Love is indispensable to it. It's at the center, and a great pleasure."

Dr. Thomas's way of speaking is very much like his way of writing, moving from the detail to the idea, as if he were trailing an ever-widening river. There are several reasons that doctors and scientists sometimes make effective writers. They are accustomed to dealing with life at its extremes. And they need to be precise, to apply precision, in a profession concerned with human health, which is quite imprecise. This, to writers, is the same relationship of language to feeling.

But the main reason, I think, is that people of medicine and science bring to literature special and concrete knowledge. They do not depend on the senses alone, or even principally, for their observations, but on a world of definite things, like cells. These things, when addressed by expansive minds, become metaphors for larger and greater things, but they are first grounded in specific reality. William Carlos Williams was a very good writer because he was a very good doctor, I believe, and the same goes for Dr. Thomas. The poetry in his writing and in his conversation derives from his knowing what an object is before he speculates on what it might become.

"If you're sure that there's no afterlife, why aren't you just as certain that the end is the absolute end?" I ask him this on a particularly bad day, when the ravages of the cancer can be read under his eyes.

"For one thing," he says, "our individual coming to an end may have some connection with the continuity of the species. It may be as important for us to die as it is for plant life to die. So we die and live in our successors. I'll tell you, I wouldn't want to live forever, even if I could. Science is tending in the direction of that possibility, keeping people alive for 140, 150 years. An appalling prospect, when you think that people will age and be fragile that much longer, and what it takes for society to take care of aging bodies. For me, frailty is a lot harder to bear than dying."

I hesitate, then ask, "What does dying feel like?"

"Weakness," he answers with a strain of bitterness. "This weakness. I'm beginning to lose all respect for my body."

"Dr. Thomas, is there an art to dying?"

"There's an art to living." He brightens a bit. "Maybe that's the same thing. One of the very important things that has to be learned around the time dying becomes a real prospect is to recognize those occasions when we have been useful in the world. With the same sharp insight that we all have for acknowledging our failures, we ought to recognize when we have been useful, and sometimes uniquely useful. All of us have had such times in our lives, but we don't pay much attention to them. Yet the thing we're really good at as a species is usefulness. If we paid more attention to this biological attribute, we'd get a satisfaction that cannot be attained from goods or knowledge. If you can contemplate the times when you've been useful, even indispensable, to other people, the review of our lives would begin to have effects on the younger generations." He pauses and reaffirms: "Plain usefulness."

"Are there any such times that come to mind for you?"

"Some things I've written and thought," he says, "they may have been useful."

He does not elaborate on this, but one assumes that he judges the life of the mind useful. In *Late Night Thoughts on Listening to Mahler's Ninth Symphony,* he imagined himself at the moment of death as a thought "drawn back into the memory of the earth." In that way, death itself is useful; thoughts are freed, as spirits, into an ineradicable—and eternally useful—life.

From time to time, Dr. Thomas comes to a full stop in something he is saying, and sits silently in his chair for a minute or two. From the street come the muffled noises of car horns and ambulance sirens. Beryl reads her book. Emma naps in a corner, her entire tiny new being pulsating in sleep. I am learning to distinguish one of Dr. Thomas's silences from another. One is merely a pause in a thought, as if he is working something through, or foraging for an opening, like a bird caught in a barn. The other silence occurs when he is too tired to continue talking, usually after an hour and a half. Lately, it is more like an hour.

He gives himself over to the silence. The conversation has gone as far as it will. I tell him I have to go, and he offers no false protest. "See ya," he says.

November 1993

The Late Afternoon

I FIRST BECAME AWARE of beauty at the age of five. The objects of my admiration were three women, called spinsters in those days, who were in their seventies and early eighties, and who lived together in an antique splendor in the apartment directly above ours in the Gramercy Park neighborhood of New York. Miss Prescott was a librarian at Columbia University. Miss Jordan was a novelist, and at one time had been an editor of *Harper's Bazaar* magazine. Miss Cutler was a painter and a potter. Her forebears came over on the *Mayflower*. It was she, I believe, who had the money.

They lived in a dark museum of an apartment, with shields and swords on the walls, and elephants carved out of ivory on the tables. At the age of five, I thought it noteworthy that people would carve ivory to make elephants, but I drew no conclusions. Framed coats of arms hung from wires on the ceilings. There was a freestanding suit of armor in the hall.

My mother, a junior high school English teacher, worked late in the afternoons, so I would go up and visit the three ladies, who would be waiting for my arrival. They would read aloud to me—*The Wind in the Willows*, *Dr. Dolittle*, Jules Verne, Mark Twain. It was from Miss Prescott, Miss Jordan, and Miss Cutler that I learned the power of the written word. And also canasta; they taught me canasta (at which they openly cheated). Miss Jordan taught me how to play the piano. Well, not exactly *how* to play the piano, since she would attack the keys as if her hands were jackhammers. But she did teach me the notes for "Londonderry Air" and the "Blue Danube Waltz."

They also taught me about beauty, though they intended no such lesson. Since they remained unmarried all their lives, they may never have thought of themselves as beautiful, perhaps as the opposite. They were beautiful to me, however, which is one of the things about beauty. It depends on who is doing the looking.

They had a wonder for life, and a passion to share that wonder, and to teach it. For that combination of qualities, the three of them were, to me, stunning.

A five-year-old is in a pretty good position to assess who is beautiful and who is not. Removed from the confusions of sexuality, he or she can judge a face as a face. Miss Cutler's face was like her work: soft like pastels and soft like clay; a Helen Hayes–ish face; a gracious welcome. Miss Prescott's face was also like her work: square edged and bony. Her voice both sang and cracked. The face of Miss Jordan was huge and severe, a giant's face. Had her body been less than huge itself, it could not have supported her head. Her eyes were dark and keen, and she was always moving in a definite direction: toward the playing cards, toward the Steinway (boom!), toward a book.

Books made up the center of our afternoons. A reading, preceded by tea, and milk and cookies for me, the four of us seated around the coffee table, they chatting and nodding, I mostly watching and listening. It never occurred to me that the ladies had arranged the late part of their day to accommodate the schedule of a five-year-old boy. I thought that this was what they did ordinarily—sit on the couch and read children's stories aloud. I thought that because they were themselves so absorbed in the stories, so visibly excited about Tom Sawyer's whitewashed fence and Mr. Toad's hall.

The shadows would lengthen in the dark museum, crawling on the antimacassars and the gold frames of the paintings. And I would watch the three of them travel into the kingdom of words, and beckon me to join them.

Many years later, when I was teaching words myself, I came across a poem by John Crowe Ransom called "Blue Girls." The poem ends with the following stanzas:

> Practise your beauty, blue girls, before it fail;
> And I will cry with my loud lips and publish

Beauty which all our power shall never establish,
It is so frail.

For I could tell you a story which is true;
I know a lady with a terrible tongue,
Blear eyes fallen from blue,
All her perfections tarnished—yet it is not long
Since she was lovelier than any of you.

Of course, I thought of Miss Jordan, Miss Cutler, and Miss Prescott, by then long dead. I did not remember them with "perfections tarnished" but as perfectly lovely, as old women. It is not an easy thing to age beautifully. It has to do with aging happily, and that, I think, has to do with continuing to see the world as an adventure, as my three ladies did.

God, they could bicker! Miss Jordan used a broadsword, and the other two, rapiers. Politely, deftly, they would pass a teacup and remind one another of errors of judgment one of them had made, or worse, errors of fact. Miss Prescott the librarian was especially good at that. They were as alive to infighting as they were to the world of events. I did not always understand the substance of their quarrels, but I could tell that this was a more stylish game than canasta, and I could see how they, who lived among swords and shields, embraced battle with both arms.

They lived for everything. For flowers, for newspapers, for literature, for warfare, for me.

Theories of beauty are usually wanting and unpersuasive. They tend to lose themselves in definitions of sublimity, or in geometry: If something is symmetrical, it must be beautiful. How then to explain why so many disparate things are considered beautiful? A mansion is beautiful, but so is a cottage. A Ferrari is beautiful, but so is a Jeep. Oddly, the element that connects these objects to one another is also the thing that accounts for their differences from one another—their originality, their unpredictability, the surprise contained within themselves.

So it is, I believe, for people, who are beautiful in youth and also beautiful in age, yet one condition looks nothing like the other. The only way a young woman can really be beautiful is when some element of difference, of strangeness, is present alongside her perfect, unblemished features. The way an older woman is beautiful has nothing to do with perfect and unblemished features, but depends rather on how her mind works—on what engages her interest, on what, and whom, she loves.

This is true for men as well. It is generally said that men get better looking with age than do women, but no one can prove it. (Maybe this is an old husbands' tale.) Common observation shows that men, like women, age well when they are lit and fired from the inside, like Yeats's aging self in "Sailing to Byzantium." His soul will "clap its hands and sing."

In short, beauty depends on the effect of character on appearance. This is true of people at any age, I suppose, but perhaps more so in the later years, when one loses the inclination to peer endlessly into mirrors. With that loss of desire comes the compensating gain of wanting to look instead at life outside the mirrors, to attend to things and to people outside oneself. That is, it comes if one wills it to come, if one deliberately, joyfully, orients one's attention toward the mystery of things, and toward those in need.

Age gracefully? Nah. Age ferociously instead. Seize everything valuable within one's reach. Extend. Question. Give. The face will follow. All the cosmetic surgeons in the world could never produce such a face.

On Christmas Eve, every Christmas Eve, Miss Prescott, Miss Jordan, and Miss Cutler would hire a car to drive them up and down Fifth Avenue, so that they could look at the displays in the shop windows. They took me with them. Slowly along the avenue the sleek black car would make its tour, the ladies sitting in the back, I in the front with the driver. They would point at the blazing windows and exclaim, rarely to me, and not exactly to one another. Each, on her own, was absorbed in something she had seen year after year, which was suddenly brand new in her eyes. Sunk deep in the leather seat, and staring straight ahead, I listened to them glow in the dark.

August 1993

Real Men Don't Die

E VEN THE POEMS are different. When women write about
dying, there is always a graceful resignation in the line, a tone of
"Ah, it's here," riding somewhere between fatalism and an embrace.
Elizabeth Bishop had a poem, "The Moose," in which she examined
the kind of "yes" said in response to tragic news:

> "Yes . . ." that peculiar
> Affirmative. "Yes . . ."
> A sharp, indrawn breath,
> Half groan, half acceptance,
> That means "Life's like that.
> We know *it* (also death)."

Place that attitude beside Dylan Thomas's instructions to his father
to "rage against the dying of the light" ("Do Not Go Gentle into That
Good Night") or Shakespeare's "The heavens themselves blaze forth
the death of princes" (*Julius Caesar*). When a man writes about
dying, he assails the act with an in-your-face.

The reason for this difference, I think, is that death is too much for
men to bear, whereas women, who are practiced in bearing the deaths

of men before their own and who are also practiced in bearing life, take death almost in stride. They go to meet death—that is, they attempt suicide—twice as often as men, though men are more "successful" because they use surer weapons, like guns. Note that to date, eight out of the nine people shepherded to the beyond by Dr. Strangelove Kevorkian were women.

In that eerie 1930s movie *Death Takes a Holiday,* a young woman actually falls in love with Death, the figure of Death as played by Fredric March, and willingly descends, like Persephone, to his dark princedom. No man, in fiction or out, would do that. With men, death is a pure calamity to be resisted—a feeling expressed either by our making great claims of how bravely we will face it or by imagining death as noble or, most often, by telling death to go fuck itself. My guess is that men use guns in suicide not just to be "safe" but to blast away at death in the process—perhaps, if lucky, to kill the beast.

Men have generally witnessed more terrible deaths close up than women have—as soldiers in wars or as cops and firemen. That may have something to do with our undisguised fear and hatred of the thing. Frequent exposure to bellies torn open, arms and legs flung from bodies like logs, is enough to put anyone off the idea that death is glorious, honorable, or, as recent books have tried to persuade us, merely a peaceful passage into a new stage of existence.

In his book *Wartime,* Paul Fussell presents the account of a British major at Normandy who joined a search party for the wounded. "Sure enough," wrote the major. "We found a poor little chap with both legs blown off above the knees, moaning softly and, I remember, he was saying, 'Oh dear! Oh dear!' The stretcher-bearer shook his head and, I thought, looked pointedly at my revolver."

The connection of death with pain is more palpable for men than for women. We take pain less well. Assurances by scientists such as the biologist-essayist Lewis Thomas that at the moment of death, pain probably goes away—that endorphins attach themselves to cells responsible for the perception of pain and dull the suffering—have never been sufficient to quash the terror most men experience at the idea not only that our life will be ended but that someone or something outside us, like a torturer or executioner, will end it for us. With AIDS, as with cancer, the torturer threatens to invade.

Samuel Johnson, who could speak of all other subjects rationally, turned away at the mention of death, though Boswell tried to get him to speculate on it. Johnson may have been thinking not so much of the pain as of the finality—the finality and the prospect of the eternally unknown. For the maker of a dictionary, who used his monumental mind defining things, the idea of a territory that lies beyond definition may have been too dreadful to dream.

With less drama in their reactions, most men feel the same way about pain, the unknown and finality: more fear of the unknown than of pain, perhaps, and more of finality than of the unknown. To enter the ultimately unknowable place may be—and has been—likened by men to an adventure, in part to make it seem that death is a test of will and cunning, a game of Dungeons and Dragons. It is telling that when Houdini vowed to return from the grave, one pictured him shattering manacles and erupting from the earth like a geyser triumphant. But when Mary Baker Eddy, founder of the Christian Science church, was said to make the same promise, it was reported that she calmly arranged to place a call from the phone she had installed in her tomb.

It's the romantic nature of men, I think, that makes us hate and fear death so much, and this nature cannot abide the notion that it's over when it's over. This feeling evidences itself in sublime circumstances such as the belief in the existence of an afterlife (shared by women, of course) and in the nuttiest situations, too. As funny as all the Elvis sightings are, I'm pretty sure that what lies behind them—behind a refusal to admit that Elvis is dead and gone—is the characteristic refusal of men to admit that they too will die and go. The more animated and adored the public figure, especially the relatively young public figure, the less thinkable it is that death can claim him.

So Elvis lives, and James Dean couldn't really die in a smashup—could he?—and when the record said, "I buried Paul," it was acceptable only because we knew that he wasn't dead; for if Paul were dead, then all the young men in the world were dead, and that was the end of the records. When John Lennon really did die, who could believe it?

While Elvis lives, Janis Joplin does not. No romantic mysticism is applied to women when they die, because by their down-to-earth nature they seem to forbid such desperate mythmaking. Men, for their part, spend much of their life in mythmaking, in particular the myth of living forever. (I wonder if Mary Shelley was not, in some way, mocking that tendency by writing *Frankenstein*.) Who mentions Mozart or Keats without thinking of their deaths "before their time"? And what exactly *is* a man's proper time, anyway? Never, that's what. There is not a whit of difference between Goethe's cry of "More light!" on his deathbed and W. C. Fields's stated preference for Philadelphia.

When I was eighteen, I certainly believed I would live forever. I would walk on the edge of a cliff or a roof without a moment's hesitation; if I fell, I'd catch a branch or a ledge; if not, I'd fly. When I was in my twenties, I would swim until my arms lay limp on the ocean. Was there any doubt that I could make it back to shore? The strength would simply come into my body like a divine wind. Even at the age of forty-five, I could play in a full-court basketball game—not well but fearlessly. And once, at that ripe age, I drove a Porsche 928S (legally a plane) at 110 miles per hour, maybe faster. Trees and highway signs shot past my ears like gunfire. I took my hands off the wheel and sang.

Now, having passed fifty (years, not mph), I know perfectly well that I can die. Attending more funerals than weddings reinforces such knowledge. Yet realizing that I can die does not in the least make me ready to clasp death to my bosom—the one I'm acquiring. And the more I think about death, the more I fear it, especially when I consider how much there is to lose—wife, children, friends, work. I'm beginning to feel death's presence too strongly, my mind occasionally hung with crepe. With a little effort, I can easily haul myself up from that cold, lightless room, but I know it's waiting.

Time can be such a menace to a man. By this age do that; by that age do better. Everything exists in a tantalizing and frequently destructive future, and if that future is not wonderful, well, then, there must be some other wonderful future somewhere, if only . . . The common rationale for older men having sudden and often pointless affairs is that, as it was put in the movie *Moonstruck,* they're afraid to die.

It is not only that everything will be over at the portal of death; everything will be equal. The idea of death as the Great Leveler is as antiromantic as that of death as the Great Ender, since—noble egalitarian sentiments aside—men spend much of their lives trying to best one another. Death both closes out the competition and says, by its inevitable equalizing presence, that the competition counted for nothing.

What all this romantic thinking comes to is that deep down, in some secret chamber not unlike a burial vault, men do not believe that we were cut out for death. It doesn't suit us. I do not mean to be sacrilegious or in any way disrespectful when I say that the story of the Resurrection of Jesus has always struck me as a perfect male invention. A young man dies, a man of such luminous goodness and powers that the designation of Messiah, long withheld from others, is gladly bestowed on him. How could his death be understood, much less accepted, by those he touched except to agree that it never happened? Real men don't die. It is a sign of virtue and power not to die. And if we must die, we will come back. And if we can't come back, we will fight like hell to keep from dying in the first place, telling death where to get off and determined to show courage when it comes reaping. Who knows? Maybe by this terrified show of nerve we actually do hold death off a bit.

A friend of mine, not much older than I, died last year. A squash champ, and a champ in all other respects, he told cancer to take a hike for a full eight years, until cancer had taken a hike through every part of his body and had nowhere else to go. Only at the very end, in the last day or so in the hospital, did tranquillity replace valor in his eyes. And then he seemed to grow serene and younger on the spot, lying among all the terrible, ridiculous tubes and gauges—as if he saw that it was game over for sure and the only way to go out was like a sport. Yet for eight more years than was ever expected, people had a good man around to love. I talk to him still.

March 1993

Dogstoevsky

THE DOG. By Roger Rosenblatt. The dog barks. By Roger Rosenblatt. The dog barks by Roger Rosenblatt who is trying to read *Crime and Punishment* by Fyodor Dostoevsky. He is trying to read *Crime and Punishment* by Fyodor Dostoevsky, but the dog barks. As Raskolnikov dodges his landlady, the dog barks. As Raskolnikov curses his sister's fate, the dog barks, too. The dog always barks. By Rodya Raskolnikov. *Dogs and Punishment* by Rodya Rosenblatt, by Roger Raskolnikov, by Fyodog Dogstoevsky. Barkbarkbarkbarkbark.

I am not crazy yet. The dog has not barked me to craziness quite yet. All I have sought to do for the past two days, sitting in the same chair in the same house with the same chocolate kisses left over from Halloween at my same left hand; all I have sought is to make some progress with *Crime and Punishment*. It is a very great book. You ought to read it sometime. I ought to read it sometime. But the dog barks, and so I cannot read *Crime and Punishment,* and so I have considered killing the dog, as Raskolnikov killed the two old women.

If you kill one dog, after all, what matters it to the balance of the world, if you know what I mean, and I think you do.

Of course, you do not hear the barking; you, swaddled in the sweet silence of your Ford Torino or your Library of Congress, you do not hear my cairn terrier with the tommy-gun voice. Nor can you hear what my cairn terrier hears. Nor can I. But I can hear her. It is a metaphysical riddle, is it not, that she barks at what she hears, but I can only hear her barking. Who then would hear the sound if I felled her with a tree in the forest?

What gets me is how little she cares for my peace of mind. She has not read *Crime and Punishment*. She knows nothing of the pleasures of sitting back with chocolate kisses on a dismal November afternoon—the trees shorn, the wind mixing with rain—and reading of starving young Russians tormenting themselves in the city of ———, in the year ———. Six long years I have owned this dog, feeding and bathing and tummy-scratching, in return for puppy barking and dog barking. Now she is not six, I remind her. She is forty-two, older than I. Time to settle down, I remind her. *Tempus fugit. Cave canem.* (Barkbarkbark.) She is not the dog I had hoped for, not that dog at all.

Not that I was hoping for Lassie, if that's what you're thinking. Nor Rin Tin Tin, nor Yukon King, nor Fala, nor Checkers, nor Him, nor Her, nor any dog that flies or takes fingerprints or says "Ruth" in bars. I was not expecting maybe Ms. Magic Dog of the Twenty-first Century, who would not only fetch me my copy of *Crime and Punishment,* but who also would have translated the book from the original. Not my dog. Not the dog of my dreams.

All I ever wanted was a good and quiet dog, like the dignified hound in Piero di Cosimo's *Death of Procris,* sitting so mournfully, so nobly at the feet of his fallen master. A dog like that would not bark more than once a month (once in his seven). A dog like that would know his place in the order of things, would state by the mere fact of his docile existence that there are those who rule and those who sit quietly, those who read *Crime and Punishment* and those who don't, and therefore do not make it impossible for those who do, just because they hear things that those who do, don't.

Damn it, dog. Am I not king of the jungle? Am I not God's reason that civilization is not going to the cairns?

Barkbarkbarkbarkbark.

There is nothing out there. I have been stalled on p. 71 for an hour, and there is nothing out there, while Raskolnikov has axed the two old women over and over again. He feels no remorse. What remorse would I feel—except to acknowledge in the foul tunnels of my heart that I am for whom the dog barks? That she barks to protect only me?

Now she is still for a moment. The brown blank eyes fixed with alarm. The head loaded, ready to fire. What can she hear? Is it the sound of an enemy I cannot hear yet? Or is it the sound of the enemy I can never hear, the sound of evil itself, of my own murderous impulse to kill the very dog who barks to keep me from killing the very dog who barks to keep me from killing me?

November 12, 1979

Enter
This House
and Let the
Ice Melt

A POET FRIEND gave Oleg the nickname Allegro, because Oleg walks and talks like a runaway note, and because Oleg's life is jazz. You might have heard him play last spring if you were around Sacramento, Milwaukee, or Rockford, Illinois. That was the first tour of the U.S.A. by the Leningradski Dixieland Band, with Yuri Borisovich Miroscnichenko on bass, Konstantin Ivanovich Dyubenck on piano, and the leader, the souped-up, the ten-steps-ahead-of-you Oleg Grigoryevich Kuvaitsev on sax. Oleg heard his first saxophone on the Voice of America in the 1950s, craved the sound, stuck a clarinet in a samovar, and it moaned like a sax. Then he organized a group that played clubs on the sly, jazz officially being Western decadence back then. Today he sings, "I got rhythm, I got music, I got my band. Who could ask for anything more?"

Allegro as ever this Thursday morning, he skitters ahead through his rainy city, the former capital of the empire, pointing out Prince Menshikov's palace and the Peter and Paul Fortress and the spot where this uprising occurred and that attempted assassination. Now he scoots into the Summer Garden built by Peter the Great, lush as the setting of Cocteau's *Beauty and the Beast*, the wide wet paths lined with statues of Justice, Mercy, and Truth. "I courted my wife in this garden," he calls back over his shoulder. "See that gate [the elegant symmetrical garden gate that looms above the Neva River]? An Englishman once sailed his ship here from Britain, and when he saw that perfect gate he said he had seen all that one ever needed to see of St. Petersburg, and he sailed home that very day. That's how I felt when I met my wife." Laugh, jump the puddles, pat the trees, move.

But the Summer Garden is merely a pause on Oleg's personal guided tour of Leningrad. As was the Naval Museum, where his metal-mustached grandfather peered out dazedly from a photograph taken aboard the *Aurora,* the cruiser that fired the shot that signaled the taking of the Winter Palace on October 25, 1917. A stop on the way, as were the Rostral Columns, studded with the prows of conquered ships, and the most rational, logical street in the world, the Street of the Architect Rossi, 220 meters long, 22 meters wide, each house 22 meters high.

"All Leningrad is logical, like a perfect plan."

"Perfect plans can be suffocating."

"Sure. But that's jazz. You improvise within the plan."

Where Oleg wants to get to is Raskolnikov's house, No. 19 Carpenter Lane, where Dostoevsky tenanted his brooding murderer. So deeply does Oleg love his Dostoevsky that he named his eldest son Fyodor, and he carries a weathered copy of *Crime and Punishment* with him. In his family are two other children and a wife like the gate of the Summer Garden, and two in-laws, all seven in three rooms. "What can you do?" He smiles and shrugs. The rain paints the city a blackened silver. "Old joke," shouts Oleg. "Out-of-towner: When do you have summer in Leningrad? Leningrader: Last year it fell on Wednesday."

Now he is here in the neighborhood of the Griboyedov Canal, approaching *the* street where *he* lived. "Yes, I know that his works were once forbidden, and other great writers are outlawed now. And yes, it bothers me. But freedom is like a girl, you know. I love her. She does not love me. Can I help but love her anyway?" Trucks hiss in the rain on what Oleg points out as the Bridge of Sixteen Balls.

"Why is it called that?"

"The statues at either end. Four horsemen. Four horses. See how much freedom you'll have to print *that.*"

Now on the street where Raskolnikov saw the woman drowning in the canal and made no move to save her, seeing that death was simple. Now past the home of Porfiry Petrovich, Raskolnikov's obsessed pursuer. Now in a potholed alley where a stranger lurched out of an archway and yelled at Raskolnikov, "You are the killer!" The archway echoes footsteps, past Nos. 27, 25, 23. At last No. 19, a yellow house at the end of the street, where sunlight cannot touch, like a secret.

Up the stairs, allegro, past the dark blue walls. One flight, two flights, three, four. Pinned to the door of the apartment next to Raskolnikov's, an official notice provided by the district designates this place as a model, well-kept apartment. An honor, a standard established by the schoolteacher state for the other residents of Raskolnikov's house, for Raskolnikov himself, if he were alive, still seething behind the door of Apartment 15.

Oleg produces his text, intending to read aloud. But then he looks up suddenly, noticing the graffiti on the wall, and belly-laughs.

"What does it say?"

" 'Raskolnikov, come back.' "

"And that one?"

" 'Raskolnikov. I was looking for you. I'll be back in an hour. Wait.' Signed 'Porfiry.' "

Loud laughter. A man opens his apartment door and shushes the intruders. Oleg whispers, giggling, that we had better leave.

"What does that one say?"

Oleg studies the wild scrawl. "It says, 'Enter this house and let the ice melt.' "

"What does it mean?"

"I don't know."

Enter this house and let the ice melt. An ambiguous injunction, applying to either one's own ice or that of the house. The injunction is difficult to follow. A first-time visitor brings an ice chip the size of a continent on his shoulder to the house of the Soviet Union. Disapproval mounts on memory, and there in the airport upon landing is all that political, historical ice at one's side: collectivism, adventurism, dissidents. Gulags, murders, antibooks, antichurch, anti-Semitism, psychological torture, denial of rights, property, humanity. You were not even aware you bore such grudge-freight with you, but flying into Moscow, circling the sudden, pleasing greenery, you understood that no Westerner can enter here, however eagerly, without a glacier in his heart.

So when the ice of hostile opinion melts, which happens over time, it melts almost in spite of itself, and it never melts entirely. Sometimes a spot that has thawed for a while refreezes in a shot, as when one, glazed-eyed, sees what one wishes to see, and then something terrible happens to mock the wisher. The open mind—that smirking journalistic god—suffers mightily in the Soviet Union. You do not arrive with an open mind, and seeking to achieve it may be an error, made usually in the interests of courtesy, since most conversations with Soviet citizens, even on heated topics, are civil, restrained, constrained. One feels either an odd sort of guilt for harboring one's chilly matter, or a fool for laying it aside.

But crossed feelings are merely one element of the game here, where the mystery is part of the solution. And the mystery itself is blatant, worn openly, since it is common knowledge in and about the Soviet Union that this is a very mysterious place, has always been a mysterious place, down through the party secretaries, and the Revolution and the czars, and past all that to the exotic mysteries of the various kingdoms that existed before they were enfolded in the larger kingdom: dolls within dolls; smiles within smiles. You get the feeling that there are *two* great secret bureaucracies in the Soviet Union: the government's and that of the people, who hide from the government out in the open and function in their own puzzling network of covert operations. And then again you get the feeling that the people were made for their government, that they could not lead lives either of resistance or of complacency, both of which offer deep satisfactions, if the government did not cooperate.

You can see at least one thing clearly at the start. The Soviet Union is as different from the United States as two places can be different, in part because the United States and the U.S.S.R. look alike in power and global interests, even in physiognomy and the varieties of nationality, and so the discovery of difference inevitably exaggerates the impression of difference. But the difference is real, and it extends to the natures of the people. Charity ads tell us that people are the same the world over, but except for biology, the evidence leans otherwise. American and Russian people both cuddle their children, lose their tempers, suffer toothaches, laugh at much the same jokes. But to believe that they are the same creatures who happen to live under antipodal political and economic theories is not only to deny that there is a logical connection between peoples and their governments but inevitably to devalue the "mutual understanding" that politicians love to tout.

If one really seeks mutual understanding with the Soviets, that understanding begins with the differences, which evidence themselves in basic characteristics. In a monthlong visit, I counted four such characteristics, never being wholly sure of anyone or anything, which was only fair, since no one could be wholly sure of me. Still, in the places I saw—Moscow, Leningrad, Kiev, Riga, Tashkent, Tbilisi, and the towns and villages around them—these four characteristics seemed to be constant: the presence of the past; the tension between the individual and the state; the mixture of love and fear with which citizens view their government; and, finally, a special beauty in the people that derives from a sense of life as grief.

"Did I see Lenin? Of course I saw Lenin. I saw Trotsky. I saw the *czar*. I saw him twice! Once was in 1913, when they celebrated the 300th anniversary of the monarchy. He stood no more than thirty meters away. The second was when a French diplomat visited the city. Nicholas. He had forty separate titles. Emperor of Russia! Duke of Finland! Always he exhorted the cossacks against the crowds. I looked upon his face."

Mikhail Petrovich Sinozersky, dressed in a white formal shirt and blue jogging pants with straps supporting his bedroom slippers, leans forward on a chair in his blue Leningrad apartment. His bald head is nearly covered by an enormous white bandage held in place by a safety pin, the result of minor surgery. "When the doctors went in, they found the fragment of a mine." He is amused by this, the eighty-four-year-old vet, who worked twelve hours a day in a factory at the age of twelve, fought in a revolution, a civil war, a world war, and only retired from his job of making gears at the age of seventy-seven. The blue eyes water slightly, but the skin on his face is taut. Head bandaged, he still looks ready for a fight.

"But yes, I saw Lenin. I saw him that second day of Easter when he came to the Finland Station. Lenin's sister Anna—historians ignore this fact—received a telegram that he was on the way, but she was able to tell only a few people of the event. Still, the word spread. We kids were just standing around when suddenly we saw a huge group of workers marching along the tramway and carrying a poster, TONIGHT LENIN IS COMING.

"Everyone at my factory knew that something big was up. The whole place, three or four thousand people, went down to meet the train. At ten o'clock the station was pitch-dark when the train pulled in. But the soldiers of the Revolution had come with searchlights and had climbed up on the roof. It was a warm night. My friends and I waited six hours. We really did not sense the significance of the event. Ninety-nine percent of the people there had never laid eyes on Lenin.

Peter the Great stood seven feet tall. Rumors spread that Lenin was taller.

"When the train arrived, Lenin climbed atop an armored car and addressed the crowd, telling them that this was the end of czarism, and more, that working people were no longer to be beaten and starved. Everyone I knew joined the Revolution—not then at the Finland Station, but before, because of the oppression, the wrongs. My own father was jailed for two years for a tussle with a policeman. We all had a reason.

"So, as the spirit of the Revolution grew in 1917, I joined. I worked as a courier, running messages to and from the Smolny Institute [formerly the convent school of Catherine the Great], where the Red Army had its headquarters. By the beginning of October, the Revolution was in the open. I reported to Smolny how many guards were in my district, where they were located at different times. Lenin remained underground. It was essential for him to know whether the soldiers would side with the provisional government or with the workers. Historians write that the provisional government just laid back and let the Revolution happen, but that is not so. Martial law was enforced. They controlled the bridges on the Neva. You needed passes in the streets. It was a dangerous time.

"Starting from October 20, the atmosphere of the entire city was heated. And still, the attack on the Winter Palace was unexpected. I was running a message to Smolny when I heard the *Aurora*'s shot, though I had no idea what it meant. A warm breeze carried the sound of the shot all over the city. I wanted to go over to the palace; my brother was there, in the first wave. He's still alive, my brother. He met Gorbachev this year. In the early morning they sent me to bring back one of the leaders.

"I was a fifteen-year-old peasant, but on the morning of October 26 at 7:00 A.M., there I was standing beneath the grand staircase of the czar's house, looking around. The air was full of dust. I poked about and entered the throne room. Three revolutionary soldiers were asleep on the throne. I called out for the leader I was sent to get, and suddenly people were treating me as an adult. They did not call me by my diminutive name. Everything was changed.

"It was not, I stress, a romantic thing that we did. We knew that we were doing something real. It worked, and it fulfilled its promise. At the Finland Station I pushed up close to the armored car to see and to hear. Lenin said, 'Everything is being done for you, for your future, your children.' I believed that."

. . .

The events recalled by Mikhail Sinozersky constitute the officially sanctified past of the Soviet present. Lenin's dicta are reproduced all over the Soviet Union, most volubly on giant metal billboards that rise from the highways and boulevards like sudden shouts. LONG LIVE LABOR; ALL PARTY DECISIONS MUST BE CARRIED OUT. Lenin's face and body are reproduced in photographs, paintings, and statuary everywhere: the friendly uncle Lenin, cap in hand and smiling; the forceful, into-the-future-that-works Lenin striding forward. In practically every office, great and small, a framed photograph of Lenin. On the bookshelf in Sinozersky's bedroom, a small pewter bust of Lenin, overseeing the old man's account of the past.

The centerpiece of this national reverence is Lenin's waxen body, lying in serene attentiveness in the Red Square tomb. No formal sight in the Soviet Union is more impressive than the lines of visitors to that tomb; day after day, an hour's wait, in all weather. The guards deliberately hook the lines in a grand sweep, not only to allow room for more people but also to give the line a quasi-religious form. All chatter diminishes rapidly as people approach the tomb that houses both a body and a statement that the revolutionary past is the best of the present. Couples on their wedding day bring flowers there for luck.

Even Stalin, acknowledged openly by most citizens now as murderous and mad, remains for many an important part of the cherished recent past. In the marble-hushed Stalin Museum in Gori, Stalin's birthplace in Georgia, hang hundreds of photographs of Stalin with Lenin, Stalin with Gorky, Stalin with Churchill and F.D.R. "Where are the photographs of Stalin with Hitler?"—a needling question to the decorous museum guide, who does not skip a beat. "Oh, those," she says. "They must be in the archives." A million people come to the museum every year, she says, not all of them Georgians and not all of them World War II veterans, although it is with veterans that Stalin's name remains least sullied. It is unsettling for Americans to realize that to Soviet citizens, it is *they* who defeated Nazi Germany, and history gives them a point.

The toll of that terrible war is part of the country's past-present as well. A memorial in Riga is half garden, half graves. In Tashkent, a statue shows a family embracing children who were orphaned in the west of the country. Outside Kiev, in Babi Yar, the memorialists were careful to dedicate the statue not to the nearly 100,000 Jews murdered there in the ravine but to the citizens of Kiev in general. Over the ravine where the murders occurred, plots of "black roses," *cherno-brivtsy,* surround a sculpture of victims clinging to one another to forestall their falling.

In Piskaryovskoye Cemetery, the war memorial in Leningrad, Maria Ivanova, in black from head to foot, comes two or three times a week to think about her husband, who died fighting outside the city. Six hundred thousand starved to death during the siege; coffins lay in the streets. In her ninth month of pregnancy when the siege began, Ivanova struggled through the 900 days, often going without food, feeding her daughter grass. She points to the grass covering the huge mounds of mass graves in the memorial; they look like enormous green beds in a hospital ward.

In the Novodevichy Cemetery in Moscow, the reverence of the past goes back further. Thousands bring their homage and flowers to lay at the graves of Gogol and Chekhov. Everywhere the past sustains the literature and the arts. Churches and entire neighborhoods are restored in Kiev and Tbilisi. In Samarkand, the old men in their square hats, *tyubetevkas,* convene to yammer folktales as old as the fourteenth-century mosques.

The presence of the past allows for feelings of enchantment, glory, inspiration, cultural moorings, reveries. It also allows for an odd sort of comfort in a country that is old-fashioned in so many ways that one would not know it for a modern power except for the missiles and rockets. This is a country where they still use the abacus and carbon paper; where, if one abandons real time, what appears is not the 1980s but the 1940s or the 1950s, with mobs hovering around the phonograph-record section of the GUM department store in Moscow, listening to Doris Day sing "Qué Será Será."

At a major basketball game in Tbilisi, the crowd of 10,000 sat in delight as ten-year-old boys in full Georgian dress performed a folk dance before the game. The style of the game itself was out of the 1950s, the Tbilisi Dynamos (pronounced dee-nah-*mos*) doing almost all the scoring from the outside. Goods in the stores look like things discovered in a warehouse unopened for fifty years. Men's gray shoes; toys that look used; vinyl raincoats made in colors that no one would choose. Cars break down. Television sets explode. High-ranking officials have four or five phones on their desks, there being no central switchboards. If the person you are phoning is not at his desk when you call, you simply will not make contact, and time will pass, and nothing will move.

In one's harshest moments, one suspects that the government has deliberately created this distortion of time so that full control of time will always reside in Moscow (all Aeroflot schedules run on Moscow time). But sometimes one also feels that this mass inefficiency and old-fashionedness is willed by the people themselves, as a means of retaining the past and of holding modernity away. In many ways all of the Soviet Union is like the old immigrant neighborhoods that once characterized America, a place at once aware of progress and intuitively resistant to it. Consciously or not, the government encourages that resistance by keeping the people ignorant of much news of the modern world, except when that news displays the violence of modernity (American murders make popular news stories).

Still, the antiquated inconveniences seem to offer the people a certain solace, as reassuring in their drabness as are the palaces in their gold leaf, that nothing will ever alter Soviet life too drastically, too frighteningly. In these *perestroika* (restructuring) times, when talk of change leaps automatically into the air, only the artists seem to take to the idea of change naturally, as a function of temperament, others showing as much wariness as pleasure at the anticipation of new structures. Even the state's former policies, now officially abjured, are part of the past that is known and oddly acceptable for that. Yet the new policies are also acceptable because the state has decided on them; the state has ordered people to be free. It sounds just like other orders in the old days. The old days prevail. Walking at her own sweet pace across a dilapidated six-lane highway near the resort town of Jurmala, an old woman in a kerchief shoulders a scythe.

"I want to explain something to you before we meet the fisherman." My journalist-guide talks cheerily as we drive toward the village of Zarmova, thirty kilometers northeast of the Latvian capital of Riga. The guide is slim as a mannequin, carefully wrapped in a sport coat and slacks. His small nose turns upward; his cheekbones seem to have driven his chin into recession. Throughout the drive he is relentless in pointing out the beauties of the countryside, the coziness of the dachas, the nobility of the working people of Latvia, of Russia.

"Before the Great Revolution," he goes on, "every fisherman in Latvia had to fish for himself. As a result, the fisherman was the poorest man in the republic."

"This particular fisherman we're going to see?"

"No, no. Fishermen in general." He does not know whether to take such questions seriously, so he takes all questions seriously.

"But *after* the Great Revolution, all the fishermen joined collective farms." He parks the car at the side of a lane. "And thanks to the Great Revolution, now they are among the *richest* people in Latvia!"

"The great *Russian* Revolution?"

"Yes." He looks briefly disconcerted. "Here we are."

At the gate of their cottage, the fisherman and his wife greet us with warm courtesy. My guide prattles on about the perfection of the fisherman's house; of his German shepherd, who stalks back and forth barking in a wire-fence-enclosed pen; of the fisherman's garden, which is indeed brilliant with daisies and roses of various colors. Inside the cottage, the couple have prepared a late-afternoon Sunday dinner of caviar, salmon, and lamprey eels. My guide's face aches with grins: "Such a table, such a table!" He gurgles with delight as he reaches for black balsam liqueur, a Latvian specialty, which is made without alcohol but kicks like a mule.

"So." The guide presents the couple again as if they were a pair of porcelain dolls. Both are in their late fifties, formally dressed, shy but at ease with the affability expected of them. "So," repeats the guide. "You may ask your questions."

"Well, for a start, could you tell me exactly how a collective farm works?" I address the fisherman.

"All the fishermen band together for the common good. Isn't that so?" my guide asks the fisherman, who nods, smiling.

"Who directs the collective farm?"

"The Fishermen's Union of the Republic of Latvia," answers the guide. "Isn't that so, Arvid?" Arvid smiles and nods again. "Of course," adds the guide, "the members of the union are elected openly, and one joins the collective farm of one's own free will."

"So," again trying to reach the fisherman directly, "the collective is joined of one's own free will. And the collective is directed—"

"Guided," corrects my guide.

"Guided, then, by the union. Who, uh, guides the union?"

"Well, of course, there is the Ministry of Fisheries in Moscow," the guide explains. "That is correct, is it not, Arvid?" By now Arvid is nodding continually.

"I want to be sure I have this straight. A fisherman can join a cooperative farm of his own free will. And the cooperative is told what to do by the union. And the union is told what to do by the ministry in Moscow."

"Correct," beams the guide.

"But the fisherman joins the cooperative farm of his own free will."

"Of course."

"And he could go to work fishing for himself."

"No," says the guide.

"So he has the free will to join the cooperative, but if he quits, he's out of a job."

The guide considers for a moment, then grins again. "No one is out of a job in the Soviet Union." Nods all around. "And there would never be a reason for the fisherman to quit the cooperative. The cooperative is not only his source of income, but his strength. Isn't that so, Arvid?"

Anxious that Arvid might nod himself to death, I change the subject to his garden, the contents of which, Arvid says for himself at last, he changes every year.

"Why do you change your garden?"

"Because it makes me feel as if I direct the flowers." His answer is pronounced very slowly.

Now the guide nods. "It is a beautiful garden, a very beautiful garden. And your ceilings, Arvid. You must not forget to show your ceilings." To me: "He has made every ceiling in this house a different design from the other."

"Why did you do that?" I ask, gazing up at the brown wooden ceiling above me, which Arvid has carved to look like the icing on a chocolate wedding cake.

"It gave me pleasure," says Arvid.

"What else do you do for your pleasure?"

"I sing," he answers. "I sing in a chorus."

"Everyone sings in Latvia," my guide chips in, eyes shining with both joy and black balsam. He has been downing the stuff steadily all afternoon, raising various enthusiastic toasts to fishermen, international friendship, and birthdays (that day happened to be mine).

Asked if he would consent to sing a Latvian folk song right now, Arvid holds back at first, but then begins in a cellolike voice that seems to come from beneath the floorboards. The song is processional. Some story is being sung.

And then, suddenly, as Arvid continues to sing, my guide joins the song in perfect thirds harmony. His squeaky speaking voice has become a flute. He looks like a different person, the face unpinched, the eyes free of strain. His contribution to the song flows like a clear stream into Arvid's.

A silence, at once contented and embarrassed, follows, in which everyone tacitly acknowledges that for a moment we have been in the presence of something disruptive. Arvid's wife gazes blushingly at the floor.

"What does the song mean?" I ask the fisherman.

The guide speaks up again, his composure regained. "It means, Oh to be alone in a boat on the open sea! Isn't that right, Arvid?" The fisherman nods.

The system in which Arvid the fisherman does his work is, like all such systems in the Soviet Union, a simple open structure operating within a complex hidden theory. Hypothetically, collective farms, whether dealing with fish or carrots, are voluntary organizations formed by people who pool resources and share profits. In fact, however, the state imposed these organizations on rural populations, and it controls them loosely or strictly, depending on location and circumstances. What my guide said about free elections is sometimes true and sometimes not. Many elected officials of unions like Arvid's are simply party appointees, and indirectly the party keeps an eye on all things related to the farm, including the fish.

The relationship of the individual to the state is thus held in place by lines that reach to him no matter if he fishes for a living, teaches, plays soccer, or practices medicine. Whatever philosophy or revision the state expresses at any given time will find its way into every segment of society through the ministry or bureau or union of this or that. The recent directives of the Twenty-seventh Congress offer perfect, if ironic, examples of these lines of connection. Viewing desperate economic straits, Gorbachev ordered up greater individual responsibility. The workers are expected to respond uniformly with individuality.

In Kiev, Boris Soldatenko, the party secretary in charge of one of the city's twelve districts, is responsible for the well-being of 300,000 citizens. In his typically spare, clean bureaucrat's office a framed photograph of Lenin is the only decoration on the walls. It looks down on a heavily built, amiable, if guarded, man of forty-one, whose main task nowadays is to build housing for the people of the district. It is an assignment that, because of his training as a construction engineer, he relishes as his meat. The Twenty-seventh Congress promised that by the year 2000 every Soviet family would have its own dwelling place. Boris is directly connected to that promise. "More attention must be given to individual incentives," he repeats the party line. "The best workers will get the best apartments first."

"Why was individual achievement ignored before?"

"It was not ignored. The country had other priorities." He cites the principle of "democratic centralism. The individual has personal responsibility for his achievements, but the overall decisions are collective."

"And what if the individual outruns the collective?"

"Lenin always said that jumping ahead too fast is destructive for the state."

Current enthusiasms aside, there is a logical conflict in all this new governmental stress on the preeminence of the individual that goes beyond the academic illogic of being ordered to be independent. Throughout its history, the Communist Party has made it clear to the people that the party and only the party understands the basic truths of Marxism-Leninism. Individuals may offer "subjective" interpretations of dogma, but the party owns the dogma's truth. When the party officially encourages individual achievements, therefore, it does so under strict control. Not only is an individual achiever always subordinate to the group, but even that balancing act is limited by the presumption that since final knowledge of all things resides in the Kremlin, no single citizen can truly comprehend the singularity he has been directed to assert.

This poses a problem for the individuals within the system who show true independent spirits. Arvid the fisherman provides an answer in his ever changing garden and ceiling designs, as does Oleg in his riffs ("You improvise within the plan"). But self-assertion need not be so private. Shota Kavlashvili, the chief architect of Tbilisi, held that post in the early 1970s but lost it between 1974 and 1978 because of his stubborn persistence in seeking to restore the mid-nineteenth-century Old Town area of the city, with its frame houses and wide, gracious balconies. After his dismissal, Shota continued to work as a rank-and-file architect, eventually securing an assignment to build a tunnel near the Old Town area. Shota completed the tunnel, but he also surreptitiously restored a couple of the old buildings nearby. If glasnost (openness) had been in effect (he smiles as he says this), he could not have been so secret or so successful.

Shota is a tall, slim, self-contained man, in his sixties now, who hardly looks like a fifth columnist, and will not admit to being one, though that is what he is. He not only works within the system, he also supervises it, taking instructions from above to build uninteresting apartment houses to complement the existing ones that look like white, square filing cabinets with laundry spilling from the drawers. Still, he pursues his own restoration dreams. As an architect he defends the necessary "free expression" of his craft. Yet he talks with equal enthusiasm about a collective good and "shared values."

"But if you had shared the values of those who did not want to see Old Town restored, nothing would have improved."

He neither agrees with this nor disagrees. "If you would like to speak with me further, call me at home in the morning. I work at home in the mornings on projects I devise for myself, not government assignments. I call that my right-hand work. In the office I do my left-hand work." He smiles only slightly again, and that is that.

The great modern Russian poet Andrei Voznesensky wrote a poem called "Antiworlds," which describes the opposition of two realities. "Long live antiworlds! They rebut/With dreams, the rat race and the rut." In the Soviet Union one senses the presence of the dreamworld in rebuttal, a sort of "other realm" that constituted paradise in the old Russian fairy tales. Perhaps that dreamworld will fuse with reality in the light of new official permissiveness. Voznesensky is delightedly shocked at how far things have gone in so short a time. At his home in Peredelkino, a woodsy artists' enclave outside Moscow, he exults about new times: "Look at the response to the Chagall exhibition." He refers to the September showing in Moscow of the formerly forbidden works of the painter, an exhibition that Voznesensky introduced. "Tens of thousands line up to ogle the paintings, and others write vicious anti-Semitic letters to the papers reviling Chagall as a Zionist. No one would have dared to write such letters years ago. Both extremes are raising their heads."

And how far will the current individual expressions go? And is not all this individuality at odds with the collective philosophy of the country, and ultimately with state power? At present the system of tight connections is still in place. In several senses, the Soviets are a nation of lines: the lines in front of the shops, the theaters, the sports palaces; the lines to the past; the verbal lines, the party slogans. But the strongest lines remain the "lines" kept on good citizens and bad, on well-kept apartments and bad; the lines that cut into telephone lines; the lines of *nomenklatura* and of *blat,* or patronage; the lines from Moscow to the fisherman, the district leader, the architect, the poet. So vast and various a country, and yet one has the feeling that on the sunniest days any citizen could be plucked from the vastness like a fish from the sea.

"I'm not supposed to talk to you, you know." We walk together toward the Moscow metro. "After you left yesterday, the department head came in and told the junior faculty that you gave a good class in literature but that you were simply cunning. She called you just another American spy."

"She was right, of course."

"Of course. She also said that since you have a Jewish name, you are undoubtedly a spy for Israel."

"For both Israel and America?"

"Yes. She must think you a very hard worker. And naturally, all you are here for is to write how badly we treat the Jews."

"How badly *do* you treat the Jews?"

"They still have trouble keeping jobs. Not long ago they were forbidden to enroll at the university."

"How difficult a position am I putting you in, talking to me?" She angles us down into the metro, heading for Red Square. "Or are you a spy too?"

"Well, yes, but it's rather complicated. You see, after I make my report on you, then someone will report that I was seen with you, and we'll both be shot."

"How difficult, seriously?"

"If you want the truth, I could lose my teaching post. But I put myself in this position, you didn't. My generation is different from the department head's. Things are different here in general. But don't exaggerate the improvements in your article. The valve that opens can close as well, little by little, so you'd hardly notice.

"And besides," walking up the metro steps into the bright cold morning, "it's Moscow Day! The first such celebration in history. Look at the people out in droves. We'll be doing our seventieth anniversary like mad all season. Like your American Constitution celebrations."

"They're going on at home right now."

"But you are here walking around Red Square. You *are* a clever spy." She looks fondly at a group of acrobats rehearsing and smiles with pleasure.

I ask her, "Younger generation or not, you believe in all this, don't you?"

"Yes, I believe. Communism is a glorious fairy tale."

"So is capitalism."

"No. Ours is a better fairy tale, if realized. People learn to rely on one another, to see the world as mutually dependent. And no one goes hungry or homeless."

"And no one reads what he wants to read. And no one travels where he wants to travel, not even in his own country." We stop to watch floats in a parade. On one of the floats the giant figure of a Western capitalist in top hat and morning coat is being beaten back by a handful of noble workers. Tonight the city will explode with fireworks, and the fascinating, grotesque Stalinist buildings that rise like mountains in the city will blaze with color. On the Moscow River, ferry boats will spew light.

"I know that we are often backward, unsophisticated," she says, watching me observe the float. "I know more about the repression than you could ever tell me. In that class you taught, there is a girl whose father lost his job only because the girl fell in love with an American boy when he was over here. But such things are not examples of Communism. They are the perversions of Communism."

"You've been living with the perversions quite a while."

"Quite a while? Seventy years? After seventy years your country was just about ready for a civil war." We glance at each other to lower the steam. "The people in the street notice you. Can you tell?"

"Why? Do I look so different?"

"You walk differently, as if you commanded the streets." In silence we study the old men wearing their war ribbons on their heavy suit jackets; the babushkas, waddling like overloaded wagons, their wheels grinding into the earth. "I know what you do not understand," she says finally. "How it is that we can love and fear our country at the same time."

"Yes. That's exactly what I can't understand."

"Do you remember what you asked the students yesterday? You asked them, 'What is a word?' getting them to say that every word, even the smallest article, is an idea and that if they concentrated on the word, every word, they would understand every idea. Last night, knowing that I would see you today and that you would ask me questions, I tried to think of a word, the idea of which I could not explain."

"What did you come up with?"

"Home."

The university teacher was right about its being hard for an American to comprehend how Soviet citizens can love the country that makes war against them. And it is not as if the fear the people have of their government is a hidden emotion. The teacher mustered real courage to speak with a forbidden American journalist, but fear rose even to her eyes when, as she entered a hotel for foreigners, a weaselly "doorman" (a probable KGB informant) made her present her passport, in an act of humiliation. In a synagogue in Kiev, one of the officers of the congregation, wearing his war ribbons and acknowledging the presence of an accompanying official, said, "Oh, no, there's no anti-Semitism in the Soviet Union. Maybe in the 1920s, but not today."

"Then why do tens of thousands of Jews want to leave?"

"Tens of thousands! Never!" He never looked at the official. "Only a handful. And they have relatives in the West. That's the only reason."

In interviews, people on the whole are extremely careful, disguising even the mildest criticisms in generalities so airy as to arouse suspicions that may be darker than the facts. (Under *perestroika,* the abstract "bureaucracy" is the acceptable bête noire.) And most interviews arranged for short-time visitors take place in the presence of a journalist-interpreter-companion who, rightly or wrongly, is assumed by those interviewed to be KGB or something close, thus inducing overwhelming courtesies but little else. At a dinner in Tashkent, a family was offered up for inspection in the presence of an official neighborhood leader, who, after answering all the questions on the mummified family's behalf and expressing many nice thoughts about world peace, began, in the amber light, to take on the appearance of a baked Alaska, her existence at once enlarging and melting over the table and onto the floor where the children sat cross-legged and silent.

But at a dinner in Kiev, at the home of Professor Gennadi Matsuka, who heads the Ukraine's Institute of Molecular Biology and Genetics, that mixture of love and fear of the country was fluid and evident. Professor Matsuka, a small man in his late sixties, wears a sad-happy face under a thick brush of gray hair. He directs an institute at the center of Soviet genetic technology, where, along with cancer and botanical research, the Soviet space experiments are shaped and conducted.

He surveyed the table his wife had prepared. "Just a little something," said his wife, a chemist, heavyset, graceful, with the face of a lively girl. "A little something," he murmured. "A little bread, a little soup, a little beef, a little herring, a little tongue, and three little cakes." Laughter among the guests, who included a nephew who drives a cab, is a painter on the side, and wants to reverse the proportions, and a female neighbor with an ethereal smile who arranges competitions for concert singers. Also present: a Great Dane with a keen interest in the dinner table, and a forty-year-old turtle with a home in one of Professor Matsuka's bedroom slippers. Flowers everywhere. "No, I did not manufacture them," said the geneticist.

The gaiety of the evening flowed naturally from the start, into moments of domestic humor, Matsuka's wife teasing him frequently, into the neighbor's questions about Van Cliburn's career, veering off into a serious discussion of Soviet artists who defected to the West. What did they feel about that? "True loss." What did Professor Matsuka feel about being a geneticist during the Stalin years, when genetics was outlawed as a field of study? He did his research in secret and waited patiently for the time when the country he favored would favor him back.

Fragments of conversations:

"During Stalin we led two lives."

"I still believe there are things we shouldn't know."

"Stalin ruined Communism."

"I was never encouraged to think for myself."

"I was always encouraged to think for myself."

"We could not have had this dinner three years ago."

An evening that touched on the oppressiveness of the government one moment and on the accomplishments of the people another, pointed with politics, smoothed over with laughter, and things in between. "Have you heard this one?" asked the nephew. "Capitalism is the exploitation of man by man; Communism just the opposite." Through all the genuine good feeling, a sense of decorum, and hope. "Now that the windows are open," said Mrs. Matsuka of *perestroika*, "they can never be shut again." All present assented. No stranger could tell whether they also saw the image of a valve opening and closing.

One source of the affection the people hold for their country is, in fact, the very orderliness that has its dark side in suppression. The subway stations in Tashkent may be the most beautiful examples of such structures in the world. One is built high with columns like an Egyptian temple. One is dedicated to an Uzbek poet and his works. One to space exploration and the cosmonauts. All are palatial, clean, and safe. What the citizens of Tashkent would make of New York City's IRT or the Bernhard Goetz case is beyond imagining. The nation that has given Tashkent Karl Marx Square has also given it civility. For passive personalities, the combination of love and fear creates no deep upheaval.

Yet even for assertive personalities, such as those of Voznesensky and the university teacher, it is clearly possible to function with that mixture of love and fear. In a sense, such people are always banking on the future, that events will allow their fears to dissipate and their love to increase and that Marxism-Leninism minus the gunshots, Marxism-Leninism as pure social and economic justice, as fairy tale come true, will prevail. Americans would find it difficult to wait, but

Americans believe that people were destined to live comfortably with their emotions as with all else. Soviet citizens, to the contrary, believe that people are meant to live uncomfortably with their emotions as with all else, and so they do it well.

"How did I know I was an actress? I didn't. I just knew I loved plays. I act in both Russian and Latvian plays. But when I play in Russian, I think in Latvian."

In her dressing room in the Riga theater, Vija Artmane sits serenely like a queen mother, her hands flying like gulls into the air when she wishes to express something forcefully, or into her hair, pure gold. They say the most famous actress in Latvia was even more beautiful as a young woman—"a Marilyn Monroe, I swear it"—but it is hard to imagine her generous, honest face more lovely than it is today. In her midfifties, she is still a star of plays and movies in the Soviet Union, doing one play tonight while rehearsing another. Her dressing room is small, uncluttered. A poster-size picture of a handsome man in Elizabethan costume fills half a wall. From time to time, an anxious stage manager comes in to alert her to curtain time.

"But I love all playwrights, all the great ones at least, no matter the language. Tennessee Williams, Albee, Arthur Miller—we know American writers pretty well. I myself played in *Night of the Iguana*. It is wonderful to work in plays that represent the world and not a single nation. Do I mean that in English—wonderful? Yes? It is wonderful to see the world; my position allows that. You may not know, I am a member of the Latvian Parliament, so I have a chance to talk peace to the officials who can do something about it. The theater gives a special kind of power, you know. Like the church."

Another actor sticks his head in the room and reminds her of something and exits. "That was my colleague. He plays Lord Cecil in *Elizabeth the Queen*, the play we are doing tonight. My husband also played Lord Cecil. That is his photograph on the wall. One year he is dead now. A beautiful actor." She stares for a moment. "A truly great actor.

"And still the government thought that the power of the theater was too strong. At least they did before, perhaps no longer. Plays are opening in Moscow now that were suppressed for fifty years, like Bulgakov's *Heart of a Dog*. Wonderful satire. For a long time, no one was allowed to touch Dostoevsky—Dostoevsky, imagine. They were afraid of 'wrong' ideas. But a play can have no damaging ideas if society is strong. And society grows strong when it has a chance to see. So trust develops. Some who would withhold certain plays from the people call it 'guidance,' but any guidance that is forced contradicts the humanistic act." Again the stage manager comes in, and again he is shooed away graciously. "I must go in a minute." She shows no anxiety.

"My favorite speech? In any play?" She is silent, thinking. "I played the heroine in a Russian play call *Blow Wind*." Her voice suddenly falls to a whisper. " 'I wore a wreath in the forest. A wreath made from my nation's flowers. But they took the wreath from my hair.' " She gathers her strength, still sitting. "The speech is of great love." She recites in Latvian, requiring no translation, but she translates nonetheless: " 'When you are taken by force the soul is killed. No one can be taken by force. No one can take by force the person who loves.'

"We are needed by our audiences here. They need a friend, and actors give them friends. Besides, everyone is an actor in some way, so we understand each other tacitly. There is no way to play something you do not have within you." She stands, extends her hand. "Now I really have to get ready." She opens her dressing-room door. "I'm afraid I sounded sadder than I intended. I am not a sad person. I like comedy as well as tragedy. Perhaps even more, life being closer to comedy, don't you think? But not a raucous comedy. A wonderful comedy. Do I mean wonderful? No. A comedy full of wonders. That is what I mean. A comedy of wonders."

The need of an audience for art, to which Vija Artmane referred, seems palpable in a country where 14,000 people will fill a stadium for a poetry reading by Voznesensky and other thousands will wait in lines overnight for an opera or a ballet. Lately need has been propelled by curiosity, since the atmosphere of *perestroika* has touched the arts, and films such as *Is It Easy to Be Young?*, which openly discusses the Soviet war in Afghanistan, and the anti-Stalinist *Repentance* draw 5,000 viewers a night. Still, the Soviet citizens' hunger for things beautiful seems abiding and general. In Tbilisi, students at the most prestigious Georgian theater school speak of the satisfactions of performing in so appreciative a country.

But the people's hunger for beautiful events or moments ought not to suggest that their ordinary lives are unbeautiful. It is only that the day-to-day beauty of the life is self-obscuring, like so much else. The beauty of Russian humor, for instance, is often hidden in hardship. At a hotel in Kiev, I sought to pay my bill, a split-second transaction in America and one that in the Soviet Union can fill an hour or more, depending on the availability of carbon paper, calculators, dollars, rubles, or clerks. In the Kiev hotel the clerk was missing, and her assistant, after much desperate searching, gamely tried her English. "Would you mind," she asked, "coming back in fifteen years?" We only laughed as hard as we did because of the dark truth in the error.

"You see, my friend, *this* is the difference between your country and mine!" On a flight from Moscow to Tashkent, an enormous man beside me has just surveyed the chicken breast and the pickle that have spilled onto his mountainous vest. The spilling has occurred because the seats on the Aeroflot plane are too close together, the food platform is too small for the tray, the tray's compartments are too small for the food, the cellophane wrappings of which are a struggle to remove, thus initiating the path of the food to the vest. "In your country," my companion explained, "airplane food is unrecognizable as food, whereas a Russian chicken is in fact a chicken, a Russian pickle a pickle. But the American tray is perfectly designed, and the seats are adequately arranged. The choice then!" He watches wanly as the pickle rolls off his vest onto the floor and away forever. "Either one is presented with an inedible meal that is easy to eat, or a delicious meal that spills in your lap."

On another Aeroflot flight from Tbilisi to Moscow, ice, great slabs of it, formed around the baggage racks. After the passengers had huddled for over an hour as if in a snowdrift, the plane's heating mechanism finally took hold, thus causing a torrent of water from above. Everyone was soaked except a woman who calmly opened her umbrella. She had come prepared for the rains.

This acceptance of day-to-day disasters makes laughter not only useful and necessary but sublime, even if the sublimity takes its form in faces turned prematurely old with weariness and the anticipation of disappointment and failure. Such weariness is more visible in Moscow than in Samarkand, more in the cities than in the villages, but it exists everywhere and is ennobling. In Leningrad there are twenty-four Rembrandts in the Hermitage, but there are many more Rembrandts in the streets. Within the gruffness and the frequent grimness of the people resides a startling innocence. In a café in Leningrad, an over-the-hill singer, hair dyed blue-black, huge green flowers splattered on her vast black dress, suffered through a repertoire of old familiar songs, the voice quavering melodramatically, the breasts heaving like bread dough, the hands crossed on her bosom. She looked a scream. Until two pink-faced soldiers barely in their twenties entered the café and sat. They were transfixed by the singer, the music. Suddenly the whole room was transfixed.

If such scenes constitute the beauty of acceptance, others, like Vija Artmane speaking up for the power of free words, constitute the beauty of rejection and rebellion. Raised hopes are the talk of every Soviet town in the *glasnost* season, but one senses from the patience of people like the geneticist Matsuka that in some citizens at least hopes were always alert to the possibility of being raised. Religions in the Soviet Union breathe freer now that the government has rather cleverly allowed official atheism to transmute into the more dignified idea of the separation of church and state. Close your ears to the Ukrainian language at an evangelical Baptist service in Kiev, and you might as well be in a Dallas suburb. The choir sang lustily "If I Had the Wings of a Dove."

Americans wonder or enjoy wondering if Soviet citizens can possibly be happy within their system. Obviously Soviets can be happy and are, but most probably would reject the standard of happiness as impertinent. Perhaps three of the perceived characteristics of the country—the presence of the past, the tension between the individual and the state, the simultaneous love and fear of the government—work in concert to produce the fourth characteristic: a sense that in life grief flows continuously in and out of happiness, and happiness in and out of grief. Americans, who on the whole have led charmed lives, have a hard time accepting that grief is anything but an aberration, but not so Soviets. For a visitor of thirty days, or perhaps even of thirty years, the recurrent mystery is how a nation founded in an illusion, just as ours was, can seem to function so steadily without illusions, how at the same time they dream and do not dream.

Of Leningrad's great Nevsky Prospekt a hundred years ago, Gogol exclaimed, "Everything you meet on the Nevsky Prospekt is brimming over with propriety: the men in long jackets with their hands in their pockets; the ladies in pink, white, or pale blue satin coats and stylish hats!" The street is different now: much of the clothing unfashionable, the heads of both men and women hung down or resolutely held aloft. On afternoons darkening into evenings, the crowd shuttles back and forth like bureau drawers, as if the entire boulevard were a convention of lines, moving in the various directed quests all at once, growing darker as the day does, in the mass.

On one such afternoon a girl of nineteen or so sits posing for a street artist in the doorway of a former church. From the distance in her eyes she could be looking at America instead of a fixed point on the Nevsky Prospekt. In her hands roll two plums, which she strokes as if they were a cat. The street artist hunches over like a tailor, trying to get the eyes right, an assertion of concentration over ability. But the girl's life is as yet undeclared. Her look shifts continually out of her control, now to a teenager fearing a math exam, now to an anxious mother, now to a widow, now to a woman who has just made love and wonders where the act went.

At last the street artist finishes; he has sketched the girl wilder than she actually appears. As she pays him, she barely glances at his work; she will study herself at home in private. The street artist, having employed his little skill, his journalistic skill, pockets his rubles and awaits new customers. The girl rolls her sketch carefully under her arm and joins the crowds on Nevsky Prospekt, disappearing part by part among the overcoats until at last she steps down into an underpass that swallows whole all who enter.

October 26, 1987

Experimental Animals

IN APRIL of this year [1975] *The New York Times* printed an open letter of protest by Alexander Dubček to the Czech government. A Czech playwright, Václav Havel, soon submitted another protest letter, releasing it simultaneously to the world press. This combination of protests made the authorities nervous and either as a result, or because they had been looking for an excuse all along, the police raided the houses of Czech writers, confiscating works in progress. Perhaps in anticipation of such reprisals, Vašek, the hero of Ludvík Vaculík's *The Guinea Pigs,* keeps his manuscript hidden in the guinea pigs' cage. The fact that the State guards seem to know his every move frightens him, "and I wouldn't want them to know about my every thought, meant for the eyes of my young readers."

The Guinea Pigs and Milan Kundera's short stories, *Laughable Loves,* are the first two reprints published by Penguin Books in an important new series, "Writers from the Other Europe." The series is under the general editorship and inspiration of Philip Roth, who has written an astute introduction to the Kundera volume. Two Polish works are due in January, *This Way for the Gas* by Tadeusz Borowski, and Tadeusz Konwicki's *A Dreambook of Our Time.* Two Yugoslav novels will be out next summer. If all the books are as good as the first two, we soon will have an abundance of genius on our hands.

The Guinea Pigs is a story of experimental animals, and is something of a guinea pig itself: tormented, playful, observant, in hiding. Vašek the bank clerk, his schoolteacher wife, Eva, and their two boys, young Vašek and Pavel, are model animals, except for the father's incubative madness. Like Dostoevsky's Golyadkin *(The Double),* another terrorized civil servant, Vašek is equally a prisoner of the State and of his feelings about being watched and noted. He decides to brighten his life by giving his children guinea pigs for Christmas.

There is nothing like a man for bringing out the animal in an animal. Here the animal emerging is two-legged; the guinea pigs are made to be afraid, resourceful, cooperative, and competitive in turns according to the growing obsessiveness of their keeper. Vašek brings the little creatures torture and reward, but uncertainty above all. He tests them—they are guinea pigs after all—but his experiments have no pattern or context outside the momentary pleasure of a mind quietly and precisely becoming murderous. The guinea pigs become something else.

In the poem "Pike" Ted Hughes made a fish so large that it was "too immense to stir" in a pond "as deep as England." Vaculík's guinea pigs also grow large, until one of them finally fills the cavernous imagination of Vašek—some size. When that happens, man and guinea pig suffer the consequences of complementarity; each fills the other's capacities. A battle follows, a duel in the dark, after which the winner/loser returns triumphant to his cage, ready to resume the business of insanity as usual.

The resumption—dogged, steady—is the core nightmare of Vaculík's fantasy. Busy busy, Vašek and his fellow bank clerks return to their cages every morning, while children and teachers return to school, revert to type. The weather changes abruptly, without nuance. Houses and conversations do not change. Animals are purchased as Christmas gifts to perk up domestic tranquillity. As with our hero's mind, the decorating is interior.

Outside the home, meanwhile, there is a national economic crisis (or is it business as usual?). For years, forever, the bank clerks have been stuffing bills in their pockets and other places, trying to make it past the guards at closing. For years the guards have caught most of them; but a lot of the stolen money is never returned to the vaults. There results a "mysterious circulation," money not accounted for, not restored to the system either at once or eventually; apparently vanished. Some fear a depression in the shape of a maelstrom.

One plot of *The Guinea Pigs* has Vašek searching to discover the nature of the mysterious circulation, and to learn if and how the maelstrom will come. As he searches he has already descended into his private maelstrom of the other plot, the tiny zoo story. He is a family man, our hero, with two boys and three guinea pigs whom he fathers with the petty tyrannies of the daddy in Joyce's "Counterparts." Little Vašek is his own counterpart who occasionally revenges himself on the old man. "Children are just like adults," said Vaculík to Antonin J. Liehm in *The Politics of Culture* (Grove Press); "the unreliable lad, the one who promised to bring a frog but didn't, is just the same now . . . except that maybe now he's a cabinet minister." Vašek is only slightly more successful at cruelty to animals than to children, but at the end of the story he still has time on his side.

The way he talks to his boys is the way they talk to each other is the way he talks to us—needling. "My dear young readers," he says early on; and as the novel simultaneously tightens and goes haywire we are reminded that we too have been put in the position of small boys and guinea pigs. Poking at us through the narrative, what plans does Vašek have for us? In fact he does torment the reader at one point, deliberately answering our worst fears, and then reversing himself—saying that the monstrosity he previously described never occurred—at which we feel no relief. Yet what have we to fear from Vašek, imprisoned Czech bank clerk, made crazy by the State, locked in his cage by the State?

Vaculík would answer that Vašek is not a prisoner of a state of government, but of a state of mind, from which we're never safe. He said as much in an interview for *The Nation* (May 21, 1973): "[I want to create] something that won't remind the readers of the regime. I want to write as if current conditions did not exist, or as if I felt at ease with them. You see, if a person feels obliged to write exclusively against the government, he has actually submitted to the government's prohibition to write about other things." This is logical, but it rings false. Richard Wilbur said the strength of the genie comes from his being in the bottle; and the strength of Vaculík (the novelist, not the interviewee) is similarly derived. Pathologically there may be no difference between a tormentor of children in a free state or a prison camp, but the difference in terms of art is enormous; the difference between little murders and tragedy.

For Vašek is a guinea pig himself, as all are guinea pigs under a government. The more abstract and unpredictable the government, the greater peril for the animals; their home life becomes shaky; they buy no cottages in the country. Under such a system everything is in miniature, except one's fears. They grow infinitely, feeding on their own mysterious circulation, and eventually may get to be as big as the ruby eye of a guinea pig in the dark.

At the outset of the story Vašek tells us that this will be a book about "Nature." Immediately he veers to the side, pretending that by Nature he means country life or the guinea pigs' behavior. But he means Nature in its most dreadful depth, the Nature known to Poe, who was an economist of a special competence, whose mysteriously circulating maelstrom whirled down in the tortured mind. Vašek the tormentor is more tormented than he knows, because he is tormented by the mind that might tell him. That he does not feel so tormented constitutes his gravest suffering, for he may prod and maim perpetually with no satisfaction. Observed externally by "an ideal observer," Vašek cannot be reached. Nothing, not even the great god guinea pig can help him.

The healthy thing to do with one's demon, said Vaculík, "is to project him outside yourself, into something external, that you can still do something with." Like a guinea pig or a novel. In a world where the police burn the novels, one can always turn to drowning guinea pigs or abusing children in order to feel alive and kicking. Then the demon is externalized ultimately, Vaculík shows us. He lives in our own sweet paws.

August 30, 1975

Portrait
of a
Prisoner

I don't think anything that has been created can be destroyed.
—SY JACKSON on immortality

HAD MARY ETTA JAQUE of Rochester, New York, been at home the night of September 16, 1958, all this might never have happened. She would have opened her front door to her boyfriend, Sylvester Jackson, then seventeen, and she would have either snuggled up or scolded him for being exuberantly drunk on Thunderbird wine. As it turned out, Mary Etta was not at home that night, and big Sy Jackson, looped and annoyed, kicked in her door. That brought the police, who, says Sy, proceeded to beat up on him in the patrol car. One cop threw a punch, Sy ducked, the cop hit his partner, Sy ran. When Sy was caught, he was beaten up some more. The charge was second-degree assault. On his lawyer's advice, Sy pleaded guilty and was committed to the Elmira Correctional Facility. So began his tour of New York State prisons. By the time he celebrated his forty-first birthday last April 18, he had spread seventeen years of his life among institutions in Elmira, Comstock, Dannemora, Auburn, Stormville, and now Attica, famous Attica.

It hardly looks troublesome these days, this odd, 1930s fortress with the Greek-echo name. In September 1971, Attica put hell on display for the nation. There are no signs of a riot today. The shock to one's system lies simply in the place itself, its main wall rising thirty

feet around fifty-three acres in the middle of dead-quiet upstate greenery. The wall is gray gray. Nothing in nature, including a rock, could
be that color. Guards say the wall goes down thirty feet in spots so
as to hold fast in the quicksand. At intervals along the flat surface,
watch turrets sit with witch-hat tops; Disney World, had it been built
by Albert Speer, would have this look. The wall encompasses five
separate cell blocks. Inside these are individual cells, seven feet from
floor to ceiling, nine feet by six feet in area, in which some 2,000 men
live among the possessions permitted them.

Sy Jackson sits hunched over at the tail end of his narrow cot. At
five feet eleven inches and slightly more than 200 pounds, he ought
easily to fill his cell, but he seems to have willed a diminished appearance in order to stay in proportion with his furnishings. Most of these
hang on the walls: a chain of beads, a pair of sunglasses, snapshots
of his three children. He has copied William Ernest Henley's poem
"Invictus" by hand and mounted it with cellophane tape. There is a
picture postcard of a sailboat at sunset below what Sy calls his "mind
stimulators," words of advice on how best to study: SURVEY, QUES-
TION, READ, REVIEW, RECITE. Between the postcard and the sunglasses
lies a poetic formula:

> You *imagine* what you desire
> You *will* what you imagine
> You *create* what you will.

For the most part Sy believes you create what you will, but he also
believes one creates what others will for him. The stony face he wears
now—the wary eyes resting on the bulging cheekbones, the rare smile
that never shows wide enough for warmth—it was not always his
look. In Elmira, he says, "I learned how to be hard and cold. I was
neither before. I used to dislike fighting so much that if I ever did get
into a fight with a kid, I couldn't even hit him in the face. That's the
God-honest truth. Then in prison I went through a transition, as if I
was beginning to understand another side of human nature, in myself
as well as others." Specifically, he learned that generosity was inter-
preted as weakness. A fellow inmate at Elmira borrowed five packs
of cigarettes and refused to pay Sy back. Sy fought him. "It wasn't my
nature, it was survival. I would have thrown that guy out the third-
floor window."

There is no doubt of it. Even today you see the indignation rising
in him as he recalls the cigarette borrower. He talks with his hands;

a swallow would be lost in them. Transferred to Comstock after the Elmira incident, Sy was involved in another fight for which he says he was given forty-five days in the "strip cell" (one meal every third day, no clothes but shorts and a T-shirt, sleep on the floor). Eventually he stopped fighting, but served five years anyway, developing a new opinion of himself. "I didn't like what I was becoming. I'm still not comfortable with me." By the time of his release at the age of twenty-two, he trusted almost no one.

With all the changes that have occurred in him since then, Sy does not say that prison made him what he is; only that it helped. After completing the first five-year term, he took a job in Rochester working for a company that makes tanks for chemicals. He fell in love, got married, had three children. Between them, he and his wife were making close to $16,000 a year; quite enough at the time. Still, he was moody, depressed. One night when his two-year-old daughter would not stop crying, he reached for a six-pack. He recalls, horrified, that he was about to fling it at her, and glances sheepishly at the photograph of smiling Alicia, now eighteen, on the cell wall. "The problem wasn't the family. It was me. The things that were in me: anger, bitterness, a lack of understanding. I don't want to get, you know, into a highly philosophical or psychological thing; but there was confusion that was not there before." (He uses "you know" when he is about to say something that does not appeal to him.) He pauses. "One day I started, you know, robbing people."

"What were you thinking when you pointed a gun at someone whose money you didn't even need?"

"I wasn't thinking. I was just acting out feelings."

"Why pick robbery?"

"I don't know. It could have been murder."

"Were you getting back at people?"

"No. I had become more *like* people." He shifts his weight on the cot and looks both certain and surprised.

For armed robbery, and because he was a two-time felony offender, they gave Sy fifteen to thirty years, of which he served eleven. During that time his wife divorced him. At Stormville he got on the wrong side of the "keepers" for speaking his mind, he contends. "This was in '71, when Attica jumped off." The reminder is suddenly chilling in this place. "They said I was trying to change people's ideas. I think any man who sees the truth is obligated to share that truth. That's what I was doing." For the effort, he says, he was handcuffed behind his back and "thrown down a couple of flights of stairs, you know. They fractured my eardrum. They fractured my left cheekbone."

He is interrupted by a rapid banging on the cell wall. He yells: "Maestro, I'm busy right now!" His neighbor Maestro is so called because he plays the guitar. No, Maestro is not his friend. Sy has no friends. The worst time of day for him is when he is let out of his cell. He finds prison life too dangerous, too unpredictable. He, who would deem it dishonorable to steal from a fellow inmate, has already had a watch and a pocket calculator stolen. He mentions this twice, angrily, in the course of two hours. "In my cell," he says, "I only have to worry about myself."

In his cell he can also do the reading he seems to need. Having recently finished *Wuthering Heights,* he concludes that "Heathcliff was one of the book's lesser villains" and that "he wasn't as strong as he appeared to be. The real Heathcliff only came through at the end." Then, with curiosity: "When Heathcliff was himself, no one understood him any more." Of Jean Valjean in *Les Misérables* Sy observes, "Any time you make a person into something other than himself, you make a monster."

He has read almost all of Richard Wright, even *The Outsider,* Wright's existential novel about a criminal who seeks to get outside everything, including morality and history. To Sy this is impossible: "You can only become so much of an outsider." One is obliged to live in the world, although "you've got to walk up your own staircase, not someone else's." Moreover, Wright, like Brontë and Hugo, was portraying a hero who was partly the victim of others, and partly of himself. When Sy says, "I want to understand whether I was the sole cause of what has happened to me," his expression is earnest to the point of desperation.

On the poem "Invictus," he says he does not believe he is "the master of my fate." The poem is on the wall because such a thing represents a goal. Sy wrote a poem himself, at the age of eighteen, when he was in Comstock. He recites it too rapidly:

> Reminiscing my childhood past
> Of the good and the bad
> The happy and the sad
> The wasted tears
> And future fears
> That all came true.

In spite of the accuracy of the poem's forecast, Sy is still bewildered by his latest crime. He is now doing six to twelve for the attempted murder of his "lady" in Poughkeepsie. After serving time for the robbery conviction, he began to work with delinquent teenagers, but he got into trouble there too, fighting with the authorities over their rough handling of the kids. "They told me: Everybody does it. I told them: *I* don't do it. *I'm* part of everybody." He lost that job and "drank and drank." Then he lost his lady, and one day he went after her where she worked—just to talk, he says. Nonetheless, he had a shotgun with him that went off in a scuffle with the woman's fellow employees. She was wounded. Sy didn't mean it. No, he does not see a parallel between this crime and his first trouble: pursuing a girl-friend and winding up in prison. "This time I was responsible." The thought does not console him.

Still, what clearly worries him more than the shooting incident is the recollection of how afraid of him the woman was. With her he had tried to make a whole life within a family of two, in a sense, as he describes it, to protect himself by building a cell on the outside. "But my lady couldn't adhere to my philosophy because she had nothing to base it on. My foundation was crumbling. I thought: Here it is, inside my unit." The "it" is threatening, but unidentified. He used to say to her: "The reason I love you is that you like the good side of me. But there is something else, and this I don't want you to see." Until the afternoon of the shooting, he had managed to stay out of jail for three and a half years.

"So here I was in the grinder again. I knew what I had to face. You get into the machine and you're just a little cog. You're nothing major." An eerie falsetto fills the corridor. An inmate walks by outside the door to Sy's cell, shouting for his ID.

"Who are you now?"

"I don't really think about myself. I don't like myself, per se, because the things I have gone through have become such a part of me." As ever, there is no touch of self-pity in his voice. He seems to regard his life scientifically, like an unknown substance. "I was thrown into a place where I couldn't develop normally," he says, quickly surveying his surroundings.

Does he think he will do something to put himself back in prison after this sentence is served? He feels that he has learned to moderate his expectations; that, he says, will help. Yet his resolution continues to be undermined by his temper. Even now he is on disciplinary report for raising a hand to a guard. He demonstrates the gesture as if to denote its casual innocence, but in fact a flick of his wrist is menacing. "I will always be in prison," he says after a while. "It was something stamped on my soul."

What are prisons for, Sy? Punishment mainly, he believes, of four distinct types. The first is one's loss of freedom. The second, the loss of a sense of responsibility: "You're expected to think for yourself and at the same time to follow orders without asking questions." The third kind of punishment he calls "sensory deprivation," the forced absence of family, of feeling. The only emotions one knows in prison, he says, are the "negatives" of anger and disappointment. And the fourth type? That, to Sy, is the most severe. "The worst punishment is being compelled to be someone other than yourself."

To see Sy Jackson from the inside is to agree that, in part, he has been compelled to be someone else. To see him from the outside, from the other end of his cot, is to acknowledge that the man is an explosive, someone to be afraid of. With that view Sy would wholeheartedly sympathize; he is afraid of himself. If the prisons in which he has spent nearly half his life have provided various punishments, they have also given him a context for looking into his own mind. Since what frightens him about his mind was nurtured in prison, the process of self-examination is as circular and enclosed as Sy's upstate odyssey. Such nonprogress may be typical of a great many prisoners, but as one discovers in a place like Attica, no inmate is typical. All the instruments of uniformity in a prison—the architecture, the outfits, the language and routine—merely emphasize the fact that here, as elsewhere, every cell contains a person.

What disturbs anyone looking at Sy, however, is not his differences from the world but his obvious membership in it. In a sense a criminal is merely a man of extremes, someone who robs gas stations rather than the dignity of a colleague, or who terrorizes with a gun rather than a bullying personality, or who murders in fact instead of with gossip. Perhaps this is why Sy feels low, but not ignoble; the laws he breaks are on the books. Yet his internal torment is that of anyone who recognizes his own guilt and self-hate, who sees in Sy's black-brown eyes all the imprisonment of the species. It is doubtful that Sy realizes this. One thing a prison does naturally is to ostracize its residents, most of whom are bound to think there is no one in the outer world remotely like them.

Sy had a dream while taking a nap the other day. It was about "a big, gigantic bird without feathers, and he came into my cell and got lodged under my cot. And I'm wondering in my dream whether to free this monster or scream for help." The problem struck him funny. He did not recognize the beast.

September 13, 1982

Black Autobiography

This life we live is a strange dream,
and I don't believe at all
any account men give of it.

—H. D. THOREAU

You might see somebody get cut or killed. I could
go out in the street for an afternoon, and I would
see so much that, when I came in the house, I'd be
talking and talking for what seemed like hours.
Dad would say, "Boy, why don't you stop that
lyin'? You know you didn't see all that. You know
you didn't see nobody do that." But I knew I had.

—CLAUDE BROWN

WHATEVER ELSE it may be, autobiography is the least reliable of genres—one person in relation to one world of that person's manufacture, which is that person in macrocosm, explained and made beautiful by that same person in the distance, playing god to the whole unholy trinity. Nevertheless, the three are lonely; they do not trust themselves any more than they trust one another, and with reason, as each is persistently reminded of his capacity to cheat and distort by the enterprise in which all are engaged. There is, in the subject, the loneliness of the oppressed; in the object, the loneliness of the oppressor; in the artist, the loneliness of the overseer, of infinite manipulation. None feels genuine kinship with anything outside its own limitations. This is why all autobiography is minority autobiography.

Perspectives notwithstanding, however, there still is such a thing as objective reality, which is where black autobiography, a minority within a minority, takes its power. The question of whether black autobiography exists as a genre can be answered in the same terms as the more frequent question concerning black fiction; it exists as a special form of literature because there are discernible patterns within black autobiographies which tie them together, and because the outer world apprehended by black autobiographies is consistent and unique, if dreadful. Black fiction is often so close to black autobiography in plot and theme that a study of the latter almost calls the existence of the former into question. The response of a reader to both genres—could this really be so?—is equally astonished and rhetorical.

Yet not all black autobiography is the rehearsal of horrors. Like fiction, black autobiography has changed both with the times and temperaments it conveyed. For the past hundred years it has fallen into roughly the same categories as the fiction. We have accommodationist autobiographies such as James D. Corrother's *In Spite of the Handicap* and William Pickens's *Bursting Bonds;* autobiographical versions of the stories of the "talented tenth": Marshall W. ("Major") Taylor's *The Fastest Bicycle Rider in the World* and Mary Church Terrell's *A Colored Woman in a White World;* autobiographies of the Harlem Renaissance: Zora Neale Hurston's *Dust Tracks on the Road,* William Stanley Braithwaite's *The House Under Arcturus,* Langston Hughes's *The Big Sea,* and Claude McKay's *A Long Way from Home;* and we have the literature of direct protest and social comment: W. E. B. DuBois's *Dusk of Dawn,* Angelo Herndon's *Let Me Live,* Richard Wright's *Black Boy,* and the contemporary autobiographies of Malcolm X, Eldridge Cleaver, Chester Himes, and Angela Davis. The material is various but the polemics are similar.

Polemics means the art of disputation, technically the use of argument to refute errors of religious doctrine. There is argument in black autobiography, but no single orthodoxy. The rights of Zora Neale Hurston are not the rights of William Stanley Braithwaite; the achievement of Malcolm X is not the achievement of Langston Hughes. Conceptions of right and achievement, as well as of failure, are as different in this literature as the minds that held them. Yet there are two elements in black autobiography which are constant, whether we are watching Major Taylor on a bicycle track or Malcolm in prison. They are the expressed desire to live as one would choose, as far as possible; and the tacit or explicit criticism of external national conditions which, also as far as possible, work to ensure that one's freedom of choice is delimited or nonexistent. These are the "arguments" of the genre. They also represent the two points where black autobiography and black fiction become inseparable and explain each other.

Both black fiction and black autobiography occur mainly in the period of modern literature. Except for slave narratives, we have very few works in either genre which go back before 1890, and the great majority of material was written after 1920. Ordinarily, we know what to expect of such material: a high degree of subjectivity, of protest against established social norms and assumptions; perhaps most prominent, an elaborately conceived and abstract sense of victimization on the part of the central character. Despite its technical modernity, neither black fiction nor autobiography gives us these things. There is social protest, of course; but it does not rely on an abstract "victim" for its medium. When the central character is black, the abuses are authentic. No black American author has ever felt the need to invent a nightmare to make his point.

This element of historic authenticity has brought both genres closer to the precincts of classical tragedy than any other modern literature, with the possible exception of Ireland's at the turn of the century. The ability of an author to count on violence, unfairness, poverty, a quashing of aspiration, denial of beauty, ridicule, often death itself, is as close to a reliance on divine inevitabilities as a modern writer can come. Blackness itself therefore becomes a variation of fate, the condition which prescribes and predetermines a life. Fictional and autobiographical heroes who go up against fate are likewise contending with their own blackness, and have just as much chance of succeeding as a person who wishes to get out of his own skin. This contest gives both genres their power and form.

The situation is, of course, essentially crazy. Why should either an actual or fictional hero be able to depend on his destruction as a given? It is very nice to congratulate Bob Jones of Chester Himes's *If He Hollers Let Him Go* on his proximity to classical tragedy, a proximity manifest in Jones's having been demoted, betrayed, beaten up, deserted, framed, jailed, and forced to enter the army for no other reason than that he is black; yet we acknowledge that no white American in similar circumstances would share such honors. Minority autobiography and minority fiction deserve their minority status not because of comparative numbers, but because of the presence of a special reality, one provided for the minority by the majority, and within which each member of the minority tries to reach an understanding both of himself and the reality into which he has been placed. When these two understandings collide, as they always do, we begin to get a clear picture of how uniquely alone our heroes are, real or imagined.

Near the end of his autobiography, *Black Boy,* Wright tells a story of his working for white men in an optical factory in Memphis. His supervisors came to him one morning and told him that Harrison, another black man working in a rival optical company across the street, held a grudge against Wright. They said that Harrison was going to kill him. Harrison's supervisors had told him the same story about Wright. When Wright and Harrison met that noon, each tried to learn why the other was angry. When they discovered the hoax, they agreed to try to let the thing pass.

But their white supervisors would not have it. They kept goading both workers, and armed the two of them with knives. Failing to antagonize them, they then urged Wright and Harrison to settle their nonexistent grudge in a bare-fist boxing match, for five dollars each. Wright refused at first, but Harrison persuaded him that this would be easy money, that they could pull punches and fool the white men. The white men were elated at the news, and offered to buy dinners for the combatants. Stripped to the waist, Wright and Harrison squared off on a Saturday afternoon in a basement before an all-white audience, jeering and shouting obscenities. They punched lightly at first; then harder and harder. Eventually they had to be pulled apart, having beaten each other senseless.

With certain symbolic additions this anecdote is re-created at least twice in black fiction: in the "Box-Seat" chapter of Jean Toomer's *Cane* and in the battle-royal scene of Ellison's *Invisible Man*. In *Cane* we are shown two dwarfs pounding each other incessantly as part of a theater performance for the amusement of a degenerate audience seeking to obliterate the savagery in themselves: one set of misfits hoisting their self-esteem by urging on the brutality of another set. In *Invisible Man,* our hero has been valedictorian of his high school class, and has been told to appear before the local white men one evening in order to receive his rewards. His rewards consist of being blindfolded and shoved into an arena with other blindfolded black boys, all outfitted with boxing gloves for a desperate free-for-all. Afterward, the boys are tossed coins on an electrified carpet. As in the Wright-Harrison anecdote they are meant to destroy themselves for the entertainment of the white citizens who would gladly pay them handsomely for their self-destruction.

The point of this story, in fact and parable, is repeated regularly; a black man seeking recognition in the white world must be brutalized to the extent that when recognition comes, it will be to him as an animal. If he decides not to fit this pattern at the outset, he will be pushed by its designers until he becomes violent in protest. Should he become violent enough, he will be considered an animal, and so satisfy his predetermination just as effectively. Either way he will be functioning according to external dictates which run counter to his will, and despite the fact that he is sane and reasonable, he will only be judged so by joining a world which is unreasonable and fundamentally mad.

Wright and Harrison would not speak to each other after their fight. They were ashamed of having been duped at the expense of each other, which was the expense of themselves and of all blacks so demeaned. Yet they had no reason to be ashamed. They had been goaded into a false and illogical act which somehow became logical and true. At the end of their fight, Wright and Harrison *did* hold a grudge against each other, just as their white supervisors had initially contended. The madness of the situation did not reside in the hysteria of the onlookers, nor even in the confusion of defeat and victory, or of power and impotency, on the parts of the boxers. It resided in the fact that a lie became the truth, and that two people who had thought they had known what the truth was wound up living the lie.

The crime which the State wishes to pin on Bigger Thomas in Richard Wright's *Native Son* is rape. By the time he is captured and jailed, Bigger has committed manslaughter on one girl, and has decapitated her body; has bashed in the head of another girl, and tossed her from a window; he has also committed burglary; yet the crime of which he is accused is rape, which in fact he did not do. De Quincey said that there is no telling what depths a man may reach having committed murder; he may drink; he may become lazy; eventually he even may not always tell the truth. In an upside-down hierarchy it is reasonable that Bigger be accused of rape rather than murder. Rape represents his self-assertion in the white world, a crime which that world would not abide.

So, in *The Autobiography of Malcolm X* Malcolm is astonished when his small band of burglars is finally caught. None of the authorities in Boston is interested in the burglaries per se, but in the fact that the band consisted of two white women and three black men: "How, where, when, had I met them? Did we sleep together? Nobody wanted to know anything at all about the robberies. All they could see was that we had taken the white man's women." There is a mirror principle operating in all of black writing, one that shows black heroes functioning in continual opposition to the white lives about them. In a sense the literature itself is a mirror into which the characters are locked. Everything they think, feel, and do seems turned the wrong way, and even when it is not, there are those available to say that it is, and, like the white citizens of Memphis or Boston, who are able to prove it.

As crazy as all of this is, it is not only true to life, but it also *rings* equally true in autobiography and fiction. "What if history were a madman?" asks the Invisible Man. In terms of the general history of black and white American relations, the question seems gratuitous. The consistency of the madness accounts not only for the correspondences between black autobiography and fiction, but for the remarkably consistent picture of white America drawn from the works of black writers. Whether we are reading the autobiographies of Du-Bois, Claude McKay, and Mary Church Terrell, or the fiction of Dunbar, Ann Petry, William Melvin Kelley, or Baldwin *(Another Country),* what we see before us is the same strange and colorless land, terrorized and confused, persistent in the hatred of its own.

Through such a place walk various autobiographical characters as classic heroes playing themselves in the theater of the absurd. From the outset they are witnesses to two versions of reality which are in perpetual friction. One is the reality of their wishful thinking. It consists of a vast yet potentially solvable puzzle which they address as children, and which they hope to conquer as grown-ups—*Yes I Can,* said Sammy Davis, Jr.—a world of reasonably constructed labyrinths, rewards, and punishments. The other is a madhouse, a hall of mirrors which, like Keats's castle, continually shifts its shape and refutes the best efforts of these autobiographical characters not to conform, but to be different and special. "I aspire to the craziness of all honest men," said LeRoi Jones. Autobiography as a genre should be the history of individual craziness, but in black autobiography the outer reality in which heroes move is so massive and absolute in its craziness that any one person's individual idiosyncrasies seem almost dull in their normality.

One of the most moving autobiographies of the twentieth century is the *Autobiography of Edwin Muir,* the British poet. It has the simple structure of all great autobiographies, and is thoroughly straightforward, particularly at moments of severe introspection. One of those moments occurred when Muir, a formal and self-contained man, underwent psychoanalysis for the first time. Watching his various coats of self-protection peel off he quietly observes: "I saw that my lot was the human lot, that when I faced my own unvarnished likeness I was one among all men and women, all of whom had the same desires and thoughts, the same failures and frustrations, the same unacknowledged hatred of themselves and others, the same hidden shame and griefs." More than an acknowledgment of personal self-discovery, this confession is a modern autobiographical device. Like most modern poetry it presumes psychological kinship with the reader, presumes not only that both confessed and confessor share the same post-Freudian world of experience, but the same conception of experience as well: that life consists of self-deception, self-revelation, and self-absolution in roughly the same linear progression for all people. The presumption was accurate for Edwin Muir, primarily because he was not only modern but white.

Angelo Herndon's autobiography, *Let Me Live,* operates on other assumptions. The Herndon case, as some may remember, was an international concern in the 1930s. The question shuttling between the Supreme Court and the courts of Georgia was whether Herndon, a young black Communist, would be sent to a chain gang for eighteen to twenty years on a trumped-up charge which in 1932 depended on the efficiency of the Anti-slave Insurrection Law of 1861. Unlike Muir, Herndon did not seek an understanding of reality through an interpretation of his dreams. This was not necessary. On July 11, 1932, Herndon was arrested and held in jail for eleven days for distributing Communist leaflets to the Atlanta unemployed. On July 22, he was formally indicted for attempting to incite insurrection on July 16, on which date he was in jail. That fact notwithstanding, or perhaps because of that fact, the two chief witnesses against Herndon were the assistant prosecutor and chief jailer. "This was one of the worst vaudeville shows I had ever seen," said Herndon of his trial; "and yet the most interesting to me, for this particular vaudeville show happened to hold my life in the balance."

The sense of circus or madhouse which controls much black autobiography inevitably controls the decisions of the main characters themselves. Recognizing an elusive and unpredictable situation, they adapt to it for survival, becoming masters of disguise, both physical and psychological, in part to avoid their hunters. Malcolm X moves from one mask to another in his autobiography. He is variously known as Malcolm, Malcolm Little, Homeboy, Detroit Red, a prison number, even Satan, until he reaches the identification of Brother, which to him is not a mask, but himself. Conversely the Invisible Man finds his identity in Rinehart, the con man and quick-change artist whose being is nonbeing, who is all things to all people. Sonny of *Manchild in the Promised Land* wears the mask of the house nigger when it serves him, as does Bigger. Both in black autobiography and fiction the final discarding of masks is a character's primary goal because such an act is a demonstration of selfhood and freedom.

Yet in autobiography as a genre this discarding can never be complete. Even Malcolm as Brother Malcolm is Malcolm in costume, as Richard Wright is in the guise of childhood in *Black Boy,* and Langston Hughes in *The Big Sea* is in the guise of writer. In autobiography one is not merely getting at the self but at reality as well, the one not existing outside its relation to the other. Malcolm's early libertinism was a way of investigating reality, a different but no less authentic way than his role as proselytizer for Allah. Every autobiographer, black or otherwise, must find a guise or voice with which to come to terms with himself and his world. If he is candid he will admit to a number of voices and guises, adopted as his mind and world enlarge. "We wear the mask," said Dunbar, "and mouth with myriad subtleties."

Ideals of the true self and the true world nevertheless persist. Against these ideals all costumes and masks are arrayed. One senses, in all autobiography, a straining toward perfection, perfection of a kind that connects the individual with a cosmic pattern which, because it is perfect in itself, verifies that individual's own potential perfection. This pattern or system is not the world created by the individual in his autobiography; it is an ideal which must be read in interstices between subject and object within the autobiography, in the particular selections of the artist-self, and, just as often, in the guesswork which we apply to all books which move us. Nor is it a flexible perfection. There is for every autobiographer an absolute ideal. Falling short of it is perhaps what inspires the autobiography in the first place; but if we are to understand the lives detailed before us we must know this ideal as fully as we know the "realities" given us.

The ideals of black autobiography are the preposterously traditional ideals of reason and consistency. Despite and within the idiosyncrasies of individual authors, all seek a structure of life, of history, which is something other than viciously circular. On the threshing floor John Grimes of Baldwin's *Go Tell It on the Mountain* hears a voice which tells him, "you got everything your daddy got." Since John's daddy, Gabriel, "got" a fearful and misshapen existence, John's future is not what one calls bright. On the morning of his father's funeral, Baldwin, just turned nineteen, was on the threshing floor of his mind:

"But as for me and my house," my father had said, "we will serve the Lord." I wondered, as we drove him to his resting place, what this line had meant for him. I had heard him preach it many times. I had preached it once myself, proudly giving it an interpretation different from my father's. Now the whole thing came back to me, as though my father and I were on our way to Sunday school and I were memorizing the golden text: And if it seem evil unto you to serve the Lord, choose you this day whom you will serve; whether the gods which your fathers served that were on the other side of the flood, or the gods of the Amorites, in whose land ye dwell; but as for me and my house, we will serve the Lord. I suspected in these familiar lines a meaning which had never been there for me before. All of my father's texts and songs, which I had decided were meaningless, were arranged before me at his death like empty bottles, waiting to hold the meaning which life would give them for me. This was his legacy: nothing is ever escaped. That bleakly memorable morning I hated the unbelievable streets and the Negroes and whites who had, equally, made them that way. But I knew that it was folly, as my father would have said, this bitterness was folly. It was necessary to hold on to the things that mattered. The dead man mattered, the new life mattered; blackness and whiteness did not matter; to believe that they did was to acquiesce in one's own destruction. Hatred, which could destroy so much, never failed to destroy the man who hated and this was an immutable law.

Baldwin's appeal at base is the appeal for sanity.

When the appeal is not answered, as it usually is not, something curious, in the Lewis Carroll sense, happens to the heroes of black autobiography; they disappear. Just as Bob Jones vanishes into the anonymity of the army at the end of *If He Hollers Let Him Go;* as James Weldon Johnson's Ex-Colored Man eliminates himself by passing for white; as the Invisible Man disappears literally; so do Richard Wright, Malcolm X, Eldridge Cleaver, and others disappear at the close of their narratives. Like Troilus, they ascend to one or another conception of heaven, ready for a new life, a life into which they have died. At the end of that life they are, as artist and individual, refined out of existence—Cleaver calling upon his "Queen," his "Black Woman" to put on her crown and "build a New City on these ruins"; Malcolm acknowledging, almost celebrating, his impending death. When the masks and disguises have been used and laid aside, nothing remains but the future, which because unknown can be thought utopian.

Every autobiography, black and white, is an extended suicide note, both announcement and vindication of the event. The life recorded is the life complete to a specific point, and therefore as good as dead. In *Metaphors of Self,* James Olney has noted the similarity of the following autobiographical statements—Darwin: "I am not conscious of any change in my mind during the last thirty years"; Mill: "From this time . . . I have no further mental changes to tell of"; Newman: "From the time that I became a Catholic, of course, I have no further history of my religious opinion to narrate." Each autobiographer tells us what a fictional character would not need to, that no further growth will occur. Each has chosen a point in his life where he could see a pattern of the whole. Having seen it, he isolates it and lays it to rest through the act of autobiography itself.

One reason for this may be the desire to bring life as close to art as possible—not merely in order to give life a lovely shape, but because art is not criticized as harshly as life. The decision to write an autobiography is never as brave as it seems, particularly in an age where nothing self-conscious can be unforgivable. In modern autobiography, one enters an arena where the rules are clear. The life theoretically laid bare before us is in fact protected by that acknowledgment. Indeed, the only autobiographies we tear apart are those that appear to be hiding something.

But this is the lesser reason. One writes autobiography not because one seeks art or safety, but out of a desire to see both a shape and end to one's life, to seek the end of everything which has been in flux and process, and at the same time to understand it all. "Everything" is, after all, every thing, all orders and disorders known and felt by the "I." When that "I" has said stop, if momentarily, to its apprehension of the world, it has likewise said stop to the world, stop to all things; it has called upon vast silence and infinite space. *Black Boy* concludes with the following lines:

> With ever watchful eyes and bearing scars, visible and invisible, I headed North, full of a hazy notion that life could be lived with dignity, that the personalities of others should not be violated, that men should be able to confront other men without fear or shame, and that if men were lucky in their living on earth they might win some redeeming meaning for their having struggled and suffered here beneath the stars.

This is Wright after his own funeral, bound for glory. His autobiography, not unlike the earliest seventeenth-century English autobiographies, describes the progress of the soul through various regions of doubt and torment toward deliverance.

The difference between Wright's statement and Darwin's, which is the difference between modern black and white autobiography generally, lies in a paradox. White autobiographers whose lives have progressed within a linear conception of history, that is, who have advanced in step with the advancement of their understanding of reality, find a stopping point and "end" their lives at it. But black autobiographers whose lives have progressed within a cyclical conception of history find no stopping point on the circle essentially different from any other point. "That's the end in the beginning and there's no encore," says Ellison. The result is that the black autobiographer in a sense spins off his circle, and is carried by the centrifugal force of the life he has led to a state which anticipates grace. Despite the fact that he has been traveling in a circle, the black autobiographer, by the invention of the autobiography itself, has managed to get somewhere. Unlike his white counterpart, he dies but has a future.

That future, which is not solely his own but that of his people and national ideals, generally seems more important to him than the life which he has gone to such pains to record. In fact, he seems to care very little for that life, regarding it like the product of molting, as an aspect of the unattractive past. Every cosmology begins in self-knowledge. Since the "argument" of black autobiography is against the existing universe of which the narrator was and is an essential, if uncomfortable, part, the "argument" of the work is extended against the self. Black autobiography annihilates the self because by so doing it takes the world with it.

At the beginning of *Black Boy*, after young Wright had set his house afire, he said, "I yearned to become invisible, to stop living." That episode incidentally bears the same tension between accident and intent as Bigger Thomas's killing of Mary Dalton. Wright's wish to obliterate himself accompanies the act of nearly destroying his house, his own family; he willingly would see everything go at once. Yet invisibility can have substance. Much later, citing the inspiration which such writers as Dreiser and Lewis provided, Wright "felt touching his face a tinge of warmth from an unseen light." His faith in that light, which is literature, is one of his reasons for writing *Black Boy*. The autobiography is an example of its own thesis, which places trust in the word, and invests it with a life of its own.

"The thought of suicide," said cheerful Nietzsche, "is a great consolation: by means of it one gets successfully through many a bad night." For most black autobiographers the night has been bad and long. After a time they have declared it finished, risen to their particular bright and morning star, and created in their suicide notes a social document. Their works are briefs in their own defenses, briefs for salvation, since suicide is a sin. But they are also briefs against the nation, which has provided false religion and false gods. Polemics means the use of argument to refute errors of doctrine. These books both depend on and dispute the Word as it has been handed down.

This said, we are nevertheless reminded every time we read one of these works that the human mind is singular. The self in autobiography is alone, but so is the reader. The autobiographer wishes the reader to be alone and counts on it, because whatever else may separate them from each other, their states of loneliness are mutually recognizable. For the black autobiographer this is a central connection; he is after all not a minority in relation to his lonely reader. They are equal in the exchange, equal because of the experience of the artifact. On this level, which is the one level where men may help each other, the artifact and the polemics are one.

Fall, 1975

Mario Cuomo

R UN!"
    "Electric chair!"
The calls blurt out like party horns from the Saint Patrick's Day
crowd, shivering twenty-deep along Fifth Avenue, staring at him
hungrily like children before a religious feast. Packed as hard as a
frozen roast in a raincoat and hat, he smiles and waves at everyone.
"That was the first time I ever heard them yell at me to go for the
presidency," he said when the parade was over. "Calls for the death
penalty, I get those all the time. But people need an occasion to set
them off, like the killing of Officer Byrne by the drug dealers." He has
reasons for opposing the death penalty, and reasons for not running
for president. Mario Matthew Cuomo, the fifty-second governor of
the state, the first Italian from Queens to hold that job, has a thousand reasons for everything.
    But when you talk to him awhile, you get the feeling that when he
is being most ineluctably logical, he is also being wrong; and when he
is most flaccidly illogical or alogical, he is right as rain. His rationale
for not seeking the 1988 Democratic nomination is impeccable: He
gave his word to the existing candidates that he would stay out of the
race, and he believes that the others are better qualified than he. The

fact (acknowledged by everyone but Cuomo) that none of the present candidates save Jesse Jackson generates an emotional response above zero does not enter Cuomo's calculus. Neither does the certainty that in TV debates he could make George Bush look like George Bush. So Cuomo is perfectly right being wrong, and you get the odd suspicion that he prefers it that way.

Whereas on the death penalty, he is wrong being right; all the statistics he raises in favor of his position pale beside the Christian faith that tells him that for the state to take a life is a sin. Remember his fame-making keynote speech to the Democratic National Convention in San Francisco? A sloppy botch of rhetoric, by his own admission, yet it brought down the national house. Why? Timing, he says, like taking a girl's hand at the right moment on the right evening in the right light. Give him that. But the hand bone is connected to the head bone, and in the end, no one but Mario Cuomo could have made that speech work: Mario of the logical illogic, the malleable-iron will, the thick-quick hands, Catholic-liberal, public-private, open-secret, love-talking Mario, whom, when it comes down to it, most people simply like.

Run. Electric chair. High in his office in the World Trade Center on Saint Patrick's Day, he displays a mind that runs perpetually between ambition and sin, as if it were caught in a rundown between third and home (the young Cuomo played minor-league baseball). He sort of relishes the trap. He remains very high all day, moving a little manically among jokes ancient and modern, flights of fancy, history, philosophy, politics, the ribbing of his staff. He is New York–funny, telling, without my asking, how his papa taught him about sex shortly before Mario married: "He takes me behind [the Cuomo grocery store in South Jamaica] and begins: 'Now, there's the bull and the cow.' In Italian. 'You know? The bull and the cow?' I said to him, 'Pa, don't worry. The priest gave me a book. The book says, This is the cow and this is the bull.' Pa says, 'You sure? Okay.' That was his lecture on sex."

Inspired, he puts in a speakerphone call to his mother, still living in the old neighborhood, ostensibly to verify the story. He says, "Ma! What did Papa tell me about the bull and the cow? A writer here wants to know." He lies with delight. The disgust of Immaculata Cuomo, eighty-six, crackles over the phone. "What kind of stupid person would ask you what your father told you about sex?" she asks. "It shows that they're all stupid. They shouldn't be writing books. They should be *reading* books."

Cuomo loves it. "Every time I go on television, she calls me up and says, 'What did you do wrong?' She figures, you're up there, so you have to do something wrong." The remark is serious. Under the skin, Cuomo, too, believes, almost as an imperative, you're up there, so you have to do something wrong. It is why his being up there appears to feel like a high-wire act: Few can do it, but who would want to? Testifying to the importance of loving ("the one thing I've learned in fifty-five years"), he springs to the preposterous, sublime analogy: "They stuck nails in my hands. But I give, nonetheless. The value is in the giving. I am trying very hard to love you, and that is the ultimate test."

Expressions of shame, self-doubt, remorse work their way into his exhilaration: When he recollects Papa, as he does frequently nowadays, he is "probably trying to compensate" for not being sufficiently appreciative when Papa was alive. When he was a kid, the church forbade girls to wear patent-leather shoes, so the boys could not look up their legs in the reflection. Shame from the start. The world was made to shun. "The monk," says Cuomo both critically and wistfully, "spends his life weaving baskets to give his hands something to do in the grim interval between birth and eternity."

But in Cuomo's lives, both as a lawyer for the little guy and as governor, the world was never for shunning. Shun the world and you are insulting God, he says. Ah, yes. But there are so many complications, as in the abortion issue, where private and civic values collide. (The Notre Dame speech on abortion, when he took on Cardinal O'Connor—now, that *was* brilliant.) The temptation of Mario: "You're tempted all the time to measure yourself by the reaction at the parade." The stations of the crossroads: "Sometimes I feel that I spend too much time thinking about what I'm thinking."

A mighty mess, to be sure, but it all rings true, even if one allows for the fact that public people in self-scrutiny generally are not to be trusted. In abstract conversation, Cuomo's dialogues between self and soul are enormously attractive. Applied to specific questions, such as whether or not he will run for president, the quality is irritating. Yet the attitude is consistent with living in mystery, which is clearly where Como is most uncomfortably comfortable. "Now, some people are confused by Christianity because they think that an act of faith means suspending intelligence," he says. "Not at all. You're simply asked to believe things you cannot *prove* with your intelligence."

• • •

The principle is illustrated by the story of his brother Frankie's five-year-old boy, who froze to death in a canal behind Frankie's house. They found him with his feet cracked through the ice, his eyes wide open, hands clinging to a rope on the bulkhead. The boy was so beautiful. Even priests cried at the funeral. The second day of the wake, Cuomo and his brother took a walk and Cuomo asked, "How do you handle this?" Frankie said, "Look. Either there is some ultimate explanation or there isn't. I'm going to choose to believe there is."

I ask, "Would Frankie be in pain if I wrote that story?"

He thinks, then answers definitely: "No."

The night of Saint Patrick's Day, at his monthly radio call-in show on CBS, we are somewhere in Black Rock, the CBS tower in midtown. The area is nearly empty at that hour, the building rising to the dark like a comic-book phantom. Cuomo is high as a kite. Before the show begins, he surveys a large poster bearing the faces of Cardinal O'Connor and Mayor Koch. Cuomo produces a black pencil and proceeds to draw a beard on the cardinal and a mustache on the mayor. Koch looks the perfect roué, a bit like Gilbert Roland. Everybody roars. Soaring still, Cuomo clamps on his earphones, a big kid in earmuffs, and takes on all callers. Ed from Buffalo. Carol from the Bronx. An Indian woman from Rochester calls to talk about the presidential election. And Don from Long Island presses Cuomo on the death penalty. *Run. Electric chair.*

His day ends a little after eight. His retinue in tow, he heads off to the car that will take him to the chopper that will fly him north to Albany in the night. I try to imagine what the governor's mansion looks like. Imperial Victorian rooms. Cuomo at his desk writing in his diary in his upstate monastery-castle-museum open to the public.

What is he like? How can you tell? A figure of the old neighborhoods, he is instantly recognizable to any New Yorker over forty, but not comprehensible. "Mario? He's okay. You know?" A person's brooding insides? The old world never looked for them. People in the neighborhoods developed a sense of privacy, of enclosure, that simply went along with whatever else one did. Play ball, be a lawyer, a governor of the state. To Cuomo, people are *supposed* to be mysteries; he does not feel the strain of those who would like to dissect him.

And yet the glimpse of a place of sadness under the exuberance, as if his life had long ago become an overwhelming dream and he, big as he is, were afraid of that dream.

"You know what I miss?" he says. "The things that are dying

away. Like my neighborhood. We had an Orthodox synagogue on one corner, our grocery store on the other. Every ethnic strain in one place. My mother's generation, the old culture, it made you intimate. You didn't have television, didn't have air-conditioning. You learned to live with each other on the stoops. 'Hey, Ma. I'm going across the street, by Paladis.' Pa-lá-dis. You always went *by* Paladis. Everything was by Paladis."

April 25, 1988

Mr. Mayor

B Y THE TIME the mayor got to the wolf, most of the chicken was
bones. The ball-shape french fries had disappeared, as had the
string beans. The people were attentive. Under nine huge chandeliers
sat the Greater Jamaica Chamber of Commerce, convened in Re-
gency House, Jamaica, Borough of Queens, for their annual "Forecast Luncheon." They were happy with their mayor, who was
running late. He would have to step on it if he was going to make
Shea Stadium in time to toss out the Opening Day ball for the Mets.
But not before getting to the wolf:

"Now I have a little story [in response to a complaint from the
audience about graffiti on the subway cars]. It is a true story. You
know graffiti is not put on as the trains are in the train stations. It is
put on in the yards. And the way you prevent the graffiti and the
vandalizing of those subway cars is to protect them when they are in
the yards. I said to Dick Ravitch [chairman of the Metropolitan
Transportation Authority], I said to Dick, 'Look. Why don't you
build a fence around the yards at night and put a dog in there to
protect those cars? And that will stop the vandals.' And he said, 'No.'
And I said, 'Why?' He said, 'The dogs might step on the third rail.'
I said, 'Dogs generally don't step on third rails. But if they do you will

replace them. However,' said I, 'if you are worried about that, then build two fences, and have the dogs run between the two fences.' He said, 'No.' I said, 'Why?' He said, 'Because somebody might climb over the fences, and the dog would bite him.' I said, 'I thought that is what dogs were for. But if you are afraid a dog will bite somebody, then use a wolf.' I said, 'There is no recorded case of a wolf attacking a human being, except if it were rabid.'

"Well, I said that, a reporter heard it, and checked it out, and he said: 'Mr. Mayor, you are only partly right. There is no recorded case of a wolf in the wild ever attacking a human being. But there are cases of wolves in captivity attacking human beings.' I said: 'Of course I was talking about wolves in the wild. I would never use a tame wolf. Take a wild wolf, put it in there, and when the wolf becomes tame, you replace it.' [The Greater Jamaica Chamber of Commerce is in stitches.]

"Now what I am telling is a true story. We are building the fence. But with the M.T.A., do you know what they have to do before they build the fence? They have to have an R.F.P.—request for proposal. Anyplace else you go out and buy a fence. Not in the City of New York. This fence, before it will be built, I will be in my third term. Do you follow what I am saying?" [Who could miss it?]

The man who brought down the house is Edward Irving Koch, fifty-six, the 105th mayor of New York, who this week [June 15, 1981] will announce, to the surprise of no one, that he hopes to remain the 105th mayor of New York for four more years (read eight). He is endorsed by his own Democrats and has already gained most of the Republican organization's endorsements as well. What the Greater Jamaica Chamber of Commerce told him in the afternoon, the Yale Club would tell him that night—that he is a sure thing. Nor did Koch tell the Yale Club anything different than he told the Greater Jamaica Chamber of Commerce, except for talking more about financial issues. Otherwise it was pure, consistent Koch, goading his listeners, giggling with malice ("heh, heh, heh"), shining among the crossed oars and dead dignitaries on the walls, as he shone everywhere else he went that day (in appearances at City Hall; Washington Square Park; at Shea; in Queens; at the Yale Club) moving right along, touting his achievements the way politicians do, but more openly, aggressively than most, the insistent nasal voice assuring all audiences equally that the city was in the very best of hands.

Those who disagree call Koch an egotist, an obsessive, a thin-skinned son of a bitch who loves nothing so much as his own prominence. They are all correct—at least to some degree—but that still leaves open the question that Koch asks anyone who looks at him: "How'm I doin'?" In terms of the city's budget, he's doing fine. In terms of the city's spirit, he's doing better—an achievement of sorcery, given that the city's so-called services include crime in the streets, garbage in the breeze, and a subway system that would operate like hell, were not hell more efficient (the wolves won't help). When Koch was officially announced over the p.a. system at the Mets' opener, he was booed to the skies, as the formalities required. Still, he is astonishingly popular in a city that usually elects mayors simply to focus its fury on a single person.

From a New Yorker's viewpoint this popularity is perfectly reasonable. Koch is New York's nut uncle, the bachelor workhorse with opinions on everything, who will not stop talking, who keeps you up all hours telling the same stories a hundred times (half with the mouth, half with the hands), and only grows drowsy when you gain your second wind. He is funny-looking, and dignified too—six feet one inch, bald as an egg, with a body that quits every day. Yet a scrupulous face, serious eyes. Everything New York does, he does. Gotta lose weight, gotta jog. Did you read *Eye of the Needle*? "Super, the best." He dines in Chinese restaurants and stands in line for movies. He loves standing in those lines. Friends persuaded him to hold movie nights at Gracie Mansion, so he tried it. "But to watch movies in your own home is boring." Koch is not boring. He awakens automatically at six o'clock every morning, hungry for his job, and lights a short fuse. A statue of him would show a fellow eating ice cream on an Exercycle, in perpetual debate with passersby.

All this translates into the sober fact that Koch is a full-time public servant whose entire being—senses, affections, intelligence—is fused with the life of his lunatic city. Like New York, Koch can be brave, hilarious, generous, protective, occasionally gracious, and more rarely, touching. He can also be arrogant, spiteful, petty, wily, and a bully. He was a bully at the Yale Club, for example, when a hapless young man rose to challenge Koch's advocacy of capital punishment. The young man put his question: "Why do you think that taking a life is a good thing?" thereby winning the disapproving sighs and groans of those about him, which Koch, of course, picked up. "When do you graduate?" he asked the kid. He would have lost nothing by a show of magnanimity (certainly not the argument, since he went on to state it forcefully), but he had the eye of the needler.

On the other hand, it is this same predisposition to face down opponents that people like in Koch. Stories of his antics at wild public meetings are enlarging New York folklore (with Koch as his own Homer). Yet it is true that Koch has refined a combative style of oratory, which appeals strongly to a city where four fifths of life is an argument. Often he does not even wait for a threat to appear before pouncing on it. "What's wrong with that?" he'll ask, out of the blue. He tells you that he buys his suits on sale at Brooks Brothers (or something equally innocuous); then suddenly: "What's wrong with that?"

Yet style and manner are not the only reasons for the mayor's foudroyant success. There is a political philosophy at work in Koch, one not fully formed, which is also at work in the country at large. Koch's basic political shift from repentant Democrat to "secret" Republican (as one antagonist, the liberal weekly *Village Voice,* calls him) is the nation's shift as well. Like the current White House occupant, the mood of the majority is in his blood.

This must seem quite strange to Koch. He certainly did not start life feeling the pulse of mainstream America. He was born in the Bronx (December 12, 1924), the second of three children of Louis and Joyce Koch, who emigrated to the United States from Poland around 1910. On their family tree hangs one Yisroel Edelstein, an orthodox Jew who, under the alias Hersh Pinyas, is said to have been the leader of a gang that stole money and jewelry from Polish noblemen and gave the loot to the poor. Koch's critics would suggest that he has reversed the family tradition.

During the Depression Louis Koch lost his fur business, and the family moved to Newark, New Jersey, where they piled into a four-room apartment with four relatives. On Saturday nights the Koches worked the cloakroom of Kreuger's Auditorium, a catering place that specialized in bar mitzvahs, confirmations, and wedding receptions. Eddie was a devoted son and an indefatigable worker, though he still recoils at the memory of cadging for tips. In 1941 the family moved back to New York—to Brooklyn. Eddie worked his way through two years of City College by selling shoes; then joined the Army, winning two battle stars and serving as a de-Nazification specialist in Bavaria. Several of his relatives were killed in the Holocaust. He is not pleased when political enemies like Victor Gotbaum, head of the city's municipal employees union, suggest that if Koch were in Hitler's Germany he would be a Nazi. (Koch calls Gotbaum "absolutely the pits.")

After the war Koch enrolled at New York University's law school; today he is vague about the reasons why. His political life began as a street speaker for Adlai Stevenson in Manhattan's Greenwich Village in 1952. In 1956 Koch moved to the Village; he still keeps a rent-controlled flat there, which he uses on weekends. He became a charter member of the Village Independent Democrats, a political reform group that doubled as an organized shouting match. Koch lost his first race for public office in 1962, when he ran for the state legislature and felt he had been "betrayed" by powerful political figures he had relied on. He wept on election night and vowed never to enter the "dirty business" of politics again. But in 1963 he was off and running once more, defeating Carmine De Sapio, the last of New York's big-time bosses, in a contest for Democratic district leader. There followed a seat on the city council and five terms in Congress, where he supported solar energy research funds, amnesty for draft resisters, aid to day-care centers, and Gene McCarthy. He received a perfect 100 percent rating from the Americans for Democratic Action, which he now abjures, calling himself "Mayor Culpa." He entered the mayoral race in late 1976 as an underdog and won in a squeak.

What is said to have changed Koch's politics was stepping into a job that requires him to pay the bills himself. He took over a city that was not unlike his family in the Depression—only in worse shape because it owed more—and so he applied a Depression mentality to it. His basic governing maxim is "Don't spend what you don't have." It sounds simple enough, but it was too difficult for Koch's predecessors, who spent a billion a year that New York did not have and pushed the city to the brink of bankruptcy. Owing is something Koch does not approve of. There is in him a moral connection between owing money and owing political favors. The personal independence he prizes, and that sometimes gets on people's nerves, is the same sort of independence he seeks for the city, which he seems to regard as an extension of himself.

His first order of business, then, was balancing the budget. "And we've done it," he says, with pride. "If you recall where we were—no credit, the seasonal loans were running out. Nobody thought we would get the federal loan guarantees we had to have. Not Felix certainly. [Felix Rohatyn, chairman of the Municipal Assistance Corporation created in 1975 to borrow for the city, and New York's chief financial strategist.] I want to give full credit to Felix for his brilliant conception of what had to be done. But I take a lot of credit for getting it done."

It must be said too that New York's economic survival has been due to circumstance as well as human genius. While federal outlays have grown at an annual rate of more than 11 percent since 1978, Koch has held his city's spending growth to less than 4 percent a year. But an inflationary economy that increases revenues—even without a real increase in city taxes—has helped.

Koch's financial success has its dark side. His cutting back has established his reputation as an enemy of the poor. In response, Koch points first to housing, citing the 26,000 major apartment rehabilitations begun in the past two years that will almost entirely benefit the lowest income groups. His main point, however, is philosophical: "We spend 56 percent of our $14 billion operating budget on services that go only to those people below the poverty line, primarily to 26 percent of the people in this city. If you have a healthy city financially, who benefits? The poor. Because if you have an unhealthy city, who leaves? The middle class. The poor can't leave." He adds that in the first half of the 1970s, before he took office, the city had lost more than half a million jobs. Since he became mayor, New York has gained more than 100,000 jobs in the private sector.

Pleased as he is about balancing the 1982 budget (at $14.7 billion), Koch believes that his city is imperiled by President Reagan's own balancing act. About one sixth of New York's budget for 1982 depends on federal largess, and if those funds are not forthcoming, Koch will face the impolitic Hobson's choice looming for most of the nation's mayors—that of raising taxes or further reducing the very services he needs to beef up. If Reagan's total proposal were to come through as is, Koch predicts that New York would stand to lose $350 million of its operating budget in the first year, and about $350 million in its capital budget. Koch agrees with Reagan in principle, so he is not about to storm the White House. He has lobbied Congress, however, on mass transit and medicaid. And his friendship with the president has paid off in at least one area. New York will receive $1.7 billion to complete its Westway construction project, a covered highway that will link midtown and downtown Manhattan.

The areas most affected by Koch's own budgetary cutbacks have been crime and education; one up, one down. Depending on his mood, Koch will sometimes make less of the city's crime situation by pointing out that New York is only ninth nationally in crime statistics and is not number 1 in rapes and murders, which is no consolation to victims, and is, in any case, misleading. Last year was a crime bonanza for New York, a record, and Koch does take that seriously. In next year's budget he calls for 1,000 new cops and 500 civilians to be added to the police force, along with thirty-seven new trial courts to try to break the gridlock of the criminal justice system. Yet the New York State Bar Association has approved only twelve of the mayor's thirty-three legislative proposals to reform the system. Two of the disapproved ideas, the most controversial, are Koch's call for pretrial jailing without bail of certain people charged with major crimes and his proposal that prosecutors be allowed to appeal, to a higher court, sentences they regard as too lenient.

As for public education, New York's problems differ from other cities' only in magnitude. Schools are dangerous; truancy is rife; classes are unwieldy; teachers can't teach. Koch emphasizes the good news: reading scores are up about 6 percent, exceeding the national average. And for 1982 he proposes the hiring of 1,100 new teachers, 400 more school guards, and an additional $9 million for new equipment and the schools' maintenance budget. Yet a central pedagogical problem must also be met. The city's economy, like the nation's, is changing from one of manufacturing to one of service. Will the schools produce students who can compete in this new market?

The mayor's most publicized problem these days is the New York transit system, which successive administrations of the M.T.A. have let go to hell, until now it has become both a mess and a high-crime district. Of the subway, Koch says that "it stinks" and that it isn't his baby. That is true: Only the governor can hire and fire the M.T.A. chairman, and Koch controls but four of the fifteen votes on the M.T.A. board.

Still, the city is Koch's baby, and the subway is a disease coursing through its arteries. Recently a panel was appointed to recommend comprehensive solutions. It had better. Responsible or not, Koch may well see much of the goodwill he has won in the past three years go down those tubes.

Of all Koch's concerns, the one that rankles and disturbs him the most personally is the accusation that he does not care about the city's blacks and Hispanics. Even his severest critics on this issue rarely accuse Koch of actually being a racist. What they do say is that the mayor, through his championship of the middle class, is exacerbating the normal racial tensions in the city by treating nonwhites as if they were not true citizens. Koch would argue that he acts toward everybody equally, but as a former aide says, "Ed treats everyone the same—badly." Nor does it help matters when Koch works himself into a state and starts hurling words at his critics like "wacko" and "ideologue."

Yet Koch's feeling about nonwhites, about blacks especially, are mixed and volatile. In 1979 the journalist Ken Auletta was researching a two-part profile of the mayor for *The New Yorker*. Koch gave Auletta permission to go through a series of oral memoirs that he had recorded for Columbia University in 1975 and 1976. Among Koch's statements on race was this: "I find the black community very anti-Semitic. I don't care what the American Jewish Congress or the B'nai B'rith will issue by way of polls showing that the black community is not. I think that's pure bull. . . . Now, I want to be fair about it. I think whites are basically antiblack. . . . But the difference is it is recognized as morally reprehensible, something you have to control."

Today Koch is sore at Auletta for printing those remarks because they showed Koch in a bad light, one that his enemies like *The Village Voice* enjoy switching on. But Koch does not deny having those feelings then, nor does he recant them now. On the other hand, he has frequently spoken out against injustice to blacks. He has appointed a higher percentage of blacks (18 percent) to top administrative positions than did any one of the three mayors who preceded him. He took the patronage out of the procedure for choosing young people for summer jobs, and raised the percentage of blacks employed for summers from about 60 percent to over 90 percent simply by making the system equitable. He has treated poverty programs evenhandedly, getting rid of ones that benefit whites as well as blacks. As for playing favorites, he took heat for removing a full-time police car protecting the leader of the Lubavitcher Hasidic sect in Brooklyn, because Koch was convinced such protection was not necessary. Still, he is regarded by many as a divisive force in the city.

Given Koch's reputation on the race issue, it would seem that he has changed a lot since the summer of 1964, when he spent eight days, his vacation, in Laurel, Mississippi, defending civil rights workers. He likes to talk about that time. The event was a sit-in at Kresge's to win equal service at the luncheonette counter. Black and white protesters were assaulted by people at the counter. Then the assailants brought charges against the protesters. Koch tells the story with helpless humor (the "heh, heh, heh") about the pixilated justice of the peace; the redneck mob; the unhelpful F.B.I. officer named Robert E. Lee, to whom Koch offered to send his intended route to Jackson, "to make it easier for you to find the bodies." And the inevitable verdict: "All my people were convicted."

The interesting thing about the story, apart from recalling Koch the liberal (as opposed to the "liberal with sanity," as he describes himself now) is that it reveals an essential part of his makeup. Civil rights was not a lost cause in 1964, but in Laurel it could appear like one. During the period Koch spent in Mississippi, the bodies of three murdered civil rights workers, Michael Schwerner, Andrew Goodman, and James Chaney, were discovered. Koch himself was in real danger, jokes aside. His defendants did not have a chance in court, as Koch well knew. He recognized a lost cause, yet he refused to concede it. One of the fundamental elements in Koch is his capacity to recognize lost causes and principles simultaneously, to wield hope against the facts—a capacity not acknowledged by those who think of him as the enemy of the hopeless.

This fact of Koch is revealed most fully in nothing political, but rather in the story of his most painful lost cause, one that required the greatest display of hope. One recent afternoon, with the light fading, Koch recalled the death of his mother. When he spoke of it, his voice at once softened and rose in pitch, as if he were imitating a boy.

He was asked: Do you picture her in any special way?

"Yes. There was a . . . [Then the voice changed] She died of cancer. And that was very painful.

"I remember the medical report. It filled 'the four quarters of the abdomen.' And ultimately the liver. [Then, spoken very quickly] And she died [like a reasonable conclusion]. It was an interesting episode.

"I dropped by the house one night. It was August 1, and it was 1960. There was my mother. She was very pleased to see me. And she said, 'I'm so glad you came, because tomorrow I'm going into the hospital.' And I said, 'What's wrong, Mama?' And she said, 'Well, I'm not feeling well. I saw my doctor and I told him there's something wrong.' He had been treating her, the doctor, for a gallbladder for five years. She was taking Pepto-Bismol. And then she said, 'But I said to him, No. I want to go in the hospital, to take whatever tests can be taken.' Quite a smart woman. [Looks up to make sure you realize this.] And the doctor said to her, 'It's gallbladder, and we'll just operate. We take it out. We'll repair it.' God knows what. [The sentences sound increasingly like Yiddish-English.]

"So . . . [long pause] she was operated on [by a different doctor]. My father and I were there. And the doctor came down. And he said, 'Uh, [almost inaudible] I've got to tell you something, now or later.' He said, 'Uh, Mr. Koch'—talking to my father—'I'm going to tell you the truth. Your wife has cancer [voice raised for bravery]. She's going to die in three months. And there's nothing I could do and there's nothing you can do [loud here] to help her. And you should let her die in dignity. I know you won't do it. I know you will run from doctor to doctor. It will not help you.' Well, that is some news. So, we take my mother home. She doesn't know. . . . They always know. . . . And just as the doctor knew we would do—my father and I, my brother, and sister, said, 'No, we can't let her die this way. We have to do something. It's ridiculous! You can't let somebody die.' "

The rest is a pilgrimage. Dragging his mother from place to place, from treatment to treatment, quack to quack. Everyone phoned with a miracle cure. His mother implored: "Why don't you let me die?" And Koch: "Oh, Mama, you're silly. You're not going to die." Then the astonishment: "She died to the day, three months; that is what is so incredible." The doctor who told the truth "was a wonderful doctor. And he didn't expect us to listen to him. It's not possible, I mean, if you're a human being." Asked to recollect his mother in happier circumstances, he said that she was very attractive, handsome, not beautiful, "because that would not be accurate." Lifting the mood, he added that she was a terrible cook.

He told his story in his office in City Hall, stretched full-length in a black leather chair to one side of the fireplace, where he customarily talks to visitors. The office is well proportioned: eighteen-foot ceilings and six high arches containing the windows and doors. The paintings vary—an uninteresting abstract consisting of parallel lines; a Matisse of a languishing nude; a study by Isabel Bishop of *Two Girls,* young women really, the one in the red hat looking concerned toward the one in the black hat, who is holding a letter, perhaps conveying bad news. The room is a trove of bric-a-brac: a bogus Oscar inscribed to "Ed Koch, Mayor of Life"; a trophy from the Friars Club; sheet music of an old song called "How'm I Doin'?" (Koch seems curiously remote from these toys, as he does from the bizarre Pee Wee, a giant black-and-white wooden rabbit that sits in his bedroom in Gracie Mansion). There is a sculpture of Romulus and Remus under the wolf, and a photo of the mayor on top of a camel in Egypt.

The mayor's desk was originally used by Fiorello La Guardia. It had to be raised for Koch, who is almost a foot taller than the only predecessor of whom he speaks admiringly—partly for his ideas, partly for his fame. Raised now, the desk is a bit too high for Koch, thus giving symbolic pleasure to those who think that the current mayor cannot hold a candle to the Little Flower. Sitting at his too high desk, Koch can gaze straight across at La Guardia in a portrait, who stares straight back with all the severity due a competitor.

Between the eras of La Guardia and Koch there is a lot of relevant
New York City history, including black and Puerto Rican immigra-
tion, the strengthening of the unions, the demise of the political
bosses. Koch has no time for history. City Hall itself, one of New
York's most beautiful monuments to the past (the architecture is
Louis XVI with sanity), seems fully functional, a museum to work in.
Outside City Hall the Wall Street area that now gambles for the
world was once the whole city, when New York was a Dutch town
veined by canals and hemmed in by a wall (thus the name of the
street). Koch shows no interest in such things, any more than he
seems to notice the plaque located on the sidewalk in front of City
Hall: "In this place 24 March 1900, Hon. Robert Van Wyck made the
first excavation for the underground railway"—the onset of one of
the mayor's great headaches commemorated under his nose.

Koch may not have time for history, but he would like to make
history, and there is a good chance that he will. History, in turn, has
made him—the immigrant boy, the shoe salesman, the Stevensonian,
civil rights–defending liberal Democrat "mugged by reality" in Irving
Kristol's phrase, until eventually, he became the most recognizable
kind of figure in modern American politics: the neoconservative, the
crypto-Republican, the Tough-Man Entrepreneur No-Nonsense
Tightwad. Oddly, this figure has assumed the most traditional American role. He is the Jew become Yankee Trader—prudent, frugal,
resourceful, strict; in Koch's case, ascetic to boot. On his shoulders
lies the mantle of New England Protestantism, the mantle scorned
and defiled by bona fide Protestants like former Mayor John Lindsay,
and now handed over to the latest pioneers.

"We went through an era when middle-class values were dumped
on," says Koch. "Honesty, integrity, hard work, patriotism, religi-
osity, all those were considered terrible things in the minds of some
ideologues who are still out there.

"Not me. I always believed they were verities then. I think they're
verities now." So, deep down, do most New Yorkers, and that is the
center of Koch's strength.

But none of this really explains Koch, who remains remarkably
mysterious for an apparently open man. Some of the mystery is due
to his living alone and keeping his own counsel. Some is due to the
fact that there are sides to Koch that do not smack of Establishment
at all—a strong egalitarian impulse that continually rises to the surface, coupled with genuine comfort in mixing with all classes and
races, without any feelings of personal superiority. Perhaps the most

telling fact about Koch is that he is a longtime resident of Greenwich Village. A Villager is a special kind of New Yorker. Anyone who chooses to live in the Village opts for the extremes of city life—squalor and elegance; beauty and danger; stoopball and art show. He also indicates that he enjoys the potential anarchy of city life—an idea that appeals to more than dare admit it.

If Koch is the elective shoo-in that he appears, however, it is not only because of what people know and see about him, but what they guess about him as well. New Yorkers know that Koch seems a hard-nose. What they guess about him is that he is not the hard-nose he seems, that he is instead a quite naive man who may have toughened up because of various treacheries and disappointments, but who remains fundamentally naive nonetheless. It is said of Koch that he trusts others too little. It is more likely that he has trusted others too much (as he trusted John Lindsay, whom he supported for mayor, and who later turned his back). And it is possible that people have affection for Koch not because he is a wised-up sucker, but because they detect that he is a sucker still, quite unwised-up, just like a great many New Yorkers who are no-nonsense on the outside and mush within.

It may thus be that New Yorkers see in Koch a political sensibility that they recognize in themselves, that of a pratical politician who has not always been that way. The 1960s were a period of extravagant idiocy, but also of great pain; and no politician who has been through that time could remain untouched by both extremes. The Koch who started out as a softy by his own account, and who then acquired a carapace, is different from a political leader who had no soft spot to begin with. With such a convert there is always the possibility (suspicion, hope) that he sympathizes more than he lets on—as in the anecdote Koch loves to tell of the judge who got mugged and then announced that it would have no effect on his future decisions. An old lady in the courtroom shouted: "Then mug him again." It always gets a big laugh. But Koch would not tell the story quite so often if he understood only the old lady.

Finally, cities tend to be sentimental about themselves, as New York's ubiquitous "I Love New York" buttons demonstrate. Koch really does love New York. For that, many people would forgive him almost anything.

Whatever the exact source of his appeal, Koch, like Ronald Reagan, has managed to persuade the citizens that happy days are here again in the face of a continent of evidence to the contrary. Part of the upsurge of feeling is due to normal human buoyancy; part to genuine signs of recovery. But most is due to Koch himself, who, no matter how well or poorly the city knows him, knows the city like the back of his hand. One thinks, for example, of his tasteless, dopey, unprincipled decision to throw a parade for the returned U.S. hostages [from Iran]. The callousness of making those people suffer yet another ceremony. The ignorance of not being able to tell when the public had had enough already. The parade was sensational.

June 15, 1981

The Dark Comedian

A T MY FIRST INTERVIEW with Richard Nixon, in his New York office in the summer of 1985, I set my tape recorder on the table beside his armchair. He stared at the machine. "That's one of those new tape recorders," he said admiringly. "They're so much better than the old tape recorders."

"Oh yes, Mr. President. These new tape recorders don't skip a minute." I did not say that. I did not even think it, caught so thoroughly off guard in the fearful comedy of his presence.

Yet it occurred to me, driving toward what was now my third interview with Nixon, at his home in Saddle River, New Jersey (I had been there once before at a dinner last spring), that in fact I had always thought of Nixon as a comic character, a dark and serious American comic character, like someone out of Twain. Comic in the Checkers speech. Comic in the "You won't have Nixon to kick around anymore" farewell following his defeat in the California gubernatorial election in 1962. In the clownish five o'clock shadow of the first Nixon-Kennedy television debate. In the "I am not a crook" protest. Lighting fires in the White House fireplace in the middle of summer. Kneeling with Henry Kissinger in prayer. Phone calls to Woody Hayes. Bebe Rebozo. Robert Abplanalp. Comic names, madcap circumstances. The man who exalted the "Enemies List," vowing not to hate his haters, waving bravely from the chopper door, then flying back to California toward a town with a name that sounds like clemency.

But see: the Checkers speech effected not Nixon's disgrace but his political *rescue;* and we *did* have Nixon to kick around some more; and if one reviews the tapes, it is easy to conclude that he actually *won* the TV debate with Jack Kennedy; and he *was* a crook. So there. With Nixon, every circumstance eventually turns out to be funnier than he is. The nation he has trod these seventy-five years, the framework for his antics, is itself a dark and serious comedy, simultaneously rejecting and accepting everything in its midst; a riot, a scream. Sometimes (rarely) Nixon laughs aloud. The gunshot laugh, the "Ha!" It is what Beckett designated the risus purus: the laugh laughing at itself in the abysmal farce, in which every part is deadly ridiculous, every line as funny as a crutch.

"Why the hell did we bug the National Committee? They never know anything. If you're going to bug anybody, you bug the McGovern headquarters!" [Drummer does a rimshot.]

"[Jesse] Jackson will have his way with the platform [the Democratic platform of 1988], and the candidate [Michael Dukakis] will ignore the platform. That's the way it happens." [Rimshot.]

"The media go on about the 'undecided voter.' Ha! Undecided voter. That's bullshit. Believe me, people decide about politics early on. You take the average guy. You know? Sipping beer and eating his pretzels. He's worrying about who he should vote for? While I'm on it, there's another myth in politics: that the American people, in their wisdom, like to divide power. That's why they vote for Republicans for president and Democrats for Congress. Because they want a balance of power. You think the average guy says, 'Gee! I'm afraid of that one, so I'm going to restrain him'? Ha! That's a political scientist talking. Know what I mean?" [Double rimshot.]

The comedian understands the average guy. To a degree, the comedian may stand on the outside, which is where Nixon has always considered Nixon to be. But he stands outside the insiders, that's all. Never outside the real, beer-and-pretzels Americans. "My mother was from Indiana. My father, from Ohio. I always did well in the Midwest." Right now, this moment, one is absolutely certain that many thousands of his countrymen would cheer him wildly from the roadsides if only they knew that it was he, Richard Nixon, seated in the back of that sedan, moving in silence every day between the

Federal Plaza office building in Lower Manhattan and the large, not-quite-hidden Saddle River house.

On the way home sometimes, he tells his driver to take the route through Harlem. "I do it mainly because I want to remind myself of what it's like. And I see those damn kids, those poor little black kids. Not to be sentimental about it, but I wonder how any of them ever make it."

Then out of Harlem, over the George Washington Bridge, the car clapping rhythmically on the breaks in the segments of pavement and, whoosh, into the average guy's New Jersey. FOR A FAMILY NIGHT OUT MAKE IT YOUR PLACE. THE GROUND ROUND. A restaurant billboard on the highway not far from Huffman Koos and Wild Bill's Paramus Chrysler and the Happy Viking furniture store. Ho-ho-kus. Paramus. Mahwah. Figments of the American road show. Past the houses with the redwood decks and the fake, unclosable shutters. Houses of no color: not-green, not-yellow, not-white. The dead plunk of the coin at the EXACT CHANGE booth and onto the parkway, where high-tech factories called InSci and Timeplex crouch like bunkers near Saddle River.

Then quiet Saddle River. Lanes are named for animals. Few kids, no litter, except where crows pick at a flattened squirrel in the road. Something on every house is out of scale. The chimney is too big, or the window, or the gate. No high protective hedges here. Residents seem to want to be assured that everyone in sight has made it.

Is this where Richard Nixon belongs? No one doubts that he has made it. Phlebitis or no, he looks terrific these days: color in the cheeks, eyes alert, on top of things. About to publish his sixth book in ten years, *1999: Victory Without War,* he has made Saddle River a Delphi for the nation's politicians. They act, he broods. In the fourteen years since his resignation-ouster, it is said that he has crafted a new base of power out of his expertise and cunning, a calculated rehabilitation. He laughs at the word *rehabilitation* as a cliché. As for the calculation, there must be a good deal of that, but Nixon could no more keep his natural ambition in check than could a beaver abstain from dam construction.

In his study (deep blue bookshelves, Oriental rugs, Chinese vase, French desk), he props his feet on a large, fluffy ottoman. The heels on his black loafers look new. The soles are white, clean as a whistle.

House beautiful: splashes of riches in pleasing, nondisruptive, conventional taste. Yet Nixon dissociates himself from the American upper class. He loathes that class, not for its money or education (he has both), but for something more painful. The loathing erupts like granite outcroppings in his conversation and in his new book. It emerges in contemptuous references to "America's leadership class," the "negativists in our great universities," and, most frequently, "the brightest and the best," for some reason always applying the word order of the hymn and inverting David Halberstam's book title, with ten times the scorn. With those "damn kids" in Harlem, he seems to feel a remote but genuine kinship—not to be sentimental about it. But at the mere thought of the Harrimans, the Bundys, the Kennedys, an excruciating anger enters his voice, reaching as deep into Richard Nixon as any feeling can reach, a fist in the entrails.

"Dukakis has to avoid being Mondale-ized. [Rimshot.] He can do it, and I'll tell you why. You see, McGovern believed all that [liberal] stuff. Dukakis does not. He is simply reflecting the Massachusetts, the M.I.T., the Harvard, the Kennedy School line, and all those people, and so forth."

What is the crime committed by all those people, and so forth? It is not as simple as their having looked down their nose at Richard Nixon. Those people do not understand Richard Nixon: "How I could be both a liberal internationalist and a conservative. You see my point?" A moment to be relished. "I remember when we went to China. Henry [Kissinger] says, 'They [liberals] are dying because you did it.' " Followed by a canny aside: "Of course, Henry is sort of an expert at that. He plays that crowd pretty well."

Even now, how that crowd gets under Nixon's skin! Much of the reason is classic American: the man who all his life had to claw and struggle to the top, seething in the presence of, under the scrutiny of, those whose prominence and power came as easily as slipping on a coat. But there is something else here. The brightest and the best also had a kind of grace that Nixon never knew. A grace of attitude, manner, form, social badinage, perhaps created out of generations of privilege, perhaps not; the unprivileged are also often born with grace. Grace did not descend on Nixon. "I was never much of an athlete, but I follow sports, you know." He of the contorted poses, the puckered face, the hunched-shoulder walk; he of the inability to lie and not get caught. Graceful people don't get caught. "Everybody tapped phones, you know. It's going on right now."

The dark and serious comedy. The graceless, awkward, stiff, stumbling character trips about in a world occupied by natural athletes and virtuoso statesmen, though once he commanded that world. Preposterous contrasts are always good for a laugh. Alone onstage in

Saddle River, the comedian raises himself to the company of heroes, soliloquizing that "it is necessary to struggle, to be embattled, to be knocked down and to have to get up." Look at history's great leaders, he says. They have all trod the wilderness at times. Churchill, De Gaulle, Adenauer. If the audience thinks such comparisons absurd, clearly the comedian does not; that is the purity of the comedy. But, whatever it may think, the audience does not laugh at this or at anything he says ("That's a new tape recorder")—because under the still alive scorn, the still alive paranoia, lives the embodiment of resilience. Homo redivivus. Degraded, insistent, recovering Man.

To be knocked down and to have to get up, that's the ticket. Never mind that it was he who arranged for most of his pratfalls; the getting up still elevates the comedian to something grand. Hard to believe. After all that one knows about Nixon, you would think it is impossible to feel admiration for him, much less affection, but then you realize that you are staring across the study at a man whom the citizens of your country elected to save it and to lead the world, not once but twice, nearly three times; who right now, today, senses enough about what America wants from its presidency to go on the stump and bring down the house. The remarkable display is not merely of will but of his mind. The swirling patterns of the world, the manipulating strategies his mind delights in. The Soviets, the Chinese, the Japanese, the Nicaraguans, NATO; he adores the map. He would play with it still if he could. Temperamentally, he seems more the monarchist French diplomat than the Republican American, yet he understands his country in his bones, half cynically, half naively, much like Gatsby. The only thing that Nixon did not understand is Nixon. (Talk about funny!) Perhaps his resilience is a function of his intelligence: "I'm fighting getting old." Perhaps he knows that in the human comedy of politics, the last man onstage is the hero.

Which makes the audience part of the comedy. "Renewal," he says at lunch. "Americans are crazy about renewal." [Rimshot.]

I mentioned that my second visit with Nixon occurred at a dinner last spring in Saddle River. The ground outside his house was soaked with rain, and no sooner had I entered the living room than I realized that I had tracked great clods of mud on the yellow-white carpet. Flustered, I called to the butler and asked him to do what he could with my destruction while I cleaned off my shoes in the bathroom. When I went back to the living room, scared to death, the carpet was spotless. Not a trace of a stain anywhere. The yellow glowed like sunshine. Several other guests were in the room now, chatting away raucously, as if nothing dirty had ever happened in their midst. The journalist simply stared at the place where the mud had been.

And then the president entered, smiling like a baby, and all rushed to welcome him into the room.

April 25, 1988

Words
on Pieces
of Paper

Picture Shallus doing the words, "engrossing" the Constitution, as the process was called, copying it out at an elegant angle
in large, legible script. The four sheets of parchment were vellum, the
skin of a lamb or a calf, stretched, scraped, and dried. The ink, a
blend of oak galls and dyes. The light, an oil lamp. The instrument,
a feather quill. All nature contributing to the assignment, human
nature in the form of Jacob Shallus, ordinary American citizen, son
of a German immigrant to Philadelphia, soldier, patriot, father of
eight, and, at the time of the Constitutional Convention, assistant
clerk to the Pennsylvania General Assembly. The convention handed
Shallus the documents for copying on September 15, 1787. He had
forty hours to transfer to four sheets of parchment 4,440 words, for
which the payment was thirty dollars, good money for moonlighting.

Two centuries later Shallus becomes history's triviality, his story
revived by a scholar, Arthur Plotnik, in a new biography. But the
words on paper are given Bicentennial parades. Amazing little artifact. What started out at one man's writing desk eventually journeyed
the country from city to city as the nation's capital moved, went into
hiding during the War of 1812, was transferred from federal department to department until it wound up in the National Archives in
Washington, sanctified in helium and watched over by an electronic

camera conceived by NASA. The quill age to the space age, and at every stage, a nation full of grateful believers making a constant noisy fuss over a piece of writing barely equivalent to a short story: much theme, no plot, and characters inferred.

Call the Constitution literature? Sarah Orne Jewett once wrote to Willa Cather, "The thing that teases the mind over and over for years, and at last gets itself put down rightly on paper . . . it belongs to literature." One would have to say that the Constitution qualifies, human minds having been teased for centuries with the possibility of making a government that would allow that mind to realize itself. The document shows other literary attributes as well: a grounding in the ideas of its time, economy of language, orderliness, symmetrical design, a strong, arresting lead sentence. Then, there's all that shapely ambiguity. Even those who have never read the document, enduring wars, debts, threats to health, privacy, equality, down to questions raised by AIDS and aid to the *contras,* are convinced that the Constitution's words foresaw all that.

Which, in a way, they did. The Constitution is more than literature, but as literature, it is primarily a work of the imagination. It imagined a country: fantastic. More fantastic still, it imagined a country full of people imagining themselves. Within the exacting articles and stipulations there was not only room to fly but also the tacit encouragement to fly, even the instructions to fly, traced delicately within the solid triangular concoction of the framers. Even 200 years after the fact, when people debate whether the Constitution is fit for so complicated and demanding a time, Americans take as granted the right to grow into themselves. They must have read it somewhere, in a fable.

Still, picture Shallus, before any of these hopes were raised or satisfied, the four skins laid out before him, the ink, the quill, and the lamp. And the words, like mysterious ciphers, handed over to him by the best minds of the age, who had just sweated out a Philadelphia summer to claim intellectual territory, which was to translate to a civilization. Did Shallus read what he had copied when he finished? Would he have understood it if he had? How could he dream that all those words, thought out so meticulously, were conceived only for him? Citizen Shallus bent over his desk in his country, deliberately, exquisitely in the act of being born.

July 6, 1987

Who
Lives
There

After all the Bicentennial's examinations of what the Constitution is, take one last look to discover who lives there. Someone lives there. The Constitution's inventors could not have produced so durable a document without a vision of the person to whom the laws and stipulations were directed. Before the season dissipates, look at the words one more time. Read them not as rules of the game but as the interior ruminations of a character, a hero, who in some strange conflicted combination of exultation and self-restraint has, for 200 years, found a way to live a life. What character? What life?

The house he occupies is as strange as he is, at once balanced and perilous, like a house of cards. The basic text of the Constitution is the main building, a symmetrical eighteenth-century structure grounded in the Enlightenment principles of reason, optimism, order, and a wariness of emotion and passion. The Constitution's architects, all fundamentally British Enlightenment minds, sought to build a home that Americans could live in without toppling it by placing their impulses above their rationality. To these men, who grew up on Swift, Hume, Locke, and Pope, stability and moderation were not only practical measures but signs of morality.

Ben Franklin, when he wrote of striving for moral perfection in the *Autobiography,* said that he originally set his ambitions in the light of an already God-perfected world. "Whatever is, is right," he quoted John Dryden; Pope used precisely the same line in "An Essay on Man." Washington, whose presence hovered over the Constitutional Convention like a muse, also advocated moderation: "We [Americans] are apt to run from one extreme to another," he wrote John Jay in 1786. As for Madison, the Constitution's principal and most elegant-minded architect, his views were straight Enlightenment dogma. "Why has government been instituted at all?" he asked. "Because the passions of men will not conform to the dictates of reason and justice, without constraint." Again: "If men were angels, no government would be necessary"—a judgment of angels as much as people.

The collective wisdom behind all such statements envisions human nature as existing in and requiring for its survival the most delicate array of balances between religion and science, reason and emotion, democracy and aristocracy, the individual and the group, self-interest and general welfare; that is, all the balances that found their way into the Constitution's basic text. On the whole, that original, unamended text is a model Enlightenment tract, carefully checking and balancing as if in imitation of the moderate universe in which eighteenth-century Europe trusted. One of the framers, John Dickinson, even saw the proposed relationship between the states and the federal government as an analogue to Newtonian physics; and why not? Whatever is, is right. If the "man" Pope considered in his "Essay" needed a body of laws, the American Constitution would do just fine.

The trouble with that original body of laws, as Henry May concluded in his study *The Enlightenment in America,* was that it reflected "all the virtues of the Moderate Enlightenment, and also one of its faults: the belief that everything can be settled by compromise." In other words, the basic Constitution was *too* balanced, and thus logically flawed: What moderate compromises are available when a nation seeks to retain the institution of slavery? The answer to the Constitution's excessive symmetry was the Bill of Rights, which did not overturn the basic document but represented a risky extension into the realms of individual freedom that many of the framers thought dangerous. So here was the Enlightenment house with an ell attached, and a riddle: yes, the main structure was perfect, and, yes, it needed continuous work.

What sort of person would live in such a house? An eighteenth-century person, in fact, but one whose mind spanned the entire century, adding the late-eighteenth-century expansiveness of Blake and Wordsworth to the wary constraints of Pope. The century that began in the Age of Reason ended in the Age of Romanticism, and the Constitution accommodated that severe transition. If the basic text is an Enlightenment document, the Bill of Rights is an homage to Romantic thought, challenging not so much the specifics of the basic Constitution as its earnest sense of permanence. Amendments did not promise answers to sentimental wishes, but they did build in rooms for restlessness. Amendments promised more, and "more" is a Romantic idea. The person who lived in the Constitution was born in the last century that equally prized both modesty and fantasy, and he shuttled naturally between the poles.

After 200 years he has changed dramatically, from an eighteenth-century Englishman to a modern African, Asian, Hispanic. But in terms of basic human nature, he remains as he was when the country began. In two centuries his equilibrium has been tested constantly in a history that includes a secession of half the country, Prohibition, a civil rights movement, burgeoning fundamentalism, and a thousand exigencies that the Constitution's framers could not possibly have foreseen. Yet, amazingly, they could foresee this character at the center of their work: the basic Enlightenment man with a capacity for explosions and a touch of dreams. Much like themselves, he was capable of sitting still as a stone and of changing utterly.

That he has survived these 200 years seems due largely to the Constitution's roominess, which has given him space to shift the furniture without destroying the house. The beauty of the Constitution is that it offers its resident a perpetual challenge to find his own equilibrium within the structure. Miraculously, to date he has managed to do that, as if he were conscious of the fact that the Constitution reflects his nature, mirroring his competing tendencies to squat adamantly and lurch suddenly. In a way, he continually rediscovers himself in that house, a brand-new American for every decade of problems.

Yet if the Constitution allows this character to create himself, he also creates the Constitution, for he existed before it was conceived, and it was built to suit his mind. Astonishing that that mind has endured, given its obvious weaknesses and failings. Perhaps its endurance has something to do with the fact that it runs on a fundamentally generous impulse, that it is the mind of a country that saw itself from the start as an institution of welcome, seeking doggedly to make good on a promise to provide a free, just home. That generous impulse is equally stabilizing and liberating, like the document that promotes it. Who lives in the Constitution? Look again. You know that face.

July 6, 1987

Is Everybody Here?

T HERE IS NO reason on earth why anyone should be anxious about President Carter's recent impromptu conference on national malaise at Camp David [July 16, 1979], and certainly no cause to wonder what went on. All conferences are alike. The trick is to assemble the proper mix of participants, such as those described below—as Mr. Carter did. Once these are in place, one conference is bound to be as successful as any other.

1. *The Academic Priest.* The Academic Priest has replaced the Battling Priest in American folklore, and like a similar change made by the Mafia, has entered the national mainstream by appearing legitimate. He accomplished this transformation by going to graduate school (in English or philosophy) after his ordination, and then by attending conferences on such topics as "Morality and Education," where he so impressed his fellow conferees by mentioning Thomas Aquinas and Angela Davis in the same sentence that eventually a well-placed conferee made him a university president. After that, no major conference has been held without him, his value lying in an uncanny ability to synthesize what has been said by others into a single sentence that includes both Thomas Aquinas and Angela

Davis, and then to top off his remarks with a delightfully salty limerick.

2. *The Wry Woman.* Like the Priest, a creation of the '60s, and often an academic herself, this conferee has spent most of her off-conference hours perfecting a facial expression invaluable to the conference. The expression consists of a combination of an almost mesmerized stare coordinated with a demi-smile at one side of the mouth that might be mistaken for paralysis were it not for the quiver. This expression inevitably unnerves other conference members, to the extent that they often interrupt their own remarks to ask the Wry Woman: "I see you disagree?" or "You have found otherwise?" At that, the Woman shrugs and turns away without comment, signaling the person across from her to pass a yellow writing pad.

3. *The Livid-but-Hopeful Black.* A true minority member, he or she seems to exist nowhere else but at conferences, and in fact may be played by a professional actor. The key to his performance is The Sudden Shift, meaning that no matter what position the participant takes at the outset of the conference, he must take the exactly opposite position by the conference's end. Usually he goes from livid to hopeful, but the other way is acceptable. Everyone nods vigorously at whatever position he takes, and he is always asked to future conferences as long as he uses such terms as "frustration," "American dream," and "soul"—in quotation marks.

4. *The Kid with a Future.* Not an absolutely necessary, but a nevertheless enchanting addition to any conference, the Kid with a Future has usually just returned from a year as a Rhodes, Marshall, or Fulbright scholar, and has been "discovered" at a conference on "The University and Moral Values" by the Academic Priest. The Kid says but two things at the conference—"You know, when I was at Harvard I thought I had all the answers" and, "You know, I truly believe my generation can make a difference"—at which the senior conferees exchange sidelong looks of deep satisfaction.

5. *The Brahmin Jew.* Taking the angry-yet-responsible approach to the topic, the Brahmin Jew almost always keynotes the conference, where he is indispensable for his treasure trove of Yiddish humor and his undisguised contempt for California. His behavior is ordinarily even-tempered, except when the Black is in his livid stage and claims that blacks are history's only sufferers, whereupon the Jew protests, whereupon the Black concedes the truth of the Jew's objection; or

when the Kid makes his generation-difference remark, whereupon the Jew flies into a modulated rage about the privileges of young people, whereupon the Kid concedes the truth of the Jew's objection. Otherwise the Brahmin Jew is a model conference member, and is the only participant allowed to mention "decency," "freedom," and "reason," without implying anything.

6. *Mr. Goodwords.* A former holder of every major government post except the presidency, Mr. G thinks it is "high time" this topic was aired in public, and that it's "just great" to be here. Occasionally he confuses the topic under discussion with another, as he participates in four conferences simultaneously, but that's all right "because we're all in the same damn mess." Mr. G has his eye on the Kid, thinks the Black is "terrific," wants to discuss something important with the Jew later on, has to leave early to catch a plane to Islip, and is "one hell of a guy."

7. *The Beloved Technician.* Indisputably the most popular conferee, the Beloved Technician claims no analytical abilities whatever, and is merely called upon once or twice to present pertinent statistics or other objective data. After his presentation, either the Jew or the Priest observes: "Well, it's a bit disconcerting to hear from someone with the facts. . . ." This is followed by raucous laughter around the table, and a hearty thank-you from the Dead Grateful (see below), at which the Beloved Technician blushes hotly.

8. *Mr. (Miss, Ms., or Mrs.) What-Am-I-Doing-Here?* An essential member of any conference, this role may be assumed by any conferee, but it is best played by a poet or a fireman or anyone regarded as representing an unheard-from, though vital, point of view. The What says but one thing at the conference: "As I sit here listening to you people, I ask myself: What am I doing here?" The effect of this remark is devastating. All conferees, with the possible exception of the Jew, apologize to the What directly or indirectly for a wide range of inferred offenses; and no further statement is made at the conference without reference to his "troubling question."

9. *The Dead Grateful.* Or Mister Conference, as he is known from Aspen to Paris to Rio, or wherever an emergency issue arises that requires a conference of knowledgeable and dedicated citizens. An indefatigable, warm, and deeply committed fellow, who is only mocked by the conferees between conferences, the Dead can do all things conference-wise, including the arrangement of subsequent con-

ferences on topics that come up during the conference at hand. But he is best simply being grateful; grateful to the people who found the time in their busy schedules to help explore so urgent a problem; and especially grateful to the Ford, Rockefeller, Lilly, Carnegie, and National Humanities foundations, without whose vision and generosity this planet of ours would be in mighty hot water.

July 16, 1979

Ronald Reagan

ON AN AFTERNOON in early December [1980], Los Angeles was in the sixties and Ronald Reagan looked like a dream. He was wearing a blue-and-green wool tartan jacket, a purple tie, white shirt, white handkerchief, black pants, and black loafers with gold along the tops. Who else could dress that way? He settled back on a couch in a living room so splurged with color that even the black seemed exuberant. A florist must have decorated it. A florist must have decorated his voice. He was talking about job hunting as a kid in his hometown of Dixon, Illinois, telling an American success story he has told a hundred times before. He seemed genuinely happy to hear it again. No noise made its way up to the house on Pacific Palisades, except for the occasional yip of a dog, and, of course, the eternal sound of California—the whir of a well-tuned car. Outside, the Secret Service patrolled the bougainvillea on streets with liquid, Spanish names. Reagan's face was ruddy, in bloom, growing younger by the second.

At week's end he would be expected at the convocation of conservatives for *The National Review*'s twenty-fifth-anniversary dinner in the Plaza Hotel in New York City. Reagan would not show—a mix-up in his calendar. Riled, his hosts would sing his praises over dessert nonetheless. He was the answer to their prayers, after all; the essential reason for the elegant, confident glow of the evening. Editor William F. Buckley, Jr., would shine quietly, modestly. Others, like publisher William Rusher, would exhort the assembled "to stamp out any remaining embers of liberalism." A war whoop was in the air— black tie, to be sure—but still the unmistakable sound of a faction reprieved, at last in power, thanks to the boyish man at the other end of the country, whose time had definitely come.

As for the cause of the celebration, his rise seems astonishing. It began in October 1964 when, as cochairman of California Citizens for Goldwater, he gave his "A Time for Choosing" television speech, a speech so tough that Goldwater himself was skittish about letting it air. Reagan ended the talk with "You and I have a rendezvous with destiny," and was at least half right. So mesmerizing was his perform- ance, so quick in its effect, that California businessmen swamped him like groupies, formed a "Friends of Ronald Reagan" committee, begged him to run for governor. He had to be pushed. Yet in 1966 the former star of *Juke Girl* snatched the governorship of California by a million votes from incumbent Edmund G. ("Pat") Brown, who must have thought he was the victim of an accident. (Reagan also starred in *Accidents Will Happen*.)

In fact, there has been a remarkably accidental air about Reagan's career; it has always borne the quality of something he could take or leave. The image of the nonpolitician running for office, antilogical as it is, has had its practical advantages, but it is also authentic. Because Reagan knows who he is, he knows what he wants. After a halfhearted run at Nixon for the Republican presidential nomination in 1968, he returned to California for a second term as governor. But in 1976, after an all-out and failed attempt to capture his party's nomination, he genuinely did not wish to be Gerald Ford's vice president. When Ford's invitation went to Bob Dole, Reagan loyalists were crestfallen, reading in that rebuff the end of their man's life in politics. Only Reagan took it well, content to settle forever on his ranch, if it came to that, but also believing (as few others did) that even at age sixty-five you can run into luck.

Four years later, his party, now confirmed in its conservatism, turned to him like a heliotrope. He was lucky to run against (Eastern, brittle) George Bush for the nomination; he was lucky to be beaten early in Iowa, before the so-called momentum against him was real; he was lucky to have Jimmy Carter as his opponent. On the night of November 4, 1980, just sixteen years after he had spoken his mind in behalf of a man too far right to be elected president, the amateur politician who will become seventy in February watched state after state turn in his direction.

For that, in part, Reagan is *Time*'s Man of the Year—for having risen so smoothly and gracefully to the most powerful and visible position in the world. He is also the idea of the year, his triumph being philosophical as well as personal. He has revived the Republican party, and has garnered high initial hopes, even from many who opposed him, both because of his personal style and because the United States is famished for cheer. On January 20 Reagan and the idea he embodies will both emerge from their respective seclusions with a real opportunity to change the direction and tone of the nation.

Reagan is also *Time*'s Man of the Year because he stands at the end of 1980 looking ahead, while the year behind him smolders in pyres. The events of any isolated year can be made to seem exceptionally grim, but one has to peer hard to find elevating moments in 1980. Only Lech Walesa's stark heroism in Poland sent anything resembling a thrill into the world. The national strike he led showed up Communism as a failure—a thing not done in the Warsaw Pact countries. Leonid Brezhnev, a different sort of strongman, had to send troops to Poland's borders, in case that country, like Czechoslovakia and Hungary before it, should prove in need of "liberation."

Otherwise, the year was consumed with the old war-and-death business. Afghanistan enters the year as a prisoner of its "liberating" neighbor; Iran and Iraq close the year at each other's throats. In between, Cambodians are starved out of existence; terrorists go about murdering eighty or more in Bologna, and a mere four outside a Paris synagogue. In Turkey, political violence kills 2,000; in El Salvador, more than 9,000 die in that country's torment. All this on top of natural disasters: Mount St. Helens erupts in Washington State; one earthquake in Algeria kills 3,000; another in Italy takes the same toll. Human enterprise is tested, and responds with black market coffins.

In February Americans flinch at an inflation rate of 18 percent that drops to a hardly bearable 12.7 percent as the year ends. February is also the month when the U.S. hockey team's victory over the Soviets ignites national pride. But in April the United States boycotts the Summer Olympic Games to protest the Soviet invasion of Afghanistan. In May Cuban refugees flee Castro, and the United States greets them at first with an "open arms" policy, then a state of emergency in Florida, then a closing of the open arms—the entire pilgrimage eventually capped off with riots at Eglin Air Force Base and later at Fort Chaffee. Vernon Jordan is shot in May as well. In June science announces a breakthrough in recombinant DNA research, raising high hopes of cancer cures along with specters of genetic engineering and Andromeda Strains. The prime lending rate at major banks soars to 21.5 percent in December, all but ensuring that 1981 will begin with a recession.

Old orders pass: Prime Minister Ohira in Japan; the Shah in Egypt; and Tito, who one thought would live forever. In the background, like presiding ghosts, the hostages in Iran serve as emblems of national impotence; Walter Cronkite's counting of the days growing weary and meaningless among Milquetoast threats and a tragic rescue fiasco. As if to sustain the world's heartache, the year heads toward Christmas with the killing of a Beatle.

In 1953 Robert Lowell said the "Republic summons Ike" because "the mausoleum [was] in her heart." In 1980 the Republic summoned Ronald Reagan. Why?

History rarely moves openly toward its main players. Usually a central figure is perceived as evolving only in retrospect, and that could well happen four years from now, when the country may acknowledge that Ronald Reagan was the only man who could possibly have pulled the United States out of its doldrums. For now, in prospect, that certainly cannot be said. Reagan is an experiment, a chance. For all the happy feelings his good nature generates, the cool fact of American life is that most of the country is still from Missouri, and much is yet to be proved.

In this light it may be useful to remember first that Reagan's ten-point popular victory was not assured until the final days of the campaign. As deeply soured on the Carter administration as most of the electorate was, it also withheld its approval of the competition until the last minute. Quietly, privately, and perhaps a little grimly, most Americans had probably decided that Carter had had it as early as eighteen months before November. Their main reason was the economy, but there was Carter himself, a man who also started out riding the country's high hopes (a *Time* Man of the Year in 1976), and who was perhaps most bitterly resented for shrinking those hopes down to the size of a presidency characterized by small people, small talk, and small matters. He made Americans feel two things they are not used to feeling, and will not abide. He made them feel puny and he made them feel insecure.

That Reagan beat such a man is a feat of circumstances as much as of personal strength. Right-wingers like to crow that the country veered sharply to the right when it turned to Reagan, but the probable truth of the matter is that most of the country had simply stepped firmly to the right of center. As conservatives sensed, the country had been an incubative conservative since the late '60s. Only Nixon's muck-up could have delayed their eventual birth and triumph. Sick and tired of the vast, clogged federal machine; sick and tired of being broke; fed up with useless programs, crime, waste, guilt; not to mention shame in the eyes of the world—derision from our enemies, dismay from our allies—fed up with all that, and to put a fine point on it, fed up with Jimmy Carter, what else would the nation do but hang a right?

The fascinating thing is how determined a swing it was. Reagan's pollster Richard Wirthlin found that voters, even at the end of the campaign, believed that Reagan was more likely to start an unnecessary war than Carter, and that Carter was much more sensitive to the poor and the elderly. Still, the right prevailed. The New Deal was out of steam; in the long run it ensured its own obsolescence by giving the workingman the wherewithal to turn Republican. Even so, his paycheck was inadequate. Everything seemed inadequate. The country had to move on, but it was not moving anywhere. Enter Reagan (with jubilation and a mandate).

That mandate is specific: to control inflation, to reduce unnecessary governmental interference in private lives and in business, to reassert America's prominence in the world. That is all there is to it, and that is plenty. The mandate does not necessarily include far-right hit lists, censorship, the absence of gun control, prayer in schools, and a constitutional amendment banning abortion. These things are significant if problematical, but they do not represent majority wishes. Nor does the Reagan mandate suggest approval of a national pulpit for Jerry Falwell's lethal sweet talk or of the National Conservative Political Action Committee (NCPAC), whose liberal-hunting leaders have been jumping up and down like Froggie the Gremlin since November 4. The majority voted for Reagan because he appeared to be a reasonable man, and a reasonable presidency is what the country expects.

Still, it is not only the anticipation of Reagan's reasonableness that has hopes high at the moment. Pennsylvania's Republican governor Richard Thornburgh explains the Reagan election in terms of ideas: "The status of the individual in society, fiscal integrity, the idea of true federalism, the idea of Government closer to the people, the idea of the toughness of the American fiber, which means a firm line with criminals at home and with our adversaries abroad. With Reagan's election, Republican principles hold the high ground, the principles which put together the real genesis of the Reagan victory. Those principles are now a majority view."

That is true enough, but Republicanism is also changing. During all the years the Democrats were in power, their party developed a kind of character, one that reached a pinnacle of form in John Kennedy—that is, the character of the *interesting* party, the party of real intellectual movement, the party of the mind. Conversely, the G.O.P. was the party of the pocketbook, the pinstripe, and the snort. Goodbye to all that. The G.O.P. is now by far the more interesting of the two parties. And much of the anticipation of the Reagan presidency has to do with the fact that people recognize that an idea is taking shape.

The man at the center of this idea appears smaller than he is. At six foot one inch, 185 pounds, his body is tight, as tight as it can be on a large frame, though there is no sign of pulling or strain. It is the body of an actor, of someone used to being scrutinized from all angles, so it has all but willed as tidy and organized an appearance as possible. His size also seems an emblem of his modesty. Lyndon Johnson used to enter a room and rape it. Reagan seems to be in a continual state of receding, a posture that makes strangers lean toward him. In a contest for the same audience, he would draw better than Johnson.

The voice goes perfectly with the body. No president since Kennedy has had a voice at once so distinctive and beguiling. It too recedes at the right moments, turning mellow at points of intensity. When it wishes to be most persuasive, it hovers barely above a whisper so as to win you over by intimacy, if not by substance. This is style, but not sham. Reagan believes everything he says, no matter how often he has said it, or if he has said it in the same words every time. He likes his voice, treats it like a guest. He makes you part of the hospitality.

It was that voice that carried him out of Dixon and away from the Depression, the voice that more than any single attribute got him where he is. On that smoky blue December afternoon in Pacific Palisades he was telling the old story again—about his job hunting in 1932, about heading for Chicago, where "a very kind woman" at NBC told him to start out in the sticks. So he drove around to radio station WOC in Davenport, Iowa, where he made his pitch to the program director, Peter MacArthur, an arthritic old Scotsman who hobbled on two canes. Reagan, of course, had that voice, and he had played football for Eureka College. But MacArthur said that he had just hired someone else, and Reagan stomped off muttering, "How the hell do you get to be a sports announcer if you can't get into a station?" The delivery is perfect—plaintive, sore. Something wonderful is bound to happen.

"I walked down the hall to the operator, and fortunately the elevator wasn't at that floor. And while I was waiting, I heard this thumping down the hall and this Scotch burr very profanely saying (in a Reagan Scotch burr), 'Wait up, ya big so and so.'" And what did MacArthur say? Something about sports, of course. And what did MacArthur ask? "Do you think you could tell me about a football game and make me see it?" And could Ronald Reagan do that then and there? On the folktale goes, fresh as a daisy, full of old hope and heartbeats.

In the pinch, Reagan fell back on describing a game he had played in for Eureka. "So when the light went on I said, 'Here we are going into the fourth quarter on a cold November afternoon, the long blue shadows settling over the field, the wind whipping in through the end of the stadium'—hell, we didn't have a stadium at Eureka, we had grandstands—and I took it up to the point in which there were twenty seconds to go and we scored the winning touchdown. As a blocking guard, I was supposed to get the first man in the secondary to spring our back loose, and I didn't get him. I missed him. And I've never known to this day how Bud Cole got by and scored that touchdown. But in the rebroadcast I nailed the guy on defense. I took him down with a magnificent block."

Cheers and laughter. Who would not hire this man? Humility, a sense of proportion, gentle humor. Bless the elevator operator; bless the crippled Scotsman. Who would doubt that even now, from time to time, the governor dreams of the fancy footwork of the ever elusive Bud Cole?

Of course, the anecdote gives everything and nothing. In the movies, *The Story of Ronald Reagan* might be built of such stuff, like the "story" of Jim Thorpe, but not a life; the life has to be discovered elsewhere. At least the facts pile up neatly: born February 6, 1911, Tampico, Illinois; son of John Edward and Nelle Wilson Reagan; younger brother of Neil Reagan, now a retired advertising executive in California. After Tampico the Reagans move around for a while and then to Dixon, a back-porch and lemonade town on the Rock River. Father is a sometime shoe salesman and a sometime alcoholic. Mother, a Scottish Protestant; father, Irish Catholic. Ronald takes the faith of his mother.

At high school in Dixon, "Dutch" plays football. His eyes are weak; he is undersized for his age; still he plays the line. He also joins the basketball team, takes part in track meets, is elected president of the student body. Along the way, he works as a lifeguard at a local river and rescues seventy-seven people, a record of sorts, preserved in notches on a log. He is Midwest perfect, down to the requisite transgression. Mellow on homemade wine one night, he mounts a traffic stand and bellows "Twinkle, twinkle, little star." On to Eureka, where he wins letters in football, track, and swimming, and joins the dramatics club. (Here the repeated good lines: "Nature was trying to tell me something. Namely, my heart is a ham loaf.") He pays his way through school, his family so poor they move into a single-bedroom apartment with an electric plate. Neighbors carry supper over to them on trays. At Eureka, he is again elected student-body president. In a regional drama competition, his performance as a shepherd wins honors. The idea of working in radio occurs to him as a halfway measure between acting and respectability. He lights out for Chicago, and the rest is folklore.

The element missing in such accounts is what it feels like to be Ronald Reagan. His autobiography, *Where's the Rest of Me?*, takes its title from the most memorable line he ever delivered as an actor, when his legs were amputated in *Kings Row*. As his presidency goes on, that title is bound to turn on him, as *Why Not the Best?* turned on Jimmy Carter, though with Reagan the question will be less accusative than mystifying. That self-diminution, the trustworthiness, the aura of the towhead, the voice—all comprise a figure one takes to the heart. But where is he in this process? What clobbers him? He offers no signs now. Back in Dixon he did offer something, however small.

He wrote a poem in high school and called it "Life," as all high school poems must be called. It went as follows:

> I wonder what it's all about, and why
> We suffer so, when little things go wrong?
> We make our life a struggle,
> When life should be a song.

Our troubles break and drench us.
Like spray on the cleaving prow
Of some trim Gloucester schooner
As it dips in a graceful bow . . .

But why does sorrow drench us
When our fellow passes on?
He's just exchanged life's dreary dirge
For an eternal life of song . . .

Millions have gone before us,
And millions will come behind.
So why do we curse and fight
At a fate both wise and kind?

We hang onto a jaded life
A life full of sorrow and pain.
A life that warps and breaks us,
And we try to run through it again.

The poem is odd, baleful—not an unusual tone for a teenager generally, but neither is it what we would expect of the peppy, clean-cut teenager that was young Dutch Reagan. Examined under a sad light, "Life" is the poem of a boy who either wants to drown or is at least considering the possibility. The first stanza is cheery enough, but it really belongs to another poem. The sense of advocated surrender in the final stanza is unmistakable. Not that Reagan would be unusual in having contemplated death as a way out of adolescence, but one does not think of his early life as having been touched with "sorrow and pain." Of course, the poem might simply have been the product of a bad moment. But even a momentary touch of desperation is interesting in such a man.

Usually, Reagan's assessments of his childhood are entirely wistful, but there was a hint of something else when he was asked recently if he ever saw his father in himself as a parent. His answer: "Yes, and maybe sometimes too much so. I don't know how to describe it because neither of my parents ever had anything in the line of a formal education, and yet there was a freedom to make decisions, and sometimes I find that maybe I go too far in that." That freedom to make decisions fits well with Reagan's political philosophy, but his answer leaves out a negative element of his own performance as a parent. A parent's philosophy of freedom leaves the parent free as well.

• • •

The main characteristics that Reagan displays—good humor, modesty, patience—are the attributes of fatherhood at its best. And from all appearances Reagan would seem to have been the compassionate father, the father to turn to in times of grief and disarray; the father of rich stories and silly jokes. Instead, his relationship with all four children—Maureen and Mike, his children with Jane Wyman, and Patti and Ron, his children with Nancy—seems to be that of deliberately created distances. The physical distances, the fact that the children were shipped off to boarding schools at young ages, seem an adjunct of the emotional distances—though the first two children lived with Wyman after she divorced him, so in their case some of the distancing was circumstantial. As for Patti and Ron, Reagan admits that he did not spend much time with them but blames his life as a celebrity and not his own desires. He tells dolefully of taking Patti to the opening of Disneyland and being beset by autograph hounds, spoiling a normal, happy family excursion.

Given that other celebrities manage to spend time with their children, Reagan's explanation does not make much sense. Still, there is no doubt that it makes sense to him. The regret he expresses about not having been more attentive to the children is sincere, if low level. Now, the children grown, they all seem much closer than before, which is interesting, as it suggests that Reagan, who bears much of the aspect of an adorable child himself, simply gets along better with grown-ups. The unceremonious wedding of young Ron a few weeks after the election offers a public sign that some vestiges of the old distances remain.

Yet in the odd child-parent pattern of the Reagan family, Ron's decision to marry suddenly with barely a last-minute word to his folks is perfectly traditional. It is widely known that Ron's parents have not managed to see a single ballet performance of their son, who is clearly very good, having been selected to the Joffrey second company, and is their son nonetheless. Ron talks of his parents with much affection. But these absences are strange and go back a ways. Son Mike was a successful motorboat racer; Reagan did not see a single race. Mike, a star quarterback at Judson School in Scottsdale, Arizona, was named Player of the Year in 1964. Reagan saw not a game.

The family tradition that he was upholding by such omissions is that his own father rarely managed to see him and Brother Neil play football. Neil Reagan notes the fact today, conceding that his father's lack of interest was odd, but consistent with the ideal of "independence" among the Reagans. Yet it takes an act of will not to watch one's children in a moment important to their self-esteem. One almost has to actively deny the desire to show pride and affection; no child could mistake the effort—unless, of course, the pride and affection were purely superficial. The great puzzlement about Ronald Reagan, in fact, is exactly how much of him lies hidden. He has lived a charmed life on the surface—many people do—but it is disconcerting, to say the least, to unravel Reagan like H. G. Wells's invisible man, only to discover that when you get the bandages off, the center is not to be seen.

Still, after listening to Reagan, it would be impossible to conclude that he did not love his children. It would be easier to conclude that he did not know how to love his children, when they were children, just as it is possible to assume that his father did not know how to love him. There is an abiding compassion in Reagan for his father, for his father's drinking—the "sickness," as his mother explained it. The story is now famous of his finding his father passed out on the front porch and bearing him inside. Nor is there any sign that Reagan's father was anything but a man of high natural instincts, like the son who inherited his looks, capable of fierce rage at racial or religious bigotry. But neither are there signs of real father-to-son love. And the fact that Reagan's father was an alcoholic, albeit "periodic," as Reagan is quick to explain, must have alloyed young Ronald's feelings for his father as much with dread as with sympathy.

One thing the children of alcoholics often have in common is an uncommon sense of control—control of themselves and control of their world, which they know from harsh experience can turn perilous at the click of a door latch. Not that Jack Reagan was known to be a mean drunk; but brutal or not, all alcoholics create states of alarm in their children. They learn a kind of easygoing formality early on, like the Secret Service, and they are often acutely alert to danger, for the very reason that the parent's binges *are* periodic. That receding look and sound of Reagan may be the hallmarks of such control. One cannot retain anger in the presence of such a man, and thus in a sense he makes fathers of us all.

In fact, Reagan seems ever to place himself in the position of being adopted. He has, in a sense, been adopted by a plethora of fathers over the years, wealthy patrons, and protectors who recognized a hope for the country's future in their favorite son. Yet Reagan is also a genuine loner. His ranch is a true retreat for him, a state of mind, and perhaps an emblem of his achievement, of the independence he was taught to prize. Solitude and self-reliance, the two essential American virtues that Emerson named, are found in him naturally. On the ranch he can be free—not "on" to audiences. The only odd thing in the picture is that such a loner would choose to give his life to lines of work that demand continuous performance.

The combination of showmanship and privacy is unusual, but the combination of that sense of control with genuine good nature is extraordinary. Conventionally, a severe sense of control is used to harness rage or malice; Reagan seems incapable of either. The effect of that combination, however, is not entirely sanguine. Twenty-five years ago, Neil dreamed up an elaborate and touching Christmas present for his kid brother. He found an impoverished family with a father who was a drunk and out of work, and Neil took the wife and child on a shopping spree. The parallels to the Reagans' own childhood are evident, and whatever moved Neil to emphasize the parallels remains obscure. But the gift was one of immense ingenuity and generosity—because the shopping spree was given in Ronald's name. Yet when it was presented to Reagan, along with a poem Neil wrote for the occasion, Ronald reacted by saying, "Gee, that's keen." It is difficult to know if he was moved or not, but he certainly did not wish to give the impression (satisfaction) of having been moved.

When campaign manager John Sears was determined to get Mike Deaver, one of the closest friends of both the Reagans, out of the 1980 organization, Reagan let it happen. He said he did not like it, but he went along anyway, choosing pragmatism over loyalty. There are other examples of cool calculation that seem out of place in what is patently a good heart. The feeling one takes from a conversation with Reagan—and it is very quiet and faint—is that his geniality is equal to his fears. What, specifically, he is afraid of is a secret, as it is with most successful people. But there is no secret about his ability to do a kind of stylistic judo on a potential threat. The voice softens to music; the eyes grow helpless, worried.

TIME: You were quoted as having said that you had read Norman Podhoretz's *The Present Danger* and thought it was a very important book. Is that accurate? Did you admire that book when it came out?

REAGAN: I read it. [Backs off at at once; eyes are shy with surprise; sounds as if he's being accused of something, or as if he is about to be tested.] I don't recall ever having anything to say about it. [Hesitates, but seeing no traps, relaxes slightly.] But I did read it [some firmness now] and do believe that it makes a great deal of sense [confidence restored]."

None of this is to suggest that Reagan resembles a haunted or threatened man. In a lifetime one does not encounter half a dozen people so authentically at ease with themselves. Reagan is a natural; he knows it. His intuitions are always in tune, and he trusts his own feelings. All his political opinions have been born of feelings—the passionate antagonism toward Big Government resulting from his boyhood observations of Dixon and his own experiences with the progressive income tax once he returned from the military; his staunch anti-communism from his days with the Screen Actors Guild in the late 1940s, when he packed a pistol for self-protection. He will read up on a subject once it has initially been proved on his pulses, but he does not take his main ideas from printed words. In that process of intellection he is classically American—the natural man whose intelligence lies not in book learning but in right instincts. Reagan regularly reads conservative journals of opinion and his share of newspapers and magazines and contemporary books about politics, but no author seems to have been especially influential in his life. Yet he is able, by employing a kind of trick of memory, to dredge up whole passages of things he read as far back as forty years ago. Like many politicians, he probably uses reading the way one might use friends. Instead of his going to books, they come to him.

This sense of his integrity, of his thoroughgoing self-knowledge is a major asset. When he was making *Dark Victory* (yes, he was there, well behind Bette Davis, George Brent, and Humphrey Bogart), the director (Edmund Goulding) bawled him out for playing a scene too simply and sincerely. "He didn't get what he wanted, whatever the hell that was," Reagan recalls, "and I ended up not delivering the line the way my instinct told me it should be delivered. It was bad."

Now, considerably freer to follow his instincts, his lines are delivered with consistent effect—simply and sincerely. At the close of the Carter television debate he posed several semirhetorical questions that are now said to have sealed his victory: "Are you better off than you were four years ago? Is it easier for you to go and buy things in the stores?" And so forth. There is first the brilliance of the baby talk—"to go and buy things in the stores." But the real power in those questions came from the delivery, which if managed by a less sensitive speaker could have produced something strident, or assured, or worse, argumentative. Instead, Reagan's pitch trembled between helplessness and fellow feeling; it was to *himself* that he was talking; *he* who could not go and buy things in the stores. The United States was in a sad mess, not an infuriating one. Only a calm though suffering voice could rescue it.

Where more hard-nosed politicians will talk ceaselessly about polling techniques or some son of a bitch in a rebellious precinct, Reagan will talk about the art of public speaking. Even though he is a virtuoso, he works at that art, primarily because he is a politician only of the essentials, and knows, as his admired Franklin Roosevelt knew, that to reach and please the public is to put first things first. One sign of his amazing success as a speaker is that his plentiful gaffes are not only forgiven; even better, they are forgotten. Speaking in Columbus last summer, he deliberately made an error, substituting the word *depression* for *recession* in order to reinforce a point. The alteration set off a small squall of technical retractions by one of his economics advisers, Alan Greenspan, but the point was reinforced. His sense of timing is almost always a thing of beauty. After the "depression" error, instead of dropping the matter, he traded on it: "If he [Carter] wants a definition, I'll give him one. [Audience is on the alert for something punchy, perhaps funny.] Recession [split-second pause] is when your neighbor loses his job. Depression [same pause; audience grows eager] is when you lose yours. [Chuckles and titters; audience wonders if there will be a third part to the definition.] And recovery [audience gears itself for a laugh] is when Jimmy Carter loses his [kaboom]."

The opposition's book on Reagan (by now a public document) is that he is always underestimated. That too is a mark of the natural man—the fox taken for a fool who winds up taking the taker. Yet there is no Volpone slyness in Reagan. If he has been underestimated, it may be that he gives every sign of underestimating himself—not as a tactic, but honestly. So wholly without self-puffery is he that he places the burden of judging him entirely on others, and since he is wholly without self-puffery, the judgment is almost always favorable. He simply appeals to people, and despite his years, there is hardly anyone of any age who would not feel protective of him, would not wish him to succeed, would not forget the mistakes, who would not corral him in the hall and give him a job. Again this is not a tactic. It may well be his soul.

Does this mean, then, that his soul is not his own? The question is urgent in the minds of those who fear that the Reagan presidency will be shaped and conducted by the God-toting religicos or the fever-swamp conservatives who exult in the hopes that they are free at last. The answer to that question is no, but it ought not necessarily put the worriers at ease. Reagan's soul is his own, yet what sort of soul is it? For those who have observed Reagan lo these many years, the answer is clearly and consistently a most conservative soul, notwithstanding the formulaic chitchat about his having once been a hemophiliac liberal, which is simply a device for implying that policies aside, his heart is still with the people. A more precise question is: What sort of mind has Reagan? How intelligent is he? But with "natural" men, intelligence is not so readily definable.

For the moment, what we can see in Reagan is a vision of America, of America's future, at once so simple and deep as to incur every emotion from elation to terror. It is a little like the vision of the Hudson River school of painting—the brooding serenity of turquoise skies, patriarchal clouds and trees, very still, doll-like people (white and red), infinite promise, potential self-deception, and, above all, perfect containment—the individual and the land, man and God locked in a snakeless Eden. James Fenimore Cooper wrote a novel, *Satanstoe,* about such a place, an ideal America in which everyone ruled his own vast estate, his own civilization. Whether or not Reagan sees Rancho del Cielo or Pacific Palisades as Satanstoe, his dream of the New World is as old as Cooper's.

At the center of that dream is the word *freedom;* it is a key word with Reagan, and it is the word at the center of all American dreams, from the beautiful to the murderous. Reagan's version seems to center largely on the question of free enterprise: "[Americans] have always known that excessive bureaucracy is the enemy of excellence and compassion." True. Therefore, freedom must be the ally of excellence and compassion. Sometimes. Since Reagan's way of understanding things is personal, he puts it thus: He dug a pond on his own property, and now if he wants to stock that pond with fish, he has to get a fishing license to catch his own fish. Bingo. If the vision of boundless freedom were to consist solely of being able to fish one's own ponds, who would have trouble siding with Reagan's idea?

But there is no particular trick in making a buffoon of federal regulations. Things grow more problematical when one tries to extend such reasonable complaints to a general political philosophy, and talk—as Reagan does talk—of putting "the Federal Government back in the business of doing the things the Constitution says are its prime functions: to keep internal order, to protect us in our national security from outside aggression, and to provide a stable currency for our commerce and trade." Very well. But such a definition omits the "general welfare" clause. And in practical terms, Reagan undoubtedly does not intend to dismantle the N.L.R.B., Social Security, unemployment insurance, and other such encroachments on pure freedom that are here to stay. So, what does he mean?

However vague and simplified Reagan's idea of freedom may be, it touches a central chord in American thought, a chord that will sound when people start to fear that the future is over, as they did during the Carter administration. The fact that Reagan speaks for the virtues of both the past and the future is reassuring, if safe, but the fact that his definition of freedom is essentially Western is more to the point. When Reagan speaks of freedom, he is speaking of freedom west of the Rockies. That is where he found his own best America; that is where he continues to find his personal and philosophical solace; that is what he wishes for the country at large—a California dream, an endless prospect of gold and greenery and don't fence me in.

That California has come to embody such a vision of boundlessness is a little strange, since the dream of California is as much the dream of disappointment as of hope—the dream of arriving at virgin territory, of messing it up, and having gone as far as one can go, of having nowhere to turn but back. As Kevin Starr pointed out in his *Americans and the California Dream,* California has always stood for something mystical in American life; it has not suffered the tragic historical burdens of the East and South, and it has seemed determined to make itself as much a folktale as a habitat. But just as it has always insisted on its eternal newness and promise, it has also represented the dead end of the New World, the end of exploration, recalling all the mistakes of every past civilization. One reason that Balboa (Keats mistakenly wrote Cortez) might have stood "silent upon a peak in Darien" is that he realized there was no place else on earth to travel to. Or as a Walt Whitman character said in "Facing West from California's Shores": "Where is what I started for so long ago? And why is it yet unfound?"

Reagan does not ask that question, nor does he stand silent upon a peak in Pacific Palisades and brood about paradise lost. His California dream remains unsullied. America is still the land of perpetual opportunity, and every man gloriously for himself. Economics fits into this vision neatly, since California happened to provide a fine justification for capitalism by producing gold from the earth like a health food. If there were a California Ocean school of painting, it would consist of avocados in the foreground and a range of office buildings behind. Perhaps that is Reagan's interior skyline.

Theoretically such a vision should produce the government that

Reagan has promised, the kind that governs least. If corporate America is part of nature—of the nature of the country, the nature of man—then it must be free to grow to its fullest capacity, like an individual. Tax cuts, reduced federal interference, and other prods to Big Business (including the corporate character of the cabinet appointments) are simply ways of making pioneers of businessmen, of restoring some of the old make-a-buck fire. Yet the character of the Reagan administration will not depend wholly on his political vision, which in any case will be modified by wary liberal Democrats in Congress, by the normal exigencies of the modern presidency, and by his own ability to compromise. Rather the Reagan years are as likely to be shaped by the temperament and intelligence of the head man, and that is precisely why those years are so difficult to envisage.

If one were to take all of Reagan's qualities—the detachment, the self-knowledge, the great voice and good looks—and project them into the White House, he would have a first-class B-movie presidency. That is no insult. The best B movies, while not artistically exquisite, are often the ones that move us most because they move us directly, through straightforward characters, simple moral conflicts, and idealized talk. Reagan once called himself "the Errol Flynn of B movies," which was astute (except that Errol Flynn was also the Errol Flynn of B movies). The president who remains above the fray yet is also capable of stirring the people is the kind of president of whose life B movies are made. After several years of *The Deer Hunter* and *All the President's Men,* perhaps *The Ronald Reagan Story* is just what the country ordered.

The trouble, however, since we are watching our lives and not a movie, is that in reality a detached presidency puts decisions in the hands of everyone else. No harm is done when the issues are trivial, but as the piecemeal nature of the cabinet appointments has demonstrated, relying so totally on advisers is a dangerous game. The prospect grows considerably more troublesome when it comes to making major decisions. And there will be plenty of those as soon as Reagan takes office—all complicated and many urgent.

For starters, he faces an economic situation growing more frightening by the moment. Almost at once he will have to decide what to cut in this year's budget and where to attack the one for fiscal 1982, which is about to be submitted by Carter. These decisions will affect his proposed tax cuts and his plans to increase money for defense. They will also bear on whether or not he will have to cut real social welfare programs, not the "fat" he is accustomed to citing. On top of these, he faces rising unemployment, monstrous interest rates, and U.S. industries (like cars) that are running on square wheels. And there are difficulties that are his, which he may not see. What happens to a black teenager in Harlem or Watts in a free enterprise system that leaves him free to go to hell?

In foreign affairs, everything in sight seems an emergency, from the hostages to the Polish frontier. Whatever happens in Poland, Reagan will not be overeager to negotiate an arms-control pact with the Soviets. What sort of agreement, then, will eventually be sought? Regarding the Third World, Reagan and his people have talked as if Soviet mischief making were the main problem, and also have come out strongly against organized terrorism, suggesting that the United States will send supplies to countries under siege by guerrillas. How does that position affect Latin America today, especially El Salvador, skidding crazily toward a possible civil war? Given Third World realities, it is all very well to support anti-Communist regimes without too much worry about how democratic they are, but what if they are so discredited with their own people that they cannot survive? For cogent reasons, Reagan and his aides seem willing to downplay the human rights issue somewhat, but how will they deal with it in the context of Soviet Jews and other dissidents?

In the Middle East, how will he continue to placate both Israelis and Arabs? How will he reassure the allies of the United State's renewed commitment? These are not the kinds of problems to be handled by subordinates, committees, or forceless task forces. They require determination but also sophistication. They are to be handled by a president who studies, considers, and knows what he wants.

In the broadest terms Reagan does know what he wants out of the next four years. But as those terms address specifics, that broad vision may prove inept. Intellectually, emotionally, Reagan lives in the past. That is where the broad vision comes from; the past is his future. But is it also the country's? Helen Lawton, a current resident of Dixon, Illinois, and a loyal Reaganite, observed of her man: "Right now, in some ways, I think he'd love to go back to the good old days. In those days he didn't even realize he was poor because so many others were poor too. He wants the good life, not in terms of material things, but so that kids can have good times and strong family relationships. Yes, I think he would like to go back to how it used to be, but it's going to be difficult." That puts it mildly.

"All our great presidents were leaders of thought at times when certain historic ideas in the life of the nation had to be clarified." So said Franklin Roosevelt, who was in a good position to know. The limits of freedom, our oldest idea, must be clarified now. Meanwhile the country is patently more hopeful about its future than it has been in a long while, much longer than the past four years; and to be fair to Jimmy Carter he was surely as much a casualty of the malaise he identified as he was its superintendent. When young man Reagan went west for the first time, the future clearly looked like the ranch or like Pacific Palisades, or perhaps both: the genteel and frontier traditions bound together by good manners and pluck. But when he turns eastward this month, the New World will be more complex, more shadowy, and more terrifying for all its magnificent possibility.

January 5, 1981

A Sense
of Where
We Are

I T TOOK A WEEK to get the picture [April 13, 1981]. First came the
gasps and "not agains"; then the nation assumed its old too-
familiar position before the tube, reluctant pros in this business by
now, ready to take in the slow-motion replays, the testimony of
experts, the edgy reporters, a bloody head, one shot-up limousine,
another, the edgy, blank-faced gunman. There was a jumble to sort
out. The president was OK. But then he wasn't. They took him to the
White House. No, to a hospital. Was it serious? Not very. Yes, very.
Maybe . . . And so on through the long Monday afternoon, the
emotions buffeted by every bulletin—sinking at the report of White
House press secretary James Brady's death; rising warily when the
report is denied; a freeze at news that the president is undergoing
surgery; a thaw when someone repeats a Reagan joke. Who was that
fool who asked if the operation was going to be filmed? More questions still—the public's tensions not at all alleviated by the figure of
Alexander Haig claiming "I am in control here," in a voice full of
jelly.

The press was hard on Haig after the recent who's-in-charge tem-
pest. Suddenly the secretary of state is playing air raid warden again
and rearranging the succession to the presidency to suit his pride. Yet

he was only trying to do what everyone wanted: to establish order and clear things up. By 7:00 P.M. there was at least the start of a clearing up. To stage center stepped Dr. Dennis O'Leary of George Washington University Hospital, a gentle, cool customer, another instant media star. Secret agent Timothy J. McCarthy was hit in the stomach, but doing well. District of Columbia policeman Thomas K. Delahanty was hit in the shoulder and neck; his condition was stable. A twenty-two-caliber bullet passed through Jim Brady's brain. And the president? He became his chest for the moment: the bullet entered here, bounced off this, settled in that. There was "oxygenation" and a "thoracotomy" and some "peritoneal lavage" to boot. But was he OK? Yes, he was fine, chipper. By nightfall the country was beginning to do some oxygenating of its own.

Within a day or two pieces were beginning to fit, even the weirdest. To the bare fact of the suspect's name, John W. Hinckley, Jr., were added the details of strangely American life, or half life. The son of oil-rich respectability quits school, takes to the road, joins the American Nazi Party, but can't make it there. He has a guitar, of course; drives a tan Plymouth with Texas plates; watches TV in cheap motels where he stops briefly. He is a traveling man. Soft-spoken and polite. He dines on Whoppers and writes love notes to a teenage movie star at Yale—while going madder by the minute, buying guns and hitting the dream cities of Denver, Nashville, Dallas, and L.A., until he arrives by Greyhound at the city of the country's heart, which he is driven to penetrate. So after a while even he becomes real. At week's end one understands not everything, but a lot more than seemed possible on frantic Monday. The people were in control here.

The interesting thing is that people can actually do this; can take a terrifying, chaotic act and eventually make some sense of it. What occurred outside the Washington Hilton was irrational and destructive. Yet the reactions it generated were both sane and helpful; and they were connected to one's best feelings about the country and the government. When the president was shot, Americans prayed very hard, not for the life of an abstraction, but for a man, one who as leader of the democracy carries something of everyone in that mortal chest. If people were ashamed and dismayed that such horrors could continue to happen in a civilized place, they were also proud and relieved that the government of that civilized place could not be rattled.

Even more basic feelings were brought out by Monday's events. Trust, for one thing: the belief that in spite of all the initial misinformation, the facts would eventually be known. Patience, for another; and a general absence of panic. Faith in science, as the doctors were relied on to tell the country what its future looked like. Faith in God, for those who have it. Faith too in the press, remarkably; the same press that is excoriated as a matter of daily habit, still counted on in a real emergency to get the truth as best it can, as fast as it can—and to tell it. A sense of national unity, in sadness and anxiety. A sense of outrage at violence. If the United States really were as fundamentally violent as it is made out, there would never be such uniform despair and disgust when violence occurred.

Then too there was kinship with the suffering, with Jim Brady, especially; old Brady "the Bear," Brady the joker, the poker-faced inventor of Goat Gap Texas Chili and Captain Brady's Nightie Night, who wasn't kidding when he described his new position as "the toughest p.r. job in the world." And kinship with life, with Sarah Brady holding her husband's hand, waiting for the squeeze to be returned.

Such feelings make it possible to survive a week like the last one. They attest to the normalities of our lives, and suggest that in the long run there is a gentleness and decency that prevails over the berserk flashes and the threats of sudden death. Yet these shootings leave scars, and they ought to. Why are all these handguns still around? Why can't creatures like Hinckley be reached before they reach others? When the president entered the hospital, he told his friend Nevada senator Paul Laxalt: "Don't worry about me. I'll make it." By the weekend the country was thinking the same thing, with the same uncertain bravery.

April 13, 1981

Ahhhhhh Wilderness!

TRUE TO HIS WORD, Ronald Reagan has taken the government out of Washington and restored it to the states. At least he has done so for the month of August [1981] by restoring himself to California, where, except for signing his tax and budget bills last Thursday and preparing for major meetings on defense and the budget next week, he will behave like most governments and do essentially nothing. Moreover, he will do it for twenty-eight days, as he rides Jeep and horse about his 688 craggy acres in the Santa Ynez Mountains, his Rancho del Cielo, 2,200 feet into the cielo, splitting firewood, clearing brush, ogling stars. A pleasant image for the public to dwell on, but it also raises some questions and a bit of a stir: Is so long a holiday fitting and proper for a president, the leader of the free world? Can Washington survive without being the center of government for so long a stretch? Is there life without news?

It helps that the nation is asking these questions at a time of year when it is otherwise busy squinting up at tennis lobs, lolling in cocoa butter, and perfecting curvature of the spine cocooned in hammocks. August is more a hiatus than a month, and the level of public anxiety ordinarily settles on such problems as whether the inner side of one's forearm is as tan as the outer. Still, some of the issues suggested by

Reagan's holiday are real, especially as they involve policy matters. This has hardly been a languid summer season so far, what with the air-traffic controllers' strike and the resurrection of the neutron bomb. The problems attending these matters have no Rancho del Cielo to escape to; and one must wonder if the nation can really be steered from the saddle.

Not that the citizenry begrudges its head of state a bit of a rest. James Thurber said that "it is better to have loafed and lost than never to have loafed at all," but Reagan seems to have lost nothing in public esteem by taking time off. In fact such behavior is tacitly expected of him. Not only is a long vacation consistent with his political philosophy of governing best by governing least; it is also part of the modus operandi he established as California's governor: in by nine, out by five. If Reagan has mastered one art in life, it is that of relaxing. He is relaxed talking to television cameras. He is relaxed striding in boots toward helicopters. He is relaxed entering a hospital lobby with a bullet in his chest. Taking a holiday comes as naturally to him as falling on a horse, because he is not merely a member of the leisure class, he is its most prominent spokesman, an embodiment in the public mind of the new American work ethic: work some, play some.

Of course, had the fate of his tax and budget bills been worse, or had popular sympathy been on the traffic controllers' side and not on Reagan's, he clearly would not have felt quite so free to head for the hills of Rancho del Cielo. He might have done so in any case, but the political damage would have been noticeable. Since life has gone pretty much as he has asked it to of late, the only thing Reagan has suffered by taking his long holiday is the dim opinion of some professional observers. Louis Masotti, a professor of political science at Northwestern University, complains: "We don't have a foreign policy, and the real issues of transportation, urban policy, and open lands have not been addressed. I don't know how a president in this day and age can take a month off." Chicago's Studs Terkel describes Reagan's vacation as an insult to "working men and women." Indirectly he makes a point; this is the sort of thing that can turn on the president if his economic policies fail dramatically.

By taking so long a rest, Reagan distinguishes himself among world leaders. Prime Minister Margaret Thatcher rarely gets away from it all for as long as ten days in Cornwall, where she relaxes among the rocks. President Ferdinand Marcos of the Philippines has not taken a real vacation in the past sixteen years, perhaps because he has always claimed that no one can yet take his place, and does not wish to put the idea to a test. Even France's new president, François Mitterrand, is merely allowing himself a brief "breath of fresh air," thus violating the ancient French custom of abandoning Paris to the tourists for much of the summer. The Soviet Union's Leonid Brezhnev may take a lengthy holiday this year (last year he took just two weeks), at his dacha in the Crimea. But Brezhnev knows better than most the penalties for lollygagging at the wrong time. It was he who replaced Nikita Khrushchev in 1964 when Khrushchev himself was on vacation.

The president's sojourn may look a bit extravagant compared with those of fellow heads of state, but in terms of American history he is, as ever, a traditionalist. President Eisenhower took a twenty-six-day holiday at the Newport, Rhode Island, naval base in September 1957. Democrats used to chivy Republicans about Eisenhower's frequent golfing vacations as well, until they were reminded (by Republicans) that their own Harry Truman was no slouch in this realm, spending much time deep-sea fishing off Key West. Calvin Coolidge, too, used to vacation as often as possible (how could they tell?). The modern record is held by Richard Nixon, who enjoyed a thirty-one-day holiday at San Clemente in 1969, although it is possible that eighteen and a half minutes were unaccounted for.

Naturally, all these presidents were at work on national business at the same time that they were dozing in the chaise. Everyone who comments on Reagan's lengthy retreat cautions that even when a president is relaxing, he is working like crazy. This is hardly startling news, since everybody gets some work done on extended holidays, along with a neurotic amount of fretting and phoning. In fact, compared with most American executives, Reagan enacts very little business while he is away. But he does have his routines: every morning National Security Adviser Richard Allen prepares a twenty-page national security briefing in Washington, where it is scrambled, telecopied, and then unscrambled at the communications trailer behind the Reagan ranch house. Shortly before 8:00 A.M. the briefing paper is ready for the president. Aide Mike Deaver, who has scanned it, phones the ranch from the Santa Barbara Biltmore. Almost all information that reaches the president goes through Deaver, who screens out everything but the essentials. They speak for fifteen to twenty minutes in the morning and again at lunchtime. Reagan approves a few appointments, mostly routine and obscure, and makes a few phone calls (last week to Transportation Secretary Drew Lewis on the air-controllers' strike, and to Philadelphia first baseman Pete Rose on his breaking Stan Musial's National League record for total hits). That is about the extent of Reagan's workday.

Robert Benchley once made a list of things to do to kill time. It included:

1. Rowing a rowboat without using the oarlocks.
2. Tooting an automobile horn in a stalled car.
3. Upsetting bookcases and then putting the books back in again, with each book opened at page 27.
4. Running just as fast as you can to the end of the room and back.

Reagan's vacation consists of none of these things. Instead of killing time, Reagan seems to fill it with the life he most enjoys. In the mornings he and Nancy ride horseback for a few hours, and in the afternoons he clears and cuts. Even with a retinue of aides and Secret Service men in constant attendance, he retains most of his privacy. Reagan's ranch is very much his world of values. It gives him solitude, independence, and a sense of making his own way—he stacks all that wood for a house heated solely by wood.

Last Tuesday he altered his schedule by cleaning out his pond, "Lake Lucky." Wearing a pair of white trunks, he jumped into the lake (a sight to gladden a former air controller's heart), and spent three and a half hours wading in mud, pulling weeds. That is the president's idea of a good time—that or his other recent projects of framing a tack room for the horses and mending a fence. Still, Reagan's concept of a vacation also includes quieter things like noticing deer, listening to frogs, and staring at the brilliant, spangled nights. Why anyone would choose such activities over munching canapés in the Hamptons is a mystery to many journalists, but then they have long found Reagan somewhat unreal.

Does the important business of government get done during this idyll? So far, apparently. Reagan seemed generally on top of things at last Thursday's bill-signing press conference, which, largely because of an eerie mist that swirled about the ranch, was suffused with an air of cozy cordiality. Nancy Reagan, in jeans and cowboy hat, was uncommonly at ease with reporters. The president touched on all the major national and world worries about the air controllers' strike, the neutron bomb, Poland, the F-16s for Israel. This week secretaries Caspar Weinberger of Defense and Alexander Haig of State will fly out for discussions on the future of the MX missile and the B-1 bomber. On Tuesday Reagan will meet with Office of Management and Budget director David Stockman to discuss future cuts in federal spending. At the Biltmore, the executive offices of the president appear to be open for business, in spite of their luxurious location in three white adobe cottages beside a putting green. Two Marine guards in full dress uniform, including white gloves, indicate that Cottage Eight is the heart of the operation. Deaver explains that originally the Marines were posted for security, but now "they remind everyone that we're not on vacation."

Actually, there is no good reason for the executive branch of government to be any more self-conscious about taking time off than either of the other two branches. The Supreme Court manages to flee Washington for the entire summer every year without a writ of apology, and Congress, as usual, has scattered until September. All this exiting has had a refreshing effect on life in the capital city, if not on its weather. Traffic flows; restaurants offer a table. The first drafts for all proposed budgets for fiscal year 1983 are due at the Office of Management and Budget by September 1, and that will keep several people at their desks in town. At the White House, presidential counselor Edwin Meese minds the mostly empty store. Reagan's other top aide, Chief of Staff James Baker, has gone fishing in Texas.

The question of whether Washington can survive with its main engine in neutral is far less urgent than whether reporters can survive a month without presidential news. One can only do so much with the story of the local rat carrying the bubonic plague, unless, of course, the plague recurs. About seventy members of the press corps are encamped in Santa Barbara, all living fairly well, that being the way to live in Santa Barbara, but some going quietly mad nonetheless, as the president cuts and clears. Whenever Deputy Press Secretary Larry Speakes announces that the president is cutting and clearing today, reporters jot down "no news." Still, reporters and photographers are a brave lot and are taking in stride events like wine-tasting excursions to nearby vineyards, when they are not peering down at Rancho del Cielo with binoculars, praying for a sign. None is forthcoming. This is August. The president is on vacation.

August 24, 1981

Gone to Soldiers Everyone

R EMOTE CONTROL. Ingenious contradiction of terms. Fits like a handshake. Aims like a gun.

There: Marlin Fitzwater, the White House press secretary, appears on the screen to announce that the "liberation of Kuwait" has begun under "Operation Desert Storm."

There: President Bush declares, "This is an historic moment." Adds: "No president can easily commit our sons and daughters to war."

There: Defense Secretary Dick Cheney and Chairman of the Joint Chiefs of Staff Colin Powell come on from the Pentagon. They use words such as "resolve," "determined," "capability," and "objective."

There: An Air Force pilot, his hair matted down by sweat, has returned from the first mission over Baghdad. He compares the rocket fire to the Fourth of July, says the city "was lit up like a huge Christmas tree."

There: CNN correspondents report on the damage from their Baghdad hotel rooms. There: The network anchormen dig in for the duration. There: The first wave of retired admirals and generals begin to analyze the action. There: The political experts. There: The pro-war rallies. There: The antiwar marches. There: The maps, the gray suits, the names of the weapons, the briefings, the world leaders, the first pictures out of Baghdad. Like Van Gogh's *The Starry Night,* the black-blue sky explodes in a silent snow.

Americans flitted from channel to channel to get hold of the story. An odd use for remote control. Usually the device operates like a missile itself, zaps the show in progress to move on to the next and obliterates the continuous narrative. Now it roved from station to station in an effort to piece together the continuous narrative.

But there: Only a few fragmented facts strung far apart like outposts on a desert, and in between each bit of news, the vast tense emptiness of a police patrol. Talk, rerun of tapes, more talk.

Until there: By Friday night the stations had resumed their regular programming, and the first SCUD missile strike on a residential neighborhood in Tel Aviv gave way to Super Bowl chatter and a rescheduled showing of the Cosby kids.

It wasn't simply the story that Americans wanted to get hold of, with their remote controls firing at will. There were feelings to get hold of and to set in order. Feelings about the war were already knotted and jumbled before the war began. If a country can suffer a collective stomachache, ours did during the days of January 13 and 14, as the deadline for Saddam Hussein to pull out of Kuwait or else approached and with it the sinking feeling that the nation was about to step logically, purposefully into chaos.

Parents with children who were over there, wives with husbands, husbands with wives, friends with friends, draft age kids and their worry-eyed families and their friends and everyone in the whole country, as far as dread could reach, arrived simultaneously at January 15 bearing an enormous burden of apprehension. It stretched from a sense of immediate danger down into a history of wars and from one people in the present to all the people who ever were. "The past is never dead," said Faulkner. "It's not even past." Suddenly (only it wasn't sudden) war, the inevitable locomotive, was steaming at the station again.

What was this mess about again? Land? Oil? Honor?

By the first "there" and the first attacks on Baghdad, America was suffused with anxiety bordering on grief. Then came an assault of emotions that were impossible to pin down and identify, they changed so quickly:

All right, we're in the thing now. Let's give 'em hell. Show no mercy. What's that? The first American down? Dead? Now let's really get 'em. Israel? They fired on Israel? Residential area? Chemical weapons? Yes? No? Iraqis are said to surrender in droves. Can't be true. Isn't true. We're sticking it to Saddam now. Tons of damage. Crippled his air force. No, we didn't. Smashed his missiles. No, we didn't. The war is a lock. It'll be over in a matter of days. No, it won't.

Within seconds of the war's beginning, almost everyone started thinking like a soldier. How did *that* happen? How did it happen that while the nation dreaded war, it also longed for it. America hated war, and when it finally got it, it wanted victory in a minute, and if that wasn't possible, it wanted to reconsider.

How did it happen that fear flowed into zeal flowed into horror flowed into anger flowed into an emotionless scientific interest in high-tech success?

There: Did you see that? A missile hit the air shaft on the nose. Can you beat that?

The remoteness of control over one's feelings was imitated by the war's technological feats. It was evident from the first moments of attack: In its initial stages, at least, this was to be a remote control war. In certain ways Americans were prepared to absorb what the new war machinery could do, but only indirectly. The movie *Top Gun* displayed the sense of speed; the video games, the sense of high-reflex accuracy. The rise of information technology in the 1980s, the development of lasers, sensors, and microchips, it was all familiar stuff.

Still, this high-tech weaponry was something else again. For the generations removed from the electronic mind, as well as for the generation who live by it, it was easy to be swept up in a rush of thoughtless amazement.

For the Pentagon and the weapons industries, the war in the Gulf offered apparent vindication. They worked: The sophisticated Patriot antimissile system; the Tomahawk cruise missiles with their preprogrammed targets. The F-4G Wild Weasel aircraft, equipped with radar-sensing and -jamming gear, also worked. As did the new LANTIRN system that permits pilots to track targets at night. Officials told of a "smart bomb" dropped from an F-117A Stealth fighter that found its way directly to the front door of a missile warehouse.

What were we learning here? That the Pentagon actually could do things right? Whatever happened to the Navy's $436 hammer and the Air Force's $7,622 coffeepot? All at once the military seemed to look as if it knew what it was doing all along. What do you make of that?

Not only did the gizmos work; they were also revolutionizing warfare. In past wars an overwhelming percentage of everything fired missed its targets. Now that same amount would strike its targets. Would this turn out to be the neatest little war ever? Machine downing machine on an electronic battlefield?

No. Nobody was buying that. There was too much experience with the realities of war, too many layers of buried knowledge. If the commander of the U.S. forces in the Gulf, Gen. Norman Schwarzkopf himself, was not going to be swept up in high-tech "euphoria" (the first cant word of the war), neither should anyone else.

There: An interviewer remarking on the astonishing accuracy of the air shaft hit asked, "Is there any sort of danger that you don't have any sense of the horrors of war here, that it is all just a game?" Schwarzkopf answered: "You didn't see *me* treating it like a game, and you didn't see me laughing and joking about it going on. There's human lives being lost when that happens."

It was hard not to be caught, clotheslined, between an appreciation of war technology and the logical consequences of using it. We seem to have had trouble with logical consequences from the start of this business. During the troop buildup in the Gulf, reservists reacted with preposterous disbelief: Gee, I knew I was in the Army, but I never thought I'd be going to war! Behind that was the logical consequence of creating armies in the first place. In Anthony Burgess's novel *The Wanting Seed,* a soldier clarifies logical consequences to the hero, Tristram:

> ". . . it stands to reason you've got to have a war. Not because anybody wants it, of course, but because there's an army. . . . Armies is for wars and wars is for armies. That's only plain common sense."
>
> "War's finished," said Tristram. "War's outlawed. There hasn't been any war for years and years and years."
>
> "All the more reason why there's got to be a war," said the [soldier], "if we've been such a long time without one."

Is that it? In some subterranean self-destructive wish was the world waiting for the Cold War to end so that it could engage in a good old-fashioned hot one?

One wasn't supposed to think that way. One was to think about the principles instead. But the principles could seem confusing too.

There: Representative Barbara Vucanovich of Nevada is saying that Saddam must be stopped right now or there will be disastrous geopolitical consequences for the region and the United States.

There: Representative Charles Rangel of New York is asking why we didn't get so all fired up about Tiananmen Square or about the Lithuanian citizens being mowed down by our new best friends, the Soviets.

The news itself could be confusing. First our military claimed to have gained general air superiority over the Iraqis. Then it said that we only achieved local superiority whenever we needed it. First we announced that Iraq's SCUD missile launching capability was almost entirely demolished. Then came the admission that those missiles were "nowhere near" being eliminated.

The language could be confusing, as it is always meant to be in a war. Writing of the First World War, Paul Fussell created a sort of dictionary in which a column of war language was set alongside a column of real language. A horse was a "steed." To die was to "perish." Legs and arms were "limbs." And so forth. Americans grew alert to linguistic manipulations during Vietnam, where an invasion became an "incursion," and war itself was described as "pacification." The language of this war was already being made swashbuckling by the use of "sortie" for an air attack.

The word "casualty" continued to disguise the maimed and dead.

Yet no one was really tricked by these obfuscations. It was not the military alone pulling the wool over our eyes. We did it ourselves. Like the romantic names of weapons, false language is a game we allow to be played to keep us remote from sorrow and revulsion.

There: Three of our downed airmen appear with faces swollen and cut up. Two denounce America in the voices of automatons.

There: The experts explicate their performances, concluding that the pilots were speaking "under duress."

"Duress?" Don't you mean torture? Don't you mean they were beaten black and blue until they knuckled under?

Most confusing were the buried thoughts about ourselves. Whatever else war is, it serves too often as an instrument of regeneration, of renewed vitality. Remember how the country felt last July? The S&L debacle and the budget outrage and the rereading of George Bush's lips on the subject of taxes? How such bad news dampened the naturally ebullient American spirit. How it threatened to make us come to grips with the prospect of a limited future—the one idea, in the land of infinite possibility, we deem impossible.

Enter then the undeniably evil Saddam Hussein, lying through his teeth, storming into poor little rich Kuwait. A devil ex machina. A respite and release from our spiritual fears and economic woes. Could it be that, in part, we got into the war to relieve ourselves from domestic frustration, lack of self-confidence, even self-hate?

Did we get into it willingly at all? Or were we pushed and pulled into the war by a president looking for an external enemy? And who exactly *was* George Bush nowadays? A newly made-over George Bush taking an unswerving stand for once without waiting for a reading of the political wind? Or was this the old George Bush who read the political wind very well and saw that in our buried dreams we wanted a way out of our troubles?

In August, remember, we seemed to be all for the aggressive approach. The buildup and rebuildup of troops in the Gulf. The hurling of the gauntlet of the January 15 deadline. Followed by the deliberate, dignified debate in Congress. Followed by a close yet inevitable vote of support. Everything had to lead to the point where there was no choice but war if Saddam refused to back down. So why when war arrived on TV did our control over events seem more remote than ever? Or was that wishful thinking too? In *Dispatches,* Michael Herr's memoir of Vietnam, the journalist wrote, "You were as responsible for everything you saw as you were for everything you did."

Who were we, anyway, watching this war unfold? Americans have never thought of themselves as a militaristic people. We have not honored our military caste with social position. We rarely elevate military heroes to power. Even Eisenhower, one of the great exceptions, spoke in favor of the rule when he warned the country against the encroachments of a "military-industrial complex."

America's glory is "built upon our freedom," said Woodrow Wilson. It "is moral, not material." Yet D. H. Lawrence said, "The essential American soul is hard, isolate, stoic, and a killer." Was that so? Were we a nation of marauders dressed as pioneers, out to "civilize" the "savages" by knocking them off?

Maybe not. Probably not. Such thoughts seemed more like the ghosts of nightmares than the nightmares themselves. There were, after all, compelling, substantial reasons for being at war this time. American myth, however disturbing in spots, did not create Saddam Hussein. Once in a blue moon, thankfully, history puts a genuine savage in power, and he has to be knocked off. Israel had said that all along. Saddam was bombing Israel's civilians. There could be no question that he would use chemical weapons in this war; he had done it before. There could be no question that he would use nuclear weapons as soon as he had them.

Now, what's *this* bit of news? Acting under orders from Saddam,

Iraqis intentionally release millions of gallons of crude oil from a Kuwaiti offshore terminal, endangering the region's water supply and despoiling the Gulf. An act of "environmental terrorism," a Pentagon spokesman calls it. Pictures of seabirds struggling in their slow black death and predictions of a permanently ruined environment.

Facts conduct feelings too. With all our habitual qualms about entering world conflicts, with the particular hesitancy brought on by Vietnam, we would not be even mildly enthusiastic about the war in the Gulf were there not the bedrock certainty that Saddam must go, however the Middle East might shake out afterward.

One of the difficulties of getting a solid hold of our feelings about the war in the beginning (if indeed we would ever get hold of them) was that everything was seen at a great distance. The war might be the first real televised war, but in the early stages it was still an abstraction of flares and booms. What would happen to public reaction when the war was shot in close-ups, in hospitals or on battle-fields, where everyone could see that limbs were in fact arms and legs and that they were blown off by all that breathtaking, accurate rocket power? When a human scream was "there" or a disconnected head, and all the specific body parts—eyes, tongues, teeth, fingers—were suddenly not there, what then would people think of the show?

The war was an amalgam of everything known and nothing known. Remote control. An illusion of control. Whatever happened in Dhahran or Tel Aviv was bulletined immediately, but the event was either censored or clouded with rumor. Gas. No gas. How many dead? How many injured? Reporters grew frustrated, enraged that they were being misled or kept in the dark. The instantaneous picture television provided was itself strangely misleading, almost surreal. One saw what was said to be happening but was unsure if it did happen. One saw not the present but a report on the present.

The idea of time became surreal. The war was theoretically telecast "live," but the real war was fought without cameras on it, or it existed on tape somewhere, being edited or suppressed. Now we saw it, now we didn't.

The surreal was epitomized in the New York Giants–San Francisco 49ers National Football Conference championship game played on Sunday, January 20. There was good old American football, with its warrior clothing and war terminology—helmets, bombs, and blitzes. And there was Dan Rather popping up on the screen to tell of a SCUD missile attack on Saudi Arabia. "We'll be back at halftime," said Dan. We were returned to the game, where people in the stands waved American flags the size of handkerchiefs and someone raised a sign reading, God Bless U GIs. Then back to Dan with an update on the missile attack. Then back to the game, with the Giants gaining ground and the 49ers retreating. Oh, the "tension," as the Giants' Matt Bahr kicked the winning field goal with time running out. "What a game!" said Dan, before he totaled up the SCUDS.

What was getting us down in this bombardment of events? By the end of the first two or three days of fighting, Americans supported the president and the war by a ratio of 4–1. Yet there was little rancor directed at those who were speaking out against the war. Perhaps the country had learned to accept protest as part of the conditions of wartime, from the days of Vietnam. Or perhaps everyone had a little protest in him along with strong feelings of support (another ratio of 4–1), because no matter how justified a war may be, it is still something that ought to be protested.

For those at home, as well as for those in battle, war is curiously disabling. The mere realization that one's country is at war poisons the bloodstream, creates an incessant mood of worry that infiltrates even the most casual moments. It sticks like a bad memory or a guilt, suffered because of something done not by oneself but by one's kind, one's species. Helplessness mixes with courage, surrender with victory.

One can be "for" an individual war but not for the entire enterprise that is, by nature, antihuman, that makes so bleak a comment on human rationality, human progress. Only a year ago, Americans were celebrating the death of communism and the prospect of peace. Well, ask the Baltic republics today about the death of communism. As for peace, it was swell while it lasted.

The contradiction of emotions the country was feeling as the war got under way was a desperate desire for victory in a desperately hated game. The bombs bursting in air might look impressive, but on the ground two questions dogged the troubled mind: What's worth a life? What's a life worth?

There: A soldier in the desert cuts up for the camera, his face red with shyness and exuberance. Behind him his buddies grunt and bellow with approval. They all look beautiful.

March 1991

Call Us Ishmael

H<small>ERE'S LITERARY RELEVANCE FOR YOU:</small>
In the first chapter of *Moby-Dick,* called "Loomings," Ishmael considers why he chose to go on that momentous whaling voyage and concludes, half-kidding, that his decision must have been part of the "grand programme of Providence that was drawn up a long time ago." He calls his adventure "a sort of brief interlude and solo between more extensive performances" and sees the providential bill as having looked like this:

Grand Contested Election for the Presidency of the United States

Whaling Voyage by One Ishmael

Bloody Battle in Afghanistan

The first headline is set in large, elegant type; the third, in bold, block type. The lettering of the middle event is small and plain, as if it were being whispered on the page.

And here we are, you and I—not about to undertake a whaling voyage, most likely, since whaling voyages are scarce and environmentally unpopular these days, but nevertheless about to undertake some small, private voyage of our own choosing, while around us, above and below, the more extensive performances of the world loom on: a grand contested election heating up [the 1980 presidential election], and some very bloody battles in Afghanistan [the Soviet attacks].

Melville chose Afghanistan because it has always seemed the most faraway place on earth, perhaps at times to the Afghans themselves. In 1851, when *Moby-Dick* was published, presidential elections must have seemed equally remote to the average citizen; thus by arranging his items on the bill, Melville was also posing a question: What could the story of one solitary citizen possibly have to do with the big and violent doings of the world? When you ask a question like that, the answer, naturally, is: everything. But you have to prove it. The connections among Ishmaels, Afghans, and presidents are rarely seen until too late, least of all by the Ishmaels who go about their solo businesses deliberately to avoid the big and violent doings.

Ishmael minimized the significance of his adventure, yet that turned out to offer as grand a contrast, as bloody a battle, as any. In fact, it turned out to be the essential journey—the pursuit of the nemesis. It was not Ishmael's nemesis being pursued, but he was on the ship, as tied to the pursuit as if he had dreamed it up himself. If Ishmael learns anything from his mad ride with Captain Ahab, it is that no performance is solo, that the one thing you may be sure of is that every human decision, no matter how slight or peculiar, is within reach of every other such decision—as near as Afghanistan.

Call us Ishmael. Before us these days are two separate pursuits of a nemesis, one in the grand contested election, the other in Afghanistan. The lesser pursuit is Teddy Kennedy's, lesser because he is unlikely to win, and so the pursuit, while sincere, has a built-in governor. You watch the senator on television and your sympathy goes out to him. Mine does. He laughs too loud at his own jokes. The jokes are feeble, the slogans faint. He shows no compulsion to gain what he seeks, except, of course, the family compulsion that shouts, "Go to it, Teddy," which Teddy does, but without heart, without the heart of an Ahab, certainly. When he loses, then down in the public mind will go the taunting connection of the Kennedys with the presidency, and for them that will be all to the good.

But the Russians are something else, as they are always something else. You may say it's inaccurate to call Afghanistan Russia's nemesis, since the historical antagonism has always been Russia's. Yet oppressors make antagonists out of those who sit still. Now, at long last, Russia ends its frustration, giving the lie to the adorable Mishka bear, pulling on its "Potemkin" boots and pawing geniuses in the streets of Moscow. It claims that its target is limited, but so did Ahab. Older and wiser, the world knows a great white whale when it sees one, especially when the whale is the world.

So the world prepares itself, stiffens. It knows in a purely moral sense that the end of the pursuit of the nemesis always spells disaster for the pursuer, but in this case that is no consolation. Legislators call for war; panic accompanies determination; and gold goes up and down, creating an image of mammonism not seen since Mammon. So much for the extensive performances.

In the middle of all this, meanwhile, are you and I, with our solos and interludes. I have no gold to sell. My daily voyages take me to the post office, the general store, and other places whose adamant serenity tries to persuade us that we are in control of Providence. Yet there was Ishmael, calmly explaining his decision to go to sea, fully aware that life could be tied to people with dark passions striding purposefully into hell.

January 28, 1980

Children
of War

The three following pieces are part of a story in Time *(January 11, 1982) called "Children of War," which I later expanded into a book. The story was divided into five sections, each covering a war zone, the three reproduced here being Northern Ireland, Lebanon, and Cambodia.*

Belfast

Our fathers and ourselves sowed dragon's teeth.
Our children know and suffer the armed men.
—Stephen Vincent Benét

I F YOU WANT the full account of Frank Rowe's murder, it will not be provided by Paul. Paul is thirteen now, was seven at the time, yet he can still only get so far into the story—to the point where "Daddy, he ran to the back, to the next house"—before he starts crying. He has a woman's face, still dimpled, along with the absolutely blue eyes of most Belfast children, and brown hair parted carelessly down the middle: the sort of face the old masters sought. His school tie hangs cockeyed; it was knotted in a hurry.

"What do you feel about your father's death now?"

His friend Joseph answers for him. Joseph, also thirteen, has a small, tight head, a high, clear voice, and his ambition is to grow up and join the Provos. "Revenge. That's what you want. Isn't it, Paul?" Paul says nothing.

"*I'd* want revenge," says Joseph, looking again to Paul.

Paul eventually nods; then says faintly: "Aye. Revenge."

As if to make his case forever, Joseph thrusts his face toward the American stranger. "You. You'd take revenge too, wouldn't you, Mister?"

The two boys sit in low plastic chairs beside each other in a classroom of the Stella Maris Secondary School, a brick-and-stucco series of afterthoughts that could pass for a warehouse. Stella Maris is in an unusual position because it is a Roman Catholic school located in a Protestant area, and it holds a special place in modern Belfast history because Bobby Sands is an alumnus. Yet the Stella Maris students make no big thing of their connection to the hunger striker. A couple of boys were once caught playing a game called Bobby Sands, but that's about the extent of it. Ask Stephen and Malachy, both fifteen, what they think of Sands's decision, and they answer simultaneously, "Brave," "Foolish."

Joseph would undoubtedly say "Brave," and he would probably urge the same answer on Paul. But alone, away from Joseph, Paul is more himself.

"That business about revenge. Is that really what you want?"

The boy looks helpless. "No. It doesn't matter who done it. Nothin's worth killing someone."

According to most accounts, Paul is a very odd, timid exception in a city that has become famous for its violent children. In fact, the reverse is true. There are plenty of violent children in Belfast, to be sure: kids who kill time stealing cars for joyrides or lobbing petrol bombs at the army. But they are a small knot of a minority. Most Belfast children are like Paul. They have not all suffered so directly from the Troubles, but their response to the Troubles is similar. They carry no hatred in their hearts, they show a will to survive, and they are exceptionally gentle with grown-ups and with one another. This seems especially remarkable when one considers the dark, moaning city of their home—the once clanging port that made great ships and sailed them down the Belfast Lough for the world to see. It is now shut tight like a corpse's mouth, its brown terrace houses strung out like teeth full of cavities, gaps, and wires.

The wires hold. Belfast is rich in wire, coiled and barbed, and in corrugated iron. (You could make your fortune in corrugated iron here.) Great sheets of it are slabbed up in front of government buildings and on the "peace line" that separates the Catholic Falls Road from the Protestant Shankill. In the centers of the streets are "dragon's teeth"—huge squares of stone arranged in uneven rows to prevent fast getaways. Downtown in the "control zone," no car may be parked unattended. Solitary figures sit like dolls behind the wheels to prove there is no bomb. Armored personnel carriers, called "pigs" by the children, poke their snouts around corners and lurch out to create sudden roadblocks. The Andersonstown police station, like a fly draped in a web, is barely visible behind what looks like a baseball backstop. The fence is slanted inward at the top, to fend off any rockets.

"O' course, there's *one* place where the Prods and Taigs [Catholics] are at peace." The cabbie grins and points to the Protestant and Catholic cemeteries that abut each other. "Yet space is tight even there. The Catholics is spillin' over on the bogland. If you bury people in that, the coffins will pop out of the ground."

To the children of the city the message is clear: Keep behind your lines; stay with your own people. In effect, the war has caged them. They have limited freedom of movement, little freedom of speech, and, in some cases, no freedom of childhood itself.

Bernadette Livingstone, for example, cannot leave the house much these days because her mother has commanded most of her attention since Julie's death. Julie was fourteen, a year younger than Bernadette when she was killed last May by a plastic bullet fired from a British army Saracen. It happened during a protest demonstration involving mostly women.

"One of the hunger strikers had just died—you know? Francis Hughes, I think it was. Yeah, it was. And Julie and her friend had just come out of a shop. And there was the bangin' of the lids [garbage can lids—a signal of mourning and anger]. Suddenly people started running. And the army Saracens came down the road—you know? Six-wheeler Saracens? And Julie dove. But when her friend tried to pick her up, she couldn't move. She was still conscious on the way to the hospital. But she wasn't all there, like, when we left her. Mommy kept ringing the doctors all night to see how she was. The thing they were afraid of was the blood leakin' into her brain."

Bernadette is a fifth-former in the Cross and Passion Secondary School—all girls—in Andersonstown, a hard-line Catholic area. The school is located next to a brewery, and the sidewalk out front bears burn marks where a car was set afire in a riot. Inside, all is composed and pleasant. Nuns shush the light chatter. The girls swish by in their green-and-yellow uniforms; their heels click on the linoleum. On the wall of the room where Bernadette sits is a Pope John Paul II calendar and a poster with the words GOD IS NEARER TO US THAN WE ARE TO OURSELVES. Bernadette holds her hands clasped below her green-and-yellow tie, except when she brushes a wisp of blond hair away from her eyes. The eyes are at once soft and stubborn.

"My mother will never get over it. She had Julie late in life—you know? My father doesn't express his feelings. I think that's worse. He used to do a bit of singin', but he doesn't sing so much any more—you know?"

You don't know, of course, but this is the way most Belfast kids tell stories. Each statement of fact is turned up at the end like a question. It isn't as if they are asking you anything that requires an answer. The statement carries the assumption that you probably already know what they have been telling you. That she and Julie didn't get along—you know? That Julie was the nervous one. That Julie was the youngest—you know? "Now I'm the youngest."

Like Paul, Bernadette seeks no revenge against the other side, not even the army men who ride the Saracens. She points out that they are not much older than herself. She does have Protestant friends, but it's difficult because of the neighborhood she lives in. The Livingstones are residents of Lenadoon, where Julie's death is memorialized by a white cross on a small green. The neighborhood is loud with graffiti: DON'T LET THEM DIE; TOUTS WILL BE SHOT; and in bold white letters across the jerry-built walls, WELCOME TO PROVOLAND. In a sense the Livingstones are a Provo family, since Bernadette's two older brothers, Patrick, thirty, and Martin, twenty-four, are serving time in the H block; one of them is up for murder. But Bernadette has her own politics: "I don't support the I.R.A. because I know what death is."

That is true two ways. Bernadette may be the youngest in her family, but Julie's death has imposed a different sort of death on her. Now her mother clings to her like death, and Bernadette must stay home with her mother and talk with her about Julie, for that is all her mother wishes to talk about. Julie used to write her name on books around the house. "Things like that bring it all back." Bernadette sounds less complaining than amazed when she says, "I can hardly get out—you know?" She has cause to be amazed. In a single shot she has been propelled into adulthood, while her mother, in Bernadette's view, has retreated to the past, and, for the time being at least, has locked her daughter in with her.

"Do you think of Julie yourself?"

"All the time," says Bernadette. "She's *everywhere.*"

Not all Belfast children have been touched by the violence. Lynn Lundy of Stella Maris smiles and says firmly, "I haven't seen anything, and I don't want to." Yet death is democratic. Eight-year-old Jonathan lives in a big house on the best side of town, and until recently the closest he came to danger was hearing a big boom one night and having a bad dream about it. The major complaint in his stately neighborhood was the stink from the nearby offal factory. Now the complaint is more topical. A few weeks ago, the Rev. Robert Bradford, M.P., was shot to death in a suburban community center not far from where Jonathan lives. Bradford's daughter Claire, seven, is Jonathan's playmate. When the incident was explained, Claire had difficulty comprehending why her father had to go to heaven to talk to people when there are so many people to talk to down here.

What has happened over the long years is that chaos has become normal, and in its normality lies a basic feature of a child's life in Belfast. Alexander Lyons, a Belfast psychiatrist, points out that in a chaotic world, antisocial behavior is acceptable. That is why he finds so little of what might be termed "emotional disturbance," in the clinical sense, among the Belfast children, since, in a way, the whole place is emotionally disturbed. The kids play war games, but there is nothing unique in that. Indeed, their war games are made more normal by the fact that the grown-ups play them too.

Of course, true insanity is in the works here as well, but it is relatively isolated. Lyons observes that among the competing terrorist groups, the Protestants seem to draw more genuine psychopaths—like the dread Butcher Gang, one of whose leaders was a real butcher, which raided Catholic areas and mutilated its victims—because the Protestant terrorists tend to operate more randomly. By comparison, the murderous insanity of the I.R.A. seems almost normal because of its putative purpose. In such an atmosphere, Lyons is far more impressed by the resilience of the children than by their fears or rampages. A girl who had three limbs blown off by a bomb managed to hold on to her mind and eventually marry. But Lyons stresses that resilience is a short-term effect. "In the long run [his voice is calm and certain] we are raising a generation of bigots."

If that is so, it is hard to see now. Bigotry is not something that people generally boast about; still, you catch almost none of it in the conversations of these children. A Catholic girl in Stella Maris expressed the deepest sorrow for the pregnant widow of a murdered Protestant policeman. "His baby will never know him." Protestant children display the same feelings. Keith Fletcher is still stunned by the story of his Catholic friend whose father, like Paul's, was murdered in his own hallway. "They walked in, very polite. The mother didn't know what they wanted. She gave them tea. They drank it. When the father came home, they shot him."

Keith and Heather Douglas are both eighteen, in their final year at Methodist College, one of the largest secondary schools in Belfast, and a life removed from Stella Maris and the Cross and Passion. For one thing, "Methody," as the students know it, is mainly financed by the state and almost wholly Protestant. For another, it is pretty. The front gate opens on a semicircular drive; neat stone urns are filled with flowers; the archways whisper Church of England; and symmetry is mandatory. Across the road sits the great Queen's University, a mere expectation away.

At a long, dark wood table in the headmaster's office, Keith and Heather sit attentively like Ph.D. candidates, each in a navy-blue blazer and a blue-and-white tie. Keith's jacket is decorated with three small badges for leadership and achievement. His face seems a work of pure logic. Heather seems a bit less organized, with her huge tinted glasses and infinite black curls.

"You have to really struggle to find the differences between the children," she says. "You can tell by the schools, of course, and by the names—Seamus versus Oliver and all that, and Long Kesh instead of the Maze. Then there's the *H* test. Have you heard of that one? I was playin' with some fellas in the park one day, and suddenly one of them stops me and makes me say the alphabet. So I go *A, B, C,* till I get to *H,* which I pronounce *aich.* That's all right. It means I'm a Prod. But if I had said *haich,* I'd have been a Taig." She laughs mockingly. "Still, most of the time it's not the children who are the bigots. It's the parents." She adds that she feels a lot closer to Catholics in Belfast than she does to Protestants in England: "You see, we have shared an experience here—a life."

It is the closeness of the lives that makes the war intense for the children, like a terrible, endless family fight, but it also confuses their feelings. Each side is carefully taught to be suspicious of the other, yet there is an unspoken affinity between the two sides as well, an affinity that does not exist between the Protestant Northern Irish and the English, or even between the Catholics in the north and south. The connections show up in indirect ways. Teenage girls in Belfast adore the romantic novels of Joan Lingard, especially *Across the Barricades* ("when Catholic Kevin and Protestant Sadie are old enough for their hitherto unacknowledged attraction to flower into love"). It is not wishful thinking, exactly; Bernadette admits she would never date a Prod, because "nothing could come of it." But the possibility exists, nonetheless—a fact that infuriates the gunmen at the doors.

What the terrorists do to keep the children in line is to use them in their battles, and the children recognize this. Here, as in Lebanon and elsewhere, children are often deliberately placed at the head of demonstrations, marches, and funeral processions. Their mere presence gives moral authority to the cause. A booklet under the prosaic title *Rubber & Plastic Bullets Kill & Maim* contains pictures and stories of child victims; the more brutal the better. Such devices work especially well in Belfast, where everyone gives the impression of knowing everyone else, where people like Paul and Bernadette achieve a dubious celebrity for having had their lives shot out from under them.

But the stories of those two are not nearly as famous as Elizabeth Crawford's. Elizabeth, sixteen, like Bernadette, goes to Cross and Passion, but even across town in Stella Maris they know all about the Crawfords. A girl in Stella Maris recalled how beautiful Patrick Crawford was—then blushes to think that she is flirting with the dead. Patrick was fifteen. He was very tall, wore his hair cut short, and resembled a policeman. They say that is how he was shot by mistake. Dead too is Elizabeth's grandfather, who was run down by a car in what appeared to be a sectarian killing. And then there was Elizabeth's mother, killed mistakenly in a crossfire between the I.R.A. and the army.

"There were ten of us at the time—seven brothers, two sisters, and myself. I can't really remember much about the happenin'. I was seven. My mother was out doin' the shoppin'. I was sittin' in a neighbor's house, and I seen my older sister being brought inside, and seen that she'd been cryin' and all. That was when we found out that Mother had been shot. And everybody kept tellin' us that she was going to be OK. Then later the doctor came in and he was tryin' to calm us down, and sain' that she was dead and gone to heaven and all this here. Just before she died, me daddy had been talkin' to her. He was very upset, he was, though he's fairly settled now. When Mother died, we all found it hard to be close to him. He was always thinkin' of her—that's the way we seen it. I don't mean to criticize him. It's just that we were left aside, like, for a while. That was only a matter of weeks. After that we began to get close again."

Elizabeth sits in the Cross and Passion office where Bernadette was sitting. Her voice is quiet, her smile hesitant. Every feature is gentle—the way the long hair waves; the way the lidded eyes give solace. She may have the face of her mother.

"Did they ever find out who did the shooting?"

"The bullets in her body were from the I.R.A. They've got two fellas in jail for it now. My father works with their fathers in the brewery. He's quite friendly with them, actually. He just has pity for the ones who done it."

The man jailed for the killing of her grandfather was a member of the militant Ulster Volunteer Force.

"And Patrick? How was he killed?"

"It was a Catholic fella. They have him locked up too." All three, then, died in different parts of the violence. "When we were younger we couldn't understand it. We didn't know where to turn or who to blame. We asked the adults, and the adults, they all had different views on it.

"I kept askin': Why is all this happenin' to *us*?"

"Did it shake your belief in God?"

"Not in God. In man."

She goes on about her life; about cooking and cleaning for her father, about the occasional movie she gets to (*Friday the 13th*—"a good scare") and the occasional book (*Across the Barricades*). She suddenly seems invested with an ancient image. She is Ireland, this girl; not Northern Ireland, but the whole strange place, that western chip of Europe stuck out in the Atlantic with no natural resources but its poetic mind and a devouring loneliness. In peacetime that loneliness is desolate but beautiful. In time of war it is merely desolate. Here is Elizabeth at the window watching rain. Or Elizabeth shopping for groceries. Or Elizabeth walking home under that tumultuous blue-black sky. Children love to be alone because alone is where they know themselves, and where they dream. But thanks to the war, Elizabeth is alone in a different way. She is not dreaming of what she will be. She looks about her and knows quite well what she will be—what her life and that of her children will be in that dread city. And like many Belfast children, she wants out. "Do you think that you could marry a Protestant boy?"

"If I find one nice enough. [A graceful laugh.] But if I ever did get married, I'd end up emigratin'. I would not want to live here, bringin' my own children up in the Troubles. 'Cause I was hurt. And I wouldn't want that to happen to them."

It is easy to picture Elizabeth as a parent because she seems a parent already. Like Bernadette, she has been rushed into adulthood. Now she must take care of her father as if she were his parent—he who does not like to talk about the Troubles, or about the past, and who seems to have settled, quite justifiably, for a life of determined peace and quiet. He may never change. A grown-up parent sees life in stages, knows fairly well when a child will outgrow or overcome this and that. But how does a child-parent know the same about grown-ups? In a sense, more patience and understanding are asked of these children than of any real parent.

You wonder, in fact, if they begin to love their parents a little less for the multitude of responsibilities imposed on them. Or, for that matter, if they love them less for the danger they all are in. In primitive worlds the high infant mortality rate is said to have inured parents against caring for their children too much. Does the same obtain in places where there is a high parent mortality rate? Perhaps the children begin to withhold some of their love from their parents as a preemptive strike against the assassins. It would be reasonable. It would be reasonable too if they loved them less simply for being grown-ups, for being partly responsible for the weeping in the streets. Yet they seem to love their parents more, not less. They only love them with greater caution. Everything these children touch may explode or disappear.

"Do you think that one side in the Troubles is more right than the other?"

"No," says Elizabeth, "neither is wrong. But they need somethin' to bring them together. I really don't know where fightin' gets anybody. It's only goin' to bring more dead, more sadness to the families."

She is told the story of Paul and Joseph.

"Don't *you* want revenge?"

"Against whom?" she says.

Like many Belfast children, Elizabeth enjoys getting out to the countryside as often as possible "for a bit of peace." On Sundays the parents of Belfast can put the city at their backs for a while and drive south to the Mournes, where the hill sheep flock like gulls, or north to the coast of Antrim, to stare across at Scotland. You don't see much of the army in the countryside, except around the Maze; and even that place, thirteen miles from town, is partly hidden from view by a pasture and a golf course. Otherwise it is all peace and greenery: swans preening on the lake shores; hedges that make quilts of the fields; grass so rich and various you can tell the country by its milk.

What is beautiful is unreal, and what is real is perilous. Yet even in the heart of the city, people work for diversions. The sparkling new Andersonstown Leisure Center won a prize as the best of its kind in the United Kingdom. Bernadette calls it "gorgeous," and 5,000 youngsters a week steam up its three swimming pools. Elizabeth plays "the badminton" there and discos on skates in the Rollerama. Children's carnivals offer another diversion. The Youth Council of Belfast sets up small amusement parks on the weekends.

On a Friday evening in September the Beechmount children's carnival begins on a hill overlooking a playing field high above the city. A constable is shot in the back that night at about the same time, but no one at the carnival has heard of it yet. This is a time for play—for joyriding in the bumper cars or knocking about in the People Mover. The cool air roars with the Beatles' "You're Gonna Lose That Girl." Parents force smiles going down the three-story Superslide, while their kids take the thrill in stride. Down on the field, boys kick a soccer ball in what is left of the light.

"Do you come from New York?" asks Sinead Doherty, fifteen, who wants to be a beautician and sports a fancy hairdo for a start.

"I do."

"Oh, I wouldn't go there. Murders everywhere."

By eight the sky is black, and the city pops on in a fluorescent amber. It has a noise, this city, like a train or a wail. Tonight the carnival's noise prevails. The place is packed, the faces glowing orange and red in the wild spinning lights. At the giant revolving swing, a man solemnly takes tickets and the children mount the seats in pairs. Slowly the machine turns; slowly the nickelodeon starts up; and the chains that hold the swings grow taut until they parallel the ground. Suddenly the children are on their sides in the air, whirling above Belfast, impelled from the center by centrifugal force.

January 11, 1982

Lebanon

You are the bows from which your children
as living arrows are sent forth.
—KAHLIL GIBRAN

PALESTINE TWITCHES on the small white mat, struggles to raise her head, and failing, falls back again; she cries, then stops. Some slice of light has caught her attention. The nurse in bright pink carries a bird cage to the mat, and for a moment Palestine is pleased by two jumpy canaries—one black, one yellow. Now she rolls back and forth. Her legs, still bowed, kick out spasmodically. You cannot tell if she hears the music in the nursery or the murmurs of the other babies, stacked up in their double-decker box cribs. She acknowledges no one. But everyone knows Palestine—if not by her blue "Space Patrol" sleep suit, then by the dark brown bruise on her right heel and, of course, by the circumstance of her birth.

For want of a standard term, the doctor on the case called the delivery a "cesarean section by explosion." It occurred last July in Beirut, during an Israeli air raid on the Fakhani Street P.L.O. offices, when Palestine's mother, nine months pregnant, rushed from her apartment house in an effort to escape the bombs. No one is certain what happened next, but when the bombing stopped, Mrs. Halaby was found dead in the rubble. Three yards away, still enveloped in the placenta, lay her new little girl.

Only a remarkable twist, like the birth of Palestine, distinguishes one explosion from another in Beirut. For the past seven years the city has known the unremitting violence of the Palestinians, Phalangists, Syrians, and Israelis; the high period was a full-scale civil war in 1975–76, which blotted out up to 60,000 lives, roughly the same number that the United States lost during fourteen years in Vietnam. For the past few years destruction has been confined to Israeli reprisals against the P.L.O.; sporadic clashes of the Syrians, Phalangists, and Palestinians; and the ordinary run of street bombings and assassinations. As the Hachette guidebook on Lebanon observes, the city of Beirut is "overflowing with activity and variety."

The odd thing is that either the Lebanese are the most durable people in the world, or they have achieved a nirvana of terror that allows them an unearthly jauntiness. The sight of a new bank in Beirut is as common as a bashed-in Mercedes. You cannot tell if a hole in the ground is the work of a bomb or a construction team. The distinguishing sound of Beirut is the car horn—not the Beethoven or Roadrunner horn, but the I-am-going-to-kill-you horn. The most popular Beirut outfits are fatigues and berets, signifying the forces of the Syrians, the Palestinians, and occasionally the Lebanese themselves.

This is the place that will make up Palestine's official home, but in her mind her true home is likely to lie elsewhere. That mind is not entirely her property even now, any more than is her story, which is told in leaflets distributed by the P.L.O. as part of its public relations.

A postcard showing Palestine in a respirator bears a printed message in French that may be mailed to friends and allies. It refers to *"Technologie Israélienne"* and swears that Palestine *"est déterminée à continuer la marche vers la liberté."* Whether or not the baby has such determination at the moment, she will probably have it in four or five years. By then she may be an instrument of determination herself, her very name a beacon to other Palestinian children who are raised in this country to inherit their parents' dreams and enemies.

The Institute of Tel Zaatar was founded to provide foster families and education for the 313 children who lost their parents in the Tel Zaatar massacre of 1976. A year before that, twenty-seven Palestinian residents of the Tel Zaatar camp were slaughtered by Christian Phalangists as they returned by bus from a rally celebrating a terrorist attack on Qiryat Shemona. In 1976 the Phalangists used 75-mm and 155-mm howitzers for a seven-week siege of the camp in which 3,000 died. Tel Zaatar was demolished.

The orphanage is a large, serene house with a façade of balconies. There are 160 children in it now, not all of them victims of Tel Zaatar. Like children elsewhere, they have rebounded quickly from their tragedies. A small boy whose mother was killed while bringing him water from a well refused at first to take water from anyone, fearing that it augured death. But after a few weeks in the home he overcame his phobia. A boy of two, who was in his father's arms when the man was shot, made no sound during his first six months in the home; now he is prattling like his peers.

Jamila, Boutros, and Mona have been at the home since it opened. Now sixteen, sixteen, and seventeen, respectively, they are considered elders, and have assumed the responsibilities of parents to the younger ones. They are sitting on a bed in a "family room"—all beds and dressers. Jamila, though in pigtails and sneakers, looks older than the other two. Her parents were killed in an Israeli shelling of Tyre. Boutros's father was killed when the Phalangists raided his poultry farm. Mona's father was killed after Tel Zaatar was destroyed:

"I was with my entire family, which divided into two groups, my mother taking shelter in one building, my father, my brother, my sister, and I hiding in another. But the Phalangists found us and started to shoot again. I fainted. I did not know what was happening until I awoke the next day and found my father, and everyone, all dead in the room with me."

Jamila observes that by losing their parents they have lost their childhood as well. Like the girls in Belfast, these three have had to grow up quickly. Asked if they believe that they have gained anything by such experiences, Boutros replies, "Power." His face seems amiable for the answer. What he means by power is something specific: "To regain our homeland." At that all three talk at once: "First we were driven from Palestine in 1948"; "The Israelis tried to exterminate us." "It's not their land. It's *our* land," says Jamila. Her voice is urgent. As the questions continue, she notices that her American visitor is sitting in an uncomfortable position. Without a word she rises and slips a pillow behind his back.

Whom do they most admire in the world? "Beside our great chairman, Arafat," says Boutros, "there are Ho Chi Minh and Castro." For Jamila it is Lenin: "Because he made a new world for his people. He made them like themselves and work together." The question of the future is raised, and the three of them talk of Palestine's certain glory. Jamila offers something more: "I would put an end to the use of all nuclear weapons."

"Do you all plan to marry and have children of your own?"

"You mean in the future?" They laugh. Mona blushes. Boutros jumps in: "When I was very young, my parents told me about their leaving Palestine. I will teach my children to be strong and to depend on themselves, as I depend on myself. I will teach them to love all those who love the Palestinians."

Much of this nationalistic fervor arises from what the children have seen firsthand as well as what they have been taught, so it is not fair to regard them solely as their elders' tools. Also their indoctrination may be indirect. The normal conversation of parents will influence children in any circumstance, and it would be a lot to ask of Palestinian parents that they display a political evenhandedness they do not feel. It may even be that for children like those in the Tel Zaatar home, this single-mindedness is not all that harmful. If there can be a benign side to indoctrination, it is that it offers a purpose; and when one's family is destroyed, any purpose, however limited, may be spiritually useful.

But the intensity of the indoctrination does not necessarily destroy one's charitable impulses either. At this stage, at least, the children are still gentler than their masters would prefer—even when their masters happen to be in the military. Samer's father is a lieutenant colonel in the P.L.O.; he controls the joint Palestinian-Lebanese forces in the region of Tyre. At the moment, Colonel Azmi controls his forces from a grass hut on stilts standing over an area bombed out by Israel last summer. The hut is furnished with red leather chairs and a Swedish-modern desk, behind which Colonel Azmi, forty, smokes Winstons and makes pronouncements:

"We are ready. We will not stop our struggle. We are not fascists. Our power is our arms. Kissinger caused this trouble. We are not Communists. Begin is a Nazi. We never intend to kill children. Till the last child we will struggle to regain our homeland." The colonel looks up. "Ah, Samer."

His son enters the hut. Samer is four years old, about three and a half feet high, and dressed in matching black-and-white checked shirt and pants and polished black laced shoes. He strides regimentally toward the Swedish-modern desk and stands before his father.

"They are so young," explains the colonel. "But they are so proud." Then to Samer: "Who is Sadat?"

"Sadat sold Palestine to Israel," says the boy, rapid-fire.

"Who is Jimmy Carter?"

"Carter supported Israel."

"Who are *you?*" asks his father with mock severity.

"I am from Palestine—from Hebron!"

"What is Israel?"

"The real name for Israel is Palestine."

The colonel invites his visitor to ask questions of his son.

"Samer, have you thought of what you would like to do when you grow up?"

"I want to marry." The colonel's men who have been sitting solemnly around the hut explode with laughter. The boy blushes with shame and confusion. His father consoles him with a gesture of the hand. Asked if he would like to live in a world that does not need soldiers, Samer says, "Yes, I would love that." At his father's signal he exits.

"Colonel, would you send Samer into war?"

"I don't want him to suffer. But he would give his blood to regain his homeland. If I am killed, my son will carry my gun."

The legatee system in which guns are passed to the children may find its pinnacle in Ahmed, a leader in a P.L.O. youth group, the *ashbals,* and in the Boy Scouts. Just fifteen, he has already made speeches for the P.L.O. in Cyprus, Egypt, East Germany, Czechoslovakia, Bulgaria, Cuba, and Moscow. The P.L.O. youth organization to which Ahmed belongs trains guerrillas from the ages of eight to sixteen, when they may graduate to the rank of full commando. The reason that Ahmed participates in both groups, explains Mahmoud Labadi, the head of P.L.O. press relations in Beirut, is that "he is so active, he doesn't want to let anything get past him." Labadi raises a hint of a smile to let Ahmed know that he is teasing him. Ahmed smiles back broadly. His red beret rests precariously on a cushion of burgeoning hair. His eyes look both inquisitive and pained. His mustache is coming along.

Ahmed is sitting at the far end of a couch in a room at the P.L.O. press office on Wafik Al Tibi Street. On quiet days, that office's routine is to pass out public relations material, like the postcard of Baby Palestine, and display Israeli weapons recovered from attacks: a rocket with Hebrew lettering, the contents of a cluster bomb lying in a helmet like a nest of brown eggs. This is not a quiet day. Twenty-four hours earlier, Wafik Al Tibi Street was almost totally obliterated by a car bomb filled with one hundred kilos of TNT and eighty liters of gasoline. Eighty-three people were killed and two hundred wounded. Labadi avoided the explosion only by uncharacteristically arriving late to work. Now he tries to catch up at his desk in the one room of the office that is not overwhelmed by the noise of the cleanup. From time to time he looks up to see if Ahmed needs a clarification in translation. On the whole, Ahmed's English is excellent.

"In 1970, when I was a child, the war began. Our family was thrown out of our house. We lived in a school for many days. Then we lived someplace else. Once the war began, every place was dangerous. No place seemed safer than another." Still, Ahmed says that he was not afraid, even at so young an age, because "I figured out that a man may only die once."

"How long do you think you will live?"

"No one can know. Maybe I'll die in a minute." There is an unnerving crash of debris on the balcony.

Ahmed hopes to study medicine one day, "because my people need doctors." Asked if he has a more personal impetus, he says that he loves science, and his expression shows it. "I love to see how the body works—the head, the stomach, the heart." Can he retain his politics and be a doctor too? "The first work of a doctor is not to be a political man." He is presented with a hypothetical situation: he is a doctor fighting in Israel; a wounded Israeli comes to him for help. "Are you a Palestinian or a doctor?"

"A doctor," he says, with no hesitation.

"What is the most beautiful thing you have ever seen?"

"Palestinian soldiers. Because they defend our people."

"Have you ever seen something beautiful that is a bit more peaceful?"

"Yes." He smiles. "My lovely girl Jomaneh." Asked to describe this Jomaneh, he considers with only mild embarrassment. "She is not black and not white. Her eyes are green, I suppose. Her hair is long and blond."

"Is she intelligent?"

He turns to Labadi. "What should I tell him?"

"The truth."

"Yes, she is intelligent. But no girls are *very* intelligent. Jomaneh is more intelligent than most." Labadi smiles, but does not look up.

The saddest thing Ahmed has ever seen, he says, is the sight of children without their parents. In the Fakhani Street air raid last summer, he came upon three such children wandering dazed in the streets. He took them to his house, where they lived until a home was found for them. Yes, he does feel older than fifteen. "Because I do a job greater than myself."

He is asked if he believes in God; his yes is awed. Is his faith at all shaken when he sees something like the devastation of yesterday's explosion? "Do you think: How could God allow such a thing to happen?" His answer is like Elizabeth's in Belfast: "No. There is no relationship between God and the people who do such things. Man does his work, God his."

"How do you see the future?"

"I do not think that war will last forever. I will work for that day." One of Labadi's assistants enters the room to curtail the interview. The funeral procession is about to begin.

Out on the street a small cannon mounted on a pickup truck shoots white clouds of disinfectant into the hot morning air. Most of the bodies were removed by midday yesterday, but in the afternoon someone discovered a detached face lying in a stairwell. Now children linger in the doorways to watch a bulldozer push along the broken bricks. The children are kept off the street itself as huge slabs of debris are thrown down from the windows of damaged buildings—glass hitting the pavement with the crash of brief, sudden applause. A strange boy in a clay-orange T-shirt skips along the sidewalk flirting with danger as the glass falls. He is bald, lost in some private game. His eyes roll back, showing only whites.

It was, they say, the worst destruction since last July's air raids.

Everyone is positive that the bomb was the work of either the Syrians, the Phalangists, the Israelis, or a combination of the above. The one group to take "credit" for the act is something called the Front for the Liberation of Lebanon from Foreigners. Within the general destruction, the front could take particular credit for the murders of Sami al-Ghoush, a member of a militant Palestinian organization, and his wife, who when the bomb exploded were just pulling up in their car, having let off their ten-year-old daughter Lara at school. The front could thus also take indirect credit for the sight of Lara in the morning, standing between, and partly held up by, two girls her size, at the head of the funeral procession now about to commence.

She has been placed at the head of the procession deliberately to symbolize the effect of the bombing, and for a while she holds her ground with courage. She wears a brownish barrette in her white-blond hair, which has been parted in the middle and drawn to the back. Her white dotted dress has short puffed sleeves and a Peter Pan collar. It is well pressed. Clearly Lara has been crying a great deal, but she is not crying now. Her eyes are hollowed with dark rings. If the girl were a dowager, you would say of her face: how beautiful she must have looked when she was young.

Then Lara breaks down again. She covers her forehead with her right hand, as if stricken with a headache. Her companions lead her away to a metal chair in front of a store, where she rests as the procession begins to move without her. She rejoins it later at the rear, half hidden behind the lines of P.L.O. soldiers, and the antiaircraft guns, and the sound trucks blaring tinny martial music. Photographs of her father and mother are displayed in the windows of an ambulance that serves as a hearse. The red lights of the ambulance spin, the siren wails at a steady pitch, and the procession of some 800 Palestinians makes its mile-long journey through the dusty marketplace, where chickens squawk in hanging cages and children clap at the parade. Now the children. Now the women in black. Now a bagpipe band, a legacy of the years of British influence.

The procession halts at a dirt clearing, where the crowd encircles a hoarse speaker: "We are following the great leader who has been killed by the enemies." Sami's coffin has been removed from the ambulance and is borne by six soldiers in helmets. Their faces shine with sweat. The coffin is wood painted silver. At first it tilts and looks about to spill—the soldiers on one side holding it higher than the others—but immediately it is righted again and draped with the

Palestinian flag. The crowd climbs mounds of earth around the speaker in order to see him better.

"He has been killed by the Phalangists and the Israelis and the CIA. Now we swear for his family: We will continue his mission. We may give up our soil, but not our weapons."

Lara is said to be nearby, but no one has seen her since the march began.

"I wonder what she is thinking [to a soldier in the crowd]."

"She is thinking: Get revenge."

January 11, 1982

Cambodia

Simon's head was tilted slightly up. His eyes could
not break away and the Lord of the Flies hung in
space before him.
"What are you doing out here all alone? Aren't
you afraid of me?"
Simon shook. "There isn't anyone to help you.
Only me. And I'm the Beast."

—WILLIAM GOLDING

T HE LEVEL OF SUFFERING among these children seems to be in direct proportion to their level of optimism. This is not surprising; adults who have endured hardships often manage a more optimistic view than their experiences would justify. What is surprising here is that some of the children who have suffered the most are not only the more optimistic; they also show the greatest amount of charity toward their fellows, including their enemies. This is true to a large extent in Belfast, and to some extent in Lebanon. It is practically universal among the Cambodians.

Why this is so is mystifying. The charity level among children who suffer economic hardship is not noticeably high; yet they, like many of the Cambodian children and the Vietnamese to follow, have been starved, brutalized, deprived of companionship, parents, love. It may have something to do with the suddenness of these assaults. Slum kids die slowly, their lives eroded at so languid a pace that even they would have trouble tracing the disintegration. To the children of war death explodes like a car bomb. They simply may not have the time to seethe or develop their hatreds. For them the exercise of charity may be an automatic protection, an instantaneous striking back with the antipode of what strikes them—kindness for cruelty, generosity for spite. In short, their goodness may be a means of survival.

Kim Seng has survived quite well for someone who, when he escaped into Thailand two years ago, was nearly dead from malnutrition. His father, a doctor, was killed by Pol Pot's Khmer Rouge soldiers. The policies of the Khmer Rouge included the execution of Cambodian intellectuals. Kim Seng watched his father being taken away in a helicopter, and for a long time in the refugee camp at Khao I Dang, all he drew were pictures of helicopters.

His mother died afterward, of starvation, with Kim Seng at her side. He was eight at the time, a member of one of the mobile work teams of children instituted by Pol Pot for their "education and well-being." The night before his mother died, he was taken to her in a nearby village. He noticed how swollen she was, how frail and tired, and that she was breathing with great difficulty. Kim Seng's mother took his hand and told him that he would very soon be an orphan. Then she said: "Always remember your father's and mother's blood. It is calling out in revenge for you."

By that time Kim Seng was already keeping a diary. He would begin his entries: "Dear friend, I turn to you in my time of sorrow and trouble . . ." On this particular night he took his diary and wrote how frightened he felt. In the morning his mother was dead. Kim Seng knelt at her bedside and prayed; then he asked a neighbor to bury his mother next to where his father lay, his father's body having been returned to the family. Kim Seng brought a shirt with him as a payment for this service.

The neighbor and his wife carried Kim Seng's mother to the burial ground, the boy walking behind them. Kim Seng was quite weak and thin. The neighbors buried his mother, burned incense, and departed. Then Kim Seng knelt by the grave and burned three incense sticks of his own. Finally he took a handful of dirt from each of his parent's graves, poured it together in his hands, and beseeched his dead parents to look after him. He then returned to the mobile team.

"Do you feel your parents' spirit inside you now?"

"Yes, it talks to me. It tells me that I must gain knowledge, and get a job. I would like to be an airplane pilot."

"Does your spirit still tell you to get revenge?"

"Yes," solemnly.

"So, will you go back to Cambodia one day and fight the Khmer Rouge?"

"No. That is not what I mean by revenge. To me revenge means that I must make the most of my life."

Kim Seng, now ten, sits at the other side of a kitchen table at the end of a long dirt-floor hut in Khao I Dang. He is visible down to the middle of his chest. The face is bright brown; the head held in balance by a pair of ears a bit too large for the rest—the effect being scholarly, not comical. Kim Seng has a special interest in France these days because he has recently learned that his older brother is there. He studies diligently, hoping to join his brother. He believes that knowledge makes people virtuous.

"What is this picture, Kim Seng?" The drawing is one of two he did upon first arriving at Khao I Dang. It is of three boys, stick figures, standing to the side of several gravestones. The background consists of a large mountain with a leering yellow moon resting on its peak. Perched on a tree is an oversized owl, whose song, says Kim Seng, is mournful.

"One day I left my mobile team to go find food for myself. I was very hungry. I met two boys, and together we came upon a mass grave of thirty bodies. The Khmer Rouge soldiers found me. I told them that I had gone for firewood. But they punished me. They bound my hands to a bamboo stick behind my back. I was tied up without food for several days."

The second drawing is of a bright orange skeleton with tears in its eyes and a grim mouth in an open frown. "I drew this after the death of my mother. I ate leaves then. That is why there is a tree in the picture."

"If you drew yourself today, would the picture be different?"

"Yes, very different. Here I have food. And there would be a smile on my face."

He is asked to do a self-portrait. He moves to a long table under a window at the far end of the hut. An elder provides him with paper and crayons, and he works in silence. The noise of the other children has abated momentarily, the only sound being an occasional squawk of a late-rising rooster. Soon the boy presents his work, which is not a self-portrait at all but a bright blue airplane with green doors, green engines, and a red nose and tail.

"But where are *you*, Kim Seng?"

"I am the pilot in the window." He points himself out enthusiastically. "We are flying to France."

Khao I Dang is one of two main refugee camps set up by the U.N. High Commissioner for Refugees at the eastern edge of Thailand. From there the refugees will be resettled. Some will return to Cambodia in an attempt to rejoin their families. The camp sits at the foot of Khao I Dang Mountain, a high, craggy hill where thousands of Cambodians have hidden in the brush before making their escape runs down into the camp. One day, the children fear, the Khmer Rouge will come hurtling down that slope to recapture them. It will not happen for a while yet. It is the end of the monsoon season. The air smells of hot mud. The sky hangs low, like a gray fishnet over the straw roofs.

The camp looks more like a Cambodian village than a refugee holding center, perhaps because some families have been here so long, awaiting resettlement, that the place has naturally taken on an ancient form. The only blatant signs of modernity are the blue mushroom-shaped water towers, the laterite roads, and the rehabilitation center, a larger hut where molds for artificial limbs lie stacked on shelves like loaves of white bread. The people mill about the wat, their Buddhist temple. Their gardens are crowded with tomatoes, scallions, cloves, lemon grass, and "Cambodian traditional"—marijuana. Squash wobbles on the latticework between the huts. A barefoot woman carries an armload of morning glories. Beside the roads grow needle flowers with pointed petals of burnished pink, and *mai-ya-rab,* a tiny fern (a weed, really) that shrinks away at the human touch, but after a while restores itself.

Nop Narith is Kim Seng's size and age. He has shaggy black hair and great buckteeth that gleam in a smile. He holds his left arm below the table. Narith had polio when he was younger, and the arm is withered. Both his parents are dead.

"When the soldiers came to my house, they took our whole family away. Me they took to a mobile team. I never saw my parents again. But I have a photograph of my father. My father was worried that I could not take care of myself. Yet I feel guarded by his spirit. I dreamed that I saw him, and he promised that his spirit would protect me. In the dream he told me to gain knowledge and to take revenge on his killers."

"Do you seek revenge against the soldiers, then?"

"Yes."

"What do you mean by revenge?"

"Revenge is to make a bad man better than before."

At first, these unorthodox interpretations of revenge seem less personal than traditional—an attitude inherited from an agrarian people accustomed to gentleness and passivity. To be sure, there was a long time, between the ninth and fifteenth centuries, when Khmer culture sustained a golden age—the period of Angkor Wat with its five peaked towers and massive stone gods. But fundamentally, Cambodia has remained a village nation, and the values of Pol Pot, not to mention his horrors, must have seemed as shocking as they were terrifying. The children in Khao I Dang have simple values. They have been taught to honor the land, the country, their dead ancestors, their parents, and their village.

Still, it is not always this way. Many children use the same wiles in the camp that they employed to survive in the jungle and elude Pol Pot. There are even stories of children denying the existence of their parents within the same camp because they have heard that an unaccompanied child stands a greater chance of being claimed by another country. One boy was desolate because his friend suddenly left camp with a family with which he had been secretly ingratiating himself for months. A ten-year-old was so eager to emigrate that he found himself wandering around back at the Cambodian border. He had stowed away on a truck that—he had persuaded himself—was bound for America.

What you have to realize, says Pierce Gerety, the director of the International Rescue Committee in Thailand, is that "their whole country has been burned over." Gerety, his wife, Marie, and Neil Boothby, a child psychologist, all of whom work steadily with these children, need continually to remind themselves that the small serious eyes that look up to them have taken in sights that should exist only in hell. A common story the children tell is of seeing pregnant women tied to trees, their stomachs then slit open by bayonets. More common still is the liver torture—the children draw pictures of this. Here the victim is also tied to a tree, and his liver is plucked out by a specially designed hook. He may survive twenty minutes in this condition.

Yet there is a kind of torment that goes deeper than such memories, and here is where their idea of revenge comes into focus. The children express this thought indirectly. Nep Phem is eighteen, and a gifted artist. His eyes tear, perhaps from a cold, and his answers are very thoughtful, introduced by long pauses. When you ask him what liberty requires, for example, he tells you "Patience." On one subject, however, his responses are rapid and automatic:

"Do you think that people learn war or is it inborn?"

"War must be born in you."

"Can the impulse to make both war and peace exist in the same person?"

"No. They cannot live together."

"Which wins out?"

"Peace always beats war."

Kim Seng says the same thing. As does Meng Mom, a puffy-cheeked twelve-year-old dancer who toys shyly with the lavender sleeve of her shirt. She is silent on all topics but one:

"Why do men make wars?"

"There are a lot of bad men in the world."

"How does someone stay good if so many men are bad?"

"Good must fight the bad."

"Can good and bad exist in the same person?"

"No. Not together. They are in separate places. The good must beat the bad."

These simple abstractions have a meaning for Cambodian children that is clearly disturbing to them. It is not as if the Khmer Rouge are an invading horde from a distant nation; the Khmer Rouge are their neighbors, their friends, themselves—which may account for the fact that so many of the children have nightmares in which they assume the roles of Pol Pot's soldiers. They have, in fact, known children who were Pol Pot's soldiers. The atrocities of the Khmer Rouge are thus acutely shocking. No, they say; the good spirit and the bad spirit cannot live within the same body. But what if they do? Here is where their definition of revenge suddenly makes perfect sense. How do you take revenge on yourself? Even at a very young age these people perceive their own capacity for evil, which is the human capacity, and they deny it with as much vehemence as fright.

Or, like Sokhar, they say nothing. Sokhar is eleven now, was eight when she first came to Khao I Dang. She too did a drawing when she arrived, but unlike Kim Seng, she did not explain it, and in fact said almost nothing at all during her first two years at the camp. Sokhar is well fed, and soft featured, though "in Cambodia I met with starvation." She has crying fits still, but is beginning to talk. It is difficult, however, to speak of her drawing, which, while primitive, requires an explanation.

She takes it in her hands, and studies what she drew: three children gathering rice in a field. A Khmer Rouge soldier has a rifle trained on them, "to keep them working." Off to the left of the picture is the device. It looks like a wheel with a hollow hub and spokes leading out to the rim. Or perhaps it is a doughnut with lines on it. Three extra lines extend from the outer rim at the bottom, giving the thing the appearance of an insect. At the top there is yet another line sticking out at an angle to the right, the end of which is attached to a small ring.

"What is happening here, Sokhar?"

"This is a picture of the Pol Pot time." She hopes to change the subject.

"Who are these people?"

"They harvest the rice."

"And what is this [the circular device]?"

"This is something you put on the head."

"Who puts it on your head?"

"The Pol Pot soldiers."

"What is its purpose?"

"To kill."

"Do soldiers do the killing?"

No answer.

"Is it the soldiers who work the device?"

She will not respond to this question. Not now. But she has answered it before. After two years of silence she at last explained the device—if not fully, at least enough to allow a guess as to how it worked. The children harvesting rice include Sokhar; she is the largest of the three. Whenever a child refused to work, he was punished with the circular device. The soldiers would place it over the child's head. Three people would hold it steady by means of ropes (the three lines at the bottom). A fourth would grab hold of the ring at the end of the other rope (the line at the top). The device worked like a camera lens, the areas between the lines in the drawing being metal blades. When the rope with the ring was pulled, the lens would close, and the child would be decapitated. A portable guillotine. But it wasn't the soldiers who worked the device. It was the children.

Outside the rain splashes down, then stops just as suddenly, and everything is hot again. The children are excited; they are about to perform a few of their folk dances. Some older boys are shooting baskets on a hard dirt court. They laugh in surprise when the American visitor blocks a shot. They did not know that defense was part of the game.

Behind the wat is a shack where the coffins are kept before cremation; and behind that, near a patch of sweet potatoes, the crematorium sits in a clearing under a shed, like a doll's chapel. There is no activity there today. But the wat itself is busy with a festival marking the last day of the Buddhist Lent. A monk in yellow sits cross-legged on a table, while children crouched in a circle burn incense. The smoke is supposed to fly to heaven in order to beckon their ancestors to descend and join them.

Other children are playing soccer in uniforms on a huge dirt field. Some enjoy the playground. A naked baby stands before a swing, perplexed as to how to work it. A few busy themselves in the arts hut, painting or carving elaborate wooden musical instruments like the *take* and the *kail*. This is where Nep Phem likes to spend his time. When asked why art is important to him, he answers: "So that I may give something to someone, and allow someone to love me in return."

But most of the children are in the theater tent now—the "Khao I Dang National Theater"—milling and chattering with expectation. Then the bright pink curtains part, showing a backdrop painting of Angkor Wat. The xylophone plays the water-drop music. The dancers enter. The boys strut, the girls cock their hands and heads and do not smile. They glow with color, their dark brown skins set off by the deep blues, reds, and greens of their sarongs and sashes. They do four dances, starting with a hunting dance in which a small boy brandishes a spear and tries to look ferocious. The coconut dance is the most fun and the most intricate, as the children clap halves of coconuts from hand to hand. They flirt, but do not touch.

The last dance is Ro Bam Kak Se Ko, the rice cultivation dance, presented in five parts. The first is the planting of seeds. The second is a dance of three scarecrows (the little ones in the audience howl at the masks). The third part is the cutting of the rice, and fourth is the tying. Finally comes the celebration of the harvest. The children prance under a full moon. Over the loudspeaker an announcer explains: It was a good year.

January 11, 1982

The Man
in the
Water

A S DISASTERS GO, this one was terrible, but not unique, certainly not among the worst on the roster of U.S. air crashes. There was the unusual element of the bridge, of course, and the fact that the plane clipped it at a moment of high traffic, one routine thus intersecting another and disrupting both. Then, too, there was the location of the event. Washington, the city of form and regulations, turned chaotic, deregulated, by a blast of real winter and a single slap of metal on metal. The jets from Washington National Airport that normally swoop around the presidential monuments like famished gulls are, for the moment, emblemized by the one that fell; so there is that detail. And there was the aesthetic clash as well—blue-and-green Air Florida, the name a flying garden, sunk down among gray chunks in a black river. All that was worth noticing, to be sure. Still, there was nothing very special in any of it, except death, which, while always special, does not necessarily bring millions to tears or to attention. Why, then, the shock here?

Perhaps because the nation saw in this disaster something more than a mechanical failure. Perhaps because people saw in it no failure at all, but rather something successful about their makeup. Here, after all, were two forms of nature in collision: the elements and human character. Last Wednesday, the elements, indifferent as ever, brought down Flight 90. And on that same afternoon, human nature—groping and flailing in mysteries of its own—rose to the occasion.

Of the four acknowledged heroes of the event, three are able to account for their behavior. Donald Usher and Eugene Windsor, a park police helicopter team, risked their lives every time they dipped the skids into the water to pick up survivors. On television, side by side in bright blue jumpsuits, they described their courage as all in the line of duty. Lenny Skutnik, a twenty-eight-year-old employee of the Congressional Budget Office, said: "It's something I never thought I would do"—referring to his jumping into the water to drag an injured woman to shore. Skutnik added that "somebody had to go in the water," delivering every hero's line that is no less admirable for its repetitions. In fact, nobody had to go into the water. That somebody actually did so is part of the reason this particular tragedy sticks in the mind.

But the person most responsible for the emotional impact of the disaster is the one known at first simply as "the man in the water." (Balding, probably in his fifties, an extravagant mustache.) He was seen clinging with five other survivors to the tail section of the airplane. This man was described by Usher and Windsor as appearing alert and in control. Every time they lowered a lifeline and flotation ring to him, he passed it on to another of the passengers. "In a mass casualty, you'll find people like him," said Windsor. "But I've never seen one with that commitment." When the helicopter came back for him, the man had gone under. His selflessness was one reason the story held national attention; his anonymity another. The fact that he went unidentified invested him with a universal character. For a while he was Everyman, and thus proof (as if one needed it) that no man is ordinary.

Still, he could never have imagined such a capacity in himself. Only minutes before his character was tested, he was sitting in the ordinary plane among the ordinary passengers, dutifully listening to the stewardess telling him to fasten his seat belt and saying something about the "no smoking sign." So our man relaxed with the others, some of whom would owe their lives to him. Perhaps he started to read, or to doze, or to regret some harsh remark made in the office that morning. Then suddenly he knew that the trip would not be ordinary. Like every other person on that flight, he was desperate to live, which makes his final act so stunning.

For at some moment in the water he must have realized that he would not live if he continued to hand over the rope and ring to others. He *had* to know it, no matter how gradual the effect of the cold. In his judgment he had no choice. When the helicopter took off with what was to be the last survivor, he watched everything in the world move away from him, and he deliberately let it happen.

Yet there was something else about the man that kept our thoughts on him, and which keeps our thoughts on him still. He was *there,* in the essential, classic circumstance. Man in nature. The man in the water. For its part, nature cared nothing about the five passengers. Our man, on the other hand, cared totally. So the timeless battle commenced in the Potomac. For as long as that man could last, they went at each other, nature and man: the one making no distinctions of good and evil, acting on no principles, offering no lifelines; the other acting wholly on distinctions, principles, and, one supposes, on faith.

Since it was he who lost the fight, we ought to come again to the conclusion that people are powerless in the world. In reality, we believe the reverse, and it takes the act of the man in the water to remind us of our true feelings in this matter. It is not to say that everyone would have acted as he did, or as Usher, Windsor, and Skutnik. Yet whatever moved these men to challenge death on behalf of their fellows is not peculiar to them. Everyone feels the possibility in himself. That is the abiding wonder of the story. That is why we would not let go of it. If the man in the water gave a lifeline to the people gasping for survival, he was likewise giving a lifeline to those who observed him.

The odd thing is that we do not even really believe that the man in the water lost his fight. "Everything in Nature contains all the powers of Nature," said Emerson. Exactly. So the man in the water had his own natural powers. He could not make ice storms, or freeze the water until it froze the blood. But he could hand life over to a stranger, and that is a power of nature too. The man in the water pitted himself against an implacable, impersonal enemy; he fought it with charity; and he held it to a standoff. He was the best we can do.

January 25, 1982

What
Should We
Lead With?

JOURNALISTS put the question in practical terms: What should we lead with? The rest of the population asks it more generally: What matters most? It comes to the same puzzle. Survey events in a given period of time and try to come up with the single moment, the headline, by which the world may be characterized, stopped in its spin. In the past couple of weeks, the press has stood chest-high in choices. In Lebanon: one more last battle for Beirut; the disintegration of the Gemayel government; the pullout of the U.S. Marines. In the Soviet Union: the death of Yuri Andropov and the succession of Konstantin Chernenko; a funeral in red. In Iowa: the small beginnings of an American presidential election; the first funny hats and toots of the horns. In Sarajevo: one more Winter Olympics done; memories on videotape; the ice dancers Torvill and Dean synchronized, as if accidentally, like birds in a wind. Four major acts, then: war, ceremony, process, grace.

What should we lead with? What matters most? Let us concede from the start that the problem is subjective, that whatever choice we settle on will be formed more by habit than by a command of history; the press is not in control of history. Getting bored with Beirut? It's not unheard of (if you don't live there). Every few weeks another upheaval; the familiar picture of a crushed Mercedes, a balcony split open like stale cake. One hears that the American people are growing tired of the Middle East as a whole. Too bad. The region matters, it's a lead. Boring or not, Beirut may be the center of the world, the place where everything comes together or apart.

So, too, for Moscow these past two weeks. After the obsequies and the miles of citizen mourners, half the world closes ranks behind another mystery. Who *is* this Chernenko, Brezhnev's former water boy turned master of the house? After Iowa, who is Mondale? Walter, we thought we knew you, but now we'd better look a bit closer at him who may become the leader of the other half of the world. Which leaves us with Sarajevo, the least important place on our current events map. Perhaps. But before we say so definitely, play it again, that ice dance performed by the two Brits. I don't think that I caught it all the first time. I think I missed one of the turns of her head, or an extension of his arm, the way they came together or apart.

Here's what one would like to say: that Torvill and Dean's routine was more important in its sublimity than all the shootings and elections time can muster; that life is short and art is long; and that the skating dance, brief and evanescent as it is, represents a perfection in which the entire universe may be encompassed. Theodore Roethke described such an effect in a poem: "A ripple widening from a single stone/ Winding around the waters of the world." Nice. It may even be true. Yet it is just as likely that Beirut is the widening ripple by which everything is framed.

What we confront in making such choices is not the events alone, but ourselves; and it is ourselves we are not able to place in order. The mind, as fickle as a southern belle, swishes rapidly from battles to dances, enthralled equally with every suitor, enthralled with itself. Tell me a story about my mind, Mr. News. Did I overturn a government this week? Did I come to power? Did I win an election? Did I skate flawlessly again? Was I murderous, decorous, triumphant, beautiful? And if I was all those things, how should I order my priorities so as to know what is truly human, the essential prevailing act? The question is not what the press decrees is this week's news. The question is us. What should we lead with? What matters most?

In another poem, Roethke suggested that the widening ripple is ourselves:

I lose and find myself in the long water;
I am gathered together once more;
I embrace the world.

We do that every week, cursing and awestruck at all we are.

March 5, 1984

The Death
of a
Columnist

JOSEPH KRAFT died on January 10. Two hundred newspapers
lost a column, one of the best in the nation. A clear light in
journalism for thirty-five years, Joe wrote books, editorials, and long
reportorial analyses, but his regular "beat" consisted of producing
two or three columns a week on national and foreign affairs. His
columns were always stately, unhurried. They stared out from the
page hard, like a good teacher absorbed in, though not quite obsessed
by, his subject, and fixed the readers to the processes of a strong, fair
mind. Presidents knew Joe, and he had power in Washington, but his
force as a writer came from his dignity. He possessed a scholar's
nature fitted to a frenzied profession; a spirit of magnanimity and
gentleness; a temperament at once high-strung and serene; a sly sense
of fun; a fierce love of words, of his work.

Strange work. Columnists take a ribbing from their fellow journalists, reporters especially, who tend to regard columnists with the
same chummy contempt that linemen show quarterbacks. Reporters
do the real work, sleep in cars, get kicked by Mafia bosses on the
courthouse steps. Even editors do some sweating (yelling is taxing).
But columnists ride the gravy train, that's what the pressroom says.
In a way, it's true. They manage to arrive home before midnight; they
dine with the brass. Their physical exercise consists of pacing all the

way to the far end of the study, and often back again. Sometimes they sit up straight.

Otherwise, they brood. Into their study every morning parade the armies of the news. A knock on the door, and there stands Heseltine resigning from Mrs. Thatcher's cabinet, Marcos on the stump, Qaddafi playing cowboy on his tractor, mummied to the nose. Come in, boys. The columnist will make sense of all this somehow. After the reporters and the editors have dumped the facts on the doorstep, the columnist, like a jigsaw addict, scoops up the pieces, studies the angles, mulls, clears his throat, and says, with as much self-assurance as possible: This piece goes here, and this one here.

And then he asks: What piece is not here? What ground is missing from this puzzling geography that would allow us to view the map redrawn, to sit back and behold the brand-new country of our concern and comprehension? The piece is not really missing, of course; you just don't see it, like the shy side of the moon. Yet the missing piece is the one that counts.

That piece must be found very quickly; the column is due tonight. Meanwhile, more facts crowd the study door like extras on a movie set, peer in, cry, "Use me!" Guatemala, Mr. T, a new novel by Bellow; Dow Jones goes down, the Columbia goes up. Say hey, Willie McCovey, you made it too. Nice hat, Mrs. Gorbachev. Hold it, please. I have to think. Didn't I read something by Octavio Paz that fits in here? Or was it Pia Zadora? Where is my authoritative, I've-studied-this-for-years lead sentence? Please, God, let me discover an apt quotation from someone other than Samuel Johnson. You have to sound as if you knew it all along. You have to shape your column too—mostly Doric, a Corinthian fluting when they least expect it. It's work. Whatever the others say, it's work.

Yet the laws of physics insist that work must move things: A pushes against B and B moves. What, besides paper, does the columnist move? He wonders that himself. Swiveling in his chair, he catches hummingbirds, bats, butterflies in flutter, pins them to the wall and whispers, "Gotcha." But he doesn't. Today Qaddafi, tomorrow the Chicago Bears. Call this history? Come Thursday, no one will remember how right he was on Tuesday, and the facts may have altered to prove that he was wrong on Tuesday after all, but who will remember that either? Twenty years after his death, maybe ten, how many readers will speak his name? Perhaps all columnists should change their names to Walter Lippmann. In the entire history of the game, only Lippmann's name survives.

So what good is effected in pointing that capacious intelligence at fast-moving targets? Why find the missing piece if even the visible pieces will vanish in a shot? Ask Joe Kraft, and he would have said that the good lies in doing it, in using the mind to grasp everything the world can throw at it, baseballs to missiles, because that is how the mind protects the body, protects itself. Understanding is protection. More: Understanding is forewarning. More: Understanding is life. The individual column does not count, because a column is not supposed to exist alone. A columnist looks to erect a whole assembly of columns, each single effort standing patiently at attention after it is created, until eventually a population emerges, a civilization emerges. The civilization is an accumulation both of the columnist's ideas and of his being; he is his collected works. More: He has shown that collecting the works is the way a life ought to be built, column by column, displaying both continuity and changes in the structure and in the architect. He has shown the way to make and use a mind.

More: There is always more, a deeper level to spot and land on, like a plane swooping down from bright white and blue into a heavy snow. People like Joe Kraft play Charles Dickens's Oliver Twist all their lives—they cannot help themselves—requesting "more" where others are horrified by, or are deaf to, or fear, or pretend not to recognize the word. The more that is sought is a statement of innocence; one believes in his heart that enlightenment will be cheering, though experience proves that more often it is punishing. Still the optimistic pursuit continues, the pursuer buoyed every morning by that barrage of knocking on the study door, the news that the news is still coming strong, and that the bonfires are still being lighted around the world, signaling that everyone is still present, still cocking their senses for the missing more.

All columnists are fifth columnists. Prominent for a moment, they rapidly go out of view, but the influence stays, and the impulse to contemplate abides. It's not a career deep down; it is a protest against being overwhelmed by the speed of things, against letting the world get away from us. When Dickens's daughter died, he was in London and his wife in the country; he wrote her a letter telling her at the outset, "You must read this letter very slowly." Joe Kraft died on January 10. You must read his death very slowly. The missing piece is the one that counts.

January 27, 1986

Do You Feel
the Deaths
of Strangers?

"A NY MAN'S DEATH DIMINISHES ME." It has always sounded excessive. John Donne expressed that thought more than 350 years ago in a world without mass communications, where a person's death was signaled by a church bell. "It tolls for thee," he said. Does it really? Logic would suggest that an individual's death would not diminish but rather enhance everybody's life, since the more who die off, the more space and materials there will be for those who remain. Before his conversion, Uncle Scrooge preferred to let the poor die "and decrease the surplus population." Scrooge may not have had God on his side, but his arithmetic was impeccable.

Are Donne's words merely a "right" thing to say, then, a slice of holy claptrap dished out at the Christmas season? What does it mean to believe that any man's death diminishes me? In what sense, diminishes? And even if one wholeheartedly accepted Donne's idea, what then? What use could one possibly make of so complete an act of sympathy, particularly when apprised of the deaths of total strangers?

Assume that at the basic minimum the process of diminishing requires a state of grief. Is it really possible to grieve for *any* person's death? A year ago in Lebanon [1983], a fanatic drove a truck bomb into the Marine compound at Beirut International Airport, killing

241. We responded to those deaths, all right; Americans grieving for Americans. The truck driver also died in the explosion. Any grief left over for him? What about all the Lebanese who have been dropping in the streets for a decade? Feel those deaths, do we? We say yes sincerely, but we only mean that we experience brief pangs of pity and sadness, especially if television shows death close enough to allow us to make identifications with the sufferers.

Last week in a place most Americans never heard of, more than 2,500 residents of Bhopal, India, were killed by leaking toxic gas. How deeply did we really feel that news? Numbers are always tossed up first in such events, but almost as a diversion; there seems a false need to know exactly how many died, how many were hospitalized; reports supersede reports. When the count is finally declared accurate, it is as if one were mourning a quantity rather than people, since the counting exercise is a way of establishing objective significance in the world. Still, we wept at the pictures, for a day or two.

Just as we wept or shook our heads sorrowfully for the citizens of Mexico City who were caught in the gas explosion and fire several weeks ago. Just as we have been weeping for the starving Ethiopians for several weeks in a row. There we could provide more than tears. There was money to send; one could do that.

But Donne seemed to be advocating a response that is deeper and more consistent: Any man's death makes me smaller, less than I was before I learned of that death, because the world is a map of interconnections. As the world decreases in size, so must each of its parts. Donne's math works too. Since the entire world suffers a numerical loss at an individual's death, then one must feel connected to the entire world to feel the subtraction equally.

The equation gets more complicated. Donne liked to think that everyone represented a world within himself. When anyone died, a planet died; messages of condolence should be flashed across the galaxy. All this intricate imagery simply provided a hard shell for soft feelings. In *The Third Man*, Harry Lime peered down from the top of a Ferris wheel at the dotlike people below, and asked who would really care if one of those dots were to stop moving. Donne saw the dots as close relatives.

For most people the difficulty may lie not in giving dollars or a moment's sympathy to a distant tragedy but in feeling a part of the world in the first place. Show me an Ethiopian mother holding her skin-sore baby—belly ballooned, limbs like an insect's—and my eyes will spill tears. Naturally. What do you take me for? But ask that I see the Ethiopian mother when she is off the screen, in the caves of my mind when I am about my business . . . ah, well. Donne's thesis was that human sympathy ought not to be what we dust off occasionally but what we display all the time. Thus would we weep not only for death at a distance but for the sufferers who are closer at hand, for the family down the street whose plight goes unnoticed and untelevised—for all those in fact whom we might actually help.

Thus, too, would we be prepared for history's surprises, so that when the species goes berserk and comes up with a Hitler or a Pol Pot, we would not turn our backs on those in danger. In his book *Language and Silence*, George Steiner was perplexed to consider how the torture-murders committed at Treblinka could be occurring at precisely the same time that people in New York were making love or going to the movies. Were there two kinds of time in the world, Steiner wondered—"good times" and "inhuman time"? The matter was troubling and confusing: "This notion of different orders of time simultaneous but in no effective analogy or communication may be necessary to the rest of us, who were not there, who lived as if on another planet. That, surely, is the point: to discover the relations between those done to death and those alive then, and the relations of both to us."

But it may not be enough to establish a relationship between those done to death and the survivors. It may be necessary to make a connection with all those who die, under any circumstances—any man's death, at any time—in order to keep one's capacity for sympathy vigilant. There may not be two kinds of time in the world, but there seem to be two kinds of sympathy: one that weeps and disappears, and one that never leaves the watch. Sympathy, unlike pity, must have some application to the future. If we do not feel deeply the deaths we are powerless to prevent, how would we be alert to the deaths we might put an end to?

Of course, this is asking a lot of you and me, who are, after all, pretty good people, who recognize despair when we see it and even respond generously when appeals are made. Especially in this season. We are very good in this season. And how realistic was Donne's idea, given human indifference and lapses of memory? Yet at times the world can feel as small as Donne's. If nothing else, we have vulnerability to share. A reporter walking about Bhopal last week remarked how on some streets people were living normally, while adjacent streets were strewn with bodies. Everything depended on where the wind was blowing.

December 17, 1984

Do You Know This Woman?

꘏꘏꘏

W HEN MADELINE ADAM, Betty's caseworker at Project
Reachout, first started working with her in 1987, Betty was
living on a bench on upper Broadway. Betty would sing for handouts
in front of Weber's Closeout Center, where sweaters go for seven
dollars. Everybody knew her. People, including other homeless, used
to leave clothing for Betty on the corner of Broadway and Seventy-
first. Father Robert O'Connor, pastor of the Church of the Blessed
Sacrament, where Betty would sometimes go for food, often walked
the neighborhood in street clothes. Betty would call out to him,
"How ya doin', Father?"

Project Reachout's staff seeks out the homeless on the Upper West
Side of New York City, wherever they live—in packing crates, in
manmade caves, among the trees in Central Park, or on benches, like
Betty. To Madeline, working with Betty was "so much fun. She'd
sing. Panhandle. Sing." Betty sang with a slight hissing sound since
the day some wild man punched her in the mouth and scattered her
teeth on the sidewalk. Her smile prevailed. At sixty-four, having
endured shock therapy at mental hospitals and years of street living,
she still had the apple cheeks of a girl.

Sometimes Betty claimed she was Dorothy Lamour. Sometimes

Elizabeth Taylor. Betty had had a Hollywood screen test. That was after she rose to fame as a show girl at the Latin Quarter. The big shots in New York, they all knew Betty. Betty was a runner-up in the Miss Cincinnati Beauty Pageant too. She'd have gone on to the Miss America Pageant in Atlantic City if she'd won.

Two weeks before Betty died, her daughter Lee came up from Baltimore in search of the mother she had never known. Lee appeared at Project Reachout with news clips and photos of her mother in the 1950s sent by Betty's brother, Joe. It was then Madeline and everybody else learned that most of what Betty had said about her life was true.

Project Reachout knew almost nothing of Betty's history until Lee showed up. The project often knows little about the people it serves since, like Betty, its clients are mentally ill, and cannot or do not wish to speak about their past. Workers often spend years persuading the homeless to "come in" for medical and psychiatric help, a room, sometimes a job. Between 80 and 100 people a day come in for help. The project also reaches out to the estimated 1,000 to 1,400 in the neighborhood who don't come in.

In December 1989, when the temperature fell to as low as six degrees, Madeline made a desperate effort to get Betty to come in. But Betty said she couldn't do it right then because she had auditions. She was the one person left on the upper Broadway benches. She wore tiger slippers over her shoes and a large red and green striped sweater. Madeline finally had her placed in Bellevue Hospital against her will.

When Betty was released, Madeline feared that Betty would resent what she had done. She brought along Betty's brand of cigarettes, but when Madeline went to get matches, she was told no smoking was permitted in the visiting room. She looked at Betty sitting with an unlit cigarette stuck in her mouth, her face alive with expectation. Later Betty told Madeline: "I saw how sorry you were you couldn't bring me those matches."

"It's very rare," says Madeline, "when our people outwardly express sympathy. They've led such isolated lives."

One of Project Reachout's clients was once an architect. One was a private secretary to a millionaire. One was a physician with a Princeton degree. And Betty Wehmeier was a show girl at the Latin Quarter.

Herman and Edith May Wehmeier raised three children in Cincinnati during the Depression. First came Joe, then Betty two years later, on

May 28, 1925, then Herman Jr. Herman Jr. died in 1973. Herman Sr. had a decorating business—wallpaper, draperies—which he ran with his brothers, Elmer and Fred. All three brothers played musical instruments. Betty sang—"at the drop of a hat," says Joe. "She loved to belt it out."

When Betty was three, the Wehmeiers went to a Christmas play at their church. Betty didn't like being told she was too young to be in the play. Her parents lost sight of her for a second. When they looked up, their daughter was onstage singing, "Baa, Baa, Black Sheep."

Joe and his brother, Herman, were the nonmusical ones in the family. They played baseball instead. Herm got real good at it. He pitched thirteen seasons with the Reds, Phillies, Cardinals, and Tigers. A news photo in a Cincinnati paper shows a deliberately posed Betty reading *The Sporting News* over brother Herm's shoulder. Her blond hair is parted in the middle, and a braid forms a crown at the back of her head.

In 1946 the Miss Cincinnati Beauty Pageant went to Lavonne Bond. Betty Wehmeier was second runner-up.

"I used to date Lavonne," says Joe. "She wound up winning Miss Congeniality at the Miss America Pageant. Tell you what: If the Cincinnati contest had been on beauty alone, Betty would have won hands down."

The first of Betty's marriages was on October 4, 1946, to Bill Lippelman, a Linotype operator. Joe says Bill's parents were overbearing. The marriage was over in less than a year.

On December 1, 1948, Betty married Bob Mueller, a dockworker for Railway Express. On July 1, 1949, Betty gave birth to Bobby Jr. That marriage fell apart August 3, 1949, with Betty given custody of Bobby.

On April 30, 1951, Betty married George Hammann, in Brookville, Indiana. George was a bartender at the Twin Lanterns nightclub, where Betty performed. On December 9, 1952, George filed for divorce. Betty left her son, Bobby, with her parents around 1953. "The show-biz fantasy was too strong," Joe explains. Betty was off to New York.

"Sure, I remember Betty Hammann," says Jeanne Tart Winding, who appeared with Betty in the Latin Quarter revue called "Made in France." "Dressed flamboyant. She showed off what she had, and she had it all. Kind of hard-looking, with a POW! appeal. Attracted men like bees to honey too. Lou Walters [owner of the Latin Quarter, father of Barbara] thought she was sensational and was mad about her.

"Betty liked a good time, all right. We took the show down to Florida in the winter, to the Latin Quarter Palm Island [in Miami]. Al Capone had his house there. The club was always filled with Mafia and Batista henchman types—all the undesirable sorts. We used to go round to the various night spots, and Betty loved to get up and sing. Before any of us heard her, she'd boast about singing here and there, and we all said, 'Yeah, yeah, yeah.' But then one night a group of us called her bluff and went to see her. She was terrific! She was just as good as she said she was!"

In 1954 Betty's parents and Herman Jr. and his wife drove to New York to visit her. "Betty took them everywhere," says Joe. "Took 'em to the Stork Club. Everybody in the place knew Betty. All those celebrities!" Joe was told that his sister went out with Joe DiMaggio. "I saw it in a gossip column."

For the period-glitter of the 1940s and early 1950s nothing could touch the Latin Quarter. Columnists like Walter Winchell worked a room packed with playboys who dangled diamonds and minks in front of the chorus girls. One of the girls, Chickee James, was offered a "three-week marriage" by playboy Tommy Manville—for $100,000. The nightly shows starred Milton Berle, Sophie Tucker, and Frank Sinatra. Arlene Dahl, like Betty, sang and danced in the chorus.

The January 24, 1955, issue of Life shows Jackie Gleason sitting at the feet of Betty Hammann. She dances on stage, arms raised as if in surrender, wearing a skirt that looks like a beach umbrella.

Sometime in the spring of 1955 Betty left the Latin Quarter and went out to Hollywood. A Cincinnati paper reported she was to have a screen test with Paramount in September. She made two calls home for money and painted a picture of her Hollywood life as exciting and happy. But years later she told Madeline of waking up in a park in Los Angeles after an all-night party, not knowing where she was. She spoke to Madeline of being at the mercy of Hollywood directors. She said a girl had to watch out for herself or the directors would just use her and toss her out.

In February or March 1956, Edith Wehmeier received a call from a psychiatric hospital in Big Springs, Texas. Betty had gotten off a bus at Big Springs, possibly on her way back to Cincinnati. She had stolen a taxicab. She did not know her name.

Joe went with his parents to bring Betty back to Ohio. She lived at home while being treated for both schizophrenia and manic depression at Rollman Psychiatric hospital. Betty left Ohio—walked away from home and hospital—the same year her father died, in 1960. Her mother died in 1986 without seeing Betty again.

Around 1962 Betty was admitted to Crownsville Hospital in Maryland. In 1963 she called George Hammann and asked him to help her get out. George, who had had a tempestuous marriage to Betty, refused. During her hospitalization she married a Victor Sherman, for whom she worked as a baby-sitter. The marriage was never dissolved. On December 7, 1964, Betty gave birth to a baby girl, not Victor Sherman's, whom she surrendered for adoption. She named the baby April Lee.

Karen Lee Anderson does not know why at age twenty-five she suddenly felt an urgent need to find her mother. Lee had always known she was adopted, but last February she accidentally discovered her birth certificate and her mother's maiden name. Lee got in touch with Joe, who lives in Lady Lake, Florida. The trail eventually led to New York and upper Broadway. Carrying a recent picture of Betty, Lee walked about, asking "Do you know this woman?" Father O'Connor told her to try Project Reachout.

"We [Lee and two friends] drove up and parked the car. Someone said that the project was at the northeast corner of Eighty-eighth and Amsterdam. But I didn't know New York, and I didn't know which way was northeast. I had a World War II compass, which my father gave me. Funny. In the end I used a compass to find my mother."

When Lee entered the Project Reachout offices, she showed Betty's picture to Madeline. Madeline told her at once that her mother was there, but warned Lee that she could not predict Betty's reaction to the reunion. Before making the introduction, Madeline took Betty aside and spoke with her of the daughter she had given up.

Lee was beckoned into a Plexiglas-walled office. Madeline introduced her to Betty as a visitor who had come a long way to see her. "How ya doin'?" said Betty. Mother and daughter looked much alike. Both wore their hair short, though Lee's was dark. Same apple cheeks, same slant of the eyebrows.

MADELINE: Betty, do you remember that baby's name when you had her twenty-five years ago? [Turning to Lee.] And how old are you?

LEE: I'm twenty-five years old.
MADELINE: Betty, do you remember what you called that baby?
BETTY: I named her April Lee. But she'd be all growed up by now.
MADELINE: Betty, I'd like to introduce you to Lee.
BETTY: Lee?
MADELINE: Yes, this is April Lee.
BETTY: April Lee?
MADELINE: Betty, this is April Lee. Your daughter.
BETTY: April Lee?
LEE: Yes, I'm April Lee. It's me.
MADELINE: She's been looking for you for a very long time, Betty. She's been worried about you. [Betty starts crying.] It's OK to cry, Betty. It's OK.
LEE: You're a hard person to find. [Betty laughs.]

Three days after her reunion with Lee, Betty participated in a round-table discussion at The Other Place, a part of Project Reachout that provides social activities for the clients. People were asked to tell about the most interesting or important event that ever happened to them. One woman told of the time she met Eartha Kitt. Another said it was when she met two girls in grade school who had exactly the same name as her own.

When asked what was the most interesting or important event that ever happened to her, Betty said she couldn't think of a thing.

Betty died in her sleep on April 26 of heart failure. Less than a month earlier she suddenly started crying. "Someone is in my cloud and is trying to kill me," she said. The next day she felt better: "I met this voodoo doctor in the grocery and he operated on my nose so I could breathe again." A couple of days before her death, Betty said she was already dead, that she was working in a beauty parlor for dead people and was doing their hair.

"It isn't fair," said Lee when she was told the news. Later, however, she spoke of her good fortune in discovering her mother. Lee and Joe were amazed at the kindness of Betty's friends among the homeless. "These are real people," said Joe. Lee said, "There are no insignificant lives."

A small man in a stained gray suit, who looks like Edward G. Robinson, stands outside Weber's these days in Betty's old spot. He panhandles in a low, almost inaudible voice. People hurry by deliberately, not wishing to deal with the question of whether or not they should give the man money. Others simply do not seem to see him. That's the way it goes with America's homeless. People are afraid of them, sometimes with good reason. Or they shun them out of an inner rage that this national blight, or this national disgrace, depending on one's point of view, has yet to be remedied.

The people walk by quickly and the homeless stand still as trees. When one learns of stories like those of the clients in Project Reachout, it is interesting to think how very close are the people who stand still to the ones who rush past. One day Betty Wehmeier or the millionaire's secretary or the architect or the doctor were the people who moved briskly and purposefully on New York's sidewalks. Then something terrible happened to them. The next day they were just standing on the sidewalks, murmuring or singing.

On the benches of upper Broadway, homeless people sit apart from one another. A black man sprawls out in a white down parka. No matter how hot it is—on a Sunday in June the temperature is in the high seventies—the homeless usually dress for winter. A small black woman wears a brown fake fur coat and a purple kerchief tied about her head. In one hand she holds a piece of French bread, in the other a chunk of butter. She butters her bread in a continuous graceful motion, and eats.

On the bench that once was Betty's, a white man with a wizened face stares forward intently, as if he has just heard a dangerous sound. He's taken off his shoes and rolled his cuffs to the knees. He sports high turquoise socks that gleam in the sunlight.

Betty's memorial service was held at the Church of the Blessed Sacrament, just down the street from Betty's bench. Over thirty homeless people who knew Betty came to the service in the dark, high-vaulted church. The mourners were scattered on the brown wooden benches. Many came from Project Reachout, including Madeline and Diane Sonde, the director of the project, and Gary Heckelman, who directs The Other Place. Lee and Joe were there. Many people spoke.

A tall black woman told of how Betty used to brighten up her day.

A man with a ponytail played the flute.

Manuel Macarrulla, Betty's caseworker at The Other Place, quoted from a friend's letter: "We do not lament the earthly passing of someone who lived gloriously." Manuel said Betty's glory lay in her sweetness.

A Cuban man speaking only Spanish approached the lectern with a woman at his side. The woman translated his wish that Betty find peace.

An older white man sang "Missing You." Father O'Connor read a prayer. Lee thanked everyone for coming.

Betty's voice, too, was heard at the memorial. With Manuel's help, Betty had made a tape recording of her singing a few weeks earlier. On the tape she sang what she called her bebop version of "What a Friend We Have in Jesus." Her voice hit every note squarely, with only the slightest rush of breathiness. She was equally strong on another number that echoed in the church with a country-and-western lilt:

> I'd rather die young
> Than grow old all alone.
> Please tell me you love me;
> Let me call you my own.
> To see someone's picture
> Where my picture hung,
> Believe me, my darling,
> I'd rather die young.

July 1990

The Quality of Mercy Killing

❦

Iₚ ɪᴛ ᴡᴇʀᴇ only a matter of law, the public would not feel
stranded. He killed her, after all. Roswell Gilbert, a seventy-six-
year-old retired electronics engineer living in a seaside condominium
in Fort Lauderdale, Florida, considered murdering his wife, Emily,
for at least a month before shooting her through the head with a
Luger as she sat on their couch. The Gilberts had been husband and
wife for fifty-one years. They were married in 1934, the year after
Calvin Coolidge died, the year after Prohibition was lifted, the year
that Hank Aaron was born. At seventy-three, Emily had Alzheimer's
disease and osteoporosis; her spinal column was gradually collapsing.
Roswell would not allow her to continue life as "a suffering animal,"
so he committed what is called a mercy killing. The jury saw only the
killing; they felt Gilbert had mercy on himself. He was sentenced to
twenty-five years with no chance of parole, which would make him
101 by the time he got out. The governor has been asked to grant
clemency. Most Floridians polled hope that Gilbert will go free.

Not that there ever was much of a legal or practical question
involved. Imagine the precedent set by freeing a killer simply because
he killed for love. Othello killed for love, though his passion was
loaded with a different motive. Does any feeling count, or is kindness

alone an excuse for murder? Or age: Maybe someone has to be seventy-six and married fifty-one years to establish his sincerity. There are an awful lot of old people and long marriages in Florida. A lot of Alzheimer's disease and osteoporosis as well. Let Gilbert loose, the fear is, and watch the run on Lugers.

Besides, the matter of mercy killing is getting rough and out of hand. Nobody seems to use poison anymore. In Fort Lauderdale two years ago, a seventy-nine-year-old man shot his sixty-two-year-old wife in the stairwell of a hospital; like Emily Gilbert, she was suffering from Alzheimer's disease. In San Antonio four years ago, a sixty-nine-year-old man shot his seventy-two-year-old brother to death in a nursing home. Last June a man in Miami put two bullets in the heart of his three-year-old daughter who lay comatose after a freak accident. An organization that studies mercy killings says that nine have occurred this year alone. You cannot have a murder every time someone feels sorry for a loved one in pain. Any fool knows that.

Yet you also feel foolish watching a case like Gilbert's (if any case can be said to be like another) because, while both feet are planted firmly on the side of law and common sense, both are firmly planted on Gilbert's side as well. The place the public really stands is nowhere: How can an act be equally destructive of society and wholly human? The reason anyone would consider going easy on Gilbert is that we can put ourselves in his shoes, can sit at his wife's bedside day after day, watching the Florida sun gild the furniture and listening to the Atlantic lick the beach like a cat. Emily dozes. He looks at her in a rare peaceful pose and is grateful for the quiet.

Or he dreams back to when such a scene would have been unimaginable: she, sharp as a tack, getting the better of him in an argument; he, strong as a bull, showing off by swinging her into the air—on a beach, perhaps, like the one in front of the condominium where old couples like themselves walk in careful slow motion at the water's edge. Since the case became a cause, photographs of the Gilbert's have appeared on television, she in a formal gown, he in tails; they, older, in a restaurant posing deadpan for a picture for no reason, the way people do in restaurants. In a way the issue here *is* age: mind and body falling away like slabs of sand off a beach cliff. If biology declares war, have people no right to a preemptive strike? In the apartment he continues to stare at her who, from time to time, still believes they are traveling together in Spain.

Now he wonders about love. He loves his wife; he tells her so; he has told her so for fifty-one years. And he thinks of what he meant by that: her understanding of him, her understanding of others, her sense of fun. Illness has replaced those qualities in her with screams and a face of panic. Does he love her still? Of course, he says; he hates the disease, but he loves his wife. Or—and this seems hard—does he only love what he remembers of Emily? Is the frail doll in the bed an impostor? But no; this is Emily too, the same old Emily hidden somewhere under the decaying cells and in the folds of the painkillers. It is Emily and she is suffering and he swore he would always look after her.

He considers an irony: You always hurt the one you love. By what act or nonact would he be hurting his wife more? He remembers news stories he has read of distraught people in similar positions, pulling the plugs on sons and husbands or assisting in the suicides of desperate friends. He sympathizes, but with a purpose; he too is interested in precedents. Surely, he concludes, morality swings both ways here. What is moral for the group cannot always be moral for the individual, or there would be no individuality, no exceptions, even if the exceptions only prove the rule. Let the people have their rules. What harm would it do history to relieve Emily's pain? A little harm, perhaps, no more than that.

This is what we see in the Gilbert case, the fusion of our lives with theirs in one grand and pathetic cliché in which all lives look pretty much alike. We go round and round with Gilbert: Gilbert suddenly wondering if Emily might get better, if one of those white-coated geniuses will come up with a cure. Gilbert realizing that once Emily is gone, he will go too, since her way of life, however wretched, was their way of life. He is afraid for them both. In *The Merchant of Venice* Portia says that mercy is "twice blessed;/ It blesses him that gives and him that takes." The murder committed, Gilbert does not feel blessed. At best, he feels he did right, which the outer world agrees with and denies.

Laws are unlikely to be changed by such cases: for every modification one can think of, there are too many loopholes and snares. What Gilbert did in fact erodes the whole basis of law, which is to keep people humane and civilized. Yet Gilbert was humane, civilized, and wrong: a riddle. In the end we want the law intact and Gilbert free, so that society wins on both counts. What the case proves, however, is that society is helpless to do anything for Gilbert, for Emily, or for itself. All we can do is recognize a real tragedy when we see one, and wonder, perhaps, if one bright morning in 1934 Gilbert read of a mercy killing in the papers, leaned earnestly across the breakfast table, and told his new bride: "I couldn't do that. I could never do that."

August 26, 1985

They Do

〜❧〜

O. BLUSHING BRIDE, daughter of Mr. and Mrs. Parents of the
Bride, of Newport, Rhode Island, and Charleston, South Car-
olina, was married yesterday to Handsome Groom III, son of Mr.
Father of the Groom, of Boston and Maine, and Mrs. Mother of the
Groom, of Baltimore and Ohio. The ceremony was performed in All
Purpose Church by the rector, Canon Dearly Beloved. Miss Sister was
the maid of honor; Mr. Brother, the best man. The bride, who made
her debut at the Desperado Cotillion, is an alumna of Small College.
The bridegroom, a graduate of Large Eastern University, is with
Substantial National Bank. The couple will reside in Bliss.

Or so it reads.

Yet now he rails at her for mispronouncing Trinitron. And she
throws a raving fit in the Kmart, of all places, because he waltzed in
late last night and spilled rye on the Cuisinart. He fingers the latest
Oui.

That, of course, comes long after the stripping of the wallpaper,
the staining of the floors, the exposure of the beams. *When those
beams are all exposed, we're going to have some joint here, I'll tell
you that. Look at those beams. Did you ever see such beams?*

Of the six marriages announced on page 83 of the Sunday paper,

2.2 will fail, 2.3 will last, 1.5 will fail and last. The lovely faces fill their squares; young women with clear, glinting eyes and miraculous teeth. *Miraculous, nothing; cost us a mint to get those teeth in line; when she was twelve, we thought she'd wind up marrying Bugs Bunny, ha ha.* Ah, Bradford Bachrach, you catch them in the pink. These are action shots, are they not? The ball at the crack of the bat; the sail just full; the trout in a pirouette, all splash and color. You sports photographer, you.

I wonder why you don't shoot the men for these announcements. Surely the men are hopeful, too; and was it not said of Handsome Groom mere hours ago that he was the luckiest man alive? Or is it presumed that only women get married, that marriage befalls only the one who wears the ivory *peau de soie* and coddles baby's breath, like a baby's breath, in her fragile arms? The man, Bachrach. You forgot the man. You forgot the *truth,* you wedding announcers, with all your Rye Country Day School and Chemical Corn. Call this responsible journalism?

The truth is that Blushing's folks did not, when it comes down to it, really "announce" the engagement of their daughter; they could barely spit out the words, so abashed were they that their little girl should throw herself away on a wimp like Groom. The truth is that Handsome's dad said the boy was marrying beneath him. The truth is that Sister is sick with envy, and Brother red with hate. The truth is that no one thinks it will work.

> Do you, Blushing?
> I do.
> Do you, Handsome?
> Oh, very much.

(While Johns Updike and Cheever, like cormorants on cliffs, watch every move.)

Go to it anyway, Bride and Groom. Damn the statistics. Full speed, deliberate speed. Strip that wallpaper, expose those beams, expose those hearts. There is no good reason on earth that you should reside happily ever after. At the same time, there is no good reason you should not. And, if the truth is that your goose is cooked at the altar, then the truth can be made wrong too, you know; can be made to look like a dope in a single, spur-of-the-moment decision to be gentle and patient—against the jeering numbers and the hoots outside. Are you game, or "Just Married"?

In the morning, in the Plaza, the two of them prop the paper up in bed against their knees. Between the melon and the sweet rolls, they agree she photographs beautifully.

November 26, 1979

The
Kitchens'
Kitchen

D ELICIOUS, ISN'T SHE," sighs Oleg Kitchen, as he observes his wife from his perch atop the wicker stool beside the garlic press, his celery green Marimekko trousers and tie-dyed T-shirt lending him more the appearance of a young Greek sailor than of the fifty-five-year-old chief of psychiatric services he is or, rather, was, until he "chucked it all" for the "very special, very private" life now shared with Frigga Kitchen. She, doused in sunlight from the kitchen skylight, hums a Finnish folk song as she beheads a red snapper— "You cannot find this outside the Bahia"—in preparation for the evening's *peixada*. "The kitchen is our life," Oleg continues. "All we have is here."

Which, from the looks of some 400 square feet of polished blond wood floors and tables, the blond wood jars and spoons, the blond wood butcher blocks and blond wood beams, from which hangs "perhaps the most comprehensive aspic mold collection in the East," is plenty. "We make our own napkins," adds Frigga. "And our own salt." She has gracefully sidled over to a bowl marked Zuppa Inglese. Her hair, the color of blond wood, is garnished with a sprig of thyme.

This remarkable kitchen almost fills the entire house of the Kitchens, who have "ruthlessly brushed aside" the original walls of their eighteenth-century saltbox to make room for what they call "our shrine to cooking, eating, and mutual respect." No longer regarding the living room as the center of the home, they have simply done without it, as they also have done without a library and even a dining room. "They are not separate things, the preparation and consumption," Oleg states emphatically, barely missing the Salton yogurt-maker with his fist. "Why have separate places for them? As for the living room"—he gestures expansively with a paring knife as he starts to stuff the *tufoli*—"that was the old life" (a veiled reference, we believe, to his six former marriages). "This is freedom."

"And honesty," Frigga adds quietly, leafing through her copy of *Cold Cuts of the Arctic*.

"Honesty above all," Oleg agrees, tenderly lowering a deveined shrimp into the mouth of the former Finnair hostess and industrial spy.

The Kitchens have made their new home in the heart of sumptuous Kitchen Synchs, the recently developed "total community" near Rye, New York. Everyone within the community is recently remarried—"reborn really"—Oleg tells us; is also a gourmet chef; and has been the subject of at least one life-at-home article in a newspaper or magazine. The residents take great pride in their kitchens, and make a point of dropping in on one another once or twice a day to compliment some goody simmering on the stove. As we are admiring the Belgian wire whisk that Frigga swears was once the property of Paul Bocuse, a neighboring couple, Art and Haute Cuisine, who look astonishingly like the Kitchens themselves, stop by in tears to report the theft of a pair of tarragon driers they had lucked into in Barcelona. And there is much saddened head-shaking over the fact that theft is not unknown in Kitchen Synchs.

"You see," Frigga explains after the Cuisines have departed, seriously shaken, "there is nothing else of real value in a place like this. To us the kitchen is not merely functional; it is [here she flounders in Finnish until Oleg provides, "spiritual"]. Exactly so," Frigga continues, "spiritual. That is why Oleg and I do everything in the kitchen, why we rarely leave, for any reason."

At that we chuckle, and ask teasingly if they sleep in the kitchen, too.

"But of course," they answer as one, to our delighted surprise. Oleg indicates several bright pots scattered on hot trays about the room. "Some of these dishes take days to prepare. You don't want to let them out of your sight for a minute."

Yet Frigga shakes an apple corer scoldingly at her husband. "Tell the truth, Oleg. It's not because we really need to watch the pots that we live in the kitchen. It's because we love each other, and we love the kitchen. Is that not so?" Whereupon Oleg hurls aside the colander, nearly toppling La Machine, and sweeps his wife into his arms as if she were a freshly baked scone. "You are right, my beet, as usual," he says. And they do a little two-step, which they call the dance of the shucked oysters, leaving us to wonder aloud if such a pair could ever become bored.

"Bored?" asks Oleg.

"Bored?" asks Frigga.

They laugh like sparkling water from the center of the earth.

October 15, 1979

The
Roy Rogers
Family
Restaurant

E VERY FOURTH OR FIFTH Sunday our children persuade my
wife and me to lead them to the Roy Rogers Family Restaurant.
This does not represent a pattern of defeat. We used to take similar
trips to McDonald's, which are more dangerous than the Roy Rogers
Family Restaurant because of their numbers. I remember driving
through towns so small that they had abandoned electricity, only to
round an apparently innocent corner and confront those great golden
arches, albeit lit by candles. The children would exclaim; my wife
would touch me gently on the shoulder; and in I would turn, ready
for the warmth of a Big Shake over my lap. Even the car trembled.

Those days are gone forever. I put my foot down after a crop of
quasi-analytical articles on McDonald's began to appear in national
magazines, and a popular song was made of the McDonald's jingle.
Then I began to realize that with every bite of a Big Mac or Tripple
Ripple [sic], I was complicit in a cultural conspiracy. I could not offer
this reasoning to my children, for fear of sounding antidemocratic.
Instead I said that I would no longer tolerate McDonald's because I
would no longer tolerate eating in the car. So much for tact. Within
days of my announcement, my family had discovered the Roy Rogers
Family Restaurant, equipped with enough tables and chairs (barrels)
for the whole wide world.

In fact it is the whole wide world that the Roy Rogers Family Restaurant claims as its province. Not alone in this ambition, it is aided by places such as Gino's, Pizza Hut, Arthur Treacher's, Burger King, Burger Chef, and of course McDonald's as well, now functioning as muse of the conspiracy, all of which, as if you hadn't noticed, have plundered every major suburb in America, and are currently heading for the cities on the airport roads. I mean this not as a call to arms; we have long ago lost the Battle of Beautiful Things. There is a quieter war in the works.

As a grown-up with grown-up's stature, I ought to bring sweat and terror to the Roy Rogers Family Restaurant every time I set my boot in the door. The professionally radiant cowgirls in their paper Stetsons and plastic cinch belts ought to stampede like strippers in a raid when I show up. The Muzak ought to stop cold. The amber-colored french fries and chicken legs ought to crash to the floor. That none of this happens, that instead the cowgirls seem to smile victoriously at my appearance, emblemizes the situation. Every time I bring my family over their "family" threshold, they whittle another notch.

The reason the word *family* is affixed to the franchise is the same reason that certain movies are designated family entertainment, certain TV programs family shows, and a recent publication, a family magazine. The idea is that the family as a unit is a low culture group. People will tell us that the "family" tag is simply meant to keep smut out of this kitchen, but this is disingenuous. A good French restaurant is never called a family restaurant. *King Lear* is not a family show. At the same time, it is conceded that *King Lear* and a good French restaurant are better, if more complicated, than family shows and family restaurants, thus implying that the American family seeks, perhaps deserves, something worse.

The Roy Rogers Family Restaurant is not a bad restaurant at all. In fact it is a good, solid, and safe restaurant. At least the food is solid. The building itself is made only to look solid, like all the other eating places of the recent blitz, with imitation fences, hand-hewn beams, pegs, barrels, wagon wheels, and brick. For protection there is an imitation Kentucky rifle on the wall, next to the imitation Confederate dollar. One of the curiosities of places like Roy Rogers and Gino's is that although they pop up overnight, their architects insist that the buildings look weathered and antique. Believers in irony, they assume that we only trust old things if they were stapled together yesterday.

But the food is sound and digestible. There is nothing wrong with it. There is nothing wrong with any aspect of the Roy Rogers Family

Restaurant, except the clatter, and the ominous poster: "Fly with the crows; get shot with the crows." There is something a little troubling about the decorators' preoccupation with the Confederate Army. There is something strange about the tiny American flag planted in the hamburgers. There is something stranger about Roy Rogers himself, who, when his horse Trigger died, had the animal stuffed. Such things do not bother the hordes of customers, however. The Roy Rogers Family Restaurant is their kind of place, they are told. A bit of the old frontier, right close to the Exxon station, where everybody says please and thank you, and no words are discouraging.

Roy Rogers costs less than most eating places, which is admirable. Its planners realized that most customers cannot afford expensive meals, particularly if four or five mouths are watering. Theoretically they also envisaged a majority of children at the tables, yet children are far outnumbered by working people at weekday lunch and by late-night snackers. Thus the restaurant while nominally devoted to a figure and ambience associated with childhood, is actually a place for grown-ups: grown-ups who think of themselves as family oriented, and grown-ups in the company of families. Grown-ups are in fact the only people in the place (including the sixteen-year-old cowgirls) who remember who Roy Rogers, Dale, Nelly-Belle, and Bullet were, and that "dern tootin'" (on another sign) was Pat Buttram's way of expressing himself.

Since this is so, items on the menu such as the Double-R-Bar-Burger and a Holster of Fries, that would seem designed for the little ones are instead meant to be spoken by the big. Daddy has liquid amusement in his voice when he asks for the "Hamburger Fixin's," yet the menu was written for him. The restaurant has thus provided him with three things: an excuse for a cheap meal in the name of nostalgia or of pleasing the children; a chance to appear fully grown in a context where he may smugly mock childhood; and childhood itself, a brief adventure backwards.

Such an adventure is precisely what the Roy Rogers people wish us to take, a fear-free adventure for the American middle class on happy trails where there are no headwaiters or other status intimidations. Just cowgirls, pardner, saying "howdy, pardner." There is no reason why a cowgirl serving food should seem saner or more natural than a man in a tux. It is simply that the cowgirl condescends to our fears, while the man in the tux deliberately aggravates them.

Like all successful businesses, the Roy Rogers Family Restaurant profits by its presumptions about people. Its main presumption is that

Americans would rather be conned quietly than openly demoralized (a thought verified by Franklin, Melville, and Twain). This accounts for that victory grin on the cowgirls' faces, both the accuracy of the presumption and the con itself. I, nearly twenty-first century, urbanized Eastern man, walk into the fake Old West restaurant with my highfalutin ways, sidle up to the counter real gentlemanlike, and ask for a Holster of Fries—not for me, you understand, for the family. In a way the Roy Rogers Family Restaurant is a work of genius; it makes a fool of you in the name of the institution it purports to celebrate.

That institution, the American family, is not well thought of generally, if its representations in popular media are to be trusted. Television in particular has had much to say about the American family since the days of *Life with Father* and *The Stu Erwin Show,* namely that the American family is stupid, and stupider in aggregate than any single member. The abilities of TV families to deal calmly and sensibly with anything is in inverse proportion to their numbers, making the recent Brady Bunch (of eight) the stupidest to date. Yet there is also safety in numbers. We allow these groups to fumble through their driving lessons and high school proms without criticism because we realize that we are not watching families of man at all, but fictional bumpkins with several heads.

I believe that the inventors of the Roy Rogers Family Restaurant have watched television carefully over the years. In their imaginations and calculations have marched the Andersons, the Nelsons, the Flintstones, the Rileys, the Danny Williamses, and others. But the Roy Rogers people did not envisage these families on television solving more problems. They saw them instead piling into the car, driving up Wisconsin Avenue, pulling into the parking lot, and bounding in the door. They even saw the old man, reluctant, fidgety, complaining about cultural conspiracies while simultaneously playing grown-up to himself and his kids. And they saw him coming back Sunday after Sunday. (Help.)

September 13, 1975

New Year's at Luchow's

L UCHOW'S is a famous old German restaurant in downtown
New York, situated just about where Irving Place and Fourteenth Street make a T. It's a bustling spot all year long, but especially
so at Christmastime, when the proprietors prop up a huge Christmas
tree for all to ogle, and a hefty group called the "Oom Pah Band"
toots "O Tannenbaum" as the customers sing. Diamond Jim Brady
proposed to Lillian Russell in Luchow's, offering her a suitcase filled
with one million dollars if she'd consent. (She didn't.) That's the kind
of place Luchow's was, and still is, as far as I know.

My parents used to take my brother and me to Luchow's every so
often, even though my father suspected the restaurant of having been
a Nazi hangout during the war. There we went, nevertheless, to stuff
our faces and gape at celebrities. I saw Jackie Gleason there once,
looking like the comics' Little King, leading a retinue including Jack
Lescoulie, of mellow memory, among the crowded tables. That was
not on New Year's Day. My family never went anywhere on New
Year's Day, though for two years running my brother and I, while
never going anywhere, still managed to spend the day at Luchow's.

You see, when my brother was in high school, he acquired his own
telephone, the number of which was but one digit removed from that

of the German eatery. At first he was annoyed by this coincidence, as calls for Luchow's and calls for my brother came in at a ratio of twenty to one. So, eventually tiring of the phrase "Wrong number," he began to accept a few reservations. This was a cruel prank, to be sure, but partly justified in his, and later my own, mind for our being on the receiving rather than the phoning end of the calls.

Returning from graduate school one Christmas vacation, I was delighted to discover my brother's new enterprise, and immediately joined his restaurant business with all the high spirits of the season. Embellishing his practice of taking reservations straight, I would ask—whenever someone called requesting a table for eight, for example—if the caller also wanted chairs. In no instance, and there were dozens, did the reservation makers treat my question as odd. As long as they thought they had Luchow's on the phone, everything was jake.

During spring vacation we adorned our business further by adding a touch of professionalism. Because of frequent requests for the Luchow's headwaiter, we learned that the man's name was Julius, which my brother, for reasons of his own, insisted on pronouncing as Hoolio, and which name he adopted whenever a call came in. I would answer the phone, and transfer the call to Hoolio, who would do most of the talking in a Spanish-German accent so difficult to penetrate that requests for tables, and chairs, often took ten minutes.

We then began to push things a bit, in part to test the limits of human credulity. We asked people if they wished to be seated in the Himmler Room, or if they wanted to try our special "Luftwaffles" instead of rolls. We asked them if they would care to try Luchow's "blitzes." These, we explained, were blintzes dropped onto one's plate from a great height. There were long pauses at the other end of the line when we would ask such things, but the answers, when they arrived, were always polite and sincere. Once we asked a fellow if he'd mind taking a table for three instead of four—one of his party could eat elsewhere, and they could all regroup for coffee. He declined our suggestion, but considered it.

Our best customers were big shots who presumed a favored relationship with the restaurant. These customers made their reservations in barks: "Julius. Mr. Van Kamp. For two. Tonight. Good." Whenever Hoolio would hear such talk, he would warm up the tone immediately, keeping Van Kemp on the line for interminable periods, as he, Hoolio, confessed his deepest, most intimate problems to his personal customer. After a while, Hoolio would lead around to the fact that he was broke. Perhaps Mr. Van Kamp could see fit to make Hoolio a gift of $500 as a token of their long friendship. No? In that case there was no table for Van Kamp.

As these transactions continued over the summer, my brother and I became more than a little ashamed at the havoc we thought we were causing. (In fact, the havoc was minimal, because we'd usually crack up toward the end of our conversations, thus blowing the ruse.) We did not stop altogether, however, until the following Christmas vacation, when we started asking people if they would mind being seated on the roof, where we had set up a cold buffet, card tables, and paper plates. This was late December, and the temperatures in New York often fell below zero, when it wasn't snowing. Still, there were one or two takers for our rooftop seats—though that was not the event that persuaded us to give up the restaurant business.

That event occurred on New Year's Day itself—this very day, thirteen years ago—when a sugar-voiced lady phoned in the morning to cancel a reservation for lunch. Hoolio was furious. How were we supposed to run a restaurant—he told her—if everyone called up to cancel reservations? No, madam, it was impossible. Under no circumstances could we accept her cancellation.

When the woman apologized and started to change her mind, we knew it was time to close shop.

January 1, 1979

Christmas
in a
Small Place

C LIMBING OVER the fence was strictly forbidden, but I can tell
you how it was done. Stand facing either the east or west gate
(the method worked for both). Place your left foot between the
wrought-iron bars directly over the lock, pull yourself up by holding
the topmost spikes firmly with both hands, swing your right foot into
one of the iron rings at the top of the gate, bring your left leg up and
around, and you're home. That's all there was to it, in terms of the
how. As for the *why,* I am not sure why the neighborhood kids
bothered to learn to climb the fence, since our parents, as local
residents, had keys to Gramercy Park. Maybe it was our way of
pretending to be like other kids in less protected neighborhoods of
New York, an unconscious gesture of expiation for the sin of growing
up in so privileged a place.

The park superintendent has made life difficult for today's fence
climbers by placing metal screening on the gates in the open space
above the locks. But little else has changed in Gramercy Park in the
past twenty-five years. The once titillating statue of the half-naked
woman (or goddess or whatever she was) at the east end of the park
has been painted dark (she was gold and white in different eras). One
of the massive elms has died. Yet the grassy areas are as they were—

four neat lawns cut in the shape of piano tops, on which no ballplaying is permitted. The gravel paths are the same, as are the benches, set at proper distances from one another to combine privacy with friendliness. Outside the park, the houses look pretty much the same as well. And the feeling of the neighborhood persists. People who have known each other for years pause on the sidewalks to chat. The cleaners and the shoe shop do not need to hand out claim checks. Dogs are greeted by name. Babies abound. Eccentrics have positions of honor.

The celebration of Christmas in Gramercy Park seems exactly as it was. Every December the Gramercy Neighborhood Associates hoist a tree on the south side of the park. A party is thrown for all the neighborhood at the National Arts Club. Clothing and toys are collected for the poor. Apartment house entrances are decorated with wreaths and lights. On Christmas Eve, the residents come together in the park around the tree, while a man with a portable organ leads them in bellowing carols against the night.

Typical small-town America? Yes and no. Gramercy Park is a bit too comfortable to be considered typical, and it has distinguishing characteristics one would not find in most small towns. An artistic tradition, for one thing. Over the 150 years of its existence the area has been home to William Dean Howells, Henry James, Edith Wharton, Horace Greeley. Herman Melville lived out his life here, embittered by the public's dismissal of *Moby-Dick*. Stephen Crane finished *The Red Badge of Courage* in his place on Twenty-third Street. Nathanael West, author of *The Day of the Locust,* worked as night manager in the Kenmore Hotel nearby. He used to sneak pals of his into the hotel, including Dashiell Hammett, who was working on *The Maltese Falcon* at the time.

John Barrymore lived in the building I grew up in, No. 36, the white one with the stonework gingerbread facade and the visored knights out front. Edwin Booth, whose statue still plays Hamlet in the center of the park, had a house remodeled by Stanford White to serve as the Players, a club for actors. When I was ten, I once waved to Charles Coburn as he emerged from the Players, and he waved back. The park's most mentioned artist-in-residence was William Sydney Porter, known as O. Henry, who lived on Irving Place and used to drink at Healy's Café, now Pete's Tavern, and still on Eighteenth Street. One of the rare continuing neighborhood disputes concerns O. Henry. The people at Pete's claim that he wrote "The Gift of the Magi" in a booth there. A plaque at Sal Anthony's a restaurant on the site of O. Henry's home, half a block from Pete's, insists that he composed the story in "two feverish hours" sitting in his wide front window—writing of the wife who sells her beautiful hair at Christmastime in order to buy a watch fob for her husband, who sells his watch in order to buy *her* a pair of combs.

The main difference between Gramercy Park and other American small towns is that this town is located in the heart of Lower Manhattan. Its character derives from its location. In a sense, the neighborhood serves as a pocket of resistance in the city, a sudden green rectangle cut out of the gray slabs, and away from the taxi horns. Yet the park needs the city, too, the way everyone needs strife to feel alive. When Christmas is celebrated here, life is celebrated, the life of a civilization huddled against itself. Nothing is really special about the people of Gramercy Park, other than that they chose Gramercy Park to live in, choosing one another's company as much as the old trees and pretty houses. Like most people, they behave better than people are generally reputed to behave, proclaiming their value, as O. Henry said of the watch fob in "The Gift of the Magi," "by substance alone and not by meretricious ornamentation."

Fair-minded people. Reserved people. Intelligent but not excessively learned or witty. People you do not notice in a crowd because they try to avoid crowds. In my day they consisted of those like my father, a neighborhood doctor, to whom the kids brought underfed cats and crippled birds, and shy Mr. Platt, who led us around on Halloween, and blind Mr. Chevigny, who wrote of his seeing-eye dog in a best-seller, *My Eyes Have a Cold Nose,* and Mr. Homer, who had a booming Bostonian voice with which he asked every child over the age of six: "When do you plan to enroll at Harvard?" These were the sorts who would gather in the park and sing. Once the caroling was finished, they would not weep or embrace or say sentimental things, but merely nod and shake hands and wish one another well.

I conducted my own small ceremony as a child on Christmas Eve. My window faced the park, and I always waited for the caroling to start before I went downstairs, so that I could, for a few moments, look down from my ninth-floor perch and take it all in—my neighbors, the music, the tree. I think I half-expected something wonderful to happen as I watched, or perhaps I dimly realized that something wonderful was already happening. On those nights, as on every Christmas Eve since they came into being, the man and wife of "The Gift of the Magi" were exchanging their gifts, which turned out to be the gifts of each other. Such is the exchange transacted frequently in this park, in this city, and in more than a few small places in the world.

December 26, 1983

A Christmas Carol

DICKENS MADE US THINK that the third ghost did the trick, but I believe it was the first. Naturally Scrooge was terrified by the image of his future death, just as he was mortified by the promise of its anonymity; after a night of whooping and rattling he was ready to swear to anything; and the prognosis for Tiny Tim undoubtedly touched his heart. Still, what really turned the tide, I think, was the first vision conjured by the Ghost of Christmas Past, the one of Scrooge as a boy sitting at his desk in the near-deserted school at Christmastime. That was Scrooge as we'd hardly known him, as he hardly knew himself, no less lonely than the man he grew into, and certainly no happier; only young.

Christmas Past is the least picturesque of Dickens's spirits. It has none of the fierce boisterousness of the Ghost of Christmas Present, none of the gray dreadfulness of the Ghost of Christmas Yet to Come. A prosaic bear-but-a-touch-of-my-hand ghost, it displays its episodes to Scrooge like a conventional historian, altering nothing, almost never stating the morals of the tales, or recriminations. The past has already happened, so what can a guide say but "there"? And it's a gentle ghost, besides; it doesn't overact like Marley.

Nevertheless it is "a strange figure" that parts Scrooge's bed curtains: "like a child; yet not so like a child as like an old man, viewed through some supernatural medium, which gave him the appearance of having receded from the view, and being diminished to a child's proportions." The ghost embodies time. It knows, as Scrooge learns, that the past is as mysterious as the future, just as out of reach, as imprecise and malleable as the present, and as likely to be falsely seen or spoken for. The past is as wide open as the future too. When the ghost shows young Scrooge to the old it has had to choose carefully. All that immense and jumbled time in the old man's life, but only certain things will affect him. The boy at the desk is the first thing Scrooge sees on his journey, and he is immediately moved to tears.

Of course the sight of oneself as a child is grossly sentimental. Dickens-haters love to trample such scenes and repeat Oscar Wilde's observation that anyone who would not laugh at the death of Little Nell must indeed have a heart of stone. A hurt and lonely child is hard enough to bear, much less when that child is you, before the fall. You want back everything you were, and there you are: able to be hurt, unable to hurt back, unencumbered by your own ill will. As superintendent of such scenes, the Ghost of Christmas Past doesn't need to hoot and holler; there's terror enough in the act—to hurl back all those years and be the future gaping at the past as if it were bright as the future.

This is happening in Scrooge's mind: both the boy at school, and Scrooge looking at the boy. The man reaches for the child and vice versa, though they are reaching for two different things—Scrooge wishing to be young, but not lonely; the child wanting to be old, but not Scrooge. Neither will have it his way, yet Scrooge weeps "to see his poor forgotten self as it used to be." Why? Does he really seek to recover all that punishing innocence?

Perhaps he sees something else in his past, something other than young Scrooge, that he wants back. It could be his imagination, so long held in check, but which, as he recalls, ran wild as a boy. Maybe his imagination is coming back to him tonight for a fling on Christmas Eve—unless you really believe in ghosts. Any mind that could fancy such a journey as Scrooge's can't be all gone. And Scrooge is not hopeless, after all. He has been caricatured by time, but looked at coldly, he is merely a bony Republican—not an honorable calling, but no devil either. Perhaps it is the past itself that reduces Scrooge to tears.

After the visitations Scrooge swears that from now on he will live in the past, present, and future, thus giving equal consideration to each ghost. But in fact Scrooge has always lived in the present and future, essential for "a good man of business"; it was the past that he had neglected, and the dead. "Old Marley was as dead as a door-nail," Dickens tells us in the first paragraph of the story; but how dead is a door-nail? As dead as a door knocker, that's for sure, yet the knocker on Scrooge's door is alive with Marley, and Marley with it. "The wisdom of our ancestors is in the simile," says Dickens. Exactly.

Dickens goes to some lengths to remind us that Marley is dead: "this must be distinctly understood, or nothing wonderful can come of the story." It must be distinctly understood that time past is time present, as Eliot's confused narrator says in *Four Quartets,* that all time is both "eternally present" and "unredeemable." Hamlet must meet his ghost, Scrooge his. Scrooge's nephew tells him that "we are all fellow-passengers to the grave," but occupants of the grave make passage too. Marley fairly shrieks at Scrooge to believe in him.

Marley, as Dickens says straight out, is the key to Scrooge's salvation. The chain he drags has the gift of metaphor; a chain is ponderous when it stands for worldly selfishness, but a chain may also link man to man, man to boy, and the past to the present and future. What do you want with me, Scrooge asks Marley, who answers, "Much." What Marley and Dickens want of Scrooge is nothing short of the awareness of eternity.

The sense of his place in time makes Scrooge weep—more than the sight of his lonely boyhood or the memory of his lost imagination. The boy in school achieves an epiphany in Scrooge's tears because he is not merely the image of one man as one child, but of all mankind deserted. When a connection is made, when Scrooge's sister Fan says that Ebenezer is welcome to come home for Christmas, that he has a home to come to, and a father, Scrooge weeps more deeply. This is the real mystery brought by the Ghost of Christmas Past: that life is bound to life, and that there is a natural order in which a strong life may tend toward a weak one, as Scrooge will finally tend toward Tiny Tim.

So Scrooge goes back in order to go forward, and when finally he goes forward, he goes back, behaving "as a schoolboy" when he discovers on Christmas morning that it is not too late to act on his repentance, that "the Time before him was his own." He says, "I'm quite a baby . . . I'd rather be a baby," which is proper in a season made for children. Then he walks around the city patting heads and questioning beggars, like Marley's ghost "abroad among his fellow-men."

He enjoys Christmas present, and we are assured that from now on he will know how "to keep Christmas well." To keep it is to preserve it as one does the past, not as in a museum case but as it really is—a state of consciousness no deader than a doornail. He knows that for Christmas to be kept in the present, it must be remembered, and when it is remembered as a time of going from loneliness to comfort, of the sudden and necessary revelation of our humanity, then it will be kept well. In time present, Scrooge the munificent strolls through London feeding the hungry and curing the lame. But he also still huddles at his school desk, waiting for a relative to take him home. Eventually he will learn that he is that relative, and weep for the life we share.

December 27, 1975

A Christmas Story

❦

What Sister Geraldine would have visitors understand is that it is not a matter of how much she gives to the people of Sunset Park but how much she gets back. The gift is their lives, she says: They trust us with their lives, and we offer them in return practical things like food and clothing, spiritual things like comfort and encouragement, hope, perhaps; sometimes we give them hope. But oh, what they give to us. Sister Mary Paul actually cried last night to realize how lucky the two of us are to be here. Don't think for a moment that these people are characterized by their poverty. They are wonderful people, wonderful. Maria. Tony and Ingrid. Rose and her six kids living in a car. Even Mallory. Yes, Mallory too, though I know you won't think so. Sure I love them. I'm supposed to love them as part of my vocation. But you can't love someone into life. They do it themselves. The process is slow but continuous. Sunset Park goes on and on. The work we do, it's not like your kind of work, not like most kinds of work, with beginnings, endings, and neat hard lines. It's not like a story.

I Mallory

The darkness has two colors: purple and gray. They float toward each other like ghosts in the hallway of Mallory's basement apartment. The darkness is absolute. Not even the walls are visible, until the door to the kitchen is pushed open and the apartment is cast in a cold silver, late afternoon light admitted through a single kitchen window. Three chairs surround a Formica table standing flush against a wall. The seats of the chairs are torn open, exposing a brown stuffing. Beside one of the kitchen chairs a gas pipe juts straight up three feet where an oven used to be. Mallory explains he has no use for an oven; the hot plate on the sink is more than adequate for Michael and him. Beneath the sink all the drawers of the kitchen cabinet have been pulled out, leaving holes. In an aluminum pie plate on the table, cigarette ashes mix with the remains of a crust. The ceiling is water-stained around a circular fluorescent bulb. The walls are yellow, sallow in the darkening room.

"Why don't you turn on the lights, Mr. Mallory?"

"Saves money." He touches a finger to his forehead to indicate shrewdness. His small dark eyes look both cold and imploring.

"Where does Michael do his homework?"

"Here, at the kitchen table. I turn on the lights at night. Don't need 'em in the day. Don't need heat, either. You feel warm enough, don't you?"

Mallory's apartment has four rooms, but he rents out the front room to a Puerto Rican mother and two children. If that family wants to use the kitchen, or the bathroom at the far end of the kitchen, they must ask Mallory's permission. On the bathroom door Mallory has posted a sign: DO NOT USE UNLESS YOU CLEAN UP AFTER YOURSELF. Of the two other rooms, one belongs to Michael and Michael's mother, Eileen. The other is Mallory's bedroom, nearly filled by a low queen-size bed with an upholstered maroon headboard into which a clock radio has been fitted. Above the headboard on a yellow wall hangs a huge novelty $1,000 bill, with Mallory's face where Grover Cleveland's would be. Beside the bed is a phone with a lock on the dial. "They want to use it," says Mallory, "they have to pay."

The room given to Michael and Eileen is packed like a storage cellar with paint cans, a battered cocktail wagon, a shopping cart, cardboard boxes full of clothing, which serve as Michael's chest of drawers, suitcases, and a single bed resting on remnants of red carpet.

"Michael's mother sleeps there."

"Where does Michael sleep?"

"On the floor under the bed. He likes it there."

"Why doesn't Eileen sleep with you?"

"I won't let her. I don't like her. I keep her here for Michael, but Michael don't like her either."

His reason for keeping Eileen in the house is to ensure that Michael, age seven, will not be taken from him again and given over to a foster home. That has happened three times, when Mallory left Michael alone in the house. Mallory was reported for neglect. He lets Eileen stay to make it appear as if the boy has a stable home, even though Mallory calls Eileen a bad mother, who will run off with anybody anytime. He cared for her once, he says, but now he cares only for Michael. He will buy Michael a bike for Christmas.

"He can read at a fourth-grade level." Mallory looks pleased again. "I taught him myself, by my own special method. If he don't know a word, I make him write it ten times. I make him read a book every night, until he's got it. I've been doing this for years. But Michael's teachers tell me not to teach him."

"Because of your method?"

"Yeah. It upsets what they teach."

"Does Michael find the two methods confusing?"

"No. He learns both ways. It's better. It's power." Mallory falls into a coughing spasm. He's had the flu for weeks, he says. At his job working as a messenger for the city government, they think that he is shirking. They want to fire him, says Mallory. But they won't get away with it. "Look at this." He produces an official letter of complaint from his employers, several pages of grievances, ranging from laziness to insubordination to petty thievery to poor hygiene and unkempt appearance. "They think they'll throw me out, but I've got a union lawyer. Let 'em try."

"Why did you seek help for Michael?"

"He gets into trouble at school. He fights a lot. It's his mother's fault. He don't have a mother, really. He's frustrated." Mallory looks troubled, puzzled. He is forty-eight, stubble bearded, but he has the face of a fearful child. "I'd like to get married." He grins. "I'm sort of playing the field."

The doorbell rings, and Mallory admits two tall black men delivering a huge brown, metal free-standing closet. They struggle to angle the closet through the darkened hallway to place it in Michael and Eileen's room. Mallory's plan is to rip out built-in drawers in the hallway, and thus widen it into a dining room. The immediate effect of the alteration is to make Michael's room impossible to enter. Mallory touches his head again. "Smart, right?"

Michael enters with Eileen. This is Veterans Day: no school. Ordinarily Michael would be in a therapy session at the Center for Family Life, an institution run by Sisters Geraldine and Mary Paul for the welfare of Sunset Park. Michael half-skips, half-struts into the kitchen, where, the afternoon gone, Mallory has finally turned on the fluorescent bulb, filling the room with fierce pink light. Eileen follows, wearing jeans and a denim jacket. She is slim and pretty, with the raw look of a teenage boy.

"You can tell that's Michael's mother," says Mallory.

"Everyone says that Michael looks like me," says Eileen.

"No. He looks like me." Mallory is amused at his joke.

"He has your nose." Eileen laughs. "That's all he has."

"He has my intelligence," says Mallory.

"I'm not talking about that. I'm talking about features. He has my feet, my hands, the color of my skin when I was a kid."

"All ugly." Mallory chuckles.

"All *ugly*? I'll punch you one, all ugly. Then why is he so beautiful?"

Mallory places a book in Michael's hands. "Read for the man, Michael." The boy rests the book on the kitchen table and stands before it, pronouncing each word as if it existed alone.

"Sam the Slug had eaten a pink petunia leaf. Night was almost over. He had time for one last bit."

"Bite." Mallory corrects his son.

"He had time for one last bite," says Michael. He continues: "Sam yawned and chewed happily. How wonderful to be a slug."

"Do you know what a petunia is, Michael?" Michael eyes the stranger.

"No." He is shown a picture of the flower next to the story.

"Do you know what a slug is?"

Again he says, "No."

"Read the page over," says Mallory. Michael starts to read more rapidly this time. His arms flap at his side like a panicked bird. But he reads the page without a hitch and looks up for approval.

"See?" says Mallory. "What did I tell you? Smart."

II   Geraldine and Sunset Park

"First, let's see the awning." Sister Geraldine squirms with anticipation in the seat beside the driver. "They just put up a new awning on the thrift shop. There. There it is." She points to a skirt-shaped burgundy awning over a doorway on Sunset Park's Fifth Avenue, the neighborhood's main shopping area. On the awning in white lettering is inscribed CENTER FOR FAMILY LIFE THRIFT SHOP. "Doesn't it look great?"

"Just like a cute boutique on Madison Avenue."

"Oh no! Do you think so? Do you think it looks too fancy for a thrift shop?" She pouts, considers, concludes that she is being teased. "It doesn't. It looks absolutely perfect."

On a bright blue afternoon the shops along Fifth Avenue spill their goods on racks onto the sidewalk, as if the shops' interiors had burst open, overstuffed. In front of a hardware store, toilet seats hang displayed like tropical leaves: lavender, pink, green, purple, yellow. A yellow seat shows a painting of a naked couple kissing in silhouette. In front of another store are racks of sweatshirts, slacks, bright-colored T-shirts. Another presents bins of Christmas lights, sandals, bogus Cabbage Patch dolls, a heap of green plastic ice buckets made in the shape of apples.

Up and down the avenue lies the history of the neighborhood, of New York, of much of the nation. In the window of a drugstore that looks preserved from the 1940s, boxes of Whitman's Samplers, chocolates, are stacked beside a cardboard cutout of a vanilla ice-cream soda. Down the avenue: a pizzeria, Ryan's bar, the Klassy Klothes Boutique. One restaurant seeks at least two populations: Comidas China Latinas y Szechuans. A clothing store, "For Latinos," shows its original name, Glass and Lieberman, embossed in the sidewalk. On other streets, other identifications: German, Polish, Korean, Finnish, Norwegian. The Scandinavians are the neighborhood elders, vestiges of the time up through World War II when Sunset Park's harbor bulged with freighters and warships.

"Half the neighborhood is Hispanic. Most of those who come to the center are Hispanic, but by no means all. Mallory is Irish, of course. Every nationality we work with has its special troubles on top of the general human variety." Geraldine (Italian) indicates the scope of her purview with a sweep of her arm. "We have a whole world here."

The world of Sunset Park holds 98,000 people, one third of whose families live below the poverty line. The neighborhood is shaped like a dog-eared rectangle, slightly over a mile wide and 2.6 miles long. Upper New York Bay creates the western boundary, across the water from which the financial towers of lower Manhattan stand bunched together like a bouquet of steel pipes. The eastern boundary is Eighth Avenue, the land rising steeply as one moves inland from the harbor. The southern boundary at Sixty-fifth Street separates Sunset Park from the middle-class neighborhood of Bay Ridge. Across Seventeenth Street, at the northern boundary, is Park Slope, a newly fashionable area where the high price of housing has driven many poor from their homes. Geraldine and Mary Paul fear this may happen in Sunset Park.

One other boundary exists inside the neighborhood. The Brooklyn-Queens Expressway, an elevated highway, extends over Third Avenue, dividing Sunset Park from itself. When the BQE opened as the Gowanus Parkway in 1941, the life under the highway was shadowed away: meat and vegetable markets, restaurants, seven movie theaters, all disappeared, along with the people. Now, to the east of Third Avenue, middle-income families, both Hispanic and white, are refurbishing brownstones with elaborate cornices and carvings. Between Third and the harbor, however, are tenements and abandoned houses spread out among bleak whitish factory buildings and the Lutheran Medical Center. On Third Avenue itself, the BQE makes a continual shushing noise, with traffic racing from Staten Island on the southwest out to the other boroughs. The vast stout legs of the expressway straddle the avenue like a gigantic millipede, around which lie stacks of dusty automobile tires and junked cars. Human life is furtive, barely visible. Under the legs of the expressway, hunched figures scavenge in metal garbage bins or simply lean against a pillar and stare.

"There's Billy." Geraldine points out a slinking figure in a black ski cap, with a gash-scar running from the corner of his right eye to his chin. "I've known him since he was a kid. Now he's an addict, a pusher too, probably." She shouts, "Hi, Billy." The figure, startled, uncoils, waves brightly, and moves on.

"It can get rough here. There's no pretending that it can't. When Mary Paul and I opened the center in 1978, youth gangs ruled the neighborhood. The Homicides. The Assassinators. Now the gangs are gone, but the pushers have taken over. The violence stays. One night two summers ago, we were closing up our Teen Jam, and I walked past this group shouting at one another. One gang trespassed on a rival gang's turf. Suddenly, a woman and a boy were shot dead. A white car sped off, chasing a wounded boy all the way to Lutheran Hospital. They fired straight through the windows of the emergency room."

Much of the greenery in Sunset Park lies in Greenwood Cemetery, one of the oldest and largest public burial grounds in America. Among the half a million interred are Currier and Ives, Samuel F. B. Morse, William ("Boss") Tweed, Horace Greeley, and Elias Howe, inventor of the sewing machine; Charles Tiffany, jeweler; Pierre Lorillard, tobacco tycoon; Edward Squibb, the pharmaceutical manufacturer; William Colgate, the soapmaker. James Kirke Paulding lies in Greenwood, the man who composed "Peter Piper picked a peck of pickled peppers," as does Frank Morgan, who played the Wizard of Oz in the 1939 movie.

They are buried among the Dutch and English, who first settled the neighborhood in the seventeenth century with farms stretching from the hill down to the water, and among those who fought under Washington in the Continental Army. Sunset Park was a major stronghold in the battle of Long Island in the summer of 1776. Some trees of Greenwood Cemetery—oak, maple, beech, white pine—are old enough to have sheltered the Canarsie Indians, who maintained a fishing station at what is now Thirty-seventh and Third. Greenwood rests above the neighborhood like a great serene estate, some of the wealthy contained in vast crypts beside decorous ponds, as stark and monumental as Egyptian tombs.

South of the cemetery is Sunset Park itself, eighteen acres of walking paths, playgrounds, graffiti-ridden benches, and a WPA-built swimming pool. From the high ground around the flagpole, neighborhood citizens may look down over the rooftops into the bay at the Statue of Liberty, sheathed in scaffolding for repairs, rising from the water like a shapeless green plant; or watch Manhattan at twilight sparkle into being.

"We use the park for our summer camp," says Geraldine. "The pool is too shallow for the bigger kids, and fights break out. But it's all we've got in the heat."

Besides the camp and the after-school programs that Michael Mallory attends, the Center for Family Life organizes a foster-grandparent program, a theater workshop, and literacy classes for adults. A dance group produces a version of *The Nutcracker* for the neighborhood Christmas show. The awninged thrift shop not only sells inexpensive goods but provides free emergency food. The center also operates an employment agency to help non-English speakers in particular. The main work of the center is counseling—group-therapy sessions, and individual meetings between staff members who are professional social workers and clients who, like Mallory, seek the center for help.

"Mallory came to us because of Michael's wild behavior in school, but that's only part of the problem, as you can see. Mallory wants to hold on to Michael. Fine. In his way, he really loves Michael. But if Michael stays with his so-called family, he may be a lot worse off. I've discussed this openly with Mallory, who, naturally, doesn't like it. The case is a mess."

The car parks at the center, a plain, deceptively large building that backs on St. Michael's Church, with its odd, elongated acorn spires. Geraldine and Mary Paul attend 8:30 mass every morning, but they have no time for other formal daily prayers. There is no religious cast whatever to the center. On the ground floor are a reception room and Geraldine's office. On the upper floors, staff offices, consultation rooms, a large "family room" used for parties and group sessions. The top floor constitutes the convent for the two nuns. This is their place of privacy.

Geraldine bustles into the center and is greeted by Zaida, a soft-spoken receptionist and a longtime resident of Sunset Park. There are many phone calls to return. Sister Mary Paul has gone to a budget hearing in the city. A Puerto Rican family of four sits on a bench, looking friendly and anxious. Geraldine leafs through her messages, then looks up suddenly. "Zaida! Wait till you see the new awning."

III Maria

I used to fight a lot, I don't know why. This girl that I hated, she hated me too, and I tried not to fight her, but then, you know, you start thinking about the person, even at night. She's always on your mind. You practice in your house. So I planned on a Monday, you know, to fight. But it didn't work out. So Tuesday I went. I had on my red Jordache. In those days it was in style. Not anymore. You like this jacket? And my sneakers and a red sweatshirt. And I saw her. Everything I had to say I told her the day before in an argument, so I ran out of words. I told my friend to tell the girl that I wanted to fight her, because I don't like her and she don't, doesn't, like me. Right? Then the girl, she pushed me. She hit me first. She called me a bitch. We started. I kept telling myself, Fight like an animal, like an animal, and don't stop, don't stop.

She bit my finger. I had her like this, you know, my arm around her head, and my hand was in her face, scratching her. I wanted to hurt her bad. The night before, I polished my fingernails to make them hard. Her father charged me with assault. That's *stupid*. But I got in trouble in school, in court, and my mother, you know, she cried when the cops came. Mothers get so nervous. But that's *stupid*. They wouldn't lock me up. I was fourteen.

That tape recorder. The light goes red when I speak. Right?

I knew something was wrong with me, you know? Me and my friend, my friend and I, started joking around. We saw a cop and we stopped in front of him, and I said, "I'm depressed," and we all started laughing. But I was really depressed. Then I went up to a lady, and I said again, "I'm depressed." And she goes, "Oh, honey. I'm depressed too. That's life." I started saying I'm depressed for a joke, but it was real. Then my friend told me, "You're crazy. You've got to talk to a psychiatrist. She told me about the center, so I came to Mary Paul and Geraldine. I was getting scared of myself. My boyfriend gave me a knife. I still have it, in a purple bag.

I hate my voice on tape recorders. I sound like a little boy.

The sisters were the first people I ever talked to about stuff like that. In my family nobody talks. They just fight. Like last week I came from gymnastics. Right? And my brother was in a bad mood or something, so he pushed me. I got mad and I pushed him. We ended up in the kitchen, and he threw me against the window, which cracked, but I didn't fall out. And my mother started screaming and pushed me to one side, and I started screaming, and my other sisters started screaming. It's always like that. When we lived on Thirty-ninth Street, my brother put his finger in my eye. I had an operation.

My father's worse. He's the worst. He drinks. He hits me. He's *stupid*. Yesterday, he came home and started fighting with my brother. I got mad at him. He says he was at my brother to give him a lesson, but he don't give anybody any lesson, doesn't; he's just mean. I smelled his breath. Smelled like liquor, and I told him. He said, "You shut up before I step on your face and throw you out of the house." And I say I'm going to leave the house on my own. And he asks, "Why would you do that?" He's so *stupid*. He almost broke my back once, punched me. Geraldine wants me to go to college. I'm applying to Purchase and Queens. I can't wait to get out of that house.

And my mother takes his side, you know? She hates him for hitting us, because she loves us. Right? But she likes him too! Like last Christmas they kissed, and I never seen them kissing, and I got embarrassed and I left. I didn't know they did that.

I think he's depressed like me. But he doesn't take depression like me. You got to take it and face it, you know?

He messes up everything. I know he's going to mess up Christmas again. Year before last, we were driving to our cousins in the Bronx. It was raining, and he gets in a fight with another driver. Last Christmas the same. We were in the car, and he's driving drunk, putting us in danger. And he starts fighting with my big sister, who can't take it. She keeps her unhappiness inside. She tried to kill herself one time by swallowing all my grandmother's asthma pills. My other sister tried to kill herself too. They had to clean out her blood in Lutheran.

My friend and I went to visit her. I said, "Hi." I was scared to kiss her. I took her hand, and she pulled it and kissed me. A lady psychiatrist was looking at me. She was wearing red high heels. I didn't like her. She was looking at me as if my sister was my fault.

You got kids? You like your kids?

He's always calling us pieces of crap. He's garbage. I hate him. When he hit my back, he took my jacket and put it over my head, and banged me against the floor. After that I thought he was finished hitting me, but yesterday he said he was going to step on my face. You want to dial the cops, but you can't. I never talk about him to my boyfriend. I didn't even want to talk to Geraldine at first. I didn't like her at first. I liked Mary Paul better. I thought Geraldine, you know, wanted too much. Then I wrote her letters. That helped. You want to see the letters?

I think two people are here. You're looking at me, and the tape recorder is looking at me.

You would have killed a father like mine. He tells me I'm good for nothing, that I won't be nothing in the future. But I'm going to be a scientist, or a medical assistant, or something. You know why he tells me I'm no good? 'Cause he's no good. Everybody always told him he's no good, and he's going to tell his children they're no good.

Last night after the fight he held the door open for me, when we were going out. I never saw him do that before. But I wouldn't go through. I just let him hold the door until he got tired of holding it, and then he went through and I went through on my own. No way I was going to let him hold that door for me.

IV Mary Paul

There was a time when Geraldine was convinced that Mary Paul was a saint. She is not at all sure now that she wasn't right about that, but Geraldine did not see the point in treating Mary Paul like a saint if she also wanted to work at her side. The glow was bound to get her down. As a young nun, Geraldine was in awe of Mary Paul's combination, as she put it, of heart and head. Still, she thought, Mary Paul is twenty years my senior. When I'm her age, I'm bound to be smarter myself. She cherishes Mary Paul's high seriousness and contemplative nature. Mary Paul cherishes Geraldine's vivacity, goodness, and sense of fun. The only severe blowup in the twenty-five years of their friendship came when Geraldine began to fear that Mary Paul would die someday, so she acted ornery as a preemptive strike.

At sixty-five, Mary Paul looks very far from dying. Her dark brown hair not only shows no gray but seems to reflect the deep blue of her habit. Her face is soft, cheeks puffed like a doll's. Her eyes, also deep blue, are a girl's eyes, her voice soft as a girl's, yet firm and untentative. She is very small. Sitting in an armchair in the upstairs convent of the center, she must lean forward so as not to be swallowed in the cushions.

"As a girl I never thought of being a nun. I wanted to be a teacher. I was a bookish little kid, very serious always. Unlike Geraldine, I did not go to Catholic school. Religion only began to interest me when I was halfway through Hunter College, and then mainly as a subject for contemplation. I read a good deal. Books such as Thomas à Kempis's *The Imitation of Christ,* which I cannot stand now. Thomas à Kempis said the more one goes into the world, the less one becomes. That's not true at all. The more you go into the world, the more you are."

Mary Paul and Geraldine belong to the Sisters of the Good Shepherd, an order founded in France in 1641 as Sisters of the Refuge to shelter banished women. The order was renamed and internationalized in 1835 under the leadership of Mother, later Saint, Maria Euphrasia, who emphasized gratitude as the basis of the order's faith and works. *"Vous avez un coeur fait pour aimer, fait pour être reconnaissant."* (You have a heart created to love and to be grateful.) Theologically, the tenet of gratitude is seen as the opposite of original sin because it grasps God as the source of all that is good. Mary Paul translates this idea into appreciation: "The staff truly appreciates the people they represent." Both she and Geraldine deemphasize the role of religion in the center's work. It never seems to be mentioned, and both staff and clients represent all faiths and none. But faith is clearly at the core of the nuns' own lives, though it is a private business with them, and both must be prodded to discuss it.

"Two things you cannot describe to anyone else," says Mary Paul. "Sex and prayer. God lives in a different realm of reality. To talk about that reaches beyond the point of talk.

"But I can talk endlessly about the center. The community set us up, in a way. As the needs evidenced themselves, we developed programs to try to meet those needs. Our employment office was a response to the fact that there's 12 percent jobless in Sunset Park, 4 percent higher than the rest of the city. You were kidding Geraldine about our building an empire here. Well, we did. We started with a dozen staff, and we never dreamed we'd grow as big as we are. But the needs are so various and complicated. Last week I did a preliminary interview with a woman who said at first that her problem was her fourteen-year-old son, who never showed up at school. The woman carried an enormous briefcase with her—all the time, I learned later—packed with every notice and letter she has ever received. She cannot read, so she carries this file around with her for reference. When I got to meet her son, he could not read either, and he didn't go to school because he was ashamed.

"Or you take Maria. Maria is smart, clever, volatile, funny, mischievous, a real piece of work. She would have us believe that she does not realize that she loves her father in spite of his awful behavior, but she does realize that. She does not need to be taught to love him, so in that she is playing a sort of game by pretending her love is a secret we all must disclose. But Maria does need to learn to live at peace with the world, because in temperament she is very much like her father. That's her real problem."

The Center for Family Life is not the sole agency of help in Sunset Park. Lutheran Hospital offers high school equivalency classes to the community, as well as medical care. Doug Heilman, a Lutheran minister, established Discipleship House in 1981, a sort of Boys Town for teenagers in trouble. Heilman's work with street kids is praised everywhere in Sunset Park; wherever he walks he is greeted warmly by young men, many of whom are former gang members. The help he provides takes the form of moral encouragement or simple solace. Heilman corresponds with a young man from the neighborhood now in prison for murdering his six-month-old child in a fit of rage. Before Heilman took to the streets, no one in Sunset Park recognized such people.

Yet Heilman, Father Thomas Haggerty, the pastor of St. Michael's, Bob Walsh, Joe Montalto—community leaders who work in different ways for Sunset Park—all agree that the center is the social engine of the neighborhood. They remember that in 1978, Sunset Park, though designated a poverty area in the 1960s, had not yet reached the point of deterioration of the South Bronx and the now destitute Bushwick section of Brooklyn. There was still a chance to pull the neighborhood back from disintegration. The center is credited for the beginnings of recovery. Mary Paul and Geraldine do not deny this, since it is demonstrably true. At the same time they are made visibly uncomfortable by any focus on themselves as individuals, and will, when so threatened, immediately draw one's attention to the others in the community and to their staff members, all of whom the sisters prize: Carol Heiney-Gonzalez, Maryanne Sabatino, Anna Nalevanko, Anita Cleary, John Kixmiller, who runs the after-school program at P.S. 314; Tom Randall; Julie Stein Brockway, who leads the theater workshop; Diana Hart-Johnson, the woman preparing the *Nutcracker* show.

"They are there for the people. They certainly don't love every one of their clients. It's hard to love wife batterers and child molesters. But they have this basic, nonjudgmental quality of acceptance."

The phone rings in the convent. Mary Paul must see a woman whose six-year-old and one-and-a-half-year-old children were discovered on a fire escape at 4:00 A.M. The woman's excuse was that she had to go buy milk. "Of course, it isn't true. The woman undoubtedly has a pattern of leaving her children in hazardous situations. Is she going to trust us enough to allow us to help?

"You wonder why the staff does this work. People who are in what we call the helping professions are curious. I think they may feel something missing in their lives. There can be a lot of ego in this profession, a lot of vicarious fulfillment. One wants to see oneself as a good and giving person. There is nothing wrong with that, but it can't be the only goal. The ultimate goal must be a change in the system in which both the giver and the taker live. Life is made better generally. I bet if you had time to interview every one of our clients, many would not attribute changes that occurred to us at all. Good things happened, and they believe they were their achievements. In many ways they were.

"People call us a charity organization. I don't like the word *charity,* except in the sense of *caritas,* love. Love is not based on marking people up by their assets and virtues. Love is based on the sense of the mystery of the person. Here we have the privilege of meeting people *in via,* as it is said, on the way. They're on a journey. The gratitude I feel is that I am able to see this particular person at this particular time. Yet the person remains an unfathomable mystery, and is going somewhere I will never know."

V Center for Family Life Theater Workshop

Sixteen teenagers in a circle run in place, snap their fingers, clap their hands under their legs as they lift them. Much giggling and groaning. Jokes about Jane Fonda. Stretch exercises on the cafeteria floor of P.S. 1. Julie, the staff leader, wears a sweatshirt reading NAGS HEAD, NORTH CAROLINA. Calls out directions: "Let's do knots." Kids divide into two huddles, all crossing arms, grasping one another. Entangled, they must work their way out by twisting until their knot unravels. "Anita's stuck again." Laughter. Julie: "Double duck-ducks, please." Kids on haunches in one large circle again. Hector, tagged "Goose," has to run outside the circle to tag Felice. Slips and collisions. Howls, exaggerated pain. Circle re-forms. Julie: "Huggy-bear two." Kids embrace in pairs. "Huggy-bear five." Kids embrace in clusters of five. Hector to observer: "Love at first sight." This is an elimination game. Last boy pretends to weep with self-pity, moans, "Rejected." Julie again: "Emotional machines." Kids make instant clusters, constructs of their bodies. In a cluster one girl cries; another spanks her; a boy rocks on the floor as he clings to the second girl's leg; another boy pulls that boy's foot. "Too easy," Julie shouts. "Take your risks, ladies and gentlemen. Family machines." A girl begins, "Gimme," and continues repeating the word as at the start of a roundelay. A boy chips in "No," and continues to say "No." Second boy: "It's mine." Second girl: "Will you stop whining?" Third boy: "Shut up." The family machine roars. Applause, whistles, whoops. Circle again. Julie: "Start a feeling." One: "I'm happy." Each follows with own intonation until "I'm happy" goes round once. Another: "I'm so frustrated." Another: "Why do you do this to me?" Julie: "Carlos, don't say it until you feel it." Another feeling starts: "I'm so cool." Another: "I've got chirasma." The whole group: "What?" Boy, confused, repeats, "I've got chirasma." Girl: "You mean you got asthma." Laughter. "You mean you got *charisma*." Julie: "Let's do it. Keep it moving. Today we've got chirasma."

VI   Maria's Letters

Geraldine:

My father is drunk again, like always, he sat in front of me. He's losing his eyesight with the alcohol. I saw his eyes, all red. He said he couldn't see very well during the day, I almost cried. I wish I wouldn't live with a person like that. Every day for years he always came home drunk, making me hate him. I know he'll soon die and that makes me cry. He gives up on life, he doesn't look for solutions. I remember when I was small he used to hug me. Things are getting worse. I got to get ready before he dies.

Geraldine:

You're not right. I'm angry at you. I know you are the one who told my mother to talk back to my father, the same thing you told me, which I won't do, cause you don't f——g know what's going on. You know, if my mother gets hurt because of listening to you, you'll get hurt too. Don't come saying things you *think* is right. My father is different. If you talk back to my father he gets dangerous . . . I f——g hate you and my stupid mother. My mother is acting like a bitch. I feel like punching her out . . . It's your fault. I see you every week and you never do nothing for me. My mother right now is close to my father, listening to him . . . I hope she dies. I hope they both die and I don't know about you.

Geraldine:

There are so many things to tell you, but I never tell you. I try my best, but I'm not happy, even though I make believe. I worry for my family which now is in danger. Don't you f——g understand? My father is dangerous. Right now he lost control. We have to get away from him, but he's then not gonna have anybody. He broke the thermometer of the apartment and the boiler is becoming into flames. I don't know if this letter will reach you. I can't sleep. He screams out of control. Everyone in the house is awake at 12:30. I don't know if we'll ever sleep today. I just can't hold on too long. Every day I think of leaving a message to some friends and teachers and throwing myself from the school's roof. I always think of that. How about my sisters? If I die it will be better because it was gonna happen anyway . . . Things will be much easier away from him, my life, my school work, my health, and my eyes. I hate. I have to kill him someday, take his brains out, slashing his face and my mother's too, if she cries.

Dear Geraldine:

Hi. I don't want to interrupt when you're busy. But I've been thinking I don't have to put up with all the garbage my father says. I know they're not true, but they really hurt. They hurt because no matter how I try to say that he's not my father, I can't say that to myself. He's my father, and he's the worst enemy I ever had.

Dear Geraldine:

The Purchase application is inside the black and blue book . . . I don't have an application from Queens. Should I call that lady? . . . I'm making a new list of applications to send. Could you review it with me?

Dear Ms. Geraldine:

I'm not trying to make you show that you care because I already know that. I want you to know that you're a good example that I will like someday to follow. If you had the time, I know you would of liked to help the whole world. Not to become *affluence*, but because it is something you enjoy to do. See, I use a big word (affluence). Geraldine, what is wrong is that I expect you to do everything for me . . . I expect you to make my decisions . . . P.S. I'm going to change because it's something I've been avoiding.

Dear Geraldine:

I'm going to write that I love you because I can't say it. You're a wonderful person, your personality and all. Before I used to think that only your own race cares for you. That's not true is it? If it's true don't tell me. Anyway I'm never forgetting about you. When I move to college I want you to visit me and I will write to you . . . P.S. If you feel that I'm talking foolishly, well too bad. If you're getting tired, tell me. And if you want to finish with me after a couple of years, tell me, O.K.? Don't hide it.

VII   Tony, Ingrid, and Maryanne

"Can you explain the process so that an outsider can understand it? What exactly happens in these counseling sessions?"

"We talk. We observe, we listen, and we talk. That's all there is to it. At our first meeting, I will introduce myself fairly formally: 'I am

Maryanne Sabatino, I'm a professional staff member here at the center,' and so forth. Then we'll begin. It's hard to see anything clearly for a while. You visited Tony and Ingrid for the first time this morning. What did you see?"

"What struck me at once was how neat their apartment was. The two of them are a lot poorer than Mallory, but their place is a palace compared with his. I gather that the main problem is that woman superintendent, who seems to be driving them crazy. She constantly yells at the two little girls. Ingrid says that Tony is after her to have it out with the woman, but Ingrid wants to solve the problem by moving. She claims that the super has become the main sore point in their marriage."

"It may be a sore point, but it isn't the heart of their troubles. In a way, Tony and Ingrid are a classic situation. They came to the center with one specific complaint, and then it opened to something wider and deeper."

"Are drugs their biggest worry, then? Ingrid is down to nothing, but Tony still uses a lot of methadone. Is Ingrid afraid that she'll get hooked again?"

"That's a problem too, of course. So is Tony's health. He coughs up blood, which he blames on the metal fragments he inhaled at the sheet-metal factory. Ingrid says he's gone down four pants sizes in a year. Also, they live together illegally even though they're married, because Ingrid's welfare check would be cut off if the government knew Tony was helping out with the support. All serious problems. But the central issue is Tony and Ingrid. I've told them that directly. Both are thirty; she may be twenty-nine. She is strong, articulate, ambitious. He is sweet and irresponsible. She feels that he is trying to hide from life. He feels she is dominating him."

"But that woman-super business. Doesn't Tony come off as the more aggressive of the two?"

"That's merely her way of bolstering him in front of a stranger. The irony there is that if Tony really wanted to stand up to the super, he would not do it through Ingrid. And she defines the problem as her responsibility, not his, merely reinforcing the circle. Even on the idea of their moving, Tony feels that he is being told what to do, not only by Ingrid but by the super, who is forcing him to make a decision. Tony avoids decisions. Ingrid has charge of the finances, the family schedules. For Tony, there is his guitar and his car. Given the chance, he would tinker with that car forever."

"He showed it off to me. A blue Cutlass. He only came to life when he talked about that car, explaining in meticulous detail how he fixed the carburetor, changed the radiator. Ingrid was with us, saying encouraging things."

"Yes, but she wants him to sell that car to help them move. Yet the car is very important to his self-esteem. And so it goes. That's Sunset Park. Real problems, poverty problems and simply problems of modern living. Tony and Ingrid are former heroin addicts living in a slum, almost wholly removed from the world. They saw their first Broadway show last year, *The Tap Dance Kid;* dinner at Howard Johnson's, a real excursion. Yet their troubles are middle-class troubles. She says: Take charge. He says: I don't take charge because you do. She says: If I let you do it, it doesn't get done. He feels resentful and excluded from the family."

"Where do you begin to help?"

"You look to understand first. You try not to judge, because inevitably judging is rejecting. You may have to make hard choices, but without judging. You look at their past. Tony and Ingrid have climbed a long way up to get to the kinds of troubles they now have. She comes from a German-Welsh background, grew up in a German section of Queens. Mother a schizophrenic, in and out of institutions. Heartbreaking for Ingrid. Father a bitter alcoholic, consumed with self-pity. Ingrid was putting needles in her arms at fourteen. She was arrested for pushing at fifteen. Yet she managed to play mother to five brothers and sisters, and eventually she stopped the drugs. That's how she met Tony: They both were on detoxification programs. I think they met at a lunch counter."

"Isn't there hope for them in the fact that Tony too showed courage? He described his childhood in Brownsville to me, how his mother would slice a banana so that each of the ten children would have something to eat. Did he tell you about his stepfather? About his hitting the kids with electric wires and cracking a thermos over Tony's head when Tony was five? Tony said the man would dip his fingers in Tabasco sauce and stick them down Tony's mouth, that he hit Tony's mother in the stomach with a baseball bat when she was eight months pregnant. As you say, they both have struggled. What do you do to keep them going?"

"Well, I give them an exercise in responsibility. This week I've suggested that Tony try paying the bills. He said I was putting him on the spot, but really I was putting them both on the spot because the exercise is also a test of whether Ingrid can ask Tony to do something in a way that will make him glad to do it."

"Even as an outsider, I could see there is a lot to Ingrid. Isn't there? As we talked it was clear that Tony couldn't care less about his sheet-metal job, but Ingrid was fascinated by the fact that the things he makes go into the Holland Tunnel and onto the Brooklyn Bridge. You could almost see her mind travel."

"Three months of working with them has shown me there is a lot to Tony too. They are both very gentle, very generous. The trouble is that she is moving much faster than he is now. And Tony simply does not believe in himself. After every session at the center, he makes a point of shaking my hand. The reason may be that I see him in a way he does not see himself."

"Funny about Tony shaking your hand. When I was leaving, they both walked me downstairs. The woman super, incidentally, was snooping at her door, and slammed it as we passed. Suddenly, Tony thanked me extravagantly for coming—patted me on the shoulder, looked at me with real affection—even though it was they who were doing the favor for me."

"You treated him like a man."

VIII   Michael

Michael bends his head so close to his notebook that his nose almost brushes the page. He insists on doing his homework, although by now he knows that these group sessions at the center are exclusively for play. Lori and Betsy, the two graduate-student group leaders, practically have to pry Michael away from the book. Ralphy, who like Michael is seven, watches the scene with interest and malice. "That your stupid old notebook?" he asks Michael. Ralphy is black. Carmen is Hispanic. Elena is white, with a broad Slavic face. All four children are the same size.

Betsy calls for the serving of refreshments. Apple juice, orange juice, popcorn, and pieces of hard candy. The children sit cross-legged on the linoleum. Michael serves the popcorn.

RALPHY: I want ten pieces.
MICHAEL: You get what I give you.
CARMEN: Ralphy, don't you live on my block?
RALPHY: Betsy Betsy Betsy Wetsy.

They are asked to say their names aloud for the benefit of the group. Ralphy refuses. Michael says his name, smiles, and looks playful. He gently places a piece of popcorn on Betsy's head.

"Who will recite the group rules?"

Michael volunteers, stands. His blond-brown hair is shaggy, emphasizing the beauty of his face. His brown pants are frayed at the bottoms and torn at the seat; he seems not to notice. Over a blue shirt, he wears a maroon sweater. He speaks to the room: "(1) Keep hands and feet to yourself; (2) don't call out; (3) be nice to each other; (4) call one another by name; (5) stay with the group."

He leaves to go to the bathroom. While he is out, Ralphy snatches a piece of Michael's candy. Lori and Betsy come down hard on him. Michael returns, takes immediate note of the theft. He says, "My candy," wanly, as if making a disinterested discovery, and takes no action. Ralphy tells him, "I took the purple one." Michael seems not to pay attention. He takes his cup of remaining candy and offers a piece to Lori: "Want candy?"

Now the children are asked to draw pictures of themselves. Each selects a Magic Marker. Michael chooses black. He draws a small circle at the top of the paper, then, unsatisfied, flips the sheet over and begins to draw a small stick figure. The two young women suggest that the children lay their heads directly on the paper; Betsy will draw an outline of their heads, and the children may fill in the features. Carmen and Elena respond at once and begin to work. Ralphy balks and starts to play elsewhere. He is taken out of the room by Lori.

With brisk strokes Michael colors the hair of his stick figure. Then he covers the entire face with hair, tosses the paper aside, and begins again. He appears not to have heard the suggestion about laying his head on the paper and instead draws his head as a large circle with slits for eyes, a button nose, and a huge mouth grinning with jack-o'-lantern teeth. He discards that paper as well. Suddenly he is out in the hall, watching Ralphy receive his lecture. He is told to return to the others, and he runs back with strange, jerky movements of his arms and legs.

Instead of addressing his own sheet of paper, he turns to one Betsy has been working on; she is occupied with Carmen. He draws a satanic face within Betsy's outline. "The devil is in her," he says to no one in particular. Elena draws a girl with a thick brown ponytail, like her own. The hair Carmen gives herself is half black, half red. Michael to Betsy: "The devil is in your heart, and he is trying to make you bad." Betsy watches as he covers the picture of her face with a cyclone of circles.

Betsy asks him calmly, "Michael, can you draw a picture of your house?" The house that Michael draws is a series of connected ladders and squares. Stick figures occupy the upper squares; they represent tenants on the upper floors. The lowest square is filled in with green. As he continues to work, the other children are asked to talk about their self-portraits. Elena is too shy. Carmen says she is pretty in her drawing. Betsy asks Michael where his self-portrait is. Michael picks up one of his discarded sheets, announces, "This is a bad guy. I'm going to make a jet." He folds the paper into a plane and lets it fly.

"Tell us about the house you drew, Michael."

"This is a Christmas tree, and this is Santa Claus at the gate." The tree is discernible; Santa Claus is not. Of a figure standing outside the ladder structure, Michael says, "This is a girl going to my house, and this is a monster kissing her." He is asked, "Where are you in the picture?" He points to the center of the green square. "I am inside the house looking out," he says.

The others continue drawing. Ralphy has returned and produces an excellent self-portrait. Michael has stopped drawing. He sits at a desk, lays his head on his arm, and stares dreamily at the window and the dark blue afternoon. He takes a swig of apple juice and is reprimanded by Lori for not asking first. "Let's play outside, Lori," he asks. Lori explains that today is meant for drawing. Michael takes more apple juice without permission. Lori says that she will tell Sister Geraldine.

"You won't tell," Michael implores her.

Lori reaffirms that she will.

"Give me one more chance?" He holds up an index finger.

"Why are you so afraid?" asks Lori.

"I'm not afraid," said with no emotion. He folds another sheet and raises and lowers it in the air. He mutters, "Bird."

Michael heads for the bathroom again, going out without asking. Lori calls after him. The session winds up. The other children are putting away their Magic Markers. Lori calls, "Michael, you'd better be back in this room by the count of five." Michael reenters at four, crushes a plastic cup under his heel, crumples his picture, and throws it into the trash can. Lori stares at him. He runs toward Ralphy and slaps Ralphy's self-portrait out of his hand. He laughs, slams the door to the room from the inside. As the other children slip on their jackets, Michael stands at the wall, looks everyone over, and turns out the lights.

IX   Sunset Park

Between the winter hours of four and six, the long avenues of Sunset Park glow like orange groves, the light trickling into the side streets the way water glints in dark canals. Each area of the neighborhood has its own light. On the older residential streets, the lights in the houses are modest, like candle glow, except where someone has decided to explode with the season and Christmas lights engulf a house to the extent that no house shows. At the harbor, the late day brings almost total darkness; the lights are on the water in the windows of the boats.

On Third Avenue, there are the lights of gas stations, garages, and used-car lots; bulbs blaring in loops. The bars glow. No light whatever shows under the BQE, where the shush of cars grows louder with the rush hour, people passing over Sunset Park on their way home to other places. Tony and Ingrid live just east of Third, across from a car wash whose walls are covered with curlicues of graffiti. At this hour, Tony is on the job at the metal plant, and Ingrid has the two girls home from school.

Maria lives just west of Third, on a dead-end street where END has been crossed off the sign. The windows in her house are blue. She heads home after a tutoring session in chemistry. Mallory lives just off Sixth Avenue, near the Park Slope line. A streetlamp sheds a pale beam in a circle in front of his house.

Where the lights come into their own is on Fourth and Fifth avenues, not only the Christmas decorations but the shops shining from inside: Santiago Grocery, De An's House of Beauty. Billy, the drug addict with the gash on his cheek, skulks in and out of these lights like an actor on a stage. He pauses at various clusters of men his age, hangs out for a while, then moves along. Everywhere there are huddles of such men, standing together and apart at once, their bodies angled away from one another while they remain close. From a shop window piled high with big box radios, Carly Simon's voice sweeps into Fifth Avenue singing "That's the Way I've Always Heard It Should Be." At the south end of the avenue, beyond Sunset Park, the Verrazano Bridge loops like a necklace in a black velvet case.

If one did not know differently, Sunset Park at this hour could be mistaken for a small New Hampshire town. The shorn trees in the park, the cemetery on the hill, the quiet churches, the low houses looking for their occupants' return at the day's end. At P.S. 314, Diana Hart-Johnson rehearses the *Nutcracker* presentation scheduled for Christmas week. Teenage boys, galoots, clomp on the stage and attempt to learn their dance as the Spirit of Winter Dreams. The smaller children make soldiers' hats. The windows of the school blaze out into the cold.

Things quicken and contract. At the Center for Family Life, Geraldine plays cards with Michael in her office, after Michael's group has dispersed. They talk in whispers. Upstairs in the convent, Mary Paul completes some paperwork, prepares a dinner of cold salad, and sits down to watch the news.

X Rose

"When we moved here we counted twenty-eight mice, and we didn't count twice. I got one cat. He died. So I was looking for a new cat now because I had mice. And I was very upset for the kids. I went all over looking. Somebody told me they were giving away cats over at the clinic at Fifty-ninth Street. I went and I got this one here, which was named Mollie, and I changed it to Jangles. When I got back, there was my girlfriend's friend waiting for me with another cat, Patches, which I had no heart to throw out, so I took him in too. So now I have Patches and Jangles. Meanwhile, my darling son Benjamin here brings home this kitten, Lucky. Lucky because he has a home. And I told Benjamin, 'You're going to be unlucky because I'm going to kick youse out.' " She wipes her brow with a dishrag. "Your *turn*, Benjamin."

Benjamin, age eight, climbs up into the kitchen sink for his evening bath, as his sister Daisy climbs out. Rose throws a towel over Daisy, shampoos Benjamin, tells Davey and Joey to get pajamas on the twins.

"I got two dogs too. Out back. You can see 'em at the window. Hear 'em too. Hah. That's Rocky and that's Bam Bam. Bam Bam will not let you near my kids."

The four smaller children file in from the outer room to present themselves to their mother before going to bed. They stall, ask for snacks. Benjamin whines about a cut finger.

"Benjamin, I'm going to shock you," Rose tells him. "I believe you're going to live."

Rose's apartment has two rooms, the kitchen and an all-purpose room where the seven of them sleep. Benjamin, Daisy, and Sabrina sleep in the bed. Davey, Joey, and Dino sleep on the floor. Rose takes the couch. They have no phone; the bathtub leaks; the ceiling is splotched with water stains. Yet this is the best place they've ever had. For a month before this, Rose and the children lived in a car, and bathing was carried out in Rose's girlfriend's apartment. Compared with then, Rose says, the sky's the limit these days. The kids go to school regularly, and they take part in the Center for Family Life's after-school programs. Rose too gets help from the center, mostly advice in practical things, like her welfare payments. She goes to school now too, to learn how to be a beautician. "I even signed up the girls for ballet lessons." When she smiles she looks baby-tough, like an East Side Kid from the movies of the 1930s. A plate hung above the kitchen door reads GOD BLESS THIS LOUSY APARTMENT.

She glowers at the lot of them: "You're getting on my *nerves,* and you know what *that* means. Yesterday I went to school without my homework done. OK? And I got yelled at just like youse would get yelled at. Now I'm telling you, not asking you. Get in bed and do not move. Good *night.*"

She pushes aside a garbage bag full of laundry and plonks down on a chair, warily eyeing the kitchen door. "It isn't paradise, but they don't go hungry. When I was a kid, I didn't eat the best either. I was raised on french fries and macaroni because that's what my mother could afford. I loved that stuff. I love it today. And I'm a healthy little woman. And macaroni is *good.* I say that because [she raises her voice deliberately to be heard in the next room] some of my kids with silver spoons in their mouth think that macaroni three or four times a week is too much." She grins and winks.

"My father died when I was nine. I lived with him in Coney Island. I don't know why I lived with my father and not my mother. He couldn't take care of me, and I remember eating hero sandwiches every day from the luncheonette, and my clothes were wrinkly, smelly, in the corner with mess and garbage. Anyway, he dies when I was nine." She glares at the door. "Sabrina, that's enough!

"My mother was sickly, very sickly, with cataracts on her eyes, diabetes, heart trouble. Name it, she had it. I played hooky a lot. I wasn't on drugs or nothin', so she didn't care. In junior high, I told my mother I didn't want to go to school anymore. The school was going to throw me out anyway. They said I was taking space. And I couldn't read, I couldn't spell. I still can't read good or spell good.

"But I could always work. Even going to beauty school, I can get work before Christmas, like I did last year in Toys R Us.

"Anyway, I met Davey's father, Davey Senior, at eighteen. I met him in an after-school center, where I played Ping-Pong every day, which I loved. Davey Senior was thrown out of his house for something, so he came to live with my mother and me. And then my grandmother moved in too. My grandmother was a rip; she used to beat up all the kids with a broom. Davey and me lived in the same house, but we didn't do nothin'—would you believe it? I was a virgin till I got married. I was a very good girl, raised myself with *honor.*" She holds her fists over her head like a winning boxer and laughs. "I didn't have no bed of roses. I came from a broken home. So what? I don't go for blaming everyone else for what you do wrong. Here's a kick: I was even a virgin the day *after* I got married. I got drunk at the wedding—nice Italian wedding—and went home and fell asleep."

A few years later, Davey Senior ran off to Florida with another woman, leaving Rose with the first of her children, Davey Junior, a boy of fifteen today. Davey's one winter jacket was stolen last week. Rose vows to get it back. Joey, the second-oldest child, was produced by Frankie, with whom Rose lived for a year. The four other children belong to Vincent, with whom, until recently, Rose has been in an on-and-off custody war. Rose won the first battle after Vincent had taken Sabrina and was sent to jail in handcuffs. "I hated to see him that way. I still had feeling for him.

"But a week later Vinnie comes and takes *all* my kids. He called B.C.W., which is the old child welfare, and tells them I'm neglecting my children and I'm beating them and they never go to school and they weren't up-to-date with their shots and dah dah dah. I tried to fight, but I wasn't ready for court. I am not a smart person by any means. They closed my welfare case because I had no children, which meant that I had no money, no electric money, food money. I got thrown out of my apartment. I would have been a goner if I hadn't been taken in by Vinnie's brother and wife. So I took care of *their* six kids while I was waiting for the court to give me back my own. I took those kids to school. I bathed them. The judge says I got to prove I'm able to be a fit mother. I got jobs. I was a cashier in Pathmark. I worked from eleven at night to eight in the morning, and then I took care of Vinnie's brother's kids, which meant I got maybe two, three hours' sleep a night. But I proved something to the judge, and I got my kids back.

"Not that my troubles were behind me. I lost my apartment because I fell behind in my rent. Day after Easter, they sent me to a welfare hotel. I could not *stand* it. That's when I lived in the car. Finally, I came to Sunset Park and I got this place, which is fine, so I think things are going to be good from now on. The kids are doing OK in school. Not great but passing. I stick with it at the beauty school. There's a lot to read, that's the trouble there, the way I read.

"When I graduate, I'm going to get a good job. If there's no good job, I'll get a bad one. You know what I'll do if there never is a job? I'll cut hair in the street and charge five bucks a head. What do you think? Will they go for it? You can't beat the price."

XI Maria

"I know that kid, Davey, that lady's son. I mean, I don't really know him, but I saw him last week after some Puerto Rican kids stole his jacket. It was a new leather jacket. They held a gun to his head. I saw him in the subway, and I gave him a hug. I didn't like him or anything. I just wanted to show him that not all Puerto Ricans were like that."

Maria walks toward her house in the early evening, her hands stuffed into the pockets of her jeans to keep off the cold. Her chemistry tutor did not pay attention today, she complains. Her grades are solid Bs, but she feels inadequate in chemistry and in English too.

"I'm afraid to go to college, you know? I think I won't belong there. But I don't care if I don't fit in with all of them. I don't want to change, you know? I like my music, my clothes. I want them to take me like I am."

The sky is unusually clear; the stars show. Maria does not notice them. Planes fly in low over Fourth Avenue, one after the other, on their way to La Guardia Airport.

"You must see those planes all the time," says her companion. "Do the jets always fly over Sunset Park?"

"I don't know. I never look."

"You'll be on one of those planes someday, on your way to California or Paris. Do you believe that?" Maria shrugs. She is still brooding about college.

"Geraldine has been good to me, you know? She helped with all my college applications."

"Why does she help you, do you think?"

"She likes me. And I think that she is sort of like me too. She has a temper, you know." Maria giggles. "The flying nun flies off the handle. But she helps me with everything. She wants me to be nice to my father, you know? But I can't do that. He's not the sort of person you talk to. I am scared to get close to him.

"But I think I'm getting a little closer to my big sister. She and my father got in an argument last night. It was four in the morning. I got up and went into her room. I said, 'Don't listen to him because he's stupid. He doesn't understand.'

"She had a pillow on her head. I said, 'I like you, so don't feel bad.' Somethin' like that. I never said that to her before. Then we started talking about college, because she's going to college now, she knows what I feel. We talked and talked, but we didn't look at each other. All the time she was looking out the window and I was looking at my sleeping brother, but we were talking to each other. I was scared to look at her face. Then I made a joke, and she started laughing. And I started laughing. And then I looked at her, and showed her that I liked her through my eyes."

On the steps of an abandoned courthouse a group of young men give Maria the once-over. She does not look up. Two boys are fighting over a bike at the corner of her street. She calls to one of them, who responds cagily, trying to determine if her walking companion is a cop.

"What happens when you and Geraldine both feel that enough progress has been made, and are ready to stop?"

"Then we'll stop. But she will still be my friend. She's part of my family. I'll grow up and I'll see her every Christmas, like that. I feel strange when I think about it. I'm happy to have her as my friend. She taught me how to learn to like yourself, and you have to learn to like yourself, you know, because if you like yourself, you can like other people."

"Do you know how she feels about you?"

"Geraldine hugged me once. In front of my mother and everyone. I got embarrassed. I hugged her once too, and then I pulled away. I haven't hugged my sister in years."

"When do you plan to hug her again?"

"When I leave for college. Or maybe when I graduate."

"That's going to be some hug."

"Geraldine has no trouble showing people she likes them, you know? She has a big heart for everyone."

"Do you think she cares for everyone equally?"

"Equally, but differently. Because everybody is different."

She approaches her house, with the blue windows. "I want you to meet my grandmother." A small, shy woman is led out into the hall in her slippers. She smiles, nods, and retreats. Maria shouts upstairs to see who is home. "You won't meet *him*. He'll be out drinking until late." She calls to her sister in Spanish. Cara, the youngest, comes downstairs in her pajamas and greets the stranger politely, as Maria's eyes suddenly shine with a prospective joke: "Cara," she says, "this is your real father."

XII Mallory

The trouble with the people who give those psychological tests is that they're trained in books, but not real life. That's what I say. So they tell me Michael has emotional problems, that he's immature. Well, what do you expect? He's young. And his mother don't exactly help either. She doesn't know how to treat kids. She talks stiff to Michael. Like when we're eating, she tells him she won't give him any food. I tell her: "Don't do that to him." I give him mine. She doesn't see what I see, you know what I mean?

I try to tell this to Sister Geraldine. She says that Eileen is intelligent. I say, "Yes, all crazy people are intelligent." I mean, they show real intelligence, but they do funny things along the way. I've known Eileen since she was eighteen. She changes: angry state one day, happy state the next. She used to take Michael to bars with her when he was a baby. She's run off eight times already, leaving me with Michael. And they say I neglected him. How you gonna help leave him alone sometimes when *you're* alone?

Tell you something else: When Michael was born, I was so happy. I didn't have any children with the woman I was married to. But when I walked into the hospital, Eileen tells the doctors that somebody not me is the father. She put down the name of some guy in New Jersey. Can you beat that? I told her she wasn't getting a dime until Michael had my name, and I went to court to make it legal. I could have murdered her then. She killed my fatherhood from the beginning, the firstborn.

And that's where Sister Geraldine is wrong again. She wants me and Eileen to stay together; she doesn't say so but I can tell from things she says that she wants it. Now Sister Geraldine is another intelligent person, but certain things she don't know anything about. I think she thinks I hit Michael, but I don't. Maybe a tap on the bottom, but that's all. I'd never hit Michael because I know how my father used to hit me, with the stick end of the plunger. I still have the marks.

I was one of twenty-one children, would you believe it? My father lived with my mother and my stepmother at the same time. He made me quit school when I was eight, so that I'd stay home and help clean house. The only one who tried to protect me was my mother. My father used to punch her in the stomach when they were in bed together. When she screamed, he said she was leaping for sex. She left when I was four. She wouldn't take me with her. I remember it today, isn't that something? I remember like it was yesterday.

Then I left home too. I ran away a lot, so they put me in Willowbrook for the crazy kids, because I was stealing bikes and radios, little things. I was fifteen. Some of the Willowbrook kids banged their heads against the wall all day, just sat and rocked and banged their heads. Some of them would get sexual and funny with me. I don't remember if they attacked me, because I didn't know what they were doing.

When I got out of Willowbrook I was twenty, and I went to live with my father. He was an old man then, seventy, but he got sexual with me too. He said it gave him strength. I felt awkward. You know what I mean? With my own father.

Excuse me for all this coughing. It's worse than when you were here before. I really have been sick; I don't care what they think at the office. My dentures are killing me too. The uppers don't fit. My gums shrink.

After six months I moved in with my mother. I think I began to grow for the first time in my life, living with her. I went to night school to learn to read and write. I started to teach myself to read in Willowbrook when they locked me up for thirty days after I jumped out the second-floor window, trying to escape. I used the detention time to try to read. I tell Michael: "Reading is the biggest thing." At night school I was doing well. I began to feel like somebody.

Nine years I lived with my mother, till I got married. I was thirty-three, she was twenty, a Jewish girl. I wanted to get married so badly. I didn't like her really. But she talked to me. I love to talk. It gets me thinking, worked up. I like talking right now like *this*.

What I'm saying is that I don't want the things that went wrong for me to go wrong for Michael. He's the happiness of my life. Yesterday he comes home with a rip in the seat of his pants. I tell him: "Throw 'em out, we'll buy new ones." Sometimes he gets upset with his lessons, rolls up the paper in a ball. I tell him: "Stop. Put the book away and relax." The only thing is I don't want him to grow up on cloud nine, which is why I make him learn. His life's got to be better than mine.

Not that my life is over yet either. Know what I mean? I'm intelligent. Don't you think I'm intelligent? And I'm still learning things and doing things and growing. I don't know where's the end of it.

XIII   Geraldine and Mary Paul

"You have to be in for the long haul. Mallory is an excellent lesson in that." Sister Geraldine hurriedly adjusts her veil and prepares to attend mass. This is the one day of the year when Sisters of the Good Shepherd all over the world renew their vows. No ceremony takes place; Mary Paul and Geraldine will reaffirm their vows in silence at the regular morning mass at St. Michael's. Geraldine calls upstairs to Mary Paul that they may be late, conjectures that Mary Paul is lost in the morning papers.

"Mallory says he wants to ditch Eileen, and I believe he means it. If he really wants to provide a new mother for Michael and if that makes for a solid loving family, I'll be glad to see it happen. Eileen certainly isn't easy to get to. I make appointments with her at the center, but she rarely shows up. She has complications of her own, and I wish we could begin to see how they impinge on her relationship with both Mallory and Michael. We call this the Center for Family Life because we believe in families as systems, that everyone touches and affects everyone else. Yet Mallory contradicts himself too. The three of them spent Thanksgiving happily at Eileen's parents' house; Mallory told me so. It speaks for the necessity of patience."

Mary Paul descends the stairs and picks up on Geraldine's last words. "You have to help people be patient with themselves, as well. Rose, whom you met, is living in an imaginary world right now, in which she tells herself that everything is going to be fine for her and the six children. But ask Anita Cleary, Rose's case worker, and you will discover things such as Rose's total inability to handle money; Anita has confronted Rose on that. Those ballet lessons Rose is so delighted with cost $500. Anita is very careful to do two things at once with Rose: to make her believe that everything is possible, and to prepare her for defeat, so that she won't collapse. That strategy applies to Mallory, Maria, Tony and Ingrid, and, I imagine, to us too."

The nuns start walking toward St. Michael's. Geraldine, no taller than five foot seven inches, appears twice the size of Mary Paul. They walk comfortably together, having done so for many years, each one's stride making automatic concessions to the other's.

"I think one must learn a different, less urgent sense of time here," says Mary Paul, "one that depends more on small moments than big ones. Today we renew our vows. It is a special day, but not as special as you might think. There are no really special days here, no momentous occasions. That even includes Christmas. I would not go so far as to say that Christmas is merely another day in Sunset Park, but in a way it is. It is necessary for us to remember that there is the day after Christmas too. Helping families to give toys is gratifying, but quite momentary. For me Christmas is special because it is a quiet day at the center, and it allows me time to meditate and replenish myself.

"And I really need these periods of reflection, because I know now how corrupting this work of ours can be. Years ago a child told me: 'You want me to succeed so much. Could you understand if I failed?' He meant: Could you love me if I failed? It is so easy for us to love someone because he is making progress and being responsive to our efforts. What about those who can't respond? It is important to learn to love someone without asking for love in return. It really is very important."

"I'm not even conscious of whether I need the response or not," says Geraldine. "It's just that I have this powerful feeling of loving, which I treat as a joke sometimes, but it is there. Maybe this work does fulfill my emotional needs, I don't know. It certainly teaches me a lot, an expansion of the heart."

"We try not to be carried away," says Mary Paul, "to give and pull back so that you can give to many, not just one or two. The long haul, as Geraldine says. When I was starting out, I heard other sisters rhapsodize about how God was in our midst when we were doing good works. I grew jaundiced at that talk. I think God is in our midst at many different times, and it does not take a surge of emotion to produce him. On the subway I look at children, look at their little blank faces, and I'm so disturbed, I'm beside myself. I wish that I could speak creatively about the beauty in those faces, in painting or music, but I can't. All I do, on the most mundane level possible, is what can be done."

Morning mass is conducted in a small chapel of St. Michael's set up with folding chairs. A cross bearing a gilded figure of Jesus hangs before the parishioners, fewer than twenty, all of whom are in their fifties and older. Most have attended mass here all their lives. Men and women in cloth coats whisper prayers to themselves before the arrival of the priest. They fill the room with soft hisses and *t*-sounds.

The two blue figures kneel beside each other in the second row and pray in silence: "My God, with all my heart I renew the vows I have made to thee to practice poverty, chastity, and obedience, and zeal for the salvation of souls, and to be faithful to thee forever."

At the entrance of the young priest the parishioners rise.

PRIEST: May the Lord be with you.
PARISHIONERS: And also with you.

XIV Sunset Park

Thirty minutes before *The Nutcracker* begins, the auditorium at P.S. 314 shows an audience of two: a pair of Hispanic fathers, wearing identical Alpine hats and somber winter coats, which they do not remove. They sit together, saying not a word to each other, and stare with pious seriousness at the tall paper Christmas tree pinned to the red curtain. A few minutes pass, and two more parents enter and find seats in the auditorium: then a jabbering group of five; then twenty; then an onrush. Grandparents with canes; mothers shoving strollers; brothers, sisters, and cousins of the performers; Geraldine and Mary Paul, who upon entering are rushed by a flock of small girls dressed as Snowflakes insisting: "Look at me! Look at me!" Maryann Sabatino takes a seat at the rear, sees Ingrid and her two daughters, and signals cheerfully.

Michael trots in at the side of Eileen, who is dressed in a maroon winter jacket and a black ski cap, from which her hair sticks out like loose hay from a bale. They take seats on the side, as Michael throws down his red school bag bearing the words BOOKS, BOOKS. Maria enters, looking sour. She has come to this performance at Geraldine's invitation, but protests that she is bored, and proceeds to search the room for kids her own age, sidling past Doug Heilman, the Lutheran minister, who sits flanked by the boys he takes care of. The auditorium is full now, loud with squeals from backstage and neighbors greeting one another. Geraldine cannot sit still, has a welcome for everyone. Julie, the theater leader, is here, as is Anita Cleary, who has come hoping to see Rose and the kids, but Rose could not make it. A woman sits down at the baby grand and begins to play background tunes. Eileen sings "White Christmas" to herself in a soft, pure voice.

Before the show, awards are presented to the seven groups in the after-school program by John Kixmiller and by other staff members and volunteers. To the stage march children in their party best, hair ribboned or slicked flat, to receive certificates for the "most improved" or for the "greatest contribution." Every child is applauded vigorously, not wildly. Eileen claps enthusiastically. Michael does not clap, but watches. From time to time he puts his face close to his mother's; she gives him a playful poke; he yanks at her cap. As *The Nutcracker* opens, the smallest children mount the stage in nightcaps and pajamas and face the audience like a UNICEF poster: white, black, Asian, Hispanic. On the faces of the audience the weariness of the workday transforms to eagerness. Maria complains to Geraldine that this show is for babies.

"They started to dream," Diana Hart-Johnson narrates on a loudspeaker. "And in their dreams they saw the most wonderful things; things you would never see when you are awake."

Groups of children appear one after the other, each with its own dances and bright costumes. Toy soldiers in blue hats; snake charmers in yellow turbans with paper emeralds on the front. At the "Waltz of the Flowers," the two fathers in Alpine hats snap to their feet simultaneously and flash pictures of their girls. The stage goes dark, and the boys representing the Spirit of Winter Dreams beckon the little children to them, make a circle about them, then stroll in a circle, casting beams with their flashlights on the children at the center and on the audience as well. One beam catches Michael, who stares back blank-faced at the light.

Diana reads, "The children clapped and cheered. Then everything became very quiet. The Spirit of Winter Dreams was calling the children deeper into their dream."

Maria slips her hand under Geraldine's arm and holds the position until the performance ends. As a finale, all the children gather onstage to lead the audience in Christmas songs: "Jingle Bells," "Santa Claus Is Coming to Town," "Rudolph the Red-nosed Reindeer," and *"Feliz Navidad."* Eileen urges Michael to sing, but he only gazes at the other children, who shout the songs at the top of their voices and inspire the audience, now packed to standing room, to do the same. Geraldine, Mary Paul, Doug, Maria, John, all sing. Mallory enters at a side door, looking dazed and disheveled. He searches the crowd, sees Eileen waving, does not return her wave but makes his way to her.

Mallory sits beside Eileen without a gesture of greeting, and Michael hops aboard his lap. The three of them huddle together as the children and the audience come to *"Feliz Navidad,"* moving smoothly between Spanish and English:

> *Feliz Navidad, Feliz Navidad*
> *Feliz Navidad, próspero año y Felicidad.*
>
> I want to wish you a Merry Christmas.
> I want to wish you a Merry Christmas.
> I want to wish you a Merry Christmas
> From the bottom of my heart.

Mallory and Eileen add their voices to the roar, tilt instinctively toward each other, and seem not to notice that Michael is singing.

December 30, 1985

Seven Days
in a
Small War

*In June 1982, I went to Lebanon during the Israeli invasion of that
country to find several children described in "Children of War,"
published in* Time *the previous January (see p. 152). The children
included a ten-year-old girl named Lara, whose parents were killed by a
car bomb in Beirut in September 1981; a fifteen-year-old boy, Ahmed, a
leader in a P.L.O. youth organization; a baby called Palestine, who was
born when her mother's stomach was slit open in a bombing raid of
Beirut in the summer of 1981; and Samer, the four-year-old son of
Colonel Azmi, head of the P.L.O. forces stationed around Tyre. The
hope was to find these children alive after three weeks of war; if not to
meet them face to face, then at least to learn of their whereabouts.
The following journal is partly an account of that search, and partly a
record of events observed in Lebanon during the week of June 28
through July 4. Although I started out on June 23, I did not arrive in
Beirut until the afternoon of June 27, due to the necessity of going first
to London, then to Cyprus, and from Cyprus by container ship from
Limassol to Junieh, a small port in northern Lebanon. On the Friday
before my arrival, the Israelis dealt West Beirut the heaviest bombing and
shelling of the war to that point. That same day Alexander Haig resigned
and a "permanent cease-fire" was announced. On June 27, Israeli jets
dropped a shower of pink leaflets, warning all civilians to get out of the
city at once. This journal began the following morning.*

Monday, June 28

The sun is high at 5:00 A.M., the air already very hot. The day begins
with a spurt of machine-gun fire and a shriek in the street, followed
by a low moaning. One learns that these sounds are normal. Late
yesterday afternoon, a car bomb exploded a few blocks from the
hotel, killing two, shooting a gray-white pillar of smoke into the sky,
which turned black before vanishing. Destruction is everywhere. An
apartment house on a corner is cracked in the middle like a bone. It
sags and heaves. Fragments of cement and wire hang from the struc-

ture at impossible angles. A carton of unopened Pepsis rests on a slab, waiting to fall. There is a hole in the building where the garage was; it gives the place the look of an ancient cave. In the rubble a bashed-in Mercedes, a book on the coronation of Queen Elizabeth, a pair of black shoes lying in the Charlie Chaplin position. The air is thick with dust and decay. There is so much glass on the ground, each step sounds like an army's.

From the outside, the hospital does not look as bad as that other building. The hospital for mental and psychological diseases was hit directly on several sides in last Friday's raid, but except for dozens of tiny smashed windows, its main damage shows in a lateral gap high on a wall, the shape of a huge expressionless mouth. When the twelve bombs hit the drab, gray structure, six people were killed and twenty injured. Two female patients sitting in the lounge were sliced to pieces by the shrapnel. It could have been worse. A rocket that hit the children's ward got entangled in a blanket and miraculously never went off.

This is a private hospital for the aged as well as the mentally handicapped and retarded. Among its patients are Lebanese, Palestinians, Maronites, Druze, Sunnis, Shi'ites, Jews; all Lebanon is here. An Armenian lies curled up on the second-floor landing. His stained white shirt hangs outside his blue pants. He wears a gray suit jacket, even in this heat. Flies collect on his bare feet. He pays no attention. He wants to sleep. "There was nothing," he explains when asked about the bombing. He is said to have gone wild when the shelling started.

In the children's quarter a wall cabinet displays a Fisher-Price xylophone, an inflated plastic goose, and a blond doll with her arms flung wide in surprise. Two beds are charred like marshmallows. No children were in their beds when the bombs fell. Still, some tried to leap through the holes the shells created.

A young woman in red cannot control her body. Her arms flail; her legs buckle; she smiles sweetly through her writhing mouth. An old woman sitting in bed confronts a round slice of bread, tearing it to small bits, which she tosses one by one on the floor; this is her project. In the bed opposite, a Bedouin wearing a white shawl and a deep purple blouse turns from side to side in fierce perplexity. On her forehead one tattoo, on her chin another. These are marks of beauty. "She did not understand what happened," says an orderly.

Neither did the children. They have been relocated near the women. Heads shaved, they seem of one sex or of none. Some are naked. They are penned in a small dark space; they smell of urine; their thighs are stained with excrement. They seem to moan continually. One boy shivers, another laughs. A legless girl spoons mush into the mouth of a younger one. A woman lurches forward and shouts in English: "I am normal!"

"This is the worst I have seen," says Hamil, seventy-five. He sits up in the bed in which he slept when the bombs fell.

"Were you in Lebanon during World War II?"

"Yes, I was here. But in that war the world was not so crazy."

At the P.L.O. press office, inquiries are made about the "children of war." There is a swift, sudden commotion. Yasser Arafat enters the room surrounded by bodyguards. He appears diminished, weary; the energy seems forced. Yes, he will take questions.

"When the war stops, what happens to the Palestinians in Lebanon?"

"They remain to put their fingers on the main spokes of the Palestinian issue, the Palestinian cause, the Palestinian rights. We are human beings, and we have the right to live like human beings, with our dignity. We have the right of self-determination. We have the right to go back to our homeland. We have the right to establish our own state."

"Will you give up your arms to the Lebanese army?"

"Would you give up *your* arms to the Lebanese army?"

A rumor of the day has five Egyptian ships on the way to Beirut to help with the proposed evacuation of the Palestinians. Arafat is asked if he gets seasick. He laughs off the idea as "silly." As for leaving a limited force in Beirut, he says that remains to be discussed with the Lebanese. Would he, under any circumstances, enter into negotiations with Israel?

"Do you think we should negotiate with the Israeli, barbarian, savage, terrorist military junta in Israel, with their hands full of blood?" His eyes strain forward. "Do you think? But I am here." He rises abruptly and goes to his car, flashing the V sign for the photographers outside.

At 5:15 that afternoon, Israeli jets roar high above the city. Two sonic booms follow in quick succession. A cloud of leaflets is produced in midair. It hangs, then floats down very slowly, like a great hive of small white birds beating their wings wildly as they fall.

Tuesday, June 29

There is news of Lara. A few months after her parents were killed, the girl was taken to live with relatives in Jordan. She is said to be well. Nothing on four-year-old Samer or the baby Palestine yet, but Ahmed has been located. He is posted somewhere on the front and is a full-fledged soldier now. His older brother Farouk will try to track him down. Farouk is more self-assured than Ahmed, a bit colder as well. At thirty-one, he holds a high rank in Al-Fatah, the largest faction within the P.L.O. He says very little to me at first, sizing up the stranger. Their taxi rolls past a fat man who has been forced to drop his pants for a search at a checkpoint in the middle of the street. He stands there helpless before a group of boy soldiers and squeals in rage and humiliation.

At Ahmed's home, his parents are warm and gracious. Within minutes, several of the family have gathered—sisters, brothers-in-law, and their children. Soldiers saunter in. The discussion starts out focusing on Ahmed's whereabouts, and soon splinters into everything, from the Syrians to the weather to abstract politics. An old soldier suggests, "People are better than governments." Farouk gets an idea where Ahmed might be, and the taxi is off again, passing a mosque with a charred black wall on which some child has painted a bright blue plane dropping bright blue bombs. Rubbish burning everywhere heats the air from below as the relentless sun works from the top. In a marketplace in a Palestinian camp, where Ahmed is thought to be located, a walleyed woman asks furiously: "What do you think of these dogs, the Arabs?" A camp security guard points out a grape arbor on a roof and explains that Palestinians create such things "to express their relationship with their native home."

Ahmed is in Shuweifat, a Palestinian stronghold (a neighborhood, really) east of the Beirut airport. Both the Israelis and the Phalangists are encamped nearby, not 500 yards away. It is close to noon. The streets are white, deserted. Overhead two jets, flying side by side, make a quotation mark as they veer. Ahmed enters the office to which he has been summoned. Thinner than in September, he is still boy-faced. He shakes hands with all the soldiers sitting around the room. He wears a camouflage suit, a pair of sneakers, and a cap that looks like a sun hat with the brim turned up, his P.L.O. badge pinned to the front of it. He plunks down on a couch with a machine gun resting in his lap. Then he gives his visitor the business for publishing the name of his girlfriend in last winter's story. His visitor tells him to watch his manners or the girl's address will be published this time.

"In September you said that you wanted to be a doctor. You also said that if you were at war with Israel and a wounded Israeli needed your help, you would behave as a doctor, not a soldier. Now that you are at war with Israel, do you say the same thing?"

"Yes." He is definite.

"What do you make of this war?"

"I cannot find the words. I don't hate the people. But I do hate the *actions* of the people."

He is all soldier now. He will not speculate on what course the P.L.O. should take. "It is up to our leaders." Asked if it came to a choice between laying down his arms and living to fight another day, or fighting it out to the end, he says: "There is no alternative. If we lose our identity, we lose everything." When pressed for a choice between reason and honor, he says, after some thought: "If I have to make priorities, I would choose honor first, but I don't know the answer, really." Sitting beside his brother, Farouk adds: "I would never place logic before dignity."

Out in the street, Ahmed points to the left, where the Phalangists are positioned, and to the Israelis on the right. At times he can see the enemy quite clearly. He can see their faces, but it disturbs him to think of them as individuals. Shuweifat is dead still; the apartment houses are still; the alleys like alleys in a painting. Suddenly there is a barrage of gunshots from the Phalangist side, but no one and nothing is hit. The P.L.O. soldiers return the fire. A skinny cat runs for cover. A chicken rapidly crosses the road, answering at least one question. More gunfire, then silence. Ahmed must return to the others. He hesitates before saying good-bye, then goes off with his comrades, trotting back for a moment to hand his visitor the badge from his cap. He apologizes that it is all he has to give.

Late that afternoon, it is learned that the baby Palestine is living safely with her father's sister's family in Syria. Oddly enough, however, a new Lebanese baby has just been born under similar circumstances. The mother, shot in the abdomen, died as the child was delivered. The father is unknown. The boy, called Samer by the nurses, is olive-skinned and weighs barely four pounds. One has to hold it close to the chest to prevent it from slipping through.

Wednesday, June 30

The news of the morning clatters through breakfast. The United States is trying to keep Israel from invading West Beirut; the Israeli cabinet will hold a special session on Lebanon today; Israel will allow the P.L.O. to leave Beirut carrying small weapons, but they *must* leave; Lebanese Christians and leftists go at each other in the mountains east of Beirut; Saudi Arabia's King Fahd telephones President Reagan. Will the day see more leaflets or the real McCoy? Reporters trade guesses around the Commodore Hotel swimming pool, itself a point of danger in Beirut. The pool is deep but empty, and there is little room to walk around its sides. By the end of the week one man will have fallen in, severely injuring his head and breaking a leg, while another, in a bizarre decision to jump to his rescue, will have broken his leg too.

Nearby, the Hotel Triomphe has been converted to an emergency hospital. In the unlit lobby restaurant, twelve beds are set out where the tables once were. A label on the door to the room states that American Express cards are welcome. There are more patients upstairs. A Lebanese man named Said was in his home when it was hit by a phosphorous bomb. His face glows pink where the layers of skin have been burned away. It seems wrapped in cellophane. Said's head is swathed in bandages. He looks surprised, open-eyed, as if amazed at the removal of his face. He makes candies for a living.

A Syrian in a crew cut was in the street when a shell hit. His right leg was blown off at the knee. He is engaged to be married. His fiancée in Syria does not know what has happened to him. He wonders if she will still love him.

An alert, handsome woman in a red-orange dress sits up in bed as a friend ceremoniously combs her wet black hair. The cluster bomb that hit her home killed her twenty-two-year-old daughter and injured the legs of her sixteen-year-old son. She was born in 1936; she knows all about war. She says she is comfortable in the Hotel Triomphe.

The Maqassed Hospital is a real hospital. Two hundred have died there since the bombing began. Twelve-year-old Houda had her stomach slit open by shrapnel, but she feels well now and smiles to show it. She does not know what this war is about. Mahmoud, also twelve, had his forehead burned by a phosphorous bomb. His black hair sticks up in points. He says that God will take revenge for him.

The emergency nature of the cases has been hard on the hospital staff. Only seven doctors were available for a hundred patients. Five specialists had to work on one patient alone, so much of the man was either injured or missing. The patients who were transferred from the shelled mental hospital presented a particular problem. They would stare at their wounds and break out in laughter, or they would tear at their bandages.

One man was brought in with part of his abdomen hanging outside his body. He was fully conscious. With his left hand he tried to scoop his intestines back inside.

A seventeen-year-old boy had his testicles blown off. He used to work in a printing office. He wants only peace.

A thirteen-year-old girl named Waffa was asleep when her home fell on top of her. She is asleep now too. Her head is shaved where they operated. Her left ear is blackened, her left eye swollen red. Below it, her cheek is sheathed in a purple-gray plaster. Her brain is damaged. She will be partly paralyzed for life. Beside her bed sits her older sister, who cannot bear to look. She stares instead at the open window.

Noon at the Palestinian cemetery. The air is unusually cool under trees that look like umbrellas. Photographs of the dead are planted over the graves instead of headstones. They look like yearbook pictures. Four new half-dug graves lie open in the red soil. The older ones are festooned with the kinds of ribbons used on candy boxes. A discarded stretcher lies off in a corner beside a green hospital mask. There is shelling to the south. Back at the Commodore a message comes through that Colonel Azmi is reported killed in Tyre. Is the boy Samer alive?

Thursday, July 1

An excursion across the Green Line into East Beirut and a new world. Shops show pretty summer dresses. Beach balls hang in clusters in the toy stores. Hibiscus glows red in the dark green hedges. It is on the high ground, East Beirut; the air is almost cold. Except for the Jeeps and the armored personnel carriers, you would not know there was a war in the vicinity.

At the bottom of a high hill the Beirut airport lies open and vacant, except for the carcasses of two scorched jets on the runway. To the left stands Shuweifat, where Ahmed is on patrol. The vantage point is Israeli headquarters, a secondary school beside a music conservatory. Armored vehicles rest in the parking lot. It is here that one must arrange for an escort to the south, to Tyre. The trip is scheduled for Sunday. The Israeli officer is helpful. He laments the war. "The world has not been fair to the Palestinians." He tells of a Palestinian mother, the wife of a P.L.O. officer, who escaped West Beirut with her baby and came to the Israeli headquarters for protection. Mother and child were cared for and escorted safely south to Nabatiyah. The story is not told to create a good impression. The officer is fifty-eight, jaded, a former air force pilot. Having survived four crashes, he claims the right to optimism.

North to Byblos. Ads for Woody Allen movies and a curious recurring road sign, BABY LOVE ME, that seems to have no reference. Here one is yet farther from the war. Not a soldier in sight. Only the ancient city and the ancient port, still protected by a Crusader fortress. Kids in bathing suits dangle their legs from the tops of the walls. Pleasure boats bob in the water where the Phoenicians once sailed. Is this Lebanon too? At lunch at the Fishing Club restaurant, one makes cheerful conversation with the owner, Pepe Abed, half Mexican, half Lebanese, who boasts pleasantly about the celebrities who have dined at his place. Producing a huge, elaborate guest book, he points out the autographs of Candice Bergen and David Niven. Below the restaurant, a museum bar displays statuettes snatched from the sea—Phoenician, Hittite, Greek, Roman, Persian—headless, armless relics of former powers.

Where did you say the war was? Or is this the real Lebanon, the restaurant civilization that has survived every invasion, every destruction, and flourished on trade? Is the customer always right?

Back in West Beirut by sundown, at the shelled stadium. The topmost stands are crumbled like stale cake. The poles, where pennants flew, are down or bent. Great fissures mark the walls. The clock and scoreboard are stopped cold. Gray stones are piled like giant's chalk, where steps were, where thousands upon thousands roared for the winners. A dog scavenges in the shadows. More shots from somewhere. Nearby, a bomb crater filled with water serves the people as a swimming hole.

At night the moon makes a perfect crescent, cradling a star between its points like an Arab flag. At 2:00 A.M. Israeli jets fly low over the hotel, creating astonishing booms. The ears ring, stunned. In the black sky two sulfurous flares glow sickly yellow, blaze momentarily, then disappear before an orange spray of machine-gun bullets.

Friday, July 2

At the P.L.O. press office again, seeing it for perhaps the last time. Residents of the apartments above it are hauling box springs and couches through the lobby. Mahmoud Labadi, chief press spokesman and a thoughtful, mysterious man, has not yet arrived. His office looks as if it had been deserted months ago, all the leaflets and propaganda material lying in dust on the shelves. Down the street, bombed so frequently, stores remain enclosed behind sheets of corrugated metal. Sandbags are piled on oil drums. An officer finally arrives to announce that there will be a press conference on the subject of cluster bombs at 1:00 P.M. The casings are on display, as are the small steel pie wedges where the "bomblets" were contained. They are spread out on a table beside a small ornate chess set. An idiot in a blue jogging suit wanders by twirling a silver automatic, which he believes to be empty.

In the Sanayeh Gardens, the public gardens, refugees from bombed-out homes encamp under strange tall trees that bulge at the top. Families make walls with rugs and laundry strung from ropes. Not long ago, this park was used almost exclusively by the city's rich. Now half-dressed babies waddle among their parents' last possessions. Shirts hang on bushes like oversize blossoms. A woman does her wash in a plastic bucket. Four elders play cards. They are ashamed of their plight and shoo strangers away.

Either there is great tragedy or great aimlessness. In another makeshift refugee camp, a modern secondary school, children drift in clusters from corner to corner in a large playground. Jomaneh, ten, explains that she had to leave her house "because all the windows were broken." The most beautiful thing in the world, she says, would be to go home. Everybody waits: the P.L.O., the Israelis, the outside world. After a week of leaflets and flares, tension verges on boredom.

The "Lebanese Forces" also wait. They have been waiting nearly eight years for the opportunity the Israelis have provided them, and now, clearly, they taste victory. Of course, they would not exactly say they were "grateful" to the Israelis. The head of "G-5" is speaking. He is a deadly serious young man with gray eyes and a low strong voice. He sits in uniform behind his desk. Not grateful; but he would say that his side could "benefit from recent actions." He explains that one must be careful with terms. For example, it would be wrong to confuse the Lebanese Forces with the name by which everyone knows them: Phalangists.

He is both better and worse than he sounds. At thirty-one, he thinks himself wise for being clever, yet he is honest, forthright, committed. And he has been through a good deal of fighting, including the battle at the Palestinian camp of Tal Zataar in 1976, which to the Palestinians was a massacre and to the Phalangists a major campaign. Not eager to answer questions, he presents the recent history of Lebanon. He is remarkably precise, naming days and months as well as years, pointing out places on the wall map, moving deliberately through the whole dreadful story of his country's pain. He talks of the shelling of Lebanese schools and hospitals by Syrians and Palestinians. He is making a verbal preemptive strike against the subject of the destruction in West Beirut now. Still, does he not think of the civilians?

"Sure. But it's a decision you have to make. You believe in something and you fight for it. And you know that from a humanitarian point of view, there are terrible consequences. But you stick to your belief. Either that, or you have no beliefs. In all the history of mankind, civilians were killed and soldiers were killed. I don't know why we should differentiate between soldiers and civilians."

"One is equipped to defend himself."

"Yes. But one also takes more risks than the other."

"Because he is a professional."

Annoyed. "I don't see myself as a professional of warfare. I was obliged to fight for my liberty. It could cost my life. It has cost the lives of many soldiers. It is the civilian who at last benefits from war. And I will have the memory of killed people in my mind." He pauses. "I am a lawyer. In eight years of war I could have made much money, had a future, a family. I missed all that for the sake of others. I missed the best part of my life. But if Lebanon is free again, I will have achieved something."

The day ends with two rumors afloat: an imminent Israeli invasion and a reported visit to West Beirut by Jane Fonda and Tom Hayden.

Saturday, July 3

The last hours in West Beirut. Tomorrow the journey south, first to Sidon, then to Tyre, to try to find Samer. It is difficult to tell why this quest remains important. A four-year-old, his father dead. What does one have to tell him? What does he have to say to anyone? Still, he offers a goal, a purpose, in a place where purposes are hard to come by or confused. This day, then, will offer one last look at the torn half city. There is an odd sense of loss and regret at the prospect of leaving. Why? Nothing is whole here. The buildings and bodies broken. Nothing is safe. What has happened so far is terrible; what may happen, more terrible still. Yet this is the center of the world for the moment. This parched, sunstruck, ruined place is where the world's heart beats. Across from the hotel, a woman mops her balcony. Finished, she stands and stares straight at the one who is staring at her.

Shortly after noon, the Palestinian poet Mahmoud Darwish comes by the Commodore. He has written no poems about the war. "I write my silence," he says. "I need distance to be a witness, not a victim." Since words are powerless against tanks, he feels that his silence is stronger than words. Still, a poem has power. Is Palestine itself a poem? "Yes," he says. "Because a poem is an unachieved desire."

Yet, at the moment, he is "fed up with poetry and refugee camps and walls." He believes that "Beirut is our last stand. From here to the grave, or to the homeland." Then he relents a bit. "We have to save the idea before we save Beirut. Beirut is not the capital of our idea." Darwish is forty. He has been a refugee four times and has been thrown in jail. "If the Palestinians find a homeland, they may discover the same dilemma as the Jews. The Jews were great creators in the abstract. Now only their army is great. Israel is the grave of Jewish greatness."

Asked what he thought when he saw that the other Arab states would desert the Palestinians, he looks stricken: "In this moment, right here, I am ashamed to belong to the world." He considers what he has said. "If we escape, however, I think a new world will be born."

The afternoon news is that the Israelis have closed the Green Line at the museum, the most frequently used crossing point. It is necessary to get to East Beirut right now, so as not to be locked in West

Beirut tomorrow. The taxi driver knows a different way across the line, around by the port. In an hour that exit will be blocked as well, and West Beirut sealed off. Once out, out totally.

From a hotel window in East Beirut, the western zone is almost entirely visible. It sparkles noiselessly in the clear night. Two images of the city recur. One is of a strange statue in the heart of West Beirut: that of a Lebanese politician. The statue is charcoal in color, about twelve feet tall, standing on a pedestal in a public circle with nothing interesting around it. The politician wears gogglelike glasses and a business suit. He looks both oracular and cartoonish, the presiding deity of the middle class.

The other image was caught this morning, in the council room of the grand mufti of Lebanon. Like parks and schools, this room too has been turned over to refugees. At 9:00 A.M. three young women lay sleeping on benches beneath an inscription from the Koran. They did not know they were observed. They looked serene and beautiful. One of them, with long black hair, stirred softly in her sleep, making a quiet sigh. Through the room's high windows, the sun touched her. Awakened by the light, she stretched and smiled.

Sunday, July 4

Time to decide who is right in this war. The Israelis, the Palestinians, and the Lebanese, to be sure; all of them are right. And their supporters are right, of course: those who pull for one side, two, or three. And the soldiers are right too; and the politicians and the poets. All are right. The dismembered are right, as are the paralyzed and the mad. The apartment houses and the stadiums are right. The bomb makers, the jets, the noise and silence. History and the future, both right. The dead are certainly right.

So it is settled, then, and not a moment too soon. The car is ready to head south by four in the morning. It takes the long way around by the Damascus Road, passing an institute for the deaf along the way. The institute was shelled. What is it like not to be able to hear the shell that falls on you? In the backseat of the car sit two Israeli soldiers, making muted conversation. Dan is the official escort. Eli goes along for the ride. He will meet up with other troops farther south.

Eli is a historian by trade, when he is not functioning as a chicken farmer on a kibbutz. He took his Ph.D. at the Sorbonne, and teaches Jewish history at Tel Aviv University. No, he does not think that this is his nation's last war: "We are always among enemies." Eli is forty, but his full beard makes him look older. He is tall and heavy in the shoulders, a powerful soldier. A major now, he has fought for Israel in three wars. His son was close to tears when the father went off to this one. Eli is not sure that this war was necessary, but he will fight it. Among the prophets, he most admires Amos, for the combination of faith and realism.

Later in the day, Dan will find Eli in despair. Eli will reach unconsciously into his breast pocket and pick out a playing card, the nine of hearts. Several days earlier he took it away from one of his men, in order to prevent card playing on duty. The soldier from whom he took it was new to battle, quite young, and scared. He made an error of judgment the next day, and was killed. Eli had forgotten about the card.

As the car rolls south, Israeli trucks roll north. One has a feeling that a push is on. The car reaches Sidon by 8:30 A.M. So much is destroyed here. Yet there was always destruction in Sidon. It is hard to tell ancient ruins from modern ruins. The historian, Eli, does not mind seeing damaged stones: "Children, yes." Dan, an artist in civilian life, says that he could never paint any of this. His hair is totally gray, but he looks younger than Eli. He rarely speaks. In the dust beside a crushed house, a one-mil coin marked PALESTINE and dated 1942 is found. When it was used as currency, the whole world was at war. One wonders who preserved the coin in Sidon.

Above the city, on a high hill, stands a ten-story statue of the Virgin holding the baby Jesus. A metal halo is riveted over the Virgin's head. One can enter the monument at the base and climb up inside it. Dan hesitates at the top because the protective wall has been shot away. This was a recent P.L.O. position. An antiaircraft gun was set up there. Below the Virgin, the Israeli army mills. "I hate war," says Dan, out of the blue.

In Tyre at last, inquiries are made at Israeli headquarters whether anyone knows where Colonel Azmi's family might be. The commander suggests that the Greek bishop would have some information; it is believed that Azmi's wife and son Samer lived with the bishop for a time after the colonel was reported killed. The bishop says no; he thinks that Mrs. Azmi stayed with a Roman Catholic priest for a while. It is so. The priest says that she and Samer lived with him two weeks, but that they left two days ago to stay with friends. He provides an address.

The apartment house is in a shady alley. Two women come to the door and appear friendly but apprehensive. Yes, Samer and Mrs. Azmi were there in the building, but they are gone now. They have moved to a town outside the city, which they name. Later it is discovered that there is no such town on the map.

An Israeli captain suggests the probable: "You will never find the boy. First, no one is absolutely sure that Azmi is dead. The burned body they discovered was only assumed to be his. So the woman will be waiting for him, and she will want to stay clear of strangers. Second, her husband was a well-known leader. She probably fears for her life. You would be looking for the kid forever."

Still, one pokes around Tyre a little while longer, peering foolishly into the faces of four-year-olds.

There is one last place to see: the roof of the bunker where Samer and Colonel Azmi were encountered last September. At the time, this roof was a room, an office, with straw walls, a straw roof, furniture, and people. Over there stood the colonel's Swedish-modern desk, disproportionately large and stylish. Red fake-leather chairs were positioned with their backs to the walls on two sides of the office. On them sat a dozen of the colonel's men—his inner circle perhaps. None spoke but the colonel, though all nodded approvingly at his harangue.

He never let up for a minute. It was *America* that brought on all this trouble. It was *America* that gave help to the Nazi Begin. *America* the warmonger . . . while the peaceful P.L.O. sought only to regain the land that was rightfully theirs, and so forth. He was a first-class haranguer, the colonel. He had the eyes for it and the fists. He could thrust his body forward like a cannon or draw back his chest in open innocence, a gesture embellished with a why-me? look. Just when you thought he was vulnerable to the point of collapse, he shot forward again, and you were hit between the eyes. Even now the pop of his words reverberates in the memory.

But only in the memory. The colonel is not here. The desk is not here. Nor the men, nor the roof, nor the walls. Nothing remains on top of this bunker anymore, including a portion of the roof itself, heaved high in a corner by an Israeli artillery hit. Where the colonel delivered his harangue, the noon sun drills. There is nothing else but silence and loose straw. No one who did not know what function the straw originally served could possibly guess that this was once a place of importance.

It was during the colonel's harangue last September that little Samer entered the office and was called to stand before his father. He wore matching checkered shirt and pants, and black laced shoes; highly polished and grown-up. He stood about three and a half feet high before the desk. The colonel put him through his paces:

"Who is Sadat?" he asked the boy.

"Sadat sold Palestine to Israel."

"Who is Jimmy Carter?"

"Carter supported Israel."

"Who are *you*?" The colonel regarded Samer with mock intensity.

"I am from Palestine," fired back his son. "From Hebron!"

Then the visitor asked Samer what he would like to be when he grew up. Samer said that he would like "to marry." The soldiers roared. The boy, not realizing that he had said something funny, froze in bewilderment. In answer to another question, Samer said that he would like to live in a world without soldiers. He said so there, standing where the Swedish-modern desk was, where the straw shifts back and forth now. After the boy left the room his father swore, "If I am killed, my son will carry my gun."

With the walls down, one can clearly see the Mediterranean from the roof, not 500 yards to the west. The mind sails it; first into the past, then north up the coast to where the past is now, to the besieged city with its sonic booms and rubbish fires and damaged children. It was for children this trip was taken in the first place. Two are known to be safely out of Lebanon. One is well in Beirut, though in a perilous position. The fourth is probably all right, in hiding with his mother, who will be protected by her people for being the widow of a warrior and hero. The story is done. Along the way, another story told itself; but that is a very old story. Everybody knows about wars.

The mind continues to sail in the white heat. Silently, in slow motion, the colonel's office comes back to its original shape. But the colonel is away today, and his men are not here either. It is Samer sitting behind the Swedish-modern desk, his head barely showing over the top. This time the visitor enters the room to stand at attention. The boy looks him over with deep curiosity. "Who are *you*?" he asks, as if he were his father. He is puzzled by the absence of an answer.

July 19, 1982

Hiroshima

The following pieces are two parts of a four-part story published in
Time *(July 29, 1985) on the fortieth anniversary of the Hiroshima*
bombing. I attempted to tell the story using different perspectives, thus
the titles, "What the Boy Saw" and "What the Physicist Saw." The other
pieces (not included here) were "What the People Saw," an essay on the
cultural consequences of Hiroshima, and "What the President Saw," on
nuclear diplomacy. This was the interview with Richard Nixon to which
I referred in the introduction. The story was published in book form by
Little, Brown in 1985.

What the Boy Saw

WHEN YOSHITAKA KAWAMOTO came to, the classroom was
very dark, and he was lying under the debris of the crushed
school building. In those days most Japanese buildings were made of
wood; when the Bomb dropped, all but one or two of the structures
that stood near the hypocenter of the explosion were flattened like
paper hats. Kawamoto's school, the Hiroshima Prefectural First Middle School, stood only 800 meters, a mere half mile, from the hypocenter. Two thirds of his classmates were killed instantly where they
sat at their desks. Some who survived were weeping and calling for
their mothers. Others began singing the school song to bolster their
courage and to let passersby know that the thirteen-year-olds were
still alive.

"But then the singing and the cries grew weaker. My classmates
were dying one by one. That made me very frightened. I struggled to
free myself from the broken fragments, and looked around. I thought
that gas tanks had exploded. Through a hole in the roof I could see
clouds swirling in a cone; some were black, some pink. There were
fires in the middle of the clouds. I checked my body. Three upper
teeth were chipped off; perhaps a roof tile had hit me. My left arm
was pierced by a piece of wood that stuck in my flesh like an arrow.

Unable to pull it out, I tied a tourniquet around my upper arm to stanch the flow of blood. I had no other injuries, but I did not run away. We were taught that it was cowardly to desert one's class-mates. So I crawled about the rubble, calling, 'Is there anyone alive?'

"Then I saw an arm shifting under the planks of wood. Ota, my friend, was moving. But I could see that his back was broken, and I had to pull him up into the clear. Ota was looking at me with his left eye. His right eyeball was hanging from his face. I think he said something, but I could not make it out. Pieces of nails were stuck on his lips. He took a student handbook from his pocket. I asked, 'Do you want me to give this to your mother?' Ota nodded. A moment later he died. By now the school was engulfed in flames. I started to walk away, and then looked back. Ota was staring at me with his one good eye. I can still see that eye in the dark."

So began Kawamoto's morning, August 6, 1945. Yoshitaka Ka-wamoto is fifty-three today, a small, solid man who dresses formally in blue or brown suits and carries himself with a quick-moving dignity. When he tells the story of what happened forty years ago, however, he can become a thirteen-year-old on the spot—suddenly springing from a chair to strike a military pose, demonstrating a march step, or hunching down like a shortstop. In his office he sang the school song that was sung by his classmates the morning of the bombing. As he did he rose automatically and snapped to attention, chin tucked, eyes forward:

> The rain pours white against the Hiroshima evening.
> Colors fade on petals just past full bloom,
> Spring is passing.
> But we stand firm, our dreams of prosperity unfading.

Only in the past two years, since he was appointed director of the Hiroshima Peace Memorial Museum, has Kawamoto begun to tell the story of his days of survival. Before then he did not want publicly to declare himself a *hibakusha,* a survivor of the bombing. He is aware of the unspoken stigma attached to being a *hibakusha,* that people often treat the survivors with a sort of sympathetic shunning. It is also unlike Kawamoto to do anything without a clearly defined reason. The museum directorship provided a reason. Kawamoto now recounts his experiences to museum visitors and groups of schoolchil-dren. He believes in his new role; people must know the facts, he says. At the same time, the retelling of the August days has caused

Kawamoto deep uneasiness. He had given little thought to Ota before the past two years. Now Ota appears in his dreams. Kawamoto explained that much guilt is connected to surviving the bombing. In the days following August 6, he lost Ota's student handbook.

Kawamoto spoke of that time, August 6–11, over a recent five-day period, telling part of his story in his office across the hall from the Peace Museum, and the rest "on location," in various places where the story occurred. His office and the museum are in a long, silvery modern building that looks like a harmonica situated at the broad end of the triangular Peace Memorial Park. At the point of the triangle sits the Aioi Bridge, a T-shaped structure spanning the Hon-kawa, the river that served as the aiming point for the *Enola Gay*. (The Bomb missed by only a block or two.) Between the point and the broad end of the triangular park lies a grassy area dotted with various memorials to peace or to specific victims of the bombing, the most sought-out of which is a rocket-shaped sculpture dedicated to a little girl who in 1955 died of leukemia attributed to radiation poisoning. According to one account, the girl made more than 900 paper cranes before she died, trusting that if she completed 1,000 her life would be spared. In Japan there is an old belief that a crane can live for 1,000 years, and that if you fold 1,000 paper cranes they will protect you from illness. Thousands of green, red, and yellow paper cranes made by schoolchildren billow out from under the rocket like the undergarments of a skirt.

At the center of the Peace Park is a stone cenotaph that looks like a covered wagon from the American prairie. It contains the names of the Hiroshima dead who have been identified—113,000 names to date. In an oblong pool before the cenotaph burns an "eternal flame" in an odd metallic structure resembling a headless figure with its arms extended; the flame burns where the head would be. On either side of the pool are red-orange and pink roses of enormous size, and trees that look as if they were formed by stacking bulbous tire-shaped hedges on top of one another. On a typical afternoon couples stroll, mothers push babies, children hand out peace buttons, pigeons swoop in low arcs like confetti, then up again over the water, the monuments, the museum.

The area's most recognizable structure is what is now called the Atomic Bomb Dome, originally Hiroshima Prefecture's Industrial Promotion Hall, a sort of chamber of commerce building and exhibition hall in 1945. The remains stand just outside the point of the park, across the Aioi Bridge. This shell is Hiroshima's Eiffel Tower, its

Statue of Liberty. Where the dome rose, only the supporting beams remain, a giant hair net capping four floors of vacant gray walls, much of their outer skin peeled away, exposing patches of brick. The interior floors are also gone, making the entire structure an accidental atrium. A front doorway leads to nowhere. A metal spiral staircase ascends to nothing. A pillar lies on its side, wires springing like wild hairs.

Yet not the dome nor the Peace Park nor the monuments—and there are dozens of monuments to victims throughout the city—give any real feeling of the devastation of August 6, 1945. Even the film that is shown visitors to the Peace Museum displays less sadness and horror than one would expect, in spite of the pictures of scorched children and hairless women lying listless in hospital beds. Far more affecting is a three-to-five-minute sixteen-mm movie in Kawamoto's possession that shows Hiroshima in 1936: men who still dressed in kimono; elegant women scooting rapidly through the streets of a shopping district; cherry blossoms; a fleeting glimpse of the Atomic Bomb Dome as it looked originally: fat, Victorian, and official.

It is the ordinariness of the city that creates the sense of loss; what a normally pleasant city Hiroshima was before the bombing, what a normally pleasant city it is today. On any summer morning, the Hiroshima Carp take infield practice in the baseball stadium; fashionably dressed young men and women walk purposefully to work; traffic builds on the city's bridges. If you would picture the layout of the center of Hiroshima, which covers much of the ground of Kawamoto's story, place your right hand palm down on a flat surface with your fingers spread wide. Your fingers are rivers. On the land between your third and fourth fingers lies the Peace Park. Between your fourth and fifth fingers Kawamoto's school was situated. The heel of your hand is Hiroshima Bay, and beyond your fingertips lie mountains and countryside.

Between your second and third fingers is where the *Enola Gay* dropped the Bomb at 8:15 A.M. on August 6. Once relieved of its nearly 9,000-pound burden, the plane thrust upward, jerking the heads of the crew. The B-29 made a 60° dive and a 158° right turn. Forty-three seconds after the Bomb was released, it detonated. The crew members watched it explode in a red core below them. Then they headed back to base, the tiny island of Tinian in the Northern Marianas, 1,600 miles to the south.

That morning had begun routinely for Kawamoto. At the time, he was living with his mother and his younger brother in Ono, now a growing suburb of 30,000, then a fishing village of fewer than 10,000, about thirty kilometers outside Hiroshima, across Hiroshima Bay. Mrs. Kawamoto had taken her two boys to Ono one year before, after her husband, an engineer, had been killed in a freak accident in an electrical factory. Until then the Kawamotos had been living in the nearby village of Kuba, where Yoshitaka and his friends swam out long distances in the bay. "They called us 'children of the sea.' " Sailors from German U-boats would wave to the boys from the subs. Kuba was a wonderful town to grow up in, Kawamoto says, a place of frogs and dragonflies. Boys would test their courage in the grave-yard at night. "In the daytime we wore uniforms, but at night we put on kimono. In the graveyard the hem of your kimono could get caught on a bush. It would feel like a hand tugging you down."

In Ono the morning routine was this: At six, Kawamoto would rise, put on his school uniform, and walk down the hill to catch the train for Hiroshima. Monday, August 6, was very hot, even that early in the day, and Kawamoto was tired. All the children his age had been conscripted by the military to clear firebreaks in Hiroshima, areas of escape or safety in case fires spread after bombing raids. Not that there had ever been major bombing raids on Hiroshima. While Tokyo and Osaka were being firebombed by the Americans in March, Hiroshima was relatively untouched, save for two bombing incidents in March and April, the second of which tore a huge hole in a street near Kawamoto's school.

August 6 had in fact begun with an air-raid alert for the city just after seven, but the B-29 soon passed over, and the all clear was sounded. This was the weather plane that advised the *Enola Gay* that the target was open. Schoolchildren looked forward to air-raid alerts, which allowed them to stop working. Kawamoto said good-bye to his mother, who told him to take care of himself. He plonked a shovel on his shoulder and strode soldierlike toward the railway station.

When the train arrived at the West Hiroshima station, Kawamoto and the other first-year boys gathered outside and, commanded by the senior boys, jogged in formation about two kilometers to the school. They jogged across the Shin Koi Bridge over the Ota River spillway, across a slim space of land to another bridge, which spanned the Tenma River, across another strip of land and the Nishi Heiwa Bridge over the Honkawa, finally crossing the Heiwa Bridge over the Motoyasu River. About a hundred meters from the school gate, Kawamoto and his classmates were ordered to halt and march regi-mentally the rest of the way.

"We arrived at school at 7:45 A.M. Morning assembly would begin in the schoolyard promptly at 8:00. As was our custom, we began the day by bowing to the picture of the emperor, and then proceeded to our classroom, where we recited the instructions for soldiers. These were rules of conduct, lessons that soldiers were always to obey. Fifteen minutes was never enough time to recite those lessons, but we could not be late for the 8:00 A.M. assembly. We went out into the yard and stood in rows. I saw B-29s flying overhead, and I thought, Maybe we won't have to work. The head teacher spoke and gave us instructions for the day. Leaving assembly, we were divided into two groups: odd- and even-numbered classes. The odd-numbered classes were to take the first shift clearing firebreaks. The even-numbered classes went inside to begin regular schoolwork. I was in the even-numbered group.

"In the classroom we immediately went to our desks. The desks were attached to chairs; we told ourselves that they were the same kind of desks used in the United States. I had a special feeling for my desk. There was a space between the desk and the chair that we could dive under in an air raid. We also had 'bulletproof' helmets, which were not bulletproof and not really helmets, but rather pointed hats of thick cloth made by our mothers. The senior boys ordered us to close our eyes and meditate. I closed my eyes, but did not meditate; I was only wondering if the seniors were going to hit us. They were always clouting us for one thing or another. I practiced making the kind of face that did not look as if it ought to be hit." Kawamoto demonstrates the expression of a blank mask.

"Then the seniors went out of the classroom, leaving the younger boys to meditate on their own. I opened my eyes. A boy named Fujimoto—I think his father was a doctor—was seated by the window. He called out, 'Look! A B-29!' My classmates kept meditating, but I was very curious, so I started to go toward the window. That was when the flash hit. I heard no sound. It was a flash like lightning. The air was shimmering, the way a television screen shimmers when it is out of order."

Then unconsciousness. Then the school song. Then Ota.

"Remember, I had only been in the middle school four months, like all first-year boys; not enough time to make many friends. Ota and I became friends because we were both short, and since students were allotted seats according to their height, Ota and I were placed beside each other in the first row. I admired Ota very much. I was just a country boy, but Ota was polished and handsome, the kind of fellow

I had always thought of as the perfect city boy. White skin, clearly defined eyebrows, a Western-type nose, not a flattish one like mine. The whites of his eyes always sparkled. And he had a husky, manly voice. Everyone looked up to him because he was so articulate. He was fun too, a very special boy.

"I left him in the fire and went out into the playground. The playground was covered with a thick, dark layer of smoke. I could see the blue sky filter through from place to place. I did not know which way to run. Out of the flames and noise, I heard a voice cry, 'Run into the wind. Run into the wind.' I picked up a fistful of sand—to this day I do not know how I thought to do this—and tossed the sand in the air to see which way the wind was blowing. There was fire everywhere. Bodies lay dead or writhing all over the playground.

"Then I saw the head teacher. So severe were his burns, I could not recognize his face, only his voice. He wore nothing but a pair of undershorts, and he was dragging a cart with some of my classmates lying on it. I helped drag the cart, but the going was extremely slow and difficult. We had to lift the cart over the other bodies, and those who were still alive grabbed at our ankles and begged for help. We had to push bodies aside to clear a path. Finally, we reached a point safe from the fires. We found several tin cans of oil. I dipped a towel in the oil and dabbed my classmates' wounds. The road was heating up terribly, either because of the sunlight or because of the bomb. [The bomb emitted a land temperature in that area of at least 3,000° C, or 5,400° F, twice the heat required to melt iron.] The head teacher and I did not talk. I was too tired to talk. I only wanted water. Two students in the cart died before my eyes."

Kawamoto has been telling this part of his story standing in a school playground that was built where his old school playground used to be. It is only four or five blocks from his office. The new playground is much larger than the old one, Kawamoto says. There are tennis courts on one side; a soccer game is in progress; over in a corner a girl puts a shot while a friend measures the distances. Kawamoto observes that children today are less disciplined than in his generation. He speaks fondly of the strong sense of unity among his classmates, how they stuck together against both the seniors and the military officers assigned to the school to conduct military exercises.

"The officers also oversaw our lunches. Our lunches usually consisted of 'Japanese flags'—a bowl of rice with a red plum in the center, the design of the national flag. But if we had too much white rice, we were hit; white rice was a sign of luxury. If we had a mixture of rice and wheat, with more wheat than rice, that was OK. Country boys had more white rice, of course, so we were hit quite often— either for that or for finishing our lunches too quickly. We were supposed to take a full hour with our rice, so we would gobble it up at first, and then slow down, trying to stretch out the hour. One of our military officers was especially strict, a real tyrant. He was in school the day of the bombing. I saw him months later working in the black market, pounding a counter in the street to attract customers."

Kawamoto did not like having the military around his school, but he appreciates the military values of discipline. He connects discipline with self-knowledge. Once, when he was a very small boy, his father took him in a boat out into the bay and threw him in, to teach the boy to swim. Kawamoto struggled and tried to grab the side of the boat, but his father pushed him off with a pole. Only when the boy sank did his father pull him back. "I asked him why he did not help me sooner. I thought my father was trying to drown me. Later I understood that he was really trying to save me, that I would only learn to swim if I came that close to death."

Of the modern generation Kawamoto says it does not possess "the kind of heart that knows how to stare into itself and discover its own strength. *Onore o shiru:* to know oneself. It is essential. People today live too much by their individual desires, and so are bound to repeat the mistakes of the past. One must vow not to repeat those mistakes. Unless you know yourself, you cannot make a vow that counts."

In the Peace Museum now, Kawamoto uses a long wooden pointer to indicate, in a large circular panorama, the route of the rest of his escape. Above the center of the panorama a bright red ball representing the hypocenter hangs by a cord. Kawamoto touches the pointer to the area of the playground, then moves it out into the city, away from the hypocenter, toward the Kyobashi River and the Miyuki Bridge.

"We were trying to get away from the fires and head for the river. On the way, I lost sight of my teacher and proceeded alone. People burned too severely to survive grabbed at me as I went along. Those who could walk stumbled over the bodies; they wore tatters and were covered with ash. I saw a living baby clinging to the breasts of its dead mother. I saw another child of three or four beating her dead mother with her fists. Perhaps she did not know that her mother was dead and in desperation and confusion was trying to wake her up.

"Near the Miyuki Bridge I met my classmate Kimura. Kimura

belonged to the odd-numbered group, so he had been working in the streets when the bomb went off. His face was charred. He lived in West Hiroshima, and he said he was going home, which meant that he was heading back toward the direction of the hypocenter. I told him that it was impossible to go back, that the area was all in flames. He was delirious and would not listen to me. He only repeated, 'I want to go home. I want to go home.' He walked away toward the flames. Later his family could not locate his ashes."

During the war people kept their own reservoirs in case of fires. The water in these reservoirs lay filthy and stagnant through the year, but Kawamoto was desperately thirsty. He started toward one of the reservoirs, but saw that people were lying dead, half in, half out of the water. Coming to the Miyuki Bridge at last, he leaped down the steep stone steps, stumbling over others plummeting down. There was a logjam of bodies at the base of the steps. "I was so scared." He tried to drink the muddy water, but spit it out. He clambered up the riverbank.

"I lay on my back in the heat. There was no shade to cool me. Thick clouds were billowing above my head. It was a thunderhead. Fires glowed in the clouds. The sky was dark. I thought, I will never see my mother again. Then I passed out."

Much of what Kawamoto saw between the school playground and the Miyuki Bridge is exhibited in the museum he directs. It is after hours now, so he is free to move easily from display case to display case, using one exhibit or another to illustrate his story. During regular hours the museum is packed with schoolchildren in uniform, pressing their noses against the windows of the cases; chattering; some horseplay from the bigger boys. On display is all that became of Hiroshima once the bomb dropped, along with historical memorabilia such as the directive from Lt. Gen. Carl Spaatz, commander in chief of the U.S. Strategic Air Force, ordering that the city be bombed; a large photo of the A-bomb known as "Little Boy," looking like a sea mammal in profile; messages of resolve or condolence from distinguished visitors; leaflets dropped by the Americans in early August 1945 that warned of some general disaster but not of the A-bomb specifically. "The Americans did warn Nagasaki about the Bomb, but not Hiroshima," says Kawamoto. "It made no difference anyway. Our military ordered the people not to read any of the leaflets, so none of our citizens knew what was coming."

Strange objects fill the display cases: testaments to the Bomb's effects on ordinary things. A twisted beam from a seven-story building; a charred tobacco pipe; a melted lump of coins; a mass of nails, of sake cups. A watch stopped at exactly 8:16 was found in the sands of the Motoyasu River. A horse is on display; its legs are missing. One case contains hair that had fallen in a clump on the ground. (Kawamoto's hair fell out after six weeks, but two months later it grew back again.) Another case contains black fingernails two or three inches in length that had grown on a hand where the skin was entirely burned off. The black nails had blood vessels in them; nothing like them was ever seen before.

And photographs of the suffering, their burned backs looking like topographical maps. And shadows of vaporized people that remained on streets after the people disappeared. And a wall streaked with "black rain," the large radioactive raindrops that fell shortly after the explosion.

The displays that touch Kawamoto most deeply are those of a middle-school uniform, much like his own, the jacket torn with one sleeve missing; and of wax models of victims walking as if stunned or asleep, their arms held out in front of them. Their skin hangs loose on their bones, like ill-fitting clothing. Their real clothes are rags. In the display case they stand blank-eyed against a backdrop of a wasteland of ashes and a fire-streaked sky. "It is the way people really looked," Kawamoto says. "They did not seem to walk voluntarily; they appeared to be pushed.

"When I regained consciousness, I found myself lying in a warehouse, which was turned into a hospital, near the Ujina port. The Ujina port is at a good distance from the Miyuki Bridge. Soldiers had carried me to the warehouse. There I waited. I remembered my fear at the sight of the bodies in the river. I saw not a single fish. That river was always full of fish. The whole area between my school and the Miyuki Bridge had looked so different. That was where Hiroshima University had stood. A railroad operated in that neighborhood. A Red Cross hospital had been there too. All gone. Children lay in the arms of dead parents, parents carried the bodies of dead children. The soldiers who brought me to the warehouse told of seeing a horse killed on the spot where it stood during the flash. There were no marks or wounds on the animal. It had died in its tracks of shock or of a scorching wind.

"It was about seven in the evening when I came to. It had taken me two and a half hours to get from the playground to the Miyuki Bridge, and this was eight or nine hours later, so I had lain unconscious for a very long time. The warehouse at Ujina ordinarily was used to store food for the soldiers. Now it stored people, who sat dazed with their backs to the walls. The first thing I saw on coming to was a soldier's face looking into mine. He gave me an affectionate pat on the head. Perhaps it was he who removed the piece of wood from my arm, for the wood was gone now, and my arm was in great pain. Another soldier who had medical training was working his way around the warehouse, going from victim to victim. When he came over to me I asked for water, but he refused. They were only giving water to the dying. By that I knew that I was expected to recover. The first soldier came by and placed a piece of ice in my mouth. I shall never forget his kindness.

"It was he who told me how I had happened to come to the warehouse. The people who originally found me by the riverbank thought I was dead, so they tossed me on top of a stack of bodies that they were about to set afire for cremation. Somehow my body slid off the pile. When a soldier tried to heave me back on top, he grabbed me by the wrist and felt my pulse."

Throughout the day, Mrs. Kawamoto had been frantic for news of her son. She had made an attempt to get into Hiroshima by train, but was turned back at the West Hiroshima station. The morning of August 7 she made a second attempt, but this time the railway station was roped off. The next day she went to the schools in the towns around Ono; she heard that bomb victims had been brought to these schools, which, like the warehouse in Ujina, had been turned into hospitals. On August 9 she got word that her son was alive on one of the islands outside the city, but she did not know where. With a group of neighbors who were also searching for their children, she hired a fishing boat to search the islands around Hiroshima.

"The soldiers tried to place me on a boat headed for the island of Ninoshima, but the people on the boat rejected me; they were already overloaded with passengers. The soldiers put me on another boat headed for the peninsula of Taibi. On Taibi I was placed in a tent that was otherwise occupied only by women. I suppose they did this because I was a child. Some of the women were with babies. Some of the women were half naked. Some showed no external wounds, but they had gone crazy from the bombing or from being parted from their families. They clung to the legs of the soldiers, imploring them, 'Where are my children?' The younger women, distraught, began climbing the tent poles, crying, 'Mother! Mother!' I could not sleep that night, or the next day, or even the next. The women cried for two days, but on the third, they were too exhausted to cry.

"The second day on Taibi, we had an air-raid alert, a false alarm. Those who could, walked to a shelter. Most people were too weak to stand. They urinated and defecated where they were lying. Soldiers, their eyes red with fatigue, passed around canned oranges. But I could not eat; I could not bear the smell in the tent. My face was burning with fever, and my eyes and lips grew swollen. By now my arm was in terrible pain, and finally a soldier took me to a doctor. The doctor wanted to amputate, but the soldier said, 'This boy is only thirteen. He has lots of things to do for our country. Please don't cut off his arm.' "

To which the doctor agreed, but said that he could not guarantee Kawamoto's life. Then he disinfected the wound. "I was not afraid now. I was sure I was going to live."

Kawamoto got word to his mother from Taibi. He did so indirectly, by invoking the name of a relative, a principal of a military school who was a powerful man in the military. A soldier, impressed by the name, called the village hall in Ono, saying that Kawamoto was alive, though he did not mention Taibi. That was when Mrs. Kawamoto hired the boat and began her search of the islands. Meanwhile, Kawamoto returned to the tent and waited, not knowing whether his mother had received his message or not. He began to get some sleep on August 9, sleeping heavily for several hours at a time in the dark tent, lit only by candles, half-waking when the women screamed.

In the Buddhist graveyard at Kuba, Kawamoto walks among the block-shaped tombstones and looks down from the steep hill at Hiroshima Bay, where he swam as a child. This was the graveyard where he and the other boys used to test their courage: "In the daytime we would come up here and leave some personal belonging. In the night we would retrieve it, which would prove to the others that we were here."

"There were mysterious stories about all these hills," he says, stories of *tanuki,* strange raccoon-dogs invested with mischievous, magical powers. He tells of a boy who used to go up into the mountains for birds' eggs; the birds nested in the mountains' muddy surface. "One day he asked me to go with him, but I was busy. By evening he had not returned home. His parents were very concerned, and they organized a search party. When the search party came upon the boy, they found him walking in a huge circle, round and round. He kept repeating, 'I have grown taller. My legs are long.' Everyone assumed that a *tanuki* had put a spell on him.

"Foxes were also supposed to be magical and troublesome. My grandfather used to tell me of a day he was walking along the 'beast path' of a mountain, a path between villages that foxes were thought to frequent. My grandfather was carrying a *bentō,* a box lunch; foxes were known to love *bentō.* Walking along, he suddenly heard the sound of straw shoes trudging in the sand behind him—*sarrah, sarrah, sarrah.* My grandfather looked back and saw what appeared to be a peasant girl in a dress, a shawl, and sandals. But foxes were known to wear such disguises. One way to be sure was to see how the creature crossed water. If it stepped across, it was a peasant girl; if it jumped, it was a fox. When my grandfather came to a stream, he crossed quickly, hid, and watched his pursuer. Sure enough the 'peasant girl' jumped the stream. I loved to hear that kind of story from my grandparents."

Reading the names on the Buddhist tombstones, Kawamoto points out those of the families he knew. He keeps a plot of ground here for his own family. Living in Ono again, he is close to both the villages of his youth, though Kuba, like Ono, has grown considerably. The hill of the graveyard had to be cut away at the base to make way for a new high school. Growth is natural, Kawamoto says, but he regrets modern disconnections from the past. "Now the future is everything." Still, he believes that the world is in many ways better off than before the war. He is glad in retrospect that the Americans won the war—a feeling expressed by many Japanese his age. Under the military regime, Japan's spirit would have perished, he says. Japan needed democracy, and it took losing the war to achieve it.

He is opposed to the existence of nuclear weapons. Both as the director of the Peace Memorial Museum and as a *hibakusha,* he can speak with authority about nuclear force, but he makes his case briefly and without evident passion. "I am not a philosopher," he says. If pressed as to what he thinks the world will do with nuclear weapons, he admits that he is worried. At the same time he ascribes his own sense of practicality to the world: "Human beings are not fools. We are not likely to destroy everything. We must leave our traditions to the generations."

Mainly he believes in what he saw those August days in 1945. He believes in the piles of bodies in the river and in the melted skin and in the fires in the sky. He believes in Ota. In the present, he believes in his wife and in his home. He would believe in children too, if he had any. But he would not have children; he was afraid they would be affected by possible genetic damage caused by radiation. He believes quite strongly in his house, onto which he has just built an additional room. The house is lovely; it sits on a hill just below his mother's house in Ono. He says that one improves one's house as one improves one's life, and that when you die, you must leave both house and life in as good shape as possible. All this, he explains, is part of the Japanese way of thinking. That all things are transitory, and that their value derives from the fact that they shine brightly before they pass away. For this reason, says Kawamoto, one must keep track of one's experiences.

On August 11, 1945, Yoshitaka Kawamoto sat in the tent in Taibi, half awake in the darkness. Suddenly his mother entered, and the two caught sight of each other. "It was the first time I cried."

What the Physicist Saw

NO, I WASN'T ON the *Enola Gay*. I was on the *Great Artiste*, the instrument plane, which measured the yield, the size of the blast. We were right next to the *Enola Gay* when she dropped the Bomb. It was I who got the pictures. I didn't take 'em. Let's say I had a hand in 'em. But I brought the films back. They were on a sixteen-mm color cassette, and the only processing facility we had out there was for black-and-white movies on reels, so they couldn't process what we had, and we didn't know if anything was on 'em or not. I had to get 'em back to the lab over Groves's dead body. Groves had a policy that everything in the field went to him first, and he tried to get the films away from me. That's a story in itself—cops 'n' robbers. So how do you keep the films from General Groves when you're going from Tinian to Kwajalein to Johnston Island to Hawaii to San Francisco to Wendover, Utah, to Albuquerque, stopping every time with some gumshoe lookin' in the plane and asking, 'Anybody on board by the name of Agnew? He has something I've been ordered by General Groves to *get*.'

"Well, I didn't put [the films] in my brassiere or up my ass, but I *got* 'em. Still, I got caught in Albuquerque. That's when they really closed in on me. But I cut a deal. We'd take the pictures to Oppie, and he'd decide what to do."

Harold M. Agnew's elbows make a pair of wings for his head, on top of which his hands fold in a clasp. The elbows are covered by suede patches sewn onto a brown tweed jacket. The collar of his brown polo shirt is worn over the jacket collar. There is a Western-style belt of silver and turquoise, and something of a belly: the paunch of a man of sixty-four who was an athlete forty years ago. He looks like Spencer Tracy now. His desk looks like a pile of raked leaves. On walls and tables in his not-too-large office are honorary university degrees; a photo taken with Attorney General Edwin Meese; another photo taken years ago on Tinian, showing Agnew and his fellow scientists at a briefing session the night before the Hiroshima bombing; and near his desk, a framed photo of his wife, Beverly, now sixty-five, looking crisp and very smart in 1939.

These mementos belong to the president of GA Technologies Inc., a company described in its brochure as one of "diverse interests and programs, ranging from the development of advanced energy conversions systems to the production of nuclear instrumentation and radiation monitoring equipment." "They still give me an office to play in," says Agnew, suggesting that his days of hands-on running the company are over. GA Technologies is a very big thing to run: 1984 sales of $160 million and 1,800 employees. Filling 350 well-tended acres behind a high wire gate near La Jolla, California, the company resembles a little village, which, instead of a school, a church, and a store, consists of a Fusion Building, Waste Yard Buildings and Experimental Area Buildings No. 1, No. 1–Bunker, and No. 2.

In fact, GA Technologies looks a good deal like the Los Alamos Scientific Laboratory, of which Agnew was once the director, succeeding Norris Bradbury, who succeeded Los Alamos's first director, J. Robert Oppenheimer, the "Oppie" of the story about the swiped films. The "Groves" is General Leslie Groves, military commander of the Manhattan Project. The films Groves was chasing were the only ones taken of the Hiroshima bomb at the moment it went off. Agnew's *Great Artiste* was one of the planes seen by the boys in Yoshitaka Kawamoto's schoolyard when assembly was held the morning of August 6. It may also have been the B-29 spotted by Kawamoto's classmate Fujimoto when Kawamoto started toward the window for a look.

Agnew was only twenty-four when he went up in the *Great Artiste*, but he had already seen a lot of the new world of split atoms. As a physics student straight out of college, he was taken by his professor to work with the people at the University of Chicago under Enrico Fermi. At the age of twenty-one, Agnew was one of forty-three people to witness the world's first man-made nuclear chain reaction, in a squash court under the football field. A few years later he was testing yield-measuring devices at Wendover Air Base in Utah, where Col. Paul Tibbets and the atom bomb crew were training in secret. What Agnew saw was much of the history of America's scientific and military progress toward the Hiroshima bombing. He also observed the close relationship that developed between science and the military after the Bomb was dropped. As director of Los Alamos from 1970 to 1979, he later superintended that relationship.

For forty years, then, Harold Agnew's life tracked the atomic age—from Chicago to Los Alamos to Hiroshima to Los Alamos to La Jolla. His perspective on Hiroshima specifically is that a bomb had to be made and a war won.

Not that any of this history occupies the forefront of Agnew's mind at the moment. These days he is steaming over the IRS, which refuses to give him a tax deduction on those films of Hiroshima. Here is what happened after he cut the deal with Groves:

"I called Oppie ahead of time to explain what was going on. And while we were negotiating, a guy from the lab grabbed the films and went to L.A. with 'em, 'cause that was the only place in the country where they could be processed. It turned out we really struck gold with those pictures. We *got* it. After that we settled the business, and gave copies to Groves. When the war was over, Oppie gave me the originals, and I'd let people use 'em.

"But then Senator [Bob] Packwood heard I had these things, and said they ought to be put in the Smithsonian. So I looked, but I decided that they'd wind up behind some stuffed owl. Then Glenn Campbell of the Hoover Institution [of War, Revolution, and Peace at Stanford University] wanted 'em, so I gave 'em to him. A few months later, I got an appraisal from Sotheby's for a deduction on my income tax. Well, since then I've been fighting the IRS. This Wednesday we're having a hearing. Seems they sent the films to Ray Hackie's Film Service. And Ray Hackie's Film Service said the films are worthless. Said they'd been taken with a hand-held camera. There's no script and no score.

"I'm not *kidding*. No script and no *score*. So I have to hire an attorney. It's funny, but it's not so *funny*. That's the IRS for you. Not a thing you can do about it. The way they're going to get their money is through the taxes the lawyer pays 'em after me payin' *him*.

"And another thing I got is the original strike orders [for the bombing], which are rather impressive. They were posted on the bulletin board in Tinian, telling us what planes to use, and when to go to breakfast, and when you take off. And the thing that gets me: You read all the way down—so many gallons of gasoline, and so on—until you get to 'Bomb: Special.' Just said 'Special.' Course, the IRS says that's worthless too. What's a country boy to *do*?"

From time to time the phone rings, and the country boy enters another imminent negotiation. He is trying to sell one of his four cars, a '66 Ford with 208,000 miles on it. Someone has just informed him that the car has a burned-out valve. "You still wanna buy it?"

He addresses the past again. "Did we have to drop the Bomb? You bet your life we did. I wrote an article a couple of years ago recounting my experiences as a member of the U.S. delegation to the United Nations General Assembly Second Session on Disarmament [June 1982]. Outside the U.S. building a group was sitting and marching in silence in memory of Hiroshima. Not Pearl Harbor but Hiroshima. No one seems to realize that without Pearl Harbor there wouldn't have *been* a Hiroshima." He goes back to the beginning:

"The way things really got started was in late '41, after Pearl Harbor. Actually for me, before that time. I was a student at the University of Denver. That's my hometown. And we were all signing up to join the Army Air Corps. Many of my classmates had run off to Canada. That was when you'd run off to Canada to get *into* a war, not stay out of one. In fact, my classmate Keith Johnson got shot down in the Battle of Britain. So we were all signing up. But a professor of mine said, 'Don't sign up in that program. I think something's happening where you can be much more useful.' That's all I knew. A couple of weeks later he said, 'You're going to Chicago.'

"In those days there were only a handful of places in the whole country that knew anything about nuclear energy—nuclear *physics*. It was just in '38 that Enrico Fermi got the Nobel Prize for his work with neutrons, so it was all really brand new. What happened was that the heads of the few places—Ernest Lawrence at Berkeley, Arthur Compton at Chicago, John Dunning at Columbia—they contacted all their former graduates and said, 'Come on back.' They were told that if they knew any semiliterate undergraduates, bring 'em too. It's for the *war*. So my professor at Denver brought me, first to Columbia, then to Chicago, to see what was going on. Not really. I don't think I knew what was going on as far as the Bomb was concerned for maybe nine months. Anyway, we went to Chicago and started building the first manmade chain reaction.

"I wrote an article about the squash court experiment too—if I can find the goddamn thing. I write lots of articles. Course, nobody ever reads 'em." After a minute, he comes up with "Early Recollections of the Manhattan Project," an address to the Society of Nuclear Medicine meeting in Chicago in June 1977. In the article he describes how Fermi and his assistants kept building up the nuclear pile to achieve a critical mass, the smallest amount of material needed to begin a chain reaction. They calculated that on the night between December 1 and December 2, 1942, the fifty-seventh layer of graphite would make the pile critical. To prevent the neutrons from multiplying and starting a reaction, the scientists used cadmium strips, which absorb neutrons. When all but one of the cadmium strips were removed, it became clear the calculations were correct. "It was a great temptation for me to partially withdraw the final cadmium strip and to be the first to make a pile chain-react. But Fermi had anticipated this possibility. He had made me promise that I would make the measurement, record the result, insert all cadmium rods, lock them all in place, go to bed, and nothing more.

"What people don't understand is that we were really running frightened of the Germans. The main thing was to get a self-sustaining chain reaction before the Germans did. All the people who were involved—Leo Szilard, John Von Neumann—the whole gaggle of 'em had just got off the boat. Fermi's wife was Jewish. The rest of the guys were Jewish. That's why they left. But all the other Huns, their colleagues, were back home, probably working on a chain reaction. So there was a lot of pressure.

"Well, anyway, we put the stuff together the next morning, and it looked as if the thing was going to go critical. Then Fermi says, 'Let's go have lunch.' You'd think he'd want to stay around and finish the damn thing. The criticality kept going up. The counters kept clicking faster and faster. You don't see anything when this happens. The counter just keeps accelerating, like in your car. Course, in a bomb it goes so fast, it blows the thing apart. But then Fermi shuts everything off and says, 'Let's have *lunch*.' So we started it all up again in the afternoon, and it went critical, and that was that.

"Let me tell you, even at this point I still didn't know what the hell this was all about. Everything was very secret. Besides the Hiroshima films and the strike orders, I got a very interesting tape by Fermi talking about secrecy. He points out that things were classified first by the *scientists*, not by the military. You hear things now about how the damn government classified science; not so. I have the tape. He even hired a guy from Yale to draw up the rules for classification. An absolute paranoid. Excellent choice."

The uneasy relationship between the scientists and the military was beginning to find its shape about the time of the Chicago chain reaction. Only three years earlier Albert Einstein, advised by his fellow refugee physicists Leo Szilard and Eugene P. Wigner that the Germans were likely to produce an atomic weapon, had addressed a letter to President Roosevelt warning of "extremely powerful bombs of a new type." Once Roosevelt was persuaded that America ought to have that bomb first, he set in motion, albeit very slow motion initially, a coordination of scientific effort that would lead inevitably to a working partnership with the American military. Watson Davis, a science editor of the 1930s, anticipated the central difficulty of that partnership in a single observation: "The most important problem before the scientific world today is not the cure of cancer, the discovery of a new source of energy, or any specific achievement. It is How can science maintain its freedom and . . . help preserve a peaceful and effective civilization?"

In a time of war against world-seizing powers, Davis's question had to lead science logically, purposefully, and enthusiastically toward a collegial relationship with the American military. Once that relationship was established it was not to be undone. After Hiroshima, with or without a war serving as matchmaker, the soldiers and the physicists were to be wedded for the rest of the century. Yet in the 1940s it was not with the military per se that many scientists believed they were forming a partnership. Rather, it was with the war as a specific and isolated entity. Agnew recalls how zealously Oppenheimer worked to keep the scientists in a draft-free status: an effort for symbolic, if not functional, independence.

For their part, most of the military had no knowledge of the atom bomb project. General Groves was in charge of the Manhattan Project at Los Alamos and on Tinian, but he served as a manager and coordinating supervisor—an exceptionally capable one, according to Agnew; an overbearing and tyrannical one, according to critics—not as a commander directly involved with the conduct of the war. Not even Gen. Douglas MacArthur, the monarchical commander in the Pacific, knew of the Bomb in the making.

Yet while these two technically separate units of physicists and soldiers trained and worked in relative isolation from each other for an event no one was sure would ever take place, and while the scientists restricted their intellectual freedom in pursuit of preserving their civic freedom, the fact is that both they and the military were working their way toward the same meeting place. That their relationship would be sealed over Hiroshima deeply troubled some of the scientists afterward, who may have read in the aerial pairing of the *Enola Gay* and the *Great Artiste* the end of their control over a universe they had disclosed. In 1943, however, most of the scientists wanted victory first, and Los Alamos was their theater.

"You want to know how I got to Los Alamos? It was my wife's good looks. We were married in May 1942, and Beverly got a job as personal secretary to R. L. Doan, the administrative head of the project in Chicago. She also handled the whole security system in Chicago—twenty-one years old, an English *literature* major. She was pretty too, and whenever Oppie came around, he liked to talk to her. Naturally, when Oppie was going to start up the lab in Los Alamos, he decided that he needed someone to work for him who had experience—like Beverly. So he asked her to come to New Mexico. And it was reasonable that I should go too. Fact is, it seemed that everyone and everything was going to Los Alamos. The Princeton guys, the Illinois people. *Tremendous* effort. People today don't appreciate how frightened we were. Things were really going down the tube in '41, '42, '43. We were losing badly in the Pacific. There was Bataan. Hong Kong fell Christmas Day. The Atlantic was just horrendous.

"Anyway, when I showed up at Los Alamos, it was a Sunday, and my wife hadn't arrived yet, 'cause she was home saying good-bye to her brother, who was off to the war. And I ran into Oppie. And all he said was 'Where's Beverly?' Which crushed me. From that day I knew exactly where I stood with *that* guy." Agnew chuckles. "I never really liked the guy, anyway. He was too smart and too rich and too handsome.

"And he was really a smoothie. We got about 128 bucks a month. The plumbers at Los Alamos were getting between $500 and $750. And the plumbers couldn't do anything the physicists couldn't do. So we went to see Oppie, about six of us, and complained. And Oppie says, 'The difference is that you know what you're doin' and the plumbers don't.' Then he walks out. And we *took* it. What an operator."

Modern Los Alamos makes it easy to picture what the town looked like in 1943, when the physicists began to arrive and settle in. Like Hiroshima, Los Alamos lives in two eras simultaneously; a road sign near Bandelier National Monument park indicates six miles to the "Atomic City. Birthplace of the Atomic Age, scientific laboratory and museum, gas-food-lodging–golf course." The makeshift wooden apartments that once housed the physicists and their families are long down, as are the PX with its cathedrallike jukebox and the commissary and the walls of bed sheets drying in the sun in front of Quonset huts. Yet photographs of all these are retained and displayed prominently in the new buildings, whose functions differ from the originals only in scope. The main business of Los Alamos is what it has been since the town popped up on a plateau just east of the continental divide forty-two years ago: the design and development of nuclear weapons. These functions are performed in a surrounding of caves, canyons, mesas, mountains, and sky so beautiful that all one has to do is look up from his work for a moment, and the day has changed.

"We came to this wonderful world," said Nobel Prize winner I. I. Rabi in a speech at Los Alamos a few years ago when the alumni reconvened. Rabi's speech was double-edged. Titled "How Well We Meant," it both recalled the necessity of nuclear weapons and lamented their subsequent expansion. But in the beginning "it happened to be one of those spring days where everything was lovely. The air was clear and mild, the Sangre de Cristo Mountains were distinct and sharp, the mesa on the other side—lovely! And the ride up on the old road, somewhat hair raising but very interesting, the old bridge, and then, of course, the Indians; we certainly seemed to enter a new world, a mystic world."

Both the mystic and the real world are exhibited in the Bradbury Science Museum. It is about the size of Kawamoto's Peace Museum, and it too tells the story of an event and its consequences. Exhibits are arranged to indicate causalities. Einstein's letter to F.D.R. is located on a wall below a newspaper headline of the times: GERMANY ANNEXES AUSTRIA. There is a letter from Groves to Oppenheimer, requesting that Oppenheimer avoid flying in airplanes: "The time saved is not worth the risk." A photograph shows the July 16, 1945, Trinity test explosion at Alamogordo, looking like a glazed white coffee cup overturned on a bed of suds.

Oddest among the exhibits are two life-size, life-shape, white plaster models of Groves and Oppenheimer: the one, thick-fleshed in an oversize Army uniform, the cast accurate to the bulge in Groves's breast pocket, perhaps made by the chocolates to which he reportedly was addicted; the other skinny, stooped, in an unpressed civilian suit and floppy hat. From hats to shoes, all white, the two of them. All white, too, is a model of "Little Boy" lying on the floor—120 inches long, 28 inches in diameter, nearly 9,000 pounds—looking like a small, friendly Moby-Dick. Another striking figure in the museum is that of "Plastic Man," described as "one of the most popular of all the laboratory's residents during the 1950s." The transparent dummy was used to test levels of radiation on human beings after an atomic blast.

The main event in the museum is a film called *The Town That Never Was,* shown on a regular schedule in a small theater where the seats are carpeted risers. Hiroshima is never mentioned in this film, which for some reason begins with voices in prayer in church and the figure of Jesus covered with blood. Then the film proceeds to show the Chicago squash court and herky-jerky conversations among Szilard, Wigner, Edward Teller, and the rest. A jalopy convertible winds up a mountain road in a scene that might have come from a Gene Autry western of the 1930s. There are sudden shots of the Statue of Liberty; sheep and golden flowers by a roadside; the Los Alamos Ranch School, which occupied the land before the lab came, a place where wealthy families sent sickly boys for toughening. The film's narrator says that "Indians willingly relinquished land for the sake of the war," and he describes the uniqueness of Los Alamos in terms of negatives: "No invalids, no idle rich, no in-laws, no unemployed, no jails, no sidewalks, no garages, no paved roads." The film ends with sailors bussing girls on the streets of New York, and references to the future of nuclear energy and "rockets to the stars."

When Agnew arrived at Los Alamos in March 1943, there were no invalids, no idle rich, no paved roads, and not much room.

"Beverly and I shared a bunkhouse with one other couple and a fella from the University of Nebraska, a guy named Jorgensen, who would eat only Chinese food. He elected himself cook. We ate Chinese food three times a day, Chinese oatmeal for breakfast. He cooked on a hot plate and slept in the hall, while the two couples had one small bedroom each. But it worked great. I loved the place. Easterners had a time getting used to all this primitive discomfort, but I was in hog heaven. It was also a completely democratic society. Oppie saw to that—big shots and flunkies like me all living together. Every week we had a colloquium in one of our two movie theaters, where we would be told what everyone was doing. Once in a while some military guy would come by and give us a pep talk.

"Soon as we got there our job was to put together an accelerator, which was brought from the University of Illinois in Champaign. A team of us—Bernie Waldman from Notre Dame and John Manley, who'd come from Illinois and Columbia, and people from Nebraska and Wisconsin—we all pitched in. We worked six days a week to get the Bomb first. There's been a lot of stories that maybe we had the Bomb and were sitting on it, that we could have used it in Germany but because we're Anglo-Saxons or whatever, that we only went against the Asians. That's not true. As soon as we got the Bomb we were ready to drop it.

"First we had to figure out how the thing would be designed. Everyone was working just as fast as possible—either on the gun-assembly method, which was used for the uranium bomb in Hiroshima, or on the implosion method, which we used for the plutonium bomb at Trinity and later in Nagasaki. [George] Kistiakowsky pooh-poohed the implosion idea at first; he was a real tough cookie. But then he got behind it. Both bombs were going ahead full steam."

As it turned out, the Hiroshima bomb would be the only one of its type America ever built or used, uranium being that much more difficult to obtain than plutonium. One of the spurs to the American atom bomb effort had been a report in 1943 that Hitler had ordered uranium shipped out of mines in Belgium. It was also taken for granted that the gun-assembly method—one piece of purified uranium (uranium-235) fired into another at terrific speed—would work, so the Hiroshima bomb was never tested till the morning it was dropped.

While the people in Los Alamos were working to produce their bomb, physicists in Japan were attempting to produce theirs. Professor Hidetake Kakihana of Sophia University in Tokyo was Agnew's age when he too was enlisted by his country in 1941 to assist with nuclear fission experiments at a secret cyclotron in Tokyo under the directorship of Yoshio Nishina, Japan's Oppenheimer. Unlike Agnew, Kakihana and many of his colleagues were reluctant to produce an atom bomb for their government because they had great distaste for the military regime. The physicists worked, Kakihana says today, with deliberate slowness.

If Japan's military regime really wanted to produce an atom bomb before the Americans, it put almost no money behind the effort, compared with the Americans' $2 billion. For their part, the Japanese physicists simply made the wrong scientific choice in their fission experiments, deciding to work with high-energy rather than low-energy neutrons. Even if they had been able to produce a chain reaction, there was very little uranium in the country and no way to get more. There is little doubt that if the Japanese had made a Bomb before the Americans, they would have used it, but the question is moot. Kakihana always believed that the United States would build the Bomb first, but he thought that the Americans would use it only in a demonstration.

"All the while," Agnew says, "I really was aching to get in the war. Pure and simple. I wanted in especially because all my classmates and my friends in Denver were in. We had an all-city softball team. My catcher got killed in the war—a guy named Howard Erikson. And all the other kids—Bob Hogan, who would have made, maybe, an All-America golf and/or football player, he got killed. *Everybody* was gettin' killed. Or they were off fighting someplace. And of course, the neighbors wanted to know where *I* was. And my parents said they really didn't know, but they knew I was doin' *something*. Well, it sounded as if I'd gone over the hill. That really bothered me. And it bothered them, but they really didn't know where we were. We had a P.O. box, that's all. So I wanted in. If I was ever asked, 'What did you do in the war, Daddy?' I could say, 'I did *this*. I didn't hide under a *bush*.'

"Luckily for me, in late '44 [fellow physicist] Luis Alvarez, who also wanted to get in the war, came up with the idea that we were neglecting our responsibilities if we didn't try to measure the yield of the Bomb while we were making it. Well, as soon as I heard about this, I went and pounded on Luis's door and said I wanted to play, and I became a member of his team. I knew that if I could handle measuring the yield, that I'd be going overseas. So did Luis. We knew too that we would get to fly on missions. We'd be as important as a tail gunner, even one who never fired a shot."

Today Agnew is glad to see a mutual understanding between the soldiers and the physicists. He is annoyed by those of his former colleagues at Los Alamos who believe that science struck a perilous bargain with the military during the war. That was the thrust of Rabi's reunion speech: "We gave away the power to people who didn't understand it and were not grown-up enough and responsible enough to realize what they had." Rabi's speech "really irritated me," says Agnew, who was at that same reunion and whose own speech declared that the Japanese "bloody well deserved" what they got. "I have always felt that science and the military *should* work together. And they *have,* from Day One, whether it was Leonardo da Vinci or Michelangelo or whoever. They were always designing things for the people in charge."

Other physicists, agreeing with Rabi, take the view that the military-scientific partnership was not only dangerous to the country but detrimental to the quality of American science as well. Philip Morrison, celebrated for his teaching at the Massachusetts Institute of Technology, carried the container of plutonium in his hands from Los Alamos to the Trinity test site and, like Agnew, was on Tinian the days of the bombings. Now he spends a good part of his intellectual life arguing for disarmament. Morrison also felt that the Bomb was needed to end the war. Looking back today, however, he says that the physicists learned something after they transferred "their science directly from the peaceable study of the ultimate structure of matter to the fearful desolation of Hiroshima . . . They learned rather quickly what had to be done next if we are to be able to survive for a long time. The statesman have not learned so quickly, but it is true that their task is a much harder one."

After Hiroshima and Nagasaki, Morrison's main concern was "how to get the Bomb into the *peace*." But once World War II was over, American scientists were inevitably associated in the public mind with war. Hiroshima had entirely changed the popular image of the unworldly professor; he had proved what he could *do*. By the end of the 1940s, the Soviets had their own atomic weapon, and by 1953, less than a year after the United States, they tested their first hydrogen bomb. Once the arms race was a fact, the United States seemed to need its physicists as saviors and protectors. Places like Los Alamos were transformed from emergency-inspired experimental labs to permanent national institutions. People like Oppenheimer and Morrison left Los Alamos to return to their universities as soon as the war was done. People like Agnew stayed on.

At Los Alamos today, Merri Wood, a tall brunet with a bright, clear-liquid voice and a designer of nuclear weapons, is in a sense Agnew's heir and creation. Not only does Wood not question the connection of her work with the military, she is pleased to have it. For one thing, that connection has provided jobs for those like herself, a former Ph.D. candidate in physics at Georgia Tech, who was specializing in particle transport and found a shop to apply her studies. (Particle transport is a general term for the motion of atomic particles through various materials.) Designing weapons is something Wood wanted to do since junior high school, when she read "everything I could lay my hands on" about the men making the first Bomb. "Out of patriotism, maybe glamour, I don't know, I really admired those people. I never dreamed that I'd be doing it. I'm tickled pink."

As a day-to-day matter, Wood has to think about the military, since the military, by making requests and assignments, gives direction to her work in "thermonuclear applications" (designing warheads). "The military wants XYZ bomb, and you give 'em the best you can." She tests a bomb's size and, like Agnew before her, measures yield. "If they [the military] say they want 2 megatons, I give 'em 2; if they want 2,000, I give 'em 2,000." The measure of success is if a bomb tests satisfactorily in Nevada and then goes into stockpile. In that case Wood works with the engineer on the final design of the weapon—"*weaponize* is the term." A bomb must be "buildable, reliable, and robust. If one little thing jiggles, it can't quit working." Design is as far as she goes. "You design it, you field it, you sit there with sweaty palms and wait for the ground to shake."

Wood enjoys the connection between her work and its military market because she sees a philosophical underpinning. The people at Los Alamos when Agnew was there were working toward something they knew was going to be used. The people at Los Alamos now work on things that are never supposed to be used. "And we don't want to use them. *Nobody* wants to see these guys used." Nor does she feel that there is something antilogical or frustrating in designing a weapon for the explicit purpose of not using it. The "in-point," she says, is in the test or in the stockpile. "We have a fellow here who hangs a peace sign from his badge.

"Now we joke: Let's nuke Tehran. But we're human beings. We live here with families. We want a good national defense, and most people believe that a nuclear deterrent is the way to go. For that reason we get satisfaction from our work by contributing to our personal and national safety. It's corny—wave the flag—but it's true." As for those who dropped the Hiroshima bomb, she says that guilt or conscience ought not to be the consideration. "If a policeman shoots a felon, there's no guilt, only regret. You just wish the world had been different."

Agnew favors the military-scientific partnership for another reason. War, he says, is "too important to be left to the young." By which he means that the existence of nuclear weapons is to be approved of because those weapons have put the politicians and generals of a nation, who arrange and orchestrate wars, at equal risk with the young people who do the actual fighting. Science has thus served as an equalizer between leaders and troops: "The young people who go around yelling 'Get rid of the Bomb!' ought to be careful, 'cause the politicians might put a bow and arrow in their hands and make the kids sally forth again, knowing that nothing is going to happen to *them* [the politicians]. With the development of nuclear weapons, the guy who says 'Go fight a war' is talking to him*self*.

"You know what I'd do to keep the world out of a nuclear war? Most of the decision makers have never seen a bomb. These guys talk about bombs—so many kilotons, so many megatons—it doesn't *mean* anything to 'em. So I say maybe every five years every world leader should have to strip down—Mrs. Thatcher in her bikini and the other guys in skivvies—and watch a multimegaton bomb go off. What'll impress them is not the flash, not the size of the cloud, and not the boom. It's the *heat*. If they're about twenty-five miles away, they will get very antsy, 'cause they'll get hotter and hotter, and they will worry that maybe somebody's made a mistake. The heat. Really scares the bejesus out of you. After that the chances of their ever using a bomb would diminish *rapidly*."

He also makes it clear that he is less opposed to the proponents of disarmament than to an attitude that suggests that in the real world the United States has no right or reason to maintain nuclear weapons, and, for that matter, that the Americans had no business bombing Hiroshima in the first place. "A few years ago, Senator [Mark] Hatfield organized a big peace exhibit in the rotunda of the Senate. So here's this big exhibit, and all it showed was the horrors of Hiroshima. [Some of the artifacts came from the Hiroshima Peace Museum.] All the burned victims. Just awful things. Melted cups. Now my objection was that in a *peace* exhibit you ought to have shown Pearl Harbor too. Then you could say, 'This is the way it started, and this is the way it ended. Let's not do this again.'"

One more phone call about the Ford. Eventually he sells it for $200. Says the *tires* are worth *that*.

"So anyway, I finally got to go to Tinian, flying from Los Alamos to San Francisco to Hawaii to Johnston Island. In Hawaii you would see where the American ships were sunk—parts of 'em sticking out of the water. And you'd see the pockmarks on the buildings. And when you got to Johnston Island, there were wrecked planes on the field. And when you got to Kwajalein, there'd been one *hell* of a battle there. I picked spent bullets right off the ground—.30 caliber, .50 caliber. Parts of airplanes and amphibious vehicles lay all over the place. The control tower was all busted up. Then we got to Tinian, and all the Japanese buildings were gutted. Remnants, standing like Coventry. You went around to these places, and you got the idea that *something* had been going on.

"I got to Tinian in March 1945, and the *Indianapolis* arrived in July with the uranium from Los Alamos. The *Indianapolis* was sunk by the Japanese after it left Tinian; if it had been hit before, no

Hiroshima. We were working six days a week on Tinian, trying to get ready for the mission. We all got jungle rot on our feet and hands. I remember going to a doctor and asking what to do. He told me, 'Scratch it.' I used to watch the B-29s, hundreds of 'em, coming back from missions like a flock of geese. Those big airplanes, coming in to land. Some smoking, some with their props feathered."

One thing Agnew and Philip Morrison do agree on: When you went to the movies on Tinian you could not hear the soundtrack for the rain beating on your helmet. Morrison remembers them always playing a follow-the-bouncing-ball sing-along of "White Christmas"—the G.I.s bellowing "White Christmas" all spring and summer. He also remembers the physicists preparing the necessary ingredients for ice cream, then sending the concoction up 30,000 feet in a B-29 to freeze the stuff: a $25,000 dessert. And he remembers the bombers going on missions before August 6. Sometimes the planes would be overloaded and would crash on takeoff. Great pillars of fire would rise on the beach, men burning alive inside them.

Of the original four runways on Tinian, two are still operable: wide, white, gleaming strips made of coral and asphalt, surrounded by orange flame trees bent by the mild wind toward the ocean, and green spongy hills, and the encroaching thick, tall grass. The island is nearly empty now, down from a population of 20,000 U.S. servicemen in 1945 to 800 Chamorro natives, who fish, raise goats, or herd cattle. Not far from the runways stands the bombed-out shell of the Japanese officers' quarters: charred timbers, a huge bomb hole in the roof, a tree blooming through the hole. Not far from there is what looks like a fresh grave, about ten feet by eighteen feet, in a grassed-over area that once was "Atomic Bomb Pit No. 1," marked by a sign that resembles a picnic-area sign in a public park. Growing on the plot are a dwarfed and twisted coconut tree and a pometia tree that looks like a stalk of grapes stripped bare. Before the plot is a stone marker shaped like a public trash can with an inscription saying that here the Bomb was loaded up into the *Enola Gay* on the afternoon of August 5. It was Agnew's day.

"And then came the night of our mission. Our B-29s had a circle with a black arrow in it as their insignia. All the other B-29s had triangles or circles with letters of the alphabet. But the night before the mission, on August 5, Tokyo Rose came on the radio and said, 'Black Arrow Squadron, we know who you are and what you are, and we are ready for you.' Early the next morning we didn't have black arrows anymore. We had triangles with letters, which I thought was chicken. But it was prudent.

"So off we went, flying near the *Enola Gay* all the way, all thirteen hours. The weather plane had returned and reported that everything was peachy keen. A little before 8:15, the area was clear, the *Enola Gay* was right on target, and we were alongside, about a quarter mile away. Then we caught the tone signal, which meant that the Bomb was armed and ready to drop. When the tone went off, that meant the Bomb was on the way down, so we dropped our measuring gauges, our own little 'bombs.' Then we saw the flash of light. And the camera was rolling. We must have been seven miles away when the shock waves hit the plane. All I remember is we sure got out of there in a hurry, which was fine by me. I just wanted to get home."

July 29, 1985

The Last Place on Earth

IF THERE WERE such a place as the last place on earth, southern Sudan is how the terrain would look: thorn trees erupting at lonely distances from one another, flattened at the top as if by an invisible hand; *Balanites aegyptiaca,* desert-date trees, which look like poor relations of weeping willows, overdressed mourners at a grave site; cactus trees—huge, aggressive things—poking their spikes at the sky; trees with thick trunks that appear to be made of cables tied in a Gordian knot. Gray bushes, looking like rolls of industrial wire, mix with the tall, gray-silver grass on the yellow land. Dry, dry; cracked pieces of old pottery. The shards of dead branches stick out in frantic directions like bones broken through skin.

What is happening to the people here mirrors the landscape—a continuum of isolations, each having its own lethal consequences. The sum total of all the isolations is leading to the destruction—the silencing—of an entire civilization. This silencing has been taking place within a region of the largest country in Africa, the region itself larger than Texas, and one of the most inaccessible places in the world. Here the White Nile extends its arms into the Sudd, Arabic for barrier—one of the world's largest swamps. Only snakes and malarial mosquitoes thrive and multiply. Otherwise, there is nothing but emptiness and danger. If this sounds like Somalia, it *is* Somalia—

with the differences that the Sudan is much harder to get help to, and too few people are trying. Southern Sudan is isolated from everything except the elements that are killing it.

There was a time when the mere mention of Khartoum, the country's capital, evoked images of billowy tents, Arabian horses, languid evenings, and that strange, flip, Kiplingesque heroism—pith helmets, the white man's burden, General Gordon, and the unsetting sun. Oppressive as colonialism was, at least it brought the country a hundred years of relative stability. Since becoming the first sub-Saharan African country to gain independence, however, the Sudan has been at war for twenty-seven of its thirty-seven years of existence.

Khartoum and northern Sudan are now ruled by the Revolutionary Command Council of Lieutenant General Omer al Bashir, who seized power in 1989. The government is fighting the Sudanese People's Liberation Army, under Dr. John Garang, which controls the countryside in the underdeveloped southern half of the nation. There are also internecine wars within the S.P.L.A., one of the more brutal being that between the Dinka tribe majority and the Nuer tribe.

No side has a claim on morality in these wars. When military convoys lose vehicles to rebel mines, they usually burn the closest village and murder its inhabitants. Soldiers routinely rape women displaced from their homes by the fighting; the S.P.L.A. has also been accused of rape and kidnapping. Both the government and the S.P.L.A. have menaced relief operations and blown up trucks carrying food and medicine. The government has amputated the limbs of prisoners of war; so has the S.P.L.A.

Yet nearly everyone agrees that the Bashir government has been the main persecutor in the wars. Muslim fundamentalists armed and inspired by Iran, they are the theocratic cleansers of their country—a twist on the ethnic cleansers in Bosnia. They seek to "Islamize" the Sudan—as indeed Iran may seek to Islamize the entire Horn of Africa—by converting or killing off all the Christians and animists in the South. Their weapons are famine, political repression, the torture of dissidents, and outright slaughter.

This latest, four-year phase of the civil war has been the most vicious and costly, with countless numbers dead, their bodies plowed under by bulldozers in communal graves, and a total of 4 million people displaced. The region is a map of upheaval and uprooting. If a stranger were to take an aerial view of southern Sudan, all he would see would be the continuous movement of children and adults in an anarchic silence.

The central figures in this mass and bewildering migration are the boys of southern Sudan—100,000 or more, aged six to fifteen, who have embarked on a long, unending journey of escape. The boys were tending cattle in the fields, as is the custom, when the government troops marched into their villages and slaughtered their families. From a distance, some saw their parents and sisters murdered; others learned what was happening, and ran.

From village after invaded village they fled—one, five, hundreds. They banded together in groups of thousands and tens of thousands. They were occasionally accompanied by adults, who were also escaping government soldiers, but most of the time they were on their own. The boys walked barefoot 200 or 500 or 1,000 miles for weeks, often months, to find camps where they would be safe—a modern reenactment of the long marches of exile in the Books of Exodus and Lamentations.

On these treks, which have lasted for four years, the boys sleep under thorn trees or in the high elephant grass, where they can hide. In the daytime they walk in the relentless heat; at night they protect themselves from the semidesert cold with a single blanket, if one is available. For food they eat leaves, roots, wild grass, berries, rats occasionally. One group reports eating wild cassavas, but they didn't know how to cook them. Boys began vomiting and writhing in pain. Fifteen died and were left on the road.

Many drown attempting to ford the swollen rivers in the rainy season. Many contract diseases from insects and from one another. Many are bitten by scorpions and snakes. Wounds cut to the bone and become infected. Those who do not die en route to the camps often die a few days after they arrive.

When government planes bomb their camps, the boys move on again. The pilots fly at altitudes too high for accuracy, but sometimes the bombardiers get "lucky." Often, the boys—most of them Dinka—are attacked by rival tribesmen. They are also hunted by hyenas, who work in packs to trap a boy; the others scramble up a tree and can do nothing but watch as the hyenas tear at and devour one of their number.

They have fled from villages such as Aweil and Wau in the southwest, where one of the first government massacres occurred, and from Kadugli in the north of the region, and Ignessana. They have trekked east into Ethiopia, where they encamped until the ruler, Colonel Mengistu, was overthrown. So the boys fled back to the Sudan, to Magus just north of Kapoeta. When Kapoeta was taken by government troops, they fled again.

They went south to Narus, then east into Kenya, where many

remain today. Others escaped to neighboring Zaire, Uganda, or the Central African Republic. But most of the boys remained in or returned to southern Sudan, in camps superintended by the Sudan Relief and Rehabilitation Association (S.R.R.A), the humanitarian wing of the S.P.L.A., the largest of which is Palotaka.

Since 1989, these boys have been in continuous aimless motion, like children spun around blindfolded in a party game—living by their wiles, moving from camp to camp, hunted, terrified, hungry, ill, benumbed. It is difficult to say which has been more of a hardship, being refugees in another country or being continually displaced in their own. Philip Thon Leek, the director of the Friends of African Children Educational (F.A.C.E.) Foundation, observes that "to be displaced in one's own land is like being lost in one's own house. You are sure you belong there, but you don't know exactly where. Or perhaps you are no longer sure you belong there, but you *are* sure you do not belong anywhere else."

And yet the plight of the lost boys is but one element of the disintegration of the entire region. Wherever one looks in southern Sudan, civilization is coming apart—in the area in which it is said that civilization originally came together. To return to the theme of isolations, the people of southern Sudan have been isolated from their villages, their culture, their education, their sense of hope, community, and dignity. They have also been isolated from the outside world, which hardly notices they are on the brink of extinction.

For years, no protests against Khartoum were made by the United States, Britain, France, Germany, Japan, the Netherlands, the European Community, or the United Nations. The international press, which fastened on Ethiopian starvation in 1984 and 1985, said almost nothing about the Sudan. The American government has provided only intermittent humanitarian aid to the Sudan, either because it is loath to interfere with a sovereign government (this is how the political situation in the Sudan differs from Somalia) or because there is no obvious geopolitical advantage in doing so in the post–Cold War environment.

Representative Frank R. Wolf (Republican, Virginia) recently returned from a fact-finding mission to the Sudan and reported the contents of a declassified State Department document to the House of Representatives on May 17. He described massacres and the selling of women and children into slavery by Khartoum. Wolf pleaded, "Where's the Congress on this issue? Where's the Clinton administration on this issue? Where's the media on this issue?"

The end product of Sudan's isolation is a region in which

silence—a vast and consuming silence—is encroaching like a season of its own, on top of the dry and rainy seasons. From time to time the silence of southern Sudan is broken by gunfire or by bombardments, and, at the more benign extreme, by occasional songs of camaraderie and the faint murmurs of individual, if ephemeral, achievement. But the silence is fathomless and overwhelming, this being the last place on earth, and eventually, give or take a few years, unless there is help from the outside, there will be no more sounds from this region.

Southern Sudan is the last place on earth not because the people are forced to eat leaves or live in huts or dress in rags, or because they have no electricity or phone lines or infrastructure, or because they are evicted from their homes or lose sight of their families forever or die of every disease that invades their territory, or because they have no medicines to combat those diseases, no books for their education, or because they often have to crawl on a sere and pitiless earth for a sip of water, or even because they are perpetually hunted by those who want either to own their souls or to bury them. Southern Sudan is the last place on earth because all these things are happening and nobody seems to care.

At the Aswa hospital, someone has painted a sign on a wall for the benefit of the American ambassador, who recently paid a visit. The sign reads, THANK YOU FOR COMING TO SEE US DYING OF DISEASE AND INJURIES.

That fairly well describes the condition of the residents of the Aswa hospital, which was built in 1983. With a 60-bed capacity, it holds anywhere between 450 and 600 patients, which means that most of the patients lie on straw mats between the beds or sit propped up against the walls of the corridors.

The walls are cracked and yellowed. The roofs leak. Windowpanes are broken. Mosquito netting has been torn out of the windows; so have most of the wooden frames. The water pipes are rusted. The sewage system is broken. Some of the ceilings have been eaten away by termites. The electrical appliances are in general working order, but many switches and wires are missing. Wounds are routinely stitched with strands from the tails of giraffes. Once, a package marked "Sterile" was opened at the hospital and a rat jumped out.

The number of patients at Aswa varies according to the number of war-wounded at any given time, and, of course, according to the rate of the dying. Most of the wounded patients survive, but one person per day dies of malnutrition. Patients come by the hundreds from displacement camps in the villages of Ame, Atepi, and nearby Aswa itself, suffering from malnutrition and a number of related diseases, and from fatigue as well, since many who were driven from their homes have walked as much as a hundred miles to get to the hospital. After the killing of three foreign relief workers and a journalist, only one agency, Norwegian People's Aid, under the direction of Helge Rohn, stayed to provide food and medical supplies to the hospital and to the area.

A good deal of surgery is performed here, but until recently not by surgeons. The hospital's first Sudanese doctor was not trained in surgery; he is better at amputations than at abdominal work. He has been joined by a Sudanese surgeon trained in Egypt and by a volunteer surgeon from Norway on a three-month mission. The Norwegian surgeon has just arrived, and while he has served in other beleaguered parts of the world, the look of amazed horror on his cheerful farm boy's face says as much about the hospital's conditions as the hard evidence.

At the moment there are 104 war wounded in the hospital. Each surgeon performs no fewer than twelve operations a day, yet the doctors agree that the wards in which the war wounded are kept are "by far the best parts of the hospital." The new Sudanese surgeon points to a corner. "Even *he* is in better shape than most of the starving." The "he" is a twenty-year-old sleeping on the floor, half his head wrapped in gauze to cover the place where a bullet entered his right eye and came out his left ear. "His right side is paralyzed and he will be mute for life, but he will survive," says the surgeon.

An eighteen-year-old named Atek is on the mend. He was shot in the left leg, which he stretches out in a splint. His black-brown skin gleams and looks healthy against the bright blue sheet on his cot. His hair glistens with beads of sweat. "First the cows of my village were taken by the soldiers," he says. "Then the houses were burned down. I saw my brother killed, and then my sister—they killed her too. They did not see me watching, so I escaped.

"I walked alone. Two months. When I got to the border of Ethiopia, there were many children there. Three hundred of us. But there were troubles for us in Ethiopia as well. They rejected us, so we had to come back to Sudan, to Kapoeta. Then the enemy came to Kapoeta. And again they killed people and took the town."

"How were you wounded?" I ask.

"On the road near here."

"Were you fighting or shot as a civilian?"

"I was fighting." Most relief workers in the area know that the S.P.L.A. is taking teenagers like Atek out of the camps and training them as soldiers—turning the victims of the war into warriors. In the camps themselves, however, there is no evidence of military training.

"So by the time you were eighteen you had a gun?"

"Yes. I was taught to defend myself."

"Did having a gun make you feel like a man?" I ask.

"Yes."

"So does having a gun make a man?"

"Yes," says Atek. "Definitely."

Atek is lucky compared with John, who is lying with his back against the wall in a corridor. At the age of thirty-eight, John looks to be at least sixty, and the position he has assumed gives him the angle of a vacationer lounging on a chaise. I would be surprised if he weighs eighty pounds, though he has to be six feet tall. He is dressed only in a blue bathing suit that might be a small boy's, and is slipping down at his hips. John's legs are thinner than most men's wrists. He complains of diarrhea, chest pains, and weakness. His headaches come and go.

"Do you remember when you felt better, John?" one of the doctors asks.

"I will never feel better," says John, anticipating a placating remark.

The principal diseases in the hospital, and throughout the region, are malaria, typhoid, dysentery, meningitis, and those related to diarrhea. Kala-azar, a wasting disease carried by sand flies, has so far been located mainly north of here, but it is characterized as a spreading epidemic. The diseases that still claim the most casualties are related to hunger.

A few yards down the corridor, a six-and-a-half-month-old baby suckles at his mother's empty breast. The mother looks at her child in his futile exercise, looks at her own flattened nipple, looks up at me as if to illustrate her plight, then back to the suckling child. His mouth makes a hushed dry gasp against his mother's breast. The Norwegian doctor tells me the baby is unlikely to survive the week, and even if he should manage to live, he will be brain damaged from the hunger.

The same prognosis is offered Philip, an orphan of two and a half years whose father was killed in the war and whose mother was killed in a car accident. In spite of his age, Philip is the size of a newborn—

but without the fat or the suppleness. People in the West have seen pictures of hundreds of babies like Philip, from Ethiopia and, more recently, Somalia. In person, they appear less like undersized babies than fully formed people of a different, diminished species. His knee joint fits easily in the circle of my thumb and index finger, and his foot measures short against my thumb. But a baby like Philip is also different to the touch. His skin does not feel like a human being's skin. Drained of normal subcutaneous fat, it feels like paper, heavy typing paper. Rubbing his back is like rubbing a page of a book.

Philip has not been able to take any food for days except sugar and water. His eyes are veiled with a thick film, indicating a constant dizziness. He moves his tongue in and out spasmodically as if attempting to taste the air.

"What you must realize about a boy like Atek," says a man in his midfifties who is visiting the Aswa hospital, "is that he has lost forever the grounding of his culture."

"And what is that?" I ask.

"Cows. The boy said it himself. Cattle. Cattle in the Sudan provide the basis of families. Cattle connect parents to children. Cattle are pledged in marriage arrangements. Now a boy like Atek thinks that the center of culture is guns. It is all turned upside down." The man looks less angry than wistful. A Dinka, a pastoralist, he has almost an inborn reverence for cattle.

"Life was more serene when you were growing up," I suggest.

"More under control, certainly. I grew up as a Christian in the North, and we were told to be afraid of Arabs, but nothing like today."

"Were you afraid of wild animals?"

"Not all animals. But lions, surely. All the kids were afraid of lions."

"Are there still lions in the Sudan?"

"Of course. But children are a lot more afraid of people today than of lions." He chuckles. "Today the lions are afraid of the people."

It is six o'clock on a Sunday morning in the camp of Palotaka, a three-hour drive from Aswa along a road composed of rocks and potholes, some two feet deep, on which time has no relation to distance. At present there are 4,000 boys in the camp. Girls, too, went on some of the treks, but when they reached places of refuge, they were located by the elders in separate camps; some rejoined their families. Many girls, of course, who were captured by the Bashir fundamentalists when their parents were killed were forced to convert or were killed themselves.

One of Palotaka's boys, an eleven-year-old named Thon, died last night from diarrhea and dehydration. He will be buried later in the day, without much ceremony. The camp elders do not encourage the younger boys to participate in burials. "It is not useful for them," says Sebit William, the camp's director, making a subtle and complex judgment.

The Catholic mass is about to begin in the large brick church. Palotaka was originally a Catholic mission set up by Italians in the early 1930s. While there are more Protestants than Catholics among the boys, the Catholic church is by far the more substantial house of worship. Many of the mission buildings are still standing, some with roofs and walls missing or partly eaten away. Four pillars of a decayed building rise to the sky, their roof long gone, like four symbolic statues. The antique European desolation of these structures stands out in strange relief against the tents, the tin shacks where the cooking is done, and the *tukuls*, the native huts of mud and wattle, in which most of the camp's residents make their homes.

The church itself, however, is in remarkably good repair, given the climate and the years. It looks to be 300 feet long and about 60 feet wide, with great high wood beams that still gleam and appear strong. A plaster statue of the Madonna and Child painted gold and a figure of Jesus on the Cross face the large hall of wooden benches. Behind the altar a dome rises, white originally, now yellow stained; there is a large brown smudge like a cloud in a corner, and a crack in the plaster running like lightning along the arc of the dome.

I sit at the end of the last bench on the left side of the aisle, and place my tape recorder beside me. A boy in the front, wearing a red sweatshirt, begins to beat a drum. In groups of two and three the other boys file in sleepily, genuflect before the altar, and find their seats. Some of their clothes are so torn and shredded that they might have just come from rolling down a hill of gravel. Several turn cautiously in their seats to look at the white man with the machine at his side.

The drummer boy begins a Dinka chant, a hymn, and the other boys join in. They sing not like an English choir, more like boys at a sports rally—a lusty noise to God. A five-year-old, still drowned in sleep, enters wearing a pair of thongs, green sweatpants with red and white stripes down the side, and a long-sleeved yellow shirt with a large rip in the front. He looks about. I come into his view. He cannot take his eyes off me. I signal for him to sit beside me.

At 6:45 the priest enters. He places a purple stole with a gold cross on each end over his white vestment, and he ties his robe at the waist with a white cord. Many boys are on their knees in the center aisle. From the cadence of the Dinka chant, I surmise that I am hearing the Lord's Prayer.

The five-year-old at my side still stares at my tape recorder, studying the string of red lights that shorten and lengthen with the volume of the chant. At last he places his mouth close to the machine and makes a hissing sound. The lights respond. He nods satisfied, and smiles.

A woman in her sixties is walking barefoot on the road leading to the entrance of the camp. She wears a faded blue jumper, and is bent at the waist, perhaps from osteoporosis, so that her body makes a right angle as she moves. Had she not the support of a long pole, she would topple over to the ground. Then she does topple over. At the garden near the entrance, she falls suddenly in a heap, rocks from side to side like a ship on a swell, and finally achieves a steady position on all fours. She searches for her pole, which has rolled out of her reach. She places a hand on her stomach, which is bloated and clearly gives her pain, though she makes no groan or sound of complaint. Her face has the look of a puzzled sheep.

The woman, Laura, has come twelve miles to Palotaka to find a doctor, but there has been no doctor here for a long while. She wants pills for her stomach; they worked before. Carried inside one of the mission houses by two men, she is offered a folding chair, but Laura prefers to sit on the stone floor, to take the pressure off her stomach. She smells sweet, of the earth and her sweat. I notice that her fingernails are perfectly trimmed. She keeps pointing to her stomach, as if it were an external weapon that was doing her harm. "Do you have the pills?" she asks me, assuming that I am a doctor. She is told by one of the camp leaders that the doctor may come today, or tomorrow.

"Her husband and children are dead. She takes care of herself," says a young man named George Okat, who has been translating Laura's words for me. George also assumes I am a doctor, and he urges me to examine his ten-year-old boy, Cirilio. I explain who I am, but he wants me to see his boy anyway; perhaps I have some useful layman's knowledge. I do not.

On the way to his *tukul,* George tells me that he and his wife are worried about Cirilio because the boy Thon died last night and Cirilio has similar symptoms. George leads Cirilio out of the *tukul* to greet me, which the boy does with as much spirit as his evident weakness allows.

We make small talk. I give him a Polaroid of himself, which pleases him for a moment. George shows me a diagnostic report on an index card filled out by a medical assistant two weeks earlier. I tell George that I can interpret these runes no better than he. "Has Cirilio improved at all since this card was made out?" I ask. George shakes his head no.

I enter the tent where they are keeping Thon, the eleven-year-old who died last night. The boy is wrapped head to foot in a green blanket with pink stripes. Sunlight shoots in on the blanket through holes in the tent; the cylinder of the blanket is so slim one would not think it contained anything. I ask to see Thon's face, which is bound in gauze like a mummy. "For the seepage," explains a man who is attending the body. He refers to the speed with which the eyes and facial tissue fall apart in this climate. Unthinking, I ask how Thon's parents are taking the death of their boy. The man gestures, indicating all the adults in the camp: "We are his parents."

A boy named John is typical of the healthy boys in Palotaka. He is fifteen now. Three years ago he saw his parents murdered by Bashir's troops in the town of Bor. He ran and found other boys, who made their way south to Mongalla, then west to Maridi, and finally east to Torit. But Torit was taken by the government, so John and the other boys moved on again.

John is lanky, in sandals and a turquoise T-shirt. He sits in a slouch and is polite but terse in his responses, like my own youngest, who is also named John. I ask if he can recall happy memories from Bor. He repeats a story his father used to tell him of a hunt for a hyena and of a clever boy who outwitted the beast. John smiles slightly at this recollection, then retrieves his alert and passive stare.

At 12:30, in the fierce silent heat of the day, two of the older boys in the camp carry Thon out into a field on an old army stretcher. Other boys notice what is happening, but they do not follow. Hens stomp about. Only the sparrows chatter as the boy in the blanket on the stretcher is carried over the field of red soil and rocks. At the grave site, near a grape arbor which is also the cemetery of the former Italian mission, four other boys are taking turns digging Thon's grave. They use a spade, a hoe, and a shovel with a handle that keeps slipping off. One boy digs until he gets tired, then the next takes over. The air is thick with heat and the thudding of the digging instruments and the heavy breathing of the gravediggers.

A tribal grave has two distinct forms of construction. One, rarely used nowadays, is a large sphere-shaped hole. The body is bound hand and foot, and is buried as if it were a ball.

The other form of grave, the one used for Thon, involves digging a rectangle about three feet deep with a six-inch shelf carved along one side. The body is placed in the deeper part of the hole, then sticks are laid across it, as close as the keys of a xylophone, from the top of the shelf to a parallel ridge cut in the other side of the grave above the body. The sticks are then covered with leaves, and the leaves with the red earth, thus creating a coffin within the grave. That way, it is explained, the body will not expand or explode.

The pastor of Thon's Episcopal church arrives, a small, neat man named Moses, dressed in a purple shirt and looking no older than eighteen. Moses stands apart from the others and thumbs through the pages of his Bible. The digging and chopping continue. Not much is said, save for some casual joking, not noticeably nervous. Someone mentions a rumor of a government bombardment near Torit, said to have occurred in the early morning.

The mountains rise like gray animals' heads in the middle distance, beyond the dry plains of the thorn trees. The deeper the digging, the darker the red earth, from apple to blood to brown. Suddenly the digging stops. Thon's body is measured with the sticks. The hole is widened by inches.

Two boys climb down into the grave. Two others carry the stretcher to the hole. Thon's body is lowered carefully so the blanket will not slip; he is placed on his side as if asleep. Then the sticks are laid over him, and the leaves on top of the sticks. The grave looks strangely beautiful, the red earth and the green leaves. Standing at the end of the grave where Thon's head is, the pastor prays as the hole is filled.

"God, we believe that you are the one who has created human beings and the one who can take human beings away. Our son is now passed back to you. We have no objections."

I ask if a marker will be made for the grave, and the answer is yes—"so if he has a relative, somewhere, he may come to see him."

• • •

The silence of approaching death is palpable in Palotaka, and is like the silence of the entire region. But there is another kind of silence in southern Sudan, a traditional and ancient silence, which is connected to the life of the country, and not to its death, and which gives the people a special grace.

Among the children there is play, but no hectic rushing about in the camps. Among the elders everything is done, every step taken, with a stately modesty and self-awareness. Athletes, who learn to fear and revere their bodies, acquire the art of moving very slowly when it is not necessary to do otherwise, to protect themselves from injury. The people of the Sudan, who have to walk their long distances on crippling terrain, have learned that same lesson of slowness and quiet.

They have also learned to stand silently, that is, with the least amount of resistance offered by their posture. Standing in groups, they are like works of perfectly balanced sculpture—mobiles on the ground. If a shoulder slants to the left, a hip is raised to the right. If the back is arched, a leg is drawn beneath it for support. The neck is absolutely conscious of the weight and shape of the head.

There is, in short, a conspiracy, a breathing together, of the land and the people, which, like the quiet of the church in Palotaka, infuses the air with a sense of religion. The silence of the mountains, the trees, the stars, commingles with the silence of the people as they go about their tasks, which, while also silent, are accomplished with total efficiency. It all gets done—the gathering of straw for a *tukul,* the discovery of a watering hole, the burying of the dead. When the boys walk single file on a long road, they become a vein in the road, a silent line drawn by pen and ink into the earth.

It is this older, traditional silence that seems to be intruded upon these days, to be attacked by the other kind of silence, incurred by the forces of destruction. Silence poisons silence. The men are almost always quiet and polite with one another, but infrequent explosions of temper are enough to suggest a constant smoldering inside, and the capacity for quick, remorseless violence. The boys in Palotaka are noiseless as they go about their work, but they are also joyless; however the camp may resemble a village, it is still a camp. There is a silence in the boys even when they are not technically silent—when they are singing in church or talking among themselves or performing songs for visitors. A song raised in all the camps—"We are so happy to see you today"—has no music in it.

In other circumstances, where the suffering is unavoidable, a certain serenity takes over, as if to confirm a compact between the living and the dead. Among the ill and the dying of southern Sudan, their silence has something of that serenity, but it also has the quality of resentment and bewilderment. These deaths are not the result of a compact with nature; they are violations of nature. There is nothing comforting, companionable, or reasonable about them. The antagonism between the two forms of silence, the welcome and unwelcome, is earsplitting.

Ayen, a woman of twenty-three, lives under a tamarind tree in Nimule, near the Ugandan border. She spends most of her time sitting on a green tarpaulin folded at the corners. Both her children are dead from malnutrition. Her husband is "away." She has tuberculosis and she has been living under this tamarind tree for a year.

The tree fans out over her like an enormous beach umbrella. In its shade she sits cross-legged, wearing a dark blue dress, over which hangs a light blue shawl, over which is draped a torn brown blanket. She holds her shaved head bowed most of the time, so it is hard to see her face. When she does look up, she has the expression of someone perpetually about to ask a question.

The tamarind tree rises a few yards in front of the TB clinic in Nimule. It is a clinic with patients suffering from both TB and leprosy, but without a regular doctor. There are more than 120 patients "housed" here, but many, like Ayen, choose to live out of doors. Those who occupy the elongated shack that serves as the clinic's sole building peer out from its darkness, coughing and staring wildly, their hands gripping the bars on the windows. "This place is for the hopeless," says a guide.

Day and night Ayen lives under her tree, surrounded by her possessions—a tin cup, a plastic bottle of water, a plastic bottle of oil to mix with sorghum, which is her food. Behind her lies a covered orange plastic bowl of tamarind nuts, bitter but rich in vitamin C, and a few large tins used for washing. In the crook of the tree, where the trunk splits into an array of branches, Ayen stores extra clothes and rags. Except for her bowed head and the incessant coughing, she might be mistaken—in her blue dress on the green tarp—for a young woman on a picnic.

"What do you think about, Ayen, under this tree?" I ask her.

"Nothing," she says. Her coughing drives the flies from her lips.

"Do you think about your children?"

"No."

"Do you think about your husband?"

"No."

"At night, under the tree, do you have dreams?"

She looks up. "Sometimes. Sometimes I have dreams."

"What do you dream about?" I ask.

She bows her head. "Nothing."

Here, in chronological order, are selections from official reports on the conditions in the Sudan since 1988, to which there has been little or no response.

· From a cable sent to the U.S. State Department by an officer of the mission in Addis Ababa, April 4, 1988:

> All [arrivals] were naked through rags around the waists; all had the dull concentration camp stare of the starving. . . . After visiting [an inpatient medical] unit, U.N. Sec. Gen. Rep. Priestly said it was the worst sight he had seen in 37 ½ years of U.N. service. . . . [The patients] compared poorly with pictures of Nazi concentration camp victims and were as bad or worse as anything seen in Ethiopia during the 1984–86 famine.

· From a radio message sent by Paride Taban, Roman Catholic bishop of Torit, to a relief-aid organization in Khartoum, September 28, 1988:

> This war in the South has become a fratricidal war. We can only compare it to the atomic bomb dropped on Japan or the Vietnam War. Both sides claim to be defending the life and rights of the civilians, but we see that the very civilians they fight for are the victims. Where will our people run to? For wherever they run in the South, their imminent death is waiting for them. Their only chance remains to run to God.

· From remarks by head of state Lt. Gen. Omer al Bashir at a public rally in Khartoum, December 3, 1989:

> I vow here before you to purge from our ranks the renegades, the hirelings, enemies of the people and enemies of the armed forces. . . . Anyone who betrays this nation does not deserve the honor of living. . . . There will be no fifth column. The masses have to purge their ranks. . . . The responsibility is really a collective one. You have authority, and are its enforcers.

· From *Sudan, a Human Rights Disaster: An African Watch Report,*
March 1990:

> The [Sudanese government] has already surpassed its predeces-
> sors in its ruthless methods. . . . Christians and Muslims, northern-
> ers and southerners, even brothers from the same family, are to be
> found fighting on opposite sides of the conflict. It is a civil war that
> has had devastating consequences for the civil society that will
> remain even when the war is eventually over. . . . The current war
> has been characterized by gross violations of human rights on a
> scale that is so substantial, it is difficult to convey the true magni-
> tude of the tragedy that is tearing Sudan apart.

· From the testimony of Roger P. Winter, director, U.S. Committee
for Refugees (U.S.C.R.), before two House of Representatives hear-
ings on African affairs, March 15, 1990, and October 25, 1990, and
before the U.S. Senate Subcommittee on African Affairs, May 14,
1991:

> With the rains already beginning in Equatoria, there are *no*
> buffer stocks of food in *any* of the areas I visited. . . . I consistently
> examined storage areas in each of the towns I entered. Nothing!
> . . . I could routinely see old women forty feet up in the tops of
> trees, picking leaves to eat. . . . I must tell you in all sincerity that
> I am scared. In Sudan today, we are confronting the possibility of
> preventable human death on a *massive* scale. . . . I believe the
> United States needs to fundamentally reconsider its posture regard-
> ing Sudan. . . . Our policy needs to be people-friendly, not govern-
> ment-friendly. . . . I spent much of last week in Ler . . . [where] I
> visited a Sudanese doctor who performs surgery, including amputa-
> tions, with the door off an abandoned refrigerator as an operating
> table. He often performs such operations at night with flashlights
> his only source of light.

· From a U.N. General Assembly resolution on the Sudan, December
2, 1992:

> The General Assembly . . . noting with deep concern reports of
> grave human rights violations in the Sudan, particularly summary
> executions, detentions without trial, forced displacement of per-
> sons and torture . . . calls on the government of the Sudan to
> comply with applicable international instruments of human rights.

· From a letter to Pope John Paul II from Philip Thon Leek, director of Friends of African Children Educational Foundation, February 6, 1993:

Your Holiness . . . over 1.5 million lives have already been lost and at least 4 million people from the Southern Sudan and the Nuba mountains have been internally displaced and over 1 million are refugees. Certainly more people will continue to die of starvation, diseases, and the government policy of ethnic cleansing conducted by the Muslim Fundamentalist forces. . . . We wonder how the international community can afford to passively look on while these atrocities are being committed against their fellow human beings in the Modern Century!

· From a statement by U.S. Representative Frank R. Wolf on February 14, 1993:

The Khartoum government conducted high altitude bombing on [Kajo Keji] when there was no military presence. I saw bomb craters where they hit huts and destroyed the market place. . . . Our government must work for relief from the Khartoum government. Pressure must be put on them to stop the bombing and stop the killing. . . . Failure to act soon will surely result in still more tragic loss of life and possibly the loss of an entire culture.

· From Situation Report No. 2, Agency for International Development (A.I.D.), February 19, 1993:

Conditions for the estimated 10,000 people in Kongor are believed to be the worst in Sudan. The resulting damage of four separate Nuer raids in Kongor from September 1991 to June 1992 and more recent counterattacks by the SPLA/Garang faction has caused "absolutely catastrophic" damage. . . . There are no children under five in the area, as they have all died.

In the huge displacement camp of Ame, forty miles to the west of Palotaka, the leader of the camp describes his realm. Jurkuch Barac is a wiry man in his early forties, with a black goatee and a tough, tight face. He looks curiously, almost accidentally, elegant in a tie-dyed Arab shirt with an intricately embroidered collar, but his manner of speaking is direct, unemotional:

"We have one clinic here. We go days without getting drug supplies. Right now, we have the meningitis. People are dying at a very high rate. We are getting no immunization program, no vaccinations, no food. Water is becoming a big problem. The people flock to the few hand pumps we have in the area. The hand pumps are not providing enough water for the population, and the streams are polluted. You can get diseases from such water. Diarrhea. Dysentery."

"How many doctors do you have in the camp?" I ask.

"We don't have any doctors, only medical assistants."

"You mean, there is not a single doctor in the camp?"

"Medical assistants only."

"How many medical assistants?"

"Six or seven. For forty-two thousand people."

"How many cases of meningitis?"

"Of meningitis? Well, it is rampant. There are many, many cases. Four deaths reported today."

"These people died last night?"

"One was this morning." He leans forward. "So this is the situation of the camp."

The ill at Ame are segregated according to gender, disease, and imminence of death. The tents in which they are housed are so dark inside it takes a full minute for one's eyes to distinguish between people and shadows.

Rebecca, one of the relatively healthy residents, came here from Kongor last year. A woman in her fifties, she stands nearly six feet tall, has high cheekbones and a gap in her front teeth, one of which is yellow. Regal in her print dress and white kerchief, she carries a tall wooden cross with her, and is known to be deeply religious. Her father was slaughtered with other villagers in Kongor, and buried by a bulldozer.

Her voice is weak. She looks down over the length of her body, as if she were examining a stranger.

"I was not like this when I grew up in Kongor. We had meat there, and fish. But here, the water . . ."

"How did that happen to your arm?" I ask, referring to a long network of scars below her elbow.

"That was shrapnel from the enemy planes," she says, staring at the wound. "My arm was cut open, and this is the way it healed. They tell me that my bone chipped. I thought my life would be different," she says matter-of-factly. "I wanted an education. I wanted to learn to talk better, in English. Then I would not need to talk to you in translation, if I had been to school."

I point out that I have been to school, yet I need to talk to *her* in translation.

"What would you have liked to do with your education?" I ask her.

"Politics. I would have liked a life in politics."

"Do Sudanese men like the idea of women in politics?" I ask. The men sitting around laugh wholeheartedly.

"They may not like it," says Rebecca, "but they will learn." Then she looks away. "But politics will not be for me. I have dysentery from the water. And amoebas. I will never leave Ame."

"What do you think about when you're alone?"

"God. I think about God. And America, of course. I think about America."

"Why America?" I ask.

"Because America brought God to our people. And where would we be without Him?"

The numerous diseases suffered by both children and adults in southern Sudan are all traceable to malnutrition. As explained by Matthew Naythons, a physician and photojournalist who founded a medical team in the Third World, malnutrition begins a chain of breakdowns. The absence of food means that the body shuts down protein synthesis. When protein synthesis stops, immune globulins (antibodies)—the patient's first line of defense against infectious agents in the environment—are no longer produced and the immune system is weakened. One of the first immune globulins to go is IgA (immune globulin A), and its loss is compounded by depletion of vitamins, which are necessary for protecting the skin, the functioning of the nervous system, repair of damaged body tissues, and the integrity of various mucosal linings such as the stomach and the intestinal tract.

When the immune system is weakened and immune globulins are low, even the most minor disorders can become life-threatening. The individual is exposed to, and ravaged by, every virus, bacterium, and parasite that exists in the contaminated environment. For the starved child, a diarrheal illness is no mere inconvenience. Unable to ward off or eliminate intestinal parasites, and lacking mucosal immunity, the child's infection becomes chronic as the gastric tract grows inflamed and ulcerated.

Tuberculosis, often "contained" by a healthy immune system, or limited to the respiratory tract, spreads throughout the body in both children and adults. In most infants, its spread to the brain leads to coma and death.

While a person in reasonably good health may merely get sick from malaria, these people die. The anemia from the malaria is compounded by anemia from hookworms, which are endemic to the Sudan, and anemia from chronic infection. Moreover, the patients lack the dietary protein and iron to replace red blood cells destroyed by the invading malarial parasites. Thousands are dying from diseases one could cure in America by going with a prescription to the corner drugstore.

The body also does a strange thing in the presence of chronic infection; it hides iron stores. It does this because bacteria and parasites thrive on iron, and the body attempts to deprive them of an element they need to reproduce. Thus the parasites lack iron, but so does the body.

No food also means no fat. If there is no fat in the diet, there is little vitamin A (a fat-soluble vitamin). Blindness due to measles (a complication resulting from vitamin A deficiency) is commonplace in the Sudan, yet unheard of in the developed world, even in the prevaccination era.

The body falls further and further behind in the production of R.B.C.'s (red blood cells), and can no longer deliver oxygen to the heart, the lungs, the brain. The patient soon can hardly move from lack of energy. The skin breaks down and is covered with sores. There is constant pain from dysentery. The stomach bloats, the limbs waste away. With malaria, the brain swells, bleeding increases, the lungs fill up with edema, impairing breathing.

This, in one form or another, is what is happening, or has already happened, inside the bodies of Ayen, John, Philip, Thon, Laura, Cirilio, and Rebecca.

The roads in southern Sudan, few as they are, create a clumsy and confusing imposition on a terrain that did without them for millions of years, and may do so again. There is no logic to their patterns; they take sudden detours around trees, split off in two or three erratic directions at once, then convene again like participants in a square dance of the mad. Often only a tremor of human instinct tells the driver whether he is still following the road or has now veered off on an illusion of a road, down where no roads go, into the endless flats. Or worse: toward one of the craterlike fissures caused by erosion that open their twisted mouths in the earth and wait for a catch.

It is somewhere between early and midmorning, the temperature is already above 100 degrees Fahrenheit, and the Land-Rover is bucking its way toward the military encampment of Dr. John Garang, the longtime leader of the S.P.L.A.

A huge black-and-white falcon swoops over the Land-Rover like a glider, then hangs motionless in the air, the embodiment of dangerous stillness. The Land-Rover spooks cattle occasionally, and the dik-diks, the miniature antelope who flee in serpentine panics, first stupidly into the middle of the road, then into the dust and the helmets of bush. Once, I happen to look over my shoulder and see a baboon glowering at us in a field, his stance and attitude that of a heavyweight boxer ready to knock my block off.

The kings and queens of this terrain live in tall, elaborate castles, but will not show themselves. They are the termite ants who have built their mud hills, like adobe villages, in enormous, imaginative shapes—some like igloos, some phallic. Many of these hills reach over twenty feet in height and have perfectly circular holes in their sides, like eyes. They are everywhere, scattered like the first efforts of a building project that ran out of cash. They are as hard as rocks. Once a light airplane brushed one of them on the landing field at Nimule and tore a gash in its wing.

One imagines the life in the hills of these termite ants. In a region where there is so little motion outside, what activities, what manipulations and intrigues, occur within these castles?

The road through southern Sudan passes village after abandoned village, the vacant *tukuls* looking like the straw sparrow nests that hang from the shorn trees. Human life shows itself on the road in the files of the young bearing rifles on their backs or water on their heads. But it is mostly empty, the land empty, the sky empty, painted with the still gray slashes of clouds. Only the hills of the termite ants have life in them. What life?

Like most leaders of people, Garang stands his ground, waiting to be approached by his visitors. Built powerfully, six feet tall, balding, with gray in his beard, he is dressed in fatigues; he carries a small firearm in a leather holster on his right side; his boots are not quite shined. He has smart, calm, tired eyes. Every soldier who approaches salutes him. Armed guards form a loose circle around him. Goats and cattle form a loose circle around the guards.

After the introductory formalities, Dr. John, as he is called, takes his position on a folding chair placed before a card table covered with a red cloth on which sits a word processor and a printer, run by a generator.

"This is my second wife," he says of the word processor.

"It can't do everything a wife can do," I offer.

He almost smiles. "No comment."

Dr. John earned his undergraduate degree at Grinnell College, the small liberal-arts school in Iowa; later returned to the United States to receive his doctorate in economics at Iowa State; joined the Sudanese Army as an officer in 1972; received military training at Fort Benning, Georgia; left the army in 1983 after attaining the rank of colonel. He has been connected with his own share of war crimes and atrocities to civilians in the ten years he has led the S.P.L.A. but is by far the lesser of the two main evils in Sudan's North-South civil war, and is now looking for a way to stop the fighting. He is also said to be a worn-out figure, and there is talk of his stepping down. In a sense he leads two armies at once: an army of soldiers and an army of shepherds for his displaced countrymen.

"What are your thoughts about what's happening to your country?" I ask him.

"That's a very difficult question to answer," he replies coolly, as if it were not difficult to answer at all. "What is the price of freedom? Wars are known through history. The Allied forces fought for freedom, for things they valued. London was virtually leveled. There was lots of suffering. Six million Jews perished. History is very cruel and wars are very bad. Civilizations die."

"What are the elements that define a civilization?"

"Culture. Language. Industry. Education. Health. A sense of history. A sense of belonging. A sense of destiny in addition to the material effects of civilization. The spirituality of it."

"Community?"

"Yes, the sense of belonging to a community."

"Family?"

"That of course is the beginning. We are a family people in Africa. It is peculiarly painful to watch these children who have now lost their families."

"So, is there anything left of civilization in southern Sudan?"

"Nothing is ever completely eradicated. I met a tribe one time that had no names, the people were not given names. 'How can you have no names?' I asked them. But these people resisted their Arab names. And at the same time, they were ashamed of their African names. So they chose nothing. No individuality. We in Sudan at least still have individuality."

"Is it religion that has gotten Sudan into so much trouble?" I ask.

"No, religion is part of the world."

"So what does one do to moderate feelings that run amok?"

"I believe in dialogue," he says. "It is possible to have dialogue between the religious communities in Sudan. The government people are not just fundamentalists per se. They are, in the first place, politicians. What set of pressures—political, economic, diplomatic, even religious—needs to be brought to bear on these people who call themselves fundamentalists so that they will compromise, will come to their senses? If their interests are threatened by these pressures, they will negotiate."

"What pressures do you mean?" I ask.

"International pressures by governments, the United Nations, by concerned people, journalists."

He bends down and draws circles in the dust with his fingers. "At a meeting with the other side, I presented three models of the Sudanese situation. The first model is where you have Sudan and you have southern Sudan within it. So, let us call this Model One. It is unworkable. It has cost us twenty-seven years of war out of thirty-seven years of independence."

Next, he draws two circles that overlap in a small eye-shaped area. He shades in this area. "Where you have these two circles—this is the North, this is the South—we have things that are common between us. This shaded area is what I call the Sudanese confederation. Anything we don't agree on, put it on one side or the other. Things we mutually agree on, put them in the shaded area."

He draws two wholly separate circles. "If that does not work, then we will go to Model Three. These are two circles that do not touch and that are only linked by normal relations between independent, completely independent countries. I call this the separation model."

"You prefer Model Two?" I ask.

"If Model Two can be brought about—that is, if we can establish this commonality as a result of dialogue between North and South to our mutual benefit—yes, this would be the ideal solution." In fact, most authorities dealing with Sudan believe that the only possible salvation of the country lies in a division of the North and South.

"And while everyone is waiting for Model One, Two, or Three, what is to be done to protect the civilians?" I ask.

"We have called for the establishment of the demilitarized zones," he says, "safe havens or safety zones to protect innocent civilians in southern Sudan while we are working this thing out, so that lives are protected."

This is the solution also recommended by Roger Winter of the U.S.C.R., Helge Rohn of the Norwegian People's Aid, and the United Nations High Commissioner for Refugees (U.N.H.C.R.). The trouble with it is that the terrorizing of civilians is the government's main strategy. For Garang, the idea of safe havens presents the government with a lose-lose proposition, so he favors it politically. If Khartoum says yes to safe havens, it only helps the S.P.L.A. If Khartoum says no, it displays a barbaric attitude toward world opinion, which it is now courting. (The government has recently hired Pagonis and Donnelly, a P.R. firm in Washington.) The solution needs the active backing of the United States and the United Nations—and neither has shown any indication of giving it. Yet the two in concert are the only hope of effectively pressuring Khartoum.

Garang goes on: "The S.P.L.A. can call for a cease-fire to provide a conducive atmosphere for peace talks. We are willing to do this."

I ask him, "What's preventing you from announcing a unilateral cease-fire right now?"

"We are doing that today." He points to the word processor. "We're printing it out."

At the end of April, the government and the Garang faction of the S.P.L.A. do in fact meet in Nigeria for talks. But at the same time, the intrafactional wars of the S.P.L.A. intensify. It is expected that the government will take advantage of the rebel infighting and move to close off Nimule and its airstrip, making future relief efforts nearly impossible. It will also undoubtedly increase the air raids on the boys, forcing them to move again.

"Why do they smile so readily?" I ask Philip Thon Leek, director of Friends of African Children Educational Foundation, who smiles quite readily himself. I refer to the children of the newly established camp at Natinga, but I am really thinking of all the southern Sudanese children I have seen.

Leek answers, "Because they regard visitors as signs of hope."

"I don't believe that," I say. "The smile seems too willing, too much a motor reflex, to have something so practical behind it."

"A smile is a strange expression, anyway," says Leek. "It appears and disappears so quickly."

"I have never seen smiling the way these children do it," I tell him.

"Never seen anything as giving and wholehearted. What do they have to smile about?"

"Nothing, of course. And if you do not smile at them, they will not smile in return. They are not fools. And they know that grown-ups are dangerous. But if you show them your friendly face, if you suggest that you wish them well . . ."

"That's it, then? They see strangers as those who wish them well?"

"Perhaps," says Leek. "Or maybe their smiling has nothing to do with anyone else."

"What do you mean?"

"Maybe their smiling simply makes them feel happy for a moment, the moment of the smile. For that one moment," says Leek, "the children live in a different world—where people smile."

The camp at Natinga has been set up hastily as a security measure. Talk of a forthcoming government offensive persuaded the S.P.L.A. that the former camps at Molitokolo and Brongole should be abandoned for a place with a terrain more difficult for government troops to penetrate. So the boys in Molitokolo and Brongole, who had trekked hundreds of miles to those camps, were sent on yet another trek, of twenty-one days and 160 miles. On the way, as usual, they sustained themselves by eating leaves and hibiscus. They eat the same things in the camp, since no food has yet arrived.

No medical supplies have arrived at the camp yet, either. Only five watering holes have been discovered so far; these are not rushing springs, but merely holes where water seeps through the ground and, every few hours, collects. The quality of this water is as yet untested.

The total number who have reached the camp is 3,978, including families and elders who serve as teachers. I ask the leaders if this new migration was really necessary. They reply that they are certain the government will bomb the former camps. But why take the political risk of bombing children, especially after Garang's peace initiative and the U.N. censure? The answer comes that Khartoum, public-relations efforts to the contrary, does not really care about world opinion; its intention is to absorb or eradicate a people. But why children? "Because the child is the heart of the people," one leader says, "and bombardment is terrorism."

The camp at Natinga is, in reality, just the first traces of a camp, the initial efforts of people trying to build a place to live out of rocks, bushes, and trees. Children carry cone-shaped bundles of straw for the *tukuls.* A young woman uses a thick pole, a *lek,* to pound grain into meal in a *dong,* a wooden vessel. There is a rhythmic beating of axes on the trees. Half-completed *tukuls* stand like hairnets on stilts. Everyone is moving slowly and methodically, as is the custom, but in the leaden evening light, the people seem to be walking underwater, each movement of an arm or leg a ritualistic gesture, like a benediction without a recipient.

A handful of boys gather on a large rock for my benefit. We talk about their ambitions, which are high. One wants to become a teacher; two, doctors. The youngest of the lot says that he will be a bishop. "Don't you have to become a priest first?" I tease him. The others laugh, but the boy insists, "I'll be a bishop."

As we talk I watch the elders of the camp as they watch the boys. Neither here nor in Palotaka could I tell how the older men regarded these boys—as objects of affection; as members of a foster family; as wards for whose moral and intellectual education they are responsible; as workers in the field; as future soldiers. There is something equally familiar and formal in the way the boys are addressed by the elders. Perhaps the closest analogy is to English public schools, but without the horseplay, and, of course, without any sense or assumption of privilege.

They certainly do not coddle these boys. A priest at Palotaka told me that he was not in the least concerned with their psychological problems. Sebit William, Palotaka's director, was definitely concerned, but even as he urges the boys to "talk out" their suffering, in Western psychological terms, he also pushes them to focus on whatever tasks are at hand. "They grow up very fast here," says William. "This is no child's experience."

The area where the settlers of Natinga have discovered the five watering holes lies at the base of a large rock, at least sixty feet high, which has been whitewashed by the repeating rains. It looks as if it is wearing clown's makeup. The rock is the kind that boys who live in easier surroundings use for games of adventure. A few of the boys here do play on the rock, but again, every move is slow and studied, and there is never any boisterous calling out. A boy has found his special niche in a large egg-shaped indentation in the rock; he has claimed it as his framework, and sits inside it like a subject in a portrait, distractedly beating a stick against one of its sides.

At the top of the rock, an older boy sits playing a handmade lyre. A triangle of sticks holds the strings in place, and is stuck into an empty oil can, which gives the instrument, called a *rabala,* its resonance. The song he plays is a repetition of chords strummed at a variety of cadences, and altered subtly from time to time. It sounds more like background music than a piece in itself.

Then, when it seems that the song will consist only of chords, the boy breaks into lyrics. A camp leader translates from the Dinka: "Mother and Father, I leave you now. I have to go away to school. Do not think about me again." Then the boy sings another song, one line of which is "Give me a pen that I may become somebody in the future."

The boy plays his *rabala* in a sitting position with his legs curled under him, exposing his feet to my view. The feet are long and narrow. They look like leatherworks into which the legs have been stuck like poles. The soles of the boy's feet are as smooth as rubbed stones. The tips of the toes are tanned marbles. There is a deep, dark crease, like one of the erosion fissures in the road, between the toes and the balls of the feet, which are flattened, showing only the hint of an arch. I think: A perfect walking instrument—as if the boy had made it with his hands, like the *rabala*.

The sky is blood orange, then dark, and the figures of the camp are gliding like hallucinations among the tents and the *tukuls*. Talk is sucked into the air; every sentence sounds like a whispered secret. A single star, the night's first, appears as a pinpoint of unpolished silver. There is an earthquake, barely a ripple, but sufficient to remind us that we are on earth.

The sudden fall of darkness alerts everyone to the necessity of flashlights. The elders of the camp sit on the ground and on benches that were made this afternoon from a tree called *kam,* used by the Nuer for spear handles because of its hardness. "A girl is straight like a *kam*" is a compliment. Of *kam,* they have also made beds for the visitors, though they have none for themselves. The talk is of stories and of storytelling. The telling of stories is not mere entertainment for these people; it is their connection to one another and to the past, a past, as one of them says, that "goes to the beginning of time." Stories cover the entire continent of Africa. Vast regions of deserts, rain forests, mountains, savannas, plateaus, and rocky areas like Natinga are held together by stories.

The main themes of the stories are hunger, danger, trickery, loyalty, custom, and community—especially community. There is a terrible story told of a man named Hornbill who disregarded the customs of his village and refused even to attend the services for the dead. When Hornbill's own child died, the other villagers would not tell him the location of the graveyard. "Where are the graves?" Hornbill asked everyone he passed as he bore his dead child on his back. But no one would tell him. So Hornbill walked the earth forever, carrying his dead child on his back, and crying, "Where are the graves?"

Every story has a moral, but the morals are not always clear. Stories that seem to have reached reasonable conclusions do not come to an end where one expects them to; underlying each tale is the idea that a narrative, like nature itself, always continues. Yes, this has happened, yet something else, perhaps even more amazing, will happen next.

"Do the boys in the camp still tell stories?" I ask.

The men are not sure about this—so many traditions have been lost in the war years. So we all go over in a group to a place near a fire where many boys have gathered for the night. They surround the elders at once, as if we had brought them a gift. Yes, they do still tell stories once in a while. They warm to the invitation, forming a large huddle. The boy storytellers step forward one by one. Each is accorded great respect and anticipation.

One boy tells of a fox who made a deal with a lion for a rabbit, and who winds up tricking the lion. Another tells a winding tale of a man who pretends to be blind to beg for money, and who, because of his greed and stupidity, is in fact made blind. The most successful story is the dirty one—about a beautiful woman made to dress scantily by her husband to lure and humiliate her lecherous suitors. The teller of this tale is expertly solemn. The boys are beside themselves with laughter.

We deliberately hold our flashlights low, away from the faces of the boys, to enhance the effects of their words in the dark. No one seems to grow tired, though it is clear that these tales have been told and retold before. The boys watch my reaction, and seem as delighted by my pleasure as they are by the stories themselves. I study the outlines of their bodies in the dark, set against the deeper darkness of the mountains behind them and a gray-purple sky now splashed with stars.

Then one of the boys invites me to tell a story, but I decline. It is not that I am unable to think of one, but the story that comes to mind is not right for the occasion, is too fragmentary and inconclusive, and, at any rate, is one they all have heard one way or another before.

It is about a young woman of twenty-three named Ayen, who lives under a tamarind tree in Nimule, and dreams of nothing.

July 1993

Things
That Do Not
Disappear

◦§§◦

——

THEY WOULD NOT go away, those pushy women circling the
Plaza de Mayo silently and sluggishly, as if under water, photographs of their sons, daughters, and husbands swinging on chains
from their necks like good-luck charms. Sometimes the women would
raise the photographs on placards; sometimes they would hold a
snapshot delicately out in front of them between the index finger and
the thumb, presenting unassailable proof to anyone who cared to
look that the subject of the picture did, at one time, exist. Every
Thursday the Mothers of Plaza de Mayo performed their half-hour
ritual across the street from the presidential Pink House, and then
dispersed for a week. But they would not go away. In many of the
photographs the children posed formally, in dresses and coats and
ties. In several, they looked saucy before the camera. That was in
better days, before the subjects came to be counted among the
desaparecidos; thousands, possibly tens of thousands of men,
women, and children who, as alleged enemies of the state, disappeared under the military government of Argentina in the late 1970s.

Not that they really disappeared. Even the powerful Argentine
generals, with so many instruments of annihilation at their fingertips,
could not actually make people disappear. They did what they could:

abduct, torture, shoot, behead, and bury their enemies in mass and secret graves. What they hoped most recently, since ending their "dirty war" of antiterrorism, was that the issue of the *desaparecidos* would itself disappear. If the newly elected president of Argentina, Raúl Alfonsín, had any sense of custom or propriety, that is precisely what would have happened. But Alfonsín seemed unaware that one does not put the military on trial; and, in any event, graves seemed to be popping up all over the countryside at an alarming rate; and there were those irritating women, of course, relentless ambulatory photograph albums. So the issue never did disappear. It must be very discouraging for the military, all that work for nothing.

They could not even dispose of the bodies, and bodies are the easiest part to dispose of. Murderers do it frequently, with a tub full of acid; even the teeth will go eventually. Ideas are something else, however. Much more difficult to get rid of them. Memories are peculiarly tenacious. Hitler may have discovered as much after the German High Command issued its *Nacht und Nebel* decree in the western occupied territories, enabling authorities to snatch citizens off the street and out of their homes under night and fog. "The prisoners will vanish without a trace," read the decree. They did not. They were traced in the minds of those who survived. Feelings are still harder to dispose of. The Argentine mothers were not patrolling the Plaza de Mayo in the name of revolutionary ideas, but because they missed those they love.

The trouble is that people simply will not disappear. There is too much stubbornness in them, too great a propensity for self-assertion. Langston Hughes's comic character Jesse B. Semple (known as Simple in Hughes's newspaper column) once boasted that he had been "cut, stabbed, run over, hit by a car, tromped by a horse, robbed, fooled, deceived, doublecrossed, dealt seconds . . . but I am still here." Not even death weakens such a stand. The power of ghosts is that they manage to retain their place in the world in spite of the final obstruction; they insist on their presence. A simple matter, but a basic one. We will do anything to stay around, and to keep others around as well, by way of monuments, ceremonies, books. During the Stalinist terror, the Russian poet Anna Akhmatova stood in line at the Leningrad prison off and on for a period of seventeen months. One day she was approached by a woman "with lips blue from the cold," who, like Akhmatova, was waiting for news of the fate of someone in the prison.

"Can you describe this?" the woman asked the poet. Akhmatova said she could. "Then something like a smile passed fleetingly over what had once been her face."

If one is truly intent on making others disappear, he is far more likely to succeed by killing his enemies outright and announcing the deed publicly. Then at least one deals out certainty, which will probably be followed by despair. By creating "disappearances" in Argentina, the military leaders not only engendered a feeling of national absence and brooding but raised a question of logic. Gone? How can anyone be gone nowadays in our small, interconnected, excessively communicative modern world? Instead of a nation of mourners, the generals created a nation of snoopers, all pawing at the ground for bones.

One wonders in the end why *they* don't go away—little tyrants, grand tyrants—all repeating themselves from year to year, reaching the same unimaginative decision about obliterating their impediments. The idea has simplicity to recommend it. "Nothing will come of nothing," King Lear told one of his daughters. He was wrong, of course. Everything comes of nothing in *King Lear,* as it tends to elsewhere, Argentina included. Technically the *desaparecidos* are nothing; the conscience and resolve of the new administration are nothing. Because of such nothings, former President Bignone is in prison this week. On the basis of those nothings does Alfonsín hope to make his nation reappear. Working toward nothing, the former leaders got rid of most left-wing terrorism in Argentina, but in terms of a stable government or a content citizenry, they achieved nothing. Perhaps they are most comfortable in the presence of nothing. Perhaps their wish from the start was to survey a wasteland from atop a reviewing stand, exquisitely alone in a world where everyone else has disappeared.

But the women of the Plaza would not let them have such a world, intruding upon them week after week. Strange figures, ghosts hunting for ghosts. Did they do it all as a political protest, or did they think that their husbands and children might actually be recognized, and returned to them safely? Do they think that still? They had nothing to hope for, they walked in a circle, and they said nothing, by which they restored much that had gone away from Argentina.

January 23, 1984

An
Inescapable
Need to Blame

YOU ARE LIKELY not to have forgotten that heartbreaking accident in East Coldenham, New York, in November 1989, when a sudden blast of wind collapsed a wall of an elementary school, killing nine young children. Such a memory is evoked by Russell Banks in *The Sweet Hereafter*—not only the circumstance of the accidental death of children, but also the tormenting helplessness of townspeople who must try to reach a rational understanding of an inexplicable calamity. In this novel the effort to rationalize takes the form of assigning blame, which brings the townspeople as much pain as do the deaths of the children.

This effort to rationalize through blame, which is the modern effort in all things, is Russell Banks's theme. It is a theme hard to find in a novel these days. The assignment of blame makes disorderly occurrences orderly, sets them within our control again. Blame is especially useful in situations in which there is no apparent villain—those moments that prove, despite our advancement of learning, how susceptible we are to high winds and wet roads.

Dolores Driscoll has been the school bus driver in the upstate New York town of Sam Dent since 1968. She and her husband, Abbott, who has had to use a wheelchair since his stroke several years ago, have lived in no other place. In July and August, Sam Dent belongs to the summer people. The remainder of the time it is populated by ordinary people who drive pickup trucks, keep neat woodpiles, and live in houses with "flapping plastic over the windows and sagging porches." The local roads, with their "boarded-up roadside diners and dilapidated motels," run among dark mountains. Dolores knows the roads of Sam Dent, "which is one of the reasons I was given this job in 1968 and rehired every year since—the other being my considerable ability as a driver, pure and simple, and my reliability and punctuality."

Those assets are called into question after one snowy morning when, with the straight part of the road shooting before her and her bus filled with children talking quietly among themselves, Dolores sees a dog move into the road, or thinks she does. She swerves right and jams the brakes, and the bus rolls downhill into an icy pond. Fourteen of the children die.

From that terrible moment the lives of the people of Sam Dent are never the same. "For us," says Billy Ansel, a former hero of the Vietnam War who now runs the town garage—and whose children die in the accident—"there was life, true life, real life, no matter how bad it had seemed, before the accident, and nothing that came after the accident resembled it in any important way. . . . For us, it was as if we, too, had died when the bus went over the embankment and tumbled down into the frozen water-filled sandpit, and now we were lodged temporarily in a kind of purgatory, waiting to be moved to wherever the other dead ones had gone." The absence of the town's children draws couples apart, drives people to drink and loneliness, makes enemies of friends, and creates a void that is soon filled by the need to blame.

Someone, something, has to be held accountable for the deaths of the children. Dolores? The bus? The seat belts? The snowfall? The roads of the state of New York?

Into the void strides Mitchell Stephens, a lawyer from New York City who specializes in accidents. To Mitchell, all accidents are the result of negligence, and he goes around Sam Dent trying to find where the responsibility lies. His job, his mission, is, he says, "to represent anger." For a while he cannot find any anger in Sam Dent. Then he half-discovers, half-creates a client in Nichole Burnell, a teenage girl who was partly paralyzed in the crash, and who agrees to pin the blame on Dolores for speeding. Nichole's motive is personal, entirely unrelated to Dolores or to the facts of the accident.

At first the townspeople want nothing to do with her lawsuit. Then they grow excited about the idea, not for the money to be gained or as a concession to the modern litigious disease but because a lawsuit is a blaming instrument. However inaccurately or inadequately, it proclaims in a public arena that an outrageous, impossible event has been understood, that it has been put in a recognizable box, that it is tamed, not mystifying, not out of human control. In a way, modernity is defined by the extent to which life has been brought under human control.

Not only Mitchell Stephens—who is not a bad guy, merely a champion of his age—but the whole town of Sam Dent wants the bus accident brought under human control. Even Dolores wants that. When she learns that she has been blamed for the children's deaths, she is actually relieved: "I felt as if a great weight that I had been lugging around for eight or nine months, since the day of the accident, had been lifted from me," she says. It is less important to her that she has been wrongly accused than that she can at last name her anguish.

But the truth of the situation—the true story of the bus accident and of the wider experience it represents—is that its cause is bewilderingly *out of* human control, just as much of modern experience is bewilderingly out of our control. At the very least the essentials, life and death, are out of our control. Not that this is really a secret; we know how helpless we can be. Yet the knowledge is resisted because it is antimodern, superstitious, a suggestion that there are certain unconquerable forces working against progress.

See the way earthquakes and hurricanes are depicted in the news. The accounts are always made in terms of the number of dead, the number of injured, the dollar amounts of the damage. To quantify is to command the event, to make the disaster less natural. Let it never be reported that a terrible fist came out of nowhere, knocked the stuffing out of us for as long as it pleased, and left us naked in the streets.

If we are not in control of our catastrophes, after all, we can only sit back and scrutinize divine justice. We can ask Job's question or ponder the suffering of the innocent or think in circles about God's plots and errors. That, too, is an effort to rationalize, but it is not as satisfying as the assignment of blame, which is reassuring and affirms free will.

What Russell Banks is saying, I think, is that our deeper satisfaction lies elsewhere: that the force of things unrationalized is the source not only of the terror but of the beauty in our lives. Instead of being humbled by the inexplicable, we can be saved by accepting it. By accepting the inexplicable we are thrown toward one another. We may even learn to sympathize with one another for the susceptibility to suffering we have in common.

Mr. Banks is too able a writer to state such things outright. But in the final scene of his novel the town rises to an acceptance of the catastrophe on its own mysterious terms.

Everyone is gathered in the grandstand to watch the last event of the annual Sam Dent Country Fair, the demolition derby. One of the entrants is Boomer, a station wagon once owned by Dolores Driscoll. The crowd cheers wildly every time Boomer takes a hit; the car is being punished as a stand-in for Dolores. Yet it continues running. One by one all the other cars and trucks drop out of the competition, but Boomer, smashed on every side, survives.

Suddenly the crowd starts chanting "Boo-mer! Boo-mer!" In the end the station wagon is the only vehicle left in the arena; it wins simply by going on. And the crowd rejoices. The townspeople, though they can never say why, are happy.

In *The Lives of a Cell,* Lewis Thomas wrote, "All of the life of the earth dies, all the time, in the same volume as the new life that dazzles us each morning, each spring." I don't know if that is a scientific observation or a religious one, but it is a great consolation in any case. Fourteen of the children in Sam Dent die, but within eight or nine months, the gestation period of Dolores Driscoll's grief, other children will be born. Things will never be the same after the accident, but they will always be the same, too, and eventually the abiding love of the people for one another will crack through the isolation of winter and create life, true life, real life again.

That also is not to be rationalized or controlled. It is the way things are in the world, and in Russell Banks's cold and merciful eye.

September 15, 1991

The
Odd Pursuit
of Teaching
Books

DOUGLAS BUSH died on March 2 [1983] at the age of eighty-six, after forty-six years as professor of English literature at Harvard and a life of devotion to *Paradise Lost*. The obituary in *The New York Times* made him out a gentle crank, quoting a complaint of Bush's that too many students attend universities these days, and thus cannot be adequately educated—the sort of hackneyed wail that Bush himself would never have dwelt on or even considered right plucked from a greater, kindlier context. Bush's world was the greater, kindlier context. Like Samuel Johnson he knew everything worth knowing. Like Johnson, too, he was born to teach books. Few people are. It is an odd pursuit. Literary study stands at the center of modern education, but when one tries to determine what happens in the relationship among book, student, and teacher, the teacher grows shadowy, eventually vanishes.

Of course, teachers of every subject suffer from obsolescence, that being almost a tool of the trade if one's students are to build on what they learn, even to the point of rejecting it at the onset of independent thinking. Good teachers yearn to be obliterated. Good teachers of literature have little choice in the matter. The *Hamlet* they pry open for the nineteen-year-old will not be the *Hamlet* that student reads at age fifty. The play will have changed because the reader's experience will have recast it—the noble, tormented boy of one's youth reappearing in middle age as something of a drip.

But even at the moment that a teacher of literature is doing his job, the work is hard to put a name to. What precisely is it that you did, Professor Bush? Every teacher knows the boredom and terror of that question. A teacher of French teaches French, a teacher of piano, piano. But a teacher of Proust, Austen, Donne, Faulkner, Joyce? Are not the writers the teachers themselves? Oh, one can see the need for a tour guide now and then: notes, terms, some scraps of biography. But surely the great books were written for people, and if they require the presence of middlemen, then they could never have been so great in the first place. So goes the cant.

In point of plain fact, a teacher of literature may do several quite different things, especially these days when universities house their own schools of thought on the subject. Some teach the formal aspects of literature, some the sociology of literature, some the politics. There are those who teach because literature tells them what it means to be human; others who hold that literature means whatever one wishes it to mean; still others who say it means nothing at all. Defenders of each fort sometimes make the newspapers, where, in argument with one another, they sound like crazed religious warriors. In a sense, the answer to "What do you do?" is "This and that." And it may be that just as there are books and books, so are there various ways of apprehending them, and thus no core of the subject to teach.

Still, something central seems to be conveyed in the teaching of literature beyond a particular point of view, something in the attitude of the teacher toward both his students and the books: his concentration, his appreciation, occasionally his awe. Awe can be a powerful pedagogical instrument, the sight of someone overwhelmed overwhelming by refraction. True, the relationship of teacher to the work of art is that of a middleman, but in the best circumstances the middleman becomes a magnifying glass ("Do you see *this*?"). Instead of intruding between Yeats and his reader, he shows Yeats in the light, reveals not only poetry but how poetry comprehends the world, thus lending his students the eyes of the poet. At full strength, the teacher is an artist himself, and not just for restorations. Treating the book as an event, he manipulates it the way the writer manipulated reality, making of literature what the writer made of life.

Curiously, this high point is precisely where the question of the teacher's usefulness sometimes turns bitter. A book says something ennobling; a teacher makes that clear. It ought to follow that students are ennobled, but the opposite often occurs. In his essay "Humane Literacy," George Steiner brooded, "We know that some of the men who devised and administered Auschwitz had been taught to read Shakespeare or Goethe, and continued to do so. This compels us to ask whether knowledge of the best that had been thought and said does, as Matthew Arnold asserted, broaden and refine the resources of the human spirit." One might wonder why a teacher of literature should worry about being unable to regulate moral actions, when no such self-recrimination haunts the teacher of, say, physics. But a work of literature, unlike a physical law, has moral content to begin with, and the teacher's inability to transfer that content may seem either a failure of his own understanding or a basic flaw of the craft.

What concerns such a teacher, the scrupulous teacher, is that he is dealing solely with words—the words of others, which are not his property, and his own words in their behalf. The matter is abstract, thus unnerving. Every word is an idea, and that may offer consolation or encouragement. But ideas are also merely represented by words, and when the teacher, who is the purveyor and curator of words, strides into the classroom and spills the words on his desk, he has no control over them, no way to enforce intelligence, charity, love, wit, or any of the elements of which the books he values are made.

So what is it he does in that mysterious classroom when the thick wood door shuts behind him and the rows of too young faces turn and rise like heliotropic plants, eager for a sign? "Today we consider Kafka." Is that in fact what "we" are considering today? Or are we considering the teacher considering Kafka, and if that is the case, what exactly is to be considered—the learned scholar stocked deep with information about "irony" and "metaphor," or the still deeper mind, which has confronted Kafka alone in a private dark, and which Kafka has confronted in turn? "How does one say that [D. H.] Lawrence is right in his great rage against the modern emotions, unless one speaks from the intimacies of one's own feelings, and one's own sense of life, and one's own worked-for way of being?" asked Lionel Trilling. The testimony is always personal. Behind the spectacles and the fuzzy coat, the teacher teaches himself.

In the end it may come to a matter of character. John Ruskin said that only a good man can make a good artist, but that notion is disproved all the time. Good teaching, however, is another matter. No one knows how virtuous a person Milton was, but the speculation becomes irrelevant when applied to *Paradise Lost,* which, like every work of art, assumed a life of its own as soon as it was finished. The writer let it go. But the teacher of *Paradise Lost* cannot let it go; he becomes its life. Whether he sees the work as a brilliant display of versification or as the story of man's fall from grace, the poem is a sacred text, the source of his intellectual or moral faith. His students thus behold the poem and the faith together, and are bound to like *Paradise Lost* in part because they admire his strength of belief.

This faith in literature cannot be easy to acquire. A teacher of books must learn to live before becoming good at his work, since literature demands that one know a great deal about life—not to have settled life's problems, but at least to recognize and accept the wide, frail world in which those problems have a home. The achievement of such perspective involves a penalty too. He who has gained that generous view inevitably moderates the books in his charge, domesticates their subversiveness, puts out the fire. As moderator he becomes a caricature, as teachers of English in fiction are always portrayed as caricatures. Who's afraid of Virginia Woolf's professor? The practice of giving apples to teachers may have originated as an unconscious mockery of their lack of experience and danger, of their apparent refusal to risk the loss of paradise.

And yet the power they generate can be enormous. Remember? One may not know exactly what happens in those classrooms, but one knows that it did happen, long after the fact, after all the classrooms and the schools are left behind. Two, perhaps three, teachers in a lifetime stick in the mind, and one of them is almost always a teacher of literature. He remains not as presiding deity but as a person, someone impassioned about words on paper. Perhaps he knows that words are all we have, all that stand between ourselves and our destruction. The teacher also intervenes. Robert Hollander, Jr., of Princeton described a class of R. P. Blackmur's, who taught Hollander the Dante he now teaches others: "The lecture gasped, tottered, and finally settled ruinously into total silence. He stood there, I thought, debating whether or not to chuck it all up, leave the room (with twenty minutes still to run before the bell), perhaps even to leave the earth." Danger enough.

Courage too, of a sort. Who but a teacher of books dares claim as his province the entire range of human experience, intuition no less than fact? Who else has the nerve? And what does he do with this vast territory he has staked out for himself? He invites us in, says in effect there has never been anything written, thought, or felt that one need be afraid to confront. A teacher of books may favor this or that author or century, but fundamentally his work is the antithesis of prejudice. Take it all, he urges; the vicious with the gentle. Do not run from anything you can read. Above all, do not become enraged at what is difficult or oblique. You too are difficult, oblique, and equally worth the effort.

It may be that such people remain with us because they were always with us from the start. Basically the enterprise of teaching literature is a hopeful one, the hope residing with the upturned faces. First faith, then hope. If words are merely words after all, then the teacher of books may be the world's most optimistic creature. No matter how he may grumble about life's decay, it is he who, year after year, trudges up the stone steps of old, dank buildings, hauls himself before the future, and announces, against all reason of experience, that "the World was all before them."

With those words, Milton approached the end of his long moral poem, and when Douglas Bush came to read those words aloud before his Harvard classes, there was nothing in his voice that betrayed a personal reverberation to the grand dismay the words contain. Bush showed none of Blackmur's visible force or Trilling's visible elegance, though like them he believed in the good that words and people are capable of. On the last day of courses at Harvard, it is the custom for students to applaud the teachers they most appreciate. After years of suffering this embarrassment, Bush would begin to pack up his books in the last minutes of the hour, so that he could time his exit from the room right at the bell. Thus when the moment arrived, and Bush was already halfway down the steps, it appeared that the students were clapping on and on for someone not there. But he was there.

March 28, 1983

Would You Mind If I Borrowed This Book?

Never lend books, for no one ever returns them:
the only books I have in my library are books
that other folk have lent me.

—ANATOLE FRANCE

OF ALL THE terrifying circumstances to which one's home is vulnerable, nothing equals that of a guest who stares straight at one's bookshelves. It is not the judgmental possibility that is frightening: the fact that one's sense of discrimination is exposed by his books. Indeed, most people would much prefer to see the guest first scan, then peer and turn away in boredom or disapproval. Alas, too often the eyes, dark with calculation, shift from title to title as from girl to girl in an overheated dance hall. Nor is that the worst. It is when those eyes stop moving that the heart too stops. The guest's body twitches; his hand floats up to where his eyes have led it. There is nothing to be done. You freeze. He smiles. You hear the question even as it forms: "Would you mind if I borrowed this book?"

(Mind? Why should I mind? The fact that I came upon that book in a Paris bookstall in April 1959—the thirteenth I believe it was, the afternoon, it was drizzling—that I found it after searching all Europe and North America for a copy; that it is dog-eared at passages that mean more to my life than my heartbeat; that the mere touch of its pages recalls to me in a Proustian shower my first love, my best dreams. Should I mind that you seek to take all that away? That I will undoubtedly never get it back? Then even if you actually return it to me one day, I will be wizened, you cavalier, and the book spoiled utterly by your mishandling? *Mind?*)

"Not at all. Hope you enjoy it."

"Thanks. I'll bring it back next week."

"No rush. Take your time. [Liar.]"

Not that there is any known way to avoid these exchanges. One has books; one has friends; they are bound to meet. Charles Lamb, who rarely railed, waxed livid on the subject: "Your borrowers of books—those mutilators of collections, spoilers of the symmetry of shelves, and creators of odd volumes." But how are such people to be put off, since *they* are often *we,* and the nonreturn of borrowed books is a custom as old as books themselves? ("Say, Gutenberg, what's *this*? And may I borrow it?") It is said that Charles I clutched a Bible as he mounted the scaffold. One shudders to imagine the last earthly question he heard.

Still, this custom confutes nature. In every other such situation, the borrower becomes a slave to the lender, the social weight of the debt so altering the balance of a relationship that a temporary acquisition turns into a permanent loss. This is certainly true with money. Yet it is not at all true with books. For some reason a book borrower feels that a book, once taken, is his own. This removes both memory and guilt from the transaction. Making matters worse, the lender believes it too. To keep up appearances, he may solemnly extract an oath that the book be brought back as soon as possible; the borrower answering with matching solemnity that the Lord might seize his eyes were he to do otherwise. But it is all a play. Once gone, the book is gone forever. The lender, fearing rudeness, never asks for it again. The borrower never stoops to raise the subject.

Can the borrowers be thwarted? There are attempts. Some hopefuls glue EX LIBRIS stickers to the inside covers (clever drawings of animals wearing glasses, and so forth)—as if the presence of Latin and the imprint of a name were so formidable as to reverse a motor reflex. It never works. One might try slipping false jackets on one's books—a cover for *The Secret Agent* disguising *Utility Rates in Ottawa: A Woman's View.* But book borrowers are merely despicable, not stupid; they tend to leaf before they pluck. Besides, the interesting thing about the feeling of loss when a book is borrowed is that the book's quality rarely matters. So mysterious is the power of books in our lives that every loss is a serious loss, every hole in the shelf a crater.

And this, of course, is the key to the sense of helplessness in this matter. Our books are ourselves, our characters, our insulation against those very people who would take away our books. There, on that wall, Ahab storms. Hamlet mulls. Molly Bloom says yes yes yes. Keats looks into Chapman, who looks at Homer, who looks at Keats. All this happens on a bookshelf continually—while you are out walking the dog, or pouting or asleep. The Punic Wars rage; Emma Bovary pines; Bacon exhorts others to behave the way he never could. Here French is spoken. There Freud. So go war and peace, pride and prejudice, decline and fall, perpetually in motions as sweeping as Milton's or as slight as Emily Dickinson considering the grass. Every evening Gatsby looks at Daisy's green light, which is green forever. Every morning Gregor Samsa discovers that he has been transformed into a giant insect.

These things are not what we have, but what we are. Leigh Hunt exulted: "Nothing can deprive me of my value for such treasures. I can help the appreciation of them while I last, and love them till I die; and perhaps, if fortune turns her face in kindness upon me before I go, I may chance, some quiet day, to lay my over-beating temples on a book, and so have the death I most envy." Plato was reputedly found dead with a book under his pillow, Petrarch in his library with his elbow resting on an open page. Books gave them more than solace. They were their lives extended, a way of touching eternity. "Go, litel book!" wrote Chaucer at the end of *Troilus and Criseyde,* sending his work on a journey that no man could complete.

Small wonder, then, that people will do almost everything for books, to acquire and preserve them, to prevent their banning or burning. Stories of manuscripts lost or destroyed are especially heartbreaking because one knows how ephemeral ideas and images are, what vast effort it takes to dust off the confusions, tune out the noise, and create those books that, for whatever inadequacies they may display, still set the mind in order for a time, giving it a spine and a binding. There may be no more pleasing picture in the world than that of a child peering into a book—the past and the future entrancing each other. Nor does anyone look quite so attractive as with a book in hand. How many people have fallen in love merely at the sight of someone reading?

All of which would appear to offer an argument that booklending ought to be encouraged. It is the supreme selfless act, after all. Should we not abjure our pettiness, open our libraries, and let our most valued possessions fly from house to house, sharing the wealth? Certain clerics with vows of poverty did this. Inside their books was printed not EX LIBRIS but AD USUM—for the use of—indicating that it is better to lend than to keep, that all life's gifts are transitory. Should we not follow the clerics? Or might we just for once summon our true feelings on this subject and, upon hearing the terrible question, smile back and speak from the heart: "Mind? I'll break your *arm,* you bastard!"

April 5, 1982

J. M. Synge

A S FAR AS I KNOW, the 1959 biography of John Synge by
David H. Green and Edward M. Stephens (Macmillan) still
gives the most thorough account of Synge's life. There have been a
number of sketches and memoirs—by Yeats, John Masefield, Lady
Gregory, and Padraic Colum, among others—and an early biography
in 1913 by Maurice Bourgeois, the first Synge scholar; but the size of
the material, critical and biographical, is very small for one of the
great playwrights in English. Even in the centennial year (1971) of
Synge's birth, the best *The New York Times* could come up with was
a short article called "Synge-Song to Resound in Ireland," that at
least gave readers a clue toward pronouncing the man's name. Were
it not for occasional revivals of *The Playboy of the Western World*
and a few stubborn admirers, Synge long ago would have passed into
the fog of the ancient Irish kings.

The account of him that gets to the heart of the matter is "With
Synge in Connemara" by Jack B. Yeats, the artist and writer, Willie's
younger brother. In this reminiscence of a walking tour Yeats made
with Synge, Yeats tells of the joy Synge took in wild scenes, and
describes the two of them in Bellmullet on St. John's Eve, watching
the fire-play. Yeats later did a drawing of this celebration: a market-

place with townspeople in the forefront hurling flaming sods of turf, white against the black sky. In the center of this drawing stand two observers, looking very much like Synge and Yeats, and watching with expressionless approval the kind of civilized frenzy of which they both made art.

Edmund John Millington Synge was born in Rathfarnham, now a Dublin suburb, on April 16, 1871. His father, a barrister, died one year later, leaving Synge to be raised by a powerhouse of a mother who trusted belligerently in the God of Protestant Ireland and who served as His emissary to her son, Johnny. As seems to be the case with many robust men, Synge was sickly as a boy. Alone most of the time, he developed an enthusiasm for natural history, and a skeptical attitude toward formal religion. He had lost the faith entirely by the time he entered Trinity College Dublin.

Synge was graduated from Trinity—by the skin of his teeth—with few prospects or accomplishments: prize exams in Hebrew and Irish; one sonnet published in the college literary magazine; a love of music, and the desire to become a musician; and a love of Cherry Matteson, the girl next door, and the second of a half dozen women who were to be central to Synge's life. Whatever else Cherry had to commend her, she was a good and ardent Christian, a fact that alone should have told Synge their situation was hopeless. But Synge was a lonely man who could brood his life into deep romantic pain.

In July 1893, he made a trip to Germany in order to study to become a professional violinist. He soon admitted that he had neither the temperament nor the ability to be a performing musician, and returned to Ireland, making one final and unsuccessful attempt to win Cherry. He then returned to the continent, making the longest stay in Rome, where he wrote translations of Petrarch's sonnets—a reasonable decision after losing his Laura. From Rome he went to Paris, where he remained from October 1896 through the winter. Events in that season were to redirect his life.

The people Synge met in the winter of 1896–97 were among the most exciting in Ireland's modern history. Young Ireland, the political club they formed in the interests of Irish independence, was equally busy, passionate, and ineffective. Maud Gonne, the mad queen of Irish nationalism, listed Synge as one of the organization's "most notable members," but Synge enjoyed the histrionics of Miss Gonne, Yeats, and the old Fenian, John O'Leary, more than participating in Young Ireland's plots and activities. As Masefield, Yeats, and Sean O'Faolain later said, Synge had no real interest in politics.

Yet he was a patriot on his terms. When doing an article, "In the Congested Districts," for *The Guardian* in 1905 he said to a friend, "I like not lifting the rags of my mother country for to tickle the sentiments of Manchester." Synge wanted Ireland free of both England and her own parochialism. In the violent public reaction to his plays he was to learn that parochialism was more adamant.

That same winter Synge discovered *The Imitation of Christ* by Thomas à Kempis. The book is central to *Étude Morbide,* a strange autobiographical piece, in which a violinist contemplating suicide over the death of one of the two women in his life, finally turns from asceticism and rejects the saint. Synge never rejected the book himself. Quotations from it frequently crop up in his diary. His review of Geoffrey Keating's history of Ireland praises Keating by comparing him to à Kempis. Yeats notes that Synge planned a translation of the *Imitation* into Irish country idiom; the first part of the Saint's speech at the end of Act One of *The Well of the Saints* sounds like such a translation.

As a conduct book the *Imitation* was attractive to Synge because it reaffirmed his own detachment from worldly things. It also implied a Socialist millennium, another appealing idea that hit Synge just when he was steeped in William Morris, *The Communist Manifesto,* and other French and English Socialist tracts. Still a more important implication was the availability of mystical experience. Synge was incapable of getting as fired up with Mme. Blavatsky and her crew as Yeats; but he read a good deal on magic and the occult. *Under Ether,* the account of a later operation, is full of mystical events, as are *Étude Morbide* and parts of *The Aran Islands,* particularly where Synge talks of the psychic memory attached to certain neighborhoods. Skeptical as Synge was about religion, he believed in miracles and in a cosmic structure capable of anything.

To verify that structure is the purpose of the *Imitation.* Behind its many prescriptions the book is a statement of supreme confidence in divine strategy: "all things are designed by God, and set in their place by the Sovereign Artist, who has left nothing disorderly in his creations." That Synge believed, though the character of this artist God remained in question. Every expression of inevitability in Synge's plays, every reference to Nature, every symbol of decay and regeneration attests to a system, but also to terrible consequences. Deaths of body and spirit fit a pattern. When characters such as the king Conchubor (pronounced Connor) of *Deirdre of the Sorrows* fall apart, they decay into Nature: "I'll walk up now into your halls," says young Deirdre, whom he covets, "and I'll say it's here nettles will be growing, and beyond thistles and docks. I'll go into your high chambers, where you've been figuring yourself stretching out your neck for the kisses of a queen of women; and I'll say it's here there'll be deer stirring and goats scratching, and sheep waking and coughing when there is a great wind from the north."

Only two of Synge's plays, *Riders to the Sea* and *Deirdre,* have people dying, and every death, except for Owens's in *Deirdre,* is anticipated. In *Riders* the sea takes the fisherman Bartley; in *Deirdre,* Naisi and his woodsmen brothers are hunted and trapped; Deirdre, the natural woman, falls into the earth. Owen appears too briefly for his death to be forecast, but for him too, life and death are accompanied by the same madness. Deirdre calls death an untidy thing, yet in fact death is a neat summing up in Synge. It is only untidy in the minds of the characters who would hold it at arm's length, and their efforts make the tragedies.

There is another aspect of à Kempis that could have affected Synge as well. The *Imitation* is a record of multiple lonelinesses. It was composed in a monastery by a man who designed rules of solitude to keep men apart from each other so as to nurture their souls that are separate from their bodies, and that trace their source to an incomprehensible system set up by an incomprehensible Creator who forbids direct communication and who is, by being unique, ultimate loneliness itself. Everything Synge wrote, including the comedies, reflects this desolation.

By spring 1897, Synge knew that he wanted to become a writer, a decision that his mother belittled. Still he had no subject. Yeats advised him to go to the Aran Islands, where Yeats had gathered material for his novel, *The Speckled Bird,* and where the life was raw and elemental. From May through June 1899, Synge made the first of his four visits to Aran, and wrote "A Story from Inishman." Between September 1899 and the winter of 1900 he made two more visits, starting to pull together *Riders to the Sea.* In April 1900 he had begun collecting his Aran sketches into a single narrative, *The Aran Islands,* which he completed in September 1901. Nothing he wrote more clearly shows the intense self-inflicted loneliness of the man: this brooding, educated member of the Ascendancy, speaking Gaelic in whispers, sitting at once among and apart from the lovely and brutal Irish peasants.

In January 1902, Fisher Unwin publishers rejected *The Aran Islands,* and in the spring of that year two of Synge's Wicklow pieces—

as strong and tight as *The Aran Islands*—were also rejected. At the age of thirty-one, Synge had sold exactly six articles, two of which were reviews. Yet he persisted; and in the summer 1902 his writing took off. Within three months he finished *Riders to the Sea,* wrote *The Shadow of the Glen* and a first draft of *The Tinkers Wedding.* The following winter he was in London, and at Yeats's urging one evening, read his plays aloud to a group that included Yeats, Masefield, G. K. Chesterton, and Lady Gregory. For the previous few years Yeats and Lady Gregory had been working to build a national Irish theater. After that evening they knew they had what they were after, and something considerably bigger.

It's a good thing that Synge did not wait for one play to be produced before starting another. The critical reception given *The Shadow of the Glen* was angry enough to have discouraged most writers. Later, in the *Playboy* riots, when Synge would look back upon mere hostile criticism as the halcyon days, he could also be sufficiently secure in the judgment of his own worth to let public condemnation go with scorn. For now he simply worked. In April 1903, he began *The Well of the Saints.* In June he read *The Shadow of the Glen* to the Theatre Group. In August he did a preliminary draft of *The Playboy of the Western World.* In September *Riders to the Sea* was published, and *The Shadow of the Glen* was in rehearsal for its opening on October 8.

As soon as the play appeared, Synge was caught in a war between the Irish press and those members of the Ascendancy such as Yeats and Lady Gregory who were heading the theater movement. *The Shadow of the Glen* is a story based on a Wicklow "hearth-tale" about Nora Burke, whose husband pretends to be dead in order to check her fidelity. The idea that an Irish country wife would ever run off with a tramp, as Nora does at the end of the play, was according to the *Irish Times* "a slur on Irish womanhood." Arthur Griffith, editor of the nationalist *United Irishman,* called *The Shadow* "decadent" and compared Synge to "any Englishman who has yet dissected us for the enlightenment of his countrymen."

Behind this anger, and the uproars to follow, there was a real issue—what was meant by a "national" drama? What theater was "good" and "right" for a nation seeking to be free? Synge's friend Stephen MacKenna, the journalist and translator of Plotinus, wrote to Synge in praise of *The Well of the Saints,* but added: "I imagine your play would be better understood in France than in these dull lands." During the controversy over *The Shadow of the Glen* he told

Synge that he believed in the "ripeness and unripeness of nations," and that "Ireland [was] blessedly unripe" for Synge's way of looking at her. MacKenna was a good index of Irish opinion on this question of propriety. Learned, sensitive, and understanding Synge's intentions, he nevertheless would rather have read Synge in a book than to have seen the plays performed for his anxious countrymen.

Synge answered MacKenna with one of the rare statements he ever made about the nature of his work. MacKenna had urged him toward a "purely fantastic unmodern . . . Cuchullainoid [sic] theatre." Synge replied that "no drama can grow out of anything other than the fundamental realities of life which are never fantastic, are neither modern nor unmodern, and as I see them rarely spring-dayish or breezy or Cuchulainoid." As for coddling immature audiences,

> Do you think that the peasantry—the people—of Norway are less blessed. . . . than the Irish? Do you think that if they are as innocent as the Irish, then Ibsen should not have been played in Norway, and therefore, have never become an efficient dramatist? Do you think that because the people I have met in the valleys of Wurzburg and the Rhine are as unripe as those of Kerry and Galway that Sudermann and Hauptmann should be driven from the boards of Berlin? The Dublin audiences who see M[me.] Rejane in Ibsen, Mrs. P[atrick] Campbell in Sudermann, Miss Olga Netherstink in Sappho etc. etc. are hardly blessedly unripe! They want to suck smut every evening and to rise up every morning and say, 'Behold we are the most virtuous nation in Europe. Thank God we are not as other men.'

On February 25, 1904, *Riders to the Sea* was performed with A.E.'s *Deirdre*. On December 27, the Abbey Theatre opened. *The Shadow of the Glen* was again performed, and the Yeats-Griffith controversy reheated. On February 4, 1905, *The Well of the Saints*—about an old blind couple who gain sight and lose their dreams—opened to little notice. By November 1906 Synge was working on *The Playboy* for a scheduled December production, later postponed. On January 8, 1907, *The Playboy* went into rehearsal and on January 26, it opened. Nothing since the arrival of Jesus has ever had such a premiere.

"On the coming out," wrote the fastidious Joseph Holloway in his diary, "Lady Gregory asked me what was the cause of the disturbance and my monosyllabic answer was 'Blackguardism'—to which she queried, on which side? 'The stage,' " said Holloway; "Synge is the evil genius of the Abbey and Yeats his able lieutenant." *The Free-man's Journal* proposed that if an English company had "attempted such an outrage the public indignation would be rightly bitter." The reviewer for the *Evening Mail* found it a pity "that such fine acting [of the Fay brothers and Sara Allgood] and such smart dialogue should be wasted on so grotesque a play." The *Irish Times* advised Synge to "sacrifice the 'remorseless truth' if his play is to be made acceptable to healthy public opinion."

Yeats and Lady Gregory disregarded public opinion, healthy and otherwise, and decided to run *The Playboy* for another week. Every night there was stamping, booing, and shouting from the audience. The police were called in, making matters worse. On Tuesday night a group of boys from Trinity College showed up "as patrons of the free drama" and sang "God Save the King." Yeats took the stage, making vain entreaties to the audience. William Boyle, the most popular and profitable Abbey playwright, withdrew his plays in protest from the company. Fistfights were normal; public debates raged; and even after that week, long after, the mere mention of *The Playboy* was enough to start a brawl. When the play toured America in 1911–12, it was attacked ferociously. Five years after Synge's death, someone signed "Observer" could still appeal to the readers of *The Freeman's Journal* by calling *The Playboy* a libel on the Irish peasant, and Synge's work "the outcome of a neurotic brain and a grovelling imagination."

The reasons for this vehemence ranged from Synge's use of the word *shift,* a woman's slip, a small shock to the audience's sensibilities, to what many saw in the play as yet another gross caricature of the stock Irishman. The most outrageous insult was the plot itself: an Irish village glorifying and protecting a young man who had killed his "da" and assaulted society; that, and the implication that there was such a thing as a deliberately loveless marriage in Ireland. There probably would have been more violent reactions to the play had the audience caught one of its slier offenses; Pegeen Mike and Shawn Kehoe are cousins, and the dispensation sought from Rome, referred to early on, is to allow the not uncommon practice of an intrafamily marriage.

Things that were important to reviewers and politicos, however, were not on Synge's mind, either when he wrote *The Playboy* or any of his work, since it is all of a piece. The key to Synge lies not in violations of taste but rather in the massive solitude from which he viewed the world, and within which he saw man's proper and lamentable place. His most important term was *desolate*. The word appears continually in his works, meaning not merely the absence of life, but the absence of life where life had once been strong. "Desolation" was caused by an establishment or hardened order, such as external nature itself. The more people resembled external nature in appearance or action, the less human, vital, they became, and the more submissive to death-in-life.

Yet there could be "splendour" in the submission if it were fought. Nora Burke goes off with the tramp so as not to resign herself to "a lonesome place." Maurya (*Riders*) gives in only when the sea has taken every man in her family. Deirdre gives in only when the legend to which she is bound prevails. Pegeen's tragedy is the prospect of a dead life with the pipsqueak Shawn. When Christie goes, she has lost not only "the only Playboy of the Western World" but the fight against custom.

Synge knew that this fight could be terribly funny, and could drive one to do strange things. In *The Well of the Saints* the Douls strive for their former blindness because they groped in the light. Nothing is as crazy as it first appears, and the comedy of the plays, often so hilarious, is a way of mocking and surviving an implacable universe. Man at his best *is* comedy standing in relief from desolation. And he is also part of the desolation with which he contends, making both more beautiful. It ought to be added, however, that this universe of Synge's was not presided over. Synge believed in God but also believed, as he said in an early unpublished play, that He cares "as little for us as we care for the sorrows of an anthill." Perhaps the Dublin audiences perceived this as well. It would explain the longevity of their hatred of the man.

On June 5, 1907, the cast of *The Playboy* stumbled into Oxford, still reeling from the winter riots. But this time there was only cheering, and from then on, outside Ireland at least, Synge's reputation was assured. At about this time he fell in love with Molly Allgood, the actress and Sara's younger sister, a stunning woman, much younger than Synge. Between June and August 1908, he and Molly had four happy weeks together before she went on tour with the theater company. Synge had begun work on *Deirdre of the Sorrows,* the story of an old king who loves a beautiful young woman to whom he represents desolation.

On April 28, 1908, doctors had discovered a lump on Synge's side. Synge had an operation on May 4 but recovered sufficiently to continue with *Deirdre*. In late September, Molly was with him again. He asked half in jest if she would attend his funeral, and her answer inspired a poem, "A Question":

> I asked if I got sick and died, would you
> With my black funeral go walking too,
> If you'd stand close to hear them talk or pray
> While I'm let down in that steep bank of clay.
> And, No, you said, for if you saw a crew
> Of living idiots pressing round that new
> Oak coffin—they alive, I dead beneath
> That board—you'd rave and rend them with your teeth.

By January, Synge's health was too low for work. On February 1, he was in the hospital again for observation. He died of Hodgkin's disease on March 24, 1909.

October 4 and 11, 1975

The "Negro Everyman" and His Humor

WHITE MEN have always supposed that black men do a great
deal of laughing, perhaps in the hope that the tag of good
humor, like the tag of a sense of rhythm, might imply happiness and
effect a kind of absolution. Many of America's earliest comedians
were black, or in blackface, or sometimes both, and it did not seem
at all contradictory to the audiences of the Georgia Minstrels that the
same people who had been forced to provide everything else for their
masters should be called upon to provide hilarity as well. The caricature of the happy darky may be one of the reasons why black authors
have put so few comic characters into black writing. There are good-
humored characters in black fiction such as Jimboy in *Not Without
Laughter* and Tea-Cake in *Their Eyes Were Watching God*, a few
witty ironists such as Bob Jones of *If He Hollers Let Him Go*,
characters such as Augie March (*God Sends Sunday*) who get caught
in comic situations, clowns such as McKay's Zeddy the Bear (*Home
to Harlem*) who are funny unintentionally; and there are pitchmen
and tricksters such as William Kelley's Cooley (*dem*), Ellison's Ras
(*Invisible Man*), and, in a way, Claude Brown (*Manchild in the
Promised Land*). But, with one exception, black literature has produced no full, self-sustaining humorous hero, either out of the desire

to avoid reproducing end men, or because end men seem out of place in the depictions of a nightmare.

The exception is Langston Hughes's Jesse B. Semple, called Simple, who was stronger and more important than any nightmare in which he functioned. Modeled on a factory worker Hughes met in a Harlem bar in the early '40s, he became known as the Negro Everyman, and during the twenty years of his prominence his commentary filled over a hundred and fifty columns of the *Chicago Defender* and the *New York Post*, five books, and a Broadway musical. He was the embodiment of an ideal intelligence, at once shrewd, generous, irreverent, resilient, contemptuous of hypocrisy, inconsistent, manly, unrefined, and frighteningly sane. He held opinions, which were rarely encumbered with facts, on everything, and he had no formal learning to choke on. In the Simple sketches Hughes pits his own college education against Simple's native sense, and as is always the case in such literary battles, the college education comes in second. The name, Jesse B. Semple (just be simple), was a combination of advice and imperative, and in his so-called simplicity Simple joined the corps of American folk hero humorists—Uncle Remus, Josh Billings, Mr. Dooley, and others—who drew laughter out of the shock and novelty of common sense. Simple may not always have been as funny as his predecessors, but he was richer and much more complicated.

He was an urban folk hero, equipped with city tastes and a city vocabulary, yet he was as ardent a regionalist as Sam Slick, Jonathan Oldstyle, Hosea Biglow, or any of the rural American humorists. It made no difference that Simple's region was Harlem and that his dialect was Harlem argot; his attitude toward his section of the country was as elaborately loyal as a Westerner's or Down Easter's, and he was just as purely a homegrown philosopher. He was brash, as are all literary regionalists, he was antiauthoritarian, and in spite of his critical stance and occasional doomsday visions, he was an optimist at heart. Where he differed from his fellow regionalists is that his region was continually under attack, because in a larger sense than Harlem his region was blackness; and so the criticisms he leveled at the nation were often informed by a sense of urgency and frustration which, until the emergence of black comedians such as Dick Gregory and Godfrey Cambridge, was unique in American humor. There was also the difference between a cracker barrel and a bar stool. The fact that Simple did his philosophizing from a local dive was designed to be one of his comic properties, but it also suggested that in order to sustain his hopeful view of the world it helped to be high, if only on beer.

Above everything, he was a race man: " 'You certainly are race-conscious,' I said. 'Negroes, Negroes, Negroes! Everything in terms of race. Can't you think just once without thinking in terms of color?' 'I am colored,' said Simple."[1] In the middle of an essay on feet ("Feet Live Their Own Life," *Mind,* p. 3) he gives a list of the places where his feet have stood—at lunch counters, WPA desks, hospitals, graves, welfare windows, craps tables, kitchen doors, social security railings, soup lines, and the draft—all of which make up the Harlemite's itinerary. When his companion asks if there is anything truly special about his feet, he tells of a night in a Harlem street riot when one of his feet was used to kick in a store window, while the other was getting set to make a run for it. Inside the playfulness there is terror and indignation, yet the playfulness prevails. He composes poems about Jim Crow, feels the beating of Emmett Till as if it were happening to himself, and still can joke about a Second Coming in which Christ kills all the whites except for Mrs. Roosevelt. He can also poke fun at his own, mocking the kinds of articles that characterized black magazines of the '50s, and vowing that if he were in charge of one of such rags he would put out a three-part series, the first installment to be called *Can Sex Pass?,* the second *Sex Seized in Passing,* the third *Please Pass the Sex.* Simple could make his readers feel angry, giddy, and abashed simultaneously and remain totally invulnerable to their feelings, like a good magician. His carapace was his honesty, not his humor, and when he said something like "I am colored," one smiled, not because the statement was funny, but because it was sublimely true.

It was this sense of the sublime in him rather than his own sense of the ridiculous which accounted for Simple's effect. The laughter his pieces inspire springs from two absolutely antithetical impulses. One is the classical state of our feeling superior to him, not because he is silly or duped—he is rarely duped—but because he has been through a mill that most of his readers are safe from, at least at the moment of reading. Yet the other side of our laughter comes from sheer

[1]Langston Hughes, *Simple Takes a Wife* (New York: Simon and Schuster, 1953), p. 22. Other Simple books quoted in this essay are *Simple Speaks His Mind* (New York: Simon and Schuster, 1950), and *Simple's Uncle Sam* (New York: Hill and Wang, 1967). References to these, abbreviated *Mind* and *Sam,* will hereafter be given in the text.

admiration and wonderment, out of our recognition that Simple is thoroughly superior to the things which have declared his inferiority. He is endurance itself. In his time, he boasts, he has been "laid off, fired, and not rehired, Jim Crowed, segregated, insulted, eliminated, locked in, locked out, locked up, left holding the bag, and denied relief . . . but I am still here" ("Census," *Sam,* p. 1). Throughout the sketches he repeats "I am still here" as if in defiance of a roll call which expected silence at his name. In a way, his humor derives from our perception that his obstinate desire to survive and flourish in the face of overwhelming odds is an absurd consistency, endurance being his humor in the Jonsonian sense. Yet we laugh more at the magnificence of the consistency than at its foolishness, as we would at the sight of something stunningly beautiful, the hah.

To create a character whom we laugh up to and down on at the same time takes an acute sense of balance. Hughes's method in the sketches was the standard one of setting up conversations between Simple and his friend, Boyd, which would serve as springboards for Simple's opinions and flights of imagination; but Hughes deviated from the pattern by giving Boyd a developed personality and a personal history. Ben Franklin's Silence Dogood, Seba Smith's Jack Downing, and other such characters who used the gimmick of letters addressed to either editors or imaginary relatives merely implied the existence of a third-party listener when they were confronting the reader directly. George W. Harris used an actual narrator for Sut Lovingood, but only as a kind of cattle prong, injecting *who*s and *why*s into Sut's monologues the way that Edgar Bergen would set up Charlie McCarthy for the punch lines. Mark Twain used a narrator in "The Celebrated Jumping Frog of Calaveras County" who, like Boyd, was more of a gentleman than the main attraction; but Twain's speaker was only a straight man, created to heighten the humor by incongruity. Mr. Dooley had his Hennessy, but Hennessy functioned solely as an interviewer who was no more educated, and a good deal duller, than his friend. In contrast to these Boyd is a lively, intelligent, likable, and completely believable man. Simple trusts and admires him, and is responsible for our doing the same. That he outshines and gets the better of Boyd only says so much more for Simple.

Occasionally, as in "Lynn Clarisse" (*Sam,* p. 83), where Boyd is trying to pick up Simple's cousin, Hughes lets his narrator out on his own, but he cannot afford to do this often for fear of dividing the reader's attention. Because Simple is the wiser and more clever of the two it is essential that he dominate the sketches, yet the interesting thing about Boyd is that Simple would not be half so effective a critic without his companion's presence. Susanne Langer points out (in *Feeling and Form*) that we tend to laugh at things in the theater which we might not think to be funny in life because we are laughing at not what the jokes mean to us but what they mean to the play. There is a kind of two-man play being performed in all the Simple pieces, a play that progresses nowhere, has no beginning, middle, and end, but that nevertheless contains a number of distinguishable players (albeit most offstage), a distinct setting, a major character, a minor character, and a series of scenes. If, when we laugh at Simple's humor, we are merely laughing at the exercise of a comic spirit within a theatrical (unreal) framework, then none of Simple's social commentary can be too painful or outrageous. But neither can it be meaningful or effective. This is clearly one reason for minimizing Boyd's time "onstage," to avoid diminishing Simple's prominence and therefore increasing the power of his direct address to the reader.

But there is also a special sense of timing in operation here. Simple rarely starts any of his protest pieces with a protest. Usually he begins griping about something inane and irrelevant, and then only after a while does he strike his theme. He cons his reader in an obvious and expectable way; but the real trick is Hughes's, because by allowing just enough dialogue to go on between Simple and Boyd before the protest theme is reached he lets his reader think he is watching a play throughout. We laugh, then, at what the humor means to the play, and we continue to laugh long after the play construction has been dropped, after Boyd has dropped out, and right on into Simple's speech (on segregation, personal ethics, or national brutality), which is not spoken to any character but ourselves. If we do not laugh outright, we are at least pleased, and it is no easy feat to please people in their own instruction.

Like every comic realist, Simple is at heart a dreamer. Boyd, who is much more of a realist, takes him up on this fact often, and Simple admits it freely. There is a connection in his mind between dreaming and optimism, yet his comic fantasies are usually ominous and baleful. His sense of the fantastic is the satirist's sense. Commenting obliquely on black people as invisible men, he envisions a demonstration in which every black in the country, including Martin King, Adam Powell, "every waitress in Chock Full o' Nuts," and the Black Muslims, would take off his clothes so that "America would be forced to scrutinize our cause" ("Pose-Outs," *Sam*, p. 109). In another piece he worries that as yet there are no Negro astronauts in space, "because if one of them white Southerners gets to the moon first, 'Colored Not Admitted' signs will go up all over heaven as sure as God made little green apples, and Dixiecrats will be asking the man in the moon, 'Do you want your daughter to marry a Nigra?' " ("The Moon," *Sam,* p. 28). His gazes into the future foresee exaggerations of the present by which the present is itself held up to ridicule. What he accomplishes with them is a projection of logical consequence, as if to say that if you doubt the craziness of the world we have now, let me show you how it will look done to a turn. Despite his fantasies, however, Simple can be as practical as Boyd. When his friend asks him if he would be the first to volunteer for the black "nude-out," Simple answers, "That honor I would leave to you."

The other device that Hughes puts to use is dialect, and Simple handles the device in a conventional way. Hughes did not indulge in the idiocy, which one often sees elsewhere, of misspelling words that his character pronounces correctly (for example, *luv*), and therefore making it appear as if the character is an illiterate writing the sketch rather than a speaking participant in it. Simple, however, does misplace *s*'s, add *-ations,* say "do" for "does," make verbs out of nouns, and generally mispronounce what is formally considered to be correct English. Such defects of language are traditionally supposed to be comic because they make the reader feel as if he possesses a higher culture and more education than the speaker. This is a particular trap for a portion of the white audience who—beneath the condescension it took to be amused by the sketches in the first place—believes all blacks to be ignorant and wants them to sound like it. One of the things that made *Amos and Andy*'s Kingfish, Rochester of the *Jack Benny Program,* and Mantan Moreland and Willie Best of the movies so hilarious to whites was the way they spoke. Accordingly, dialect was a peculiarly touchy device for Hughes to employ because he knew how his black readers would resent anything that smacked of stereotype. (In "Summer Ain't Simple" he digs at certain white representations of black life by having Simple observe that his papa wasn't rich, nor was his mama good-looking). What Hughes did with dialect was what Twain had done with Huck and Henry Shaw had done with Josh Billings; he made it an integral part of his hero's intelligence. All the mistakes of diction which Simple makes are subsumed in that intelligence, are neutralized by it, and indeed are transformed. Not only does Simple dignify dialect, he makes the King's English seem awkward in comparison.

Under the surface of Simple's way of speaking is the implicit American contempt for education, which is both black and white and is attached vaguely to the romantic conception of a free man. As a folk hero, humorist or otherwise, Simple is expected to outwit Boyd because Boyd is only "colleged," while Simple has had his education where it counts, in the streets. Although this feeling runs high and deep in American literature it has a particular quality when a black author expresses it, because for black people the question of the value of a formal education has less of a mythic and more of a practical base. For blacks in this country neither education nor the lack of it has provided much opportunity for advancement or freedom. The only reason for opting for street schools over colleges may be that the former take less time and effort to arrive at the same place, which is usually nowhere. Hughes handled this theme in his novel *Not Without Laughter,* where at the end the bright and promising Sandy is going to head for college and save his soul. But the ending seems tacked on and unconvincing. There is a much more realistic conclusion earlier in the book when Sandy takes a job running an elevator, just as Richard does in Baldwin's *Go Tell It on the Mountain* before he kills himself, because an elevator like a formal education is the perfect vehicle for providing the illusion of progress without the fact. When Will Rogers used "ain't" for "isn't" he was implying that moral and wise men have an eloquence of their own, but when Simple does the same thing he is not so much saying that the wrong words are better than the right ones as he is pointing to the futility of worrying about the problem.

I am beginning to refer to black and white readers under the assumption that Simple's audiences are distinct and show distinguishable responses. This assumption would not be true for "serious" black writing, either poetry or fiction, because in those cases the writer writes for an inner audience which is largely color-blind. In *Native Son,* for example, Wright may have considered the effects of his story on white and black readers separately, hoping for different kinds of awakening in each, but one still feels that such consideration was secondary to the professional and private exercise of his craft. With Hughes, however, the question of audience becomes more pertinent because in writing humor one must always theoretically be facing outward in order to court the laughter which is the only sort of approbation available. Simple is a black man, not making fun of black life, yet making fun out of it. When a white man laughs at this fun, is it the guilty laugh, the sympathetic laugh, Beckett's "dianoetic" laugh (*Watt*), or is it punitive? When the black man laughs, is it nervousness, embarrassment, revenge, or magnanimity?

At one point in the "Census" sketch Simple complains that, because the census taker was white, he did not understand when Simple was making a joke. It is not true that white readers do not understand when Simple is joking, but the problem is what they understand those jokes to mean. For a black reader the impulse to laugh at "Feet" may be informed by commiseration or by a feeling of exhilaration in sharing the episode vicariously. For the white reader the reasons may be similar, but they can never be the same, and it is more likely that he laughs out of shame than anything else. The black reader too may feel shame, but it is the shame of what has happened to him, not at what he has caused to happen. Yet it also may be that no group feeling is present at all.

Bergson believed that the act of laughter suggests a complicity with other laughers, but in reading Simple it is questionable whether such complicity is felt. It seems more often than not that Simple is addressing the private best in our black or white selves, which we always assume to be in opposition to the public (or group) worst. Whenever he indicates that the nation is made up of fools, we read "the rest of the nation." He often does not appeal to fellow feeling in his readers as much as he does to the personal and isolated situation and, in a sense, to individual vanity, which is an educable element. Whether or not there is a color line in his audience it is fascinating, and a credit to Hughes, to note that as a character Simple does not seem to care in the least who his readers are or what they think. With most humorists, literary or real, we always get the sense of how fragile they are, that after three consecutive jokes without raising a chuckle they would disintegrate. But Simple seems entirely careless of our appraisal. He may appeal to our vanity, but he sustains himself on pride.

In *The Book of Negro Humor,* which Hughes edited, Roi Ottley records an anecdote about Robert S. Abbott, the founder and editor of the *Chicago Defender.* A judge named Abernathy in a small Georgia town was running for reelection on a hate-Negro platform. Blacks in the town sent Abernathy's campaign literature to Abbott, who instructed his staff to pillory Abernathy in an editorial. Abbott then sent five hundred copies of the editorial back to Abernathy's town for distribution, but when Abernathy's opponent reprinted the editorial for one of his own pamphlets, and acknowledged the source,

Abernathy was reelected by a landslide. The would-be heroes of the story, Abbott and the *Defender* staff, are hoist with their own petard, a classically comic circumstance. The unexpected occurs, Abernathy turns the tables on his enemies, and as in cartoons where the chased outwits the chasers, the audience is supposed to laugh at the triumph of a lucky scoundrel. Yet, all the humor in the anecdote derives from hatred: the judge's hatred of blacks, the town's hatred of blacks and their Northern newspaper, Abbott's hatred of Abernathy, and our own hatred of hatred as well. What we are laughing (or more likely smiling) at is only partly the irony of the judge's good fortune. That is a reflex laugh, the situation demands it. But we are laughing primarily at our disappointment in humanity generally, and in ourselves. The anecdote is a pathetic story. It is funny largely because of its pathos, which we appreciate because of our confidence in the inevitable perseverance of human idiocy. In a sense our reaction defies the Bergsonian rule, because instead of laughing at the unexpected in the tale, we laugh at the all too readily expected. But the all too readily expected can be as much of an aberration as total surprise. Given enough time even the consistency of bigotry becomes laughable.

Nobody understood this phenomenon more fully than Hughes, who continually drew laughter from the unlaughable. Hazlitt ("On Wit and Humour") has said that humor makes the ludicrous lead us to the pathetic, and in his choice of subject matter this is precisely what Simple does. He jokes about poll taxes, segregation, governmental corruption and neglect, disenfranchisement, unemployment, hunger, ignorance, ghetto living conditions, the Ku Klux Klan, in short, about everything that is inherently unfunny. Hughes himself said that "humor is what you wish in your heart were not funny."[2] To Simple there was nothing so terrible in the world that it could not be made to seem ridiculous. He is purely and unrelentingly a social critic. As Benchley took his humor from the upper reaches of the middle class, from the perils of tennis games and hotel suites, Simple took his from the harassment of his people and the continuation of their servitude. Surprisingly for a literary figure, he only rarely deals in literary jokes—in "Matter for a Book" (*Mind*), he wants to follow on Frank Yerby's success with *The Foxes of Harrow* by writing *The Wolves of Harlem*—and even more rarely is he witty or ironic. Nor

[2]Langston Hughes, *The Book of Negro Humor* (New York: Dodd, Mead, 1966), p. vii.

will he indulge in savage or cruel comedy; the episode of the street riot is a joke about escape, not destruction. What he cares about exclusively are the troubles of being black, and like some of Synge's Wicklow and West Kerry men he makes laughter out of his own mistreatment.

Yet, along with being an ordinary man of his people, there is also an evangelical strain in Simple, a strain which is evident in the low key preaching he does, and in the structure of the sketches themselves. Each of these pieces is built as a sermon. Not all of them deal with references to religion, though many do; but every one of them is modeled on the revivalist pattern of the preacher making an opening statement, which is followed by a pause in which the congregation says "amen" or an equivalent, which is in turn followed by the preacher's expansion of the topic at hand using examples usually drawn from his own experience. The use of this structure for comic rather than devotional purposes has been part of American stand-up comedians' routines for a long time. When Red Buttons began his act with "Strange things are happening," or when Rodney Dangerfield starts out by saying, "Nobody gives me any respect," the idea was, and is, for the audience to think "amen," and then gear itself for the jokes to follow. Twain said that he was always preaching when he wrote, that if the humor emerged as part of the sermons, fine, but that he would have written the sermons in any case. We get something of this feeling with Simple. His sermons are part of himself and so they are humorous naturally, but because like Twain he is first a moral man, then a humorist, we realize that amusement is not the most important reaction intended.

There is a complication, however, in Simple's use of the religious framework which would probably not exist if he were white. Whenever he cracks jokes or fantasizes about heaven or angels or God, he is working within the convention of gently irreverent, folksy, and familiar humor, the kind that *Green Pastures* is made of. The main difference is tone, and Simple's tone on this subject is affected by his suspicion that he may be joking about someone else's God, a white one. There is a sketch called "God's Other Side" (*Sam*) in which Simple says that he would prefer to sit at the left hand of God instead of the right, like everyone else, so as to get more attention; but light-hearted as this piece is, underlying it there is the intimation that Simple and all blacks must always pay court to God's other side. In "Empty Houses" he recalls wondering if the white Jesus he had learned to pray to as a child "cared anything about a little colored boy's prayers" (*Sam,* p. 15). In all the sketches the religious joking lacks confidence, and without confidence the jokes develop an edge. Similarly his religious satires can sound heavy-handed, as is the case with "Cracker Prayer" (*Sam*), which when compared to something as finely controlled as John Betjeman's "In Westminster Abbey" seems ominous and seething.

No single aspect of black life in America has affected black literature as deeply as religion. In *Another Country* Ida, who is bent on revenge against the white world, remarks that she "learned all [her] Christianity from white folks."[3] She speaks bitterly because the God acquired was a God imposed, and along with the acquisition came a thousand crimes committed in His name. There is no major black author who has not grappled with the ambiguity of trying to believe in a religion which was transfused as a mollifying instrument for slaves, which promises future salvation while contributing to present isolation and torment (Bigger Thomas noticed that the crosses burning outside his jail were no different from the one hanging around his neck), and which may, for all its promises, contain a heaven for whites only and be a hoax. This is the background to Simple's religious humor. When he speaks of Saint Peter and the Pearly Gates it is not the voice of a man who trusts what he's making fun of, but of a man who is making a joke of something because he is supposed to trust it, yet does not. By poking fun at heaven Simple is partly poking fun at himself and all black people for whom heaven may be unattainable. There is fear behind this humor, but there is safety too; for if heaven and God do not exist for him after all, laughter may create the perspective to anticipate the loss.

The most remarkable thing about Simple is that he can be edgy or shaky in his humor or opinions, he can be grumpy or sour, digressive, illogical, wrongheaded, he can even be dull without losing our affection or attention or anything in himself. There is so much fluidity and grace in his makeup that the subjects he discusses and the tricks he employs roll on and off him like water beads, always leaving him to seem larger than the sum total of his effects and defects as well. At the end of a piece called "Dog Days" he simply runs out of ideas, but instead of stopping neatly he suddenly switches the topic from dogs to a dogwood tree and a girl whom he once kissed under it. When the consecutive-minded Boyd asks, "why did you bring that up," Simple

[3]James Baldwin, *Another Country* (New York: Dell, 1968), p. 237.

says "to revive my remembrance" (*Sam*, p. 106). The feat of these touches is that they regularly remind us that Simple is more of a human being than a pundit. In this he comes much closer to a folk hero like Davy Crockett (though luckily he did not have a crazy living model to depend on) than to a closet wit such as Jonathan Oldstyle, because he has a life apart and distinguishable from his sense of humor. If one were to imagine an instance when Mr. Dooley were publicly proven wrong in his judgment of an important issue, it is likely that Mr. Dooley's reputation would suffer because his whole being relies on the accuracy of his wit. This is not the case with Simple. He is more interesting than his intelligence, and he outlives it. Nothing can shake him, no mishap and no mistake.

He is, first of all, a completely honest man, about himself particularly; and because his brand of honesty is so scarce it becomes one of his comic attributes. As deeply as he is committed to the causes of civil rights, it is not an ethereal subject with him, and he shows nothing but melancholy derision for senseless martyrdom. In "Swinging High" he comments upon the death of a white Cleveland minister who, as part of a protest against racial discrimination, lay down behind a bulldozer: "I gather there are some things you would not do for a cause," said Boyd. "I would not lay down behind a bulldozer going backwards," (*Sam*, p. 7) said Simple. His candor also extends to the way he makes his points, loosely and without apparent premeditation. The sketch "Bomb Shelters" (*Sam*) deals with the inanity of planning shelters for a Harlem tenement whose quarters are so cramped that the shelters would not be able to accommodate all the tenants, and which is probably about to collapse anyway. Simple imagines a situation in which he is battling his neighbors to get inside the shelter, a notion which undoubtedly would have appealed to James Thurber. But what Thurber would have done with it would have been to invent a fable (riotous, of course) in which would be exhibited all the selfishness people, or animals, are capable of, selfishness akin to the evil that creates the necessity of bomb shelters in the first place. Simple's style, on the other hand, is to avoid the moral. He builds his theme haphazardly, letting the laughs arise where they may, creating a full scene. By this he suggests that nothing is funny or sad in isolation, himself included.

The honesty Simple uses to aid his humor works for other effects as well. When he feels prejudiced, he says so directly (he is unquestionably one of the most die-hard male chauvinists in literature). When he feels sanctimonious or sentimental he is equally open. He gets away with total candor because he is recognizably a good man, good enough even to laugh at his own virtue: "now me, my specialty is to walk on water" ("Soul Food," *Sam,* p. 111). His goodness is intimately bound to his simplicity—which, at its conventional level, merely takes the shape of wanting to strip the frills from things, of disliking high tone and preferring soul food to French cooking, natural hairdos to wigs, gospel to Italian opera, the Apollo Theater to the Met, and so on. But in a more fundamental way Simple's simplicity represents his effort to discover who he is and where he has come from. It is the classic circumstance in black literature of the hero's search for roots. By giving Simple his name Hughes implies that for a black man to be simple is a most difficult achievement. It means holding on to a sense of self and manhood in a strange land that conspires daily against your doing so.

In the piece "Concernment" Simple and Boyd have a rare squaring off, triggered when Boyd gets bogged down trying to remember the exact word in a quotation. Simple says, "Boyd, your diploma is worth every penny you paid for it. Only a man who is colleged could talk like that. Me, I speaks simpler myself" (*Sam,* p. 152). Boyd counters by observing that sometimes simplicity can be more devious than erudition, to which Simple answers, "of course." As usual Simple gets the last word, but by agreeing with Boyd he also makes a point. The reason Simple maintains his simplicity is not because he cannot fathom complications. Indeed, he gives the impression of already having been through the complications of a subject, which have allowed him finally to arrive at his simple conclusion. What comes through instead of a contempt for complexities is a weariness of talking about them, of devising subordinate clauses and qualifying phrases which diffuse the energy of the central thought. The kind of maxim Simple coins is "greater love hath no man than that he lay down his life to get even" ("Junkies," *Sam,* p. 98). The kind of wisdom he lives by is that "there is no way for a man to commit bigamy without being married" ("Simple on Women," *Book of Negro Humor,* p. 146). If there are exceptions to his rules he takes them up one by one, but he refuses to be caught with the all-encompassing thesis on anything because such things carry a complacency which is alien to his nature and also impose a rigidity of their own.

Unlike the pseudoinnocent boy observers of American humor, Simple is a full-fledged grown-up. He has been married and separated, is seeking and eventually obtains a divorce (which on principle he refuses to pay for), is courting one respectable woman while having an occasional fling with another less respectable one, has been, as he says, "cut, stabbed, run over, hit by a car, tromped by a horse, robbed, fooled, deceived, double-crossed, dealt seconds" ("Census," *Sam,* p. 2), can hold his liquor, believes very little he hears, and is beginning to go gray. As an adult he is not burdened by demands that his behavior or thinking be consistent. In separate sketches he toasts Harlem as paradise and condemns it as hell. He deplores warfare, composes a beautiful prayer against it, but admits "I would not mind a war if I could win it" ("A Toast to Harlem," *Mind,* p. 34). On the race issue he can, in different moods, sound like Gandhi or Rap Brown. He lives most of his time in a dreamworld and yet values nothing as highly as money and possessions. Having no use for education himself, he nevertheless would establish a fund to send all the young people in Harlem to college. He is a confirmed capitalist, yet fantasizes about the coming of a socialist millennium. At one point he brags to Boyd, "I am the toughest Negro God's got" ("Family Tree," *Mind,* p. 26). In a quieter spirit he confesses that he drinks because "I'm lonesome inside myself" ("Conversation on the Corner," *Mind,* p. 20).

There is a moment in the movie *Humoresque* when Oscar Levant turns to John Garfield or Joan Crawford, I forget who, and says, "Don't blame me, I didn't make the world; I barely live on it." The sense Simple gives us is just that: of a man who can take anything, who can roll with the punches, bounce back, punch back if aroused, and at the same time who seems to be living on a better and cleaner plane than the world he contends with. In his "Character Notes" to the play *Simply Heavenly,* Hughes describes Simple as Chaplinesque. Nothing could be more apt. Like Chaplin, Simple was the complete humorous creation. There has never been a character in black literature like him, nor is there likely to be another in the future. For all his combativeness Simple was a standard American dreamer who believed in progress within the system, and his optimism would have been incompatible with the present-day mood. Moreover, in a time of real and verbal militancy humor is judged to be a harmful distraction, or "counterproductive." Yet he could not have been born in a period earlier than he was, either; not in the late '20s and early '30s when black writers were bent on producing serious books and establishing the Harlem Renaissance, and certainly not before then, when whatever black writing existed was done by apologists. Simple came, flourished, and went at just the right time. Even a few years before Hughes's death in 1967 he was beginning to sound a little out of things, a little forced.

Everyone knows that humorists perish rapidly, that unlike tragedy, which endures from age to age, humor generally thrives only within the lifetime of a particular taste. If Simple turns out to be the exception to this rule it will not be because the jokes he made held their flavor, but because the image of man he represented was important to hold on to. On the level of vital statistics no one could have stood further from the packaged ideal of American heroism. He was disqualified from this designation by his loose love life, his upbringing, his habits, his age, his physique, his disrespectful attitude, his friends, his absence of prospects, and especially his color. Yet from a no less idealistic viewpoint Simple was more the embodiment of the all-American boy than a dozen Frank Merriwells or Jack Armstrongs. He was the fighter who knew when to quit, the resourceful, canny mind that could wax poetic on an impulse, the man unencumbered by possessions, the free man, the generous Joseph, the stumbler who admitted his mistakes, the survivor and the dreamer. To Schiller "the aim of comedy [was] the same as the highest destiny of man,"[4] which was a liberation from all violence, cruelty, and stupidity. If Simple was more skeptical about such liberation being man's destiny, at least he felt it was worth a try. For himself he sought nothing but human decency between the races. When so simple a wish was persistently denied, he had to laugh.

Spring, 1972

[4] Friedrich Schiller, "On Simple and Sentimental Poetry," in *The Comic in Theory and Practice*, ed. John Enck, Elizabeth Forter, and Alvin Whitley (New York: Appleton-Century-Crofts, 1960), p. 23.

My
Wild
Irish
Rosenblatt

EVERYBODY AGREES that Robert E. Lee got what was coming to him, which was his own name, Robert Earl Lee, or rather it was coming back to him, since he tried to get rid of it by calling himself Roberto Eduardo Leon. He claimed Leon because he also wanted to claim minority privileges under an affirmative action program in Montgomery County. But the Montgomery County officials would have none of that. They told Mr. Lee he could call himself anything he pleased, including the names everyone else was calling him privately, but for purposes of affirmative action he was no more Spanish than is a french fry French.

That disappointed Mr. Lee, who is patently a conniver, and deserves no sympathy. Yet you can't blame a fellow for wishing to change his name on general grounds alone. You couldn't blame Issur Danielovitch Demsky for changing his name to Kirk Douglas. And you couldn't blame Tula Finklea for changing her name to Cyd Charisse, or Edda Hepburn van Heemstra for Audrey Hepburn, or Francesca Mitzi Marlene de Charney von Gerber for Mitzi Gaynor. If Joe Yule, Jr., wanted to call himself Mickey Rooney, that was his business, as it was Norma Dolores Eggstrom's when she became Peggy Lee.

All of which is to lead gently to the announcement that I too changed my name, and I did so a long time ago, for the following reasons:

The name Rosenblatt is the name I was born with, and is the name I write under, and the name used by the people at Reader's Digest sweepstakes when they let me know that I am about to win two houses or $100,000 in cash; but it is not the name by which I think of myself. That name came to me in Ireland in 1965, after twenty-four hard years dealing with Rosenblatt, which is a sonorous name, but unwieldy. There is the *Rosen,* which is musical enough and redolent of flowers. But there is also the *blatt,* which, while merely meaning a leaf or a sheet of paper in German, here has the sound of an overripe pumpkin dropped to the sidewalk from the roof of a cheap hotel.

Yet I lived fairly comfortably with my Rosenblatt throughout childhood, when there were plenty of familial Rosenblatts around me; and I had a grandfather Maximilian Rosenblatt and a grandmother Rose Rosenblatt compared to whose names my own sounded like Cabot. Inevitably there were a few "Rosenfat"s and "Rosenbrat"s hurled by taunting kids. But on the whole, I kind of liked my name, which, for all its weight, had a rather nice roll to it, like Roy Rogers or Robin Roberts, or Robert Redford, who was growing up too.

In teenagehood, however, life got a bit rougher. For one thing, there was a tennis tournament at a private club in Maine that I was not allowed to enter because my name was Rosenblatt. And since my disqualification had less to do with my name than what my name signified, I learned the hard way what's in a name. Then there was a time or two when important people like girls would shiver with giggles at the mere sound of my name. One girl on a beach, with the mellifluous name of Gabrielle, laughed so hard when I said "Rosenblatt," I wanted to tell her I was kidding.

In college I actually did change my name, on several exam papers, for a whole term—to Roger Craig Lawrence, which I thought had a fine New England gong to it. Professors recognizing my exams by the low grades handed back the papers unerringly without ever saying a word to me, or to my friend Peter Weissman, who changed his name to Peter Scott Douglas. (We had another friend, Bob Lichtenfeld, who changed his name to Van Wyck Klingerman, thus missing the point.) But that was mere collegiate game playing, and I toted old Rosenblatt into graduate school without altering a letter.

There I started to grow happy with my name once again, for by coincidence there were four other Rosenblatts in school at the time, including a Rand Rosenblatt and another Roger, whose existence I discovered when his pals at Princeton wrote to say they were coming to spend the weekend with me. At first the idea of another Roger Rosenblatt was eerie. Dostoevsky and Poe have both written stories about people haunted by exact doubles who bear their names, and do them in. I kept my alter-Roger at a distance. Otherwise I was encouraged by the presence of so many Rosenblatts, whose number provided not only safety but also a faint sort of pride.

That was short-lived. In adulthood, as I entered it, there were no more taunts and giggles at the name, but there was something as bad, or maybe worse, in the perverse confusion of my name with those that sound like it—the implication being that when you've seen one Rosensomething you've seen them all. And then I went to live in Ireland for a year, where—in spite of the fact that Ireland is the most hospitable country on earth—I encountered the last straw; where my name was so alien, so odd-sounding (as compared with Nic Shiubhlaigh and Gillhooley) that the postman would fake a coughing fit when he said "Good morning," so as not to get past the "Mr."

But his painful courtesy was not what finally persuaded me to change my name. That occurred at a Dublin book auction, the first (and last) I ever attended, where I brought my meager pennies to bid on a small pile of books, which I actually won. "What's the name?" shouted the auctioneer's assistant over the throng. "Rosenblatt," I answered, followed by general murmuring and bewilderment.

"The name, sir?" repeated the assistant.

"Rosenblatt. With two t's," as if that were the issue.

"Once more, please?"

"Rosenblatt," said I, loud and clear. And suddenly emboldened, "Rosenblatt" again. And yet another "Rosenblatt," until the full weight of the ancient name, both the Rosen and the blatt, filled the musty hall, thumping on the ceiling, heaving against the walls, the name like a colossus, so big that it extended back in time to Berlin and Heidelberg, to my father and Maximilian and Rose, and all the Rosenblatts forever. I had been challenged in public, and I had risen to it, obliterating all present and former embarrassments, as I, Rosenblatt, stepped forward to claim my pile of books.

There next to the books was a tag on which the assistant had inscribed my name—Frozenwemm. With two m's. And I have kept it to this day.

May 7, 1979

Hair Piece

G ONE. I do not need to look. A mere forefinger gently on the spot, circling clockwise in the tiniest circumference, tells me all I need to know, tells me what I knew would be, eventually, when I started rubbing that spot, several inches above the left eyebrow, several months ago. Then there was a hair at that spot, a lone hair at the frontier, a hair that *was* the frontier of what used to be my widow's peak, and is now my widow's walk. The hair was long and wavy, like the hair of my youth. But it was also frail—I could feel that—frail from living on the edge, and on the run. I knew it was dying. Now it is gone, and there is nothing in its place. Only my forehead, pushing back, as it has been pushing back relentlessly, my last frontier.

I wish I had never singled out that hair. For years friends had been bellowing: "Hey, you know, you're going bald!" as if they had just discovered artichokes or the Comstock Lode, instead of the source of man's discomfort. But I refused to believe them. I was always possessed of a high forehead, a sign of nobility, my mother said. And had not my faithful barber answered, "Nah," when asked if it were true? "Your hairline is where it has always been."

Not so. I know now he was being kind, or practical, now that I am sitting here circling the spot blindly like the Cyclops, groping for a hero. But there is no hero. And I am growing more like the Cyclops every day: a man without hair, like a man with one eye, admired only for what is absent.

When should I openly call myself bald? Having pussyfooted around like J. Alfred Prufrock so long, having lied to the world that nothing was missing, is it incumbent on me now to make some official public declaration—"I am going bald"? Should I have it notarized? This is a major cultural decision. The world is made up solely of those with hair and those without. And those without are called "skinheads" and "billiard balls," and those with are called people.

If I do declare myself bald, will I then have to act bald? Bald people usually act either too brash or too meek. Will I have to choose? Will I have to dress especially neat so as not to compound my baldness, and watch my weight in order to prevent my becoming known as fat *and* bald? Will I learn to make jokes about my own baldness, preempting others? Or will I flee in the streets at the drop of a snigger, pulling oversize hats about my ears?

Hugh Troy, the millionaire practical joker, once bought out the first twenty rows in the orchestra of the Metropolitan Opera, sending most of the tickets to friends with hair, and some particular tickets to friends without. He had arranged the seats so that he, observing from the balcony, could read a dirty word spelled out by the hairless heads. I used to think that clever. No more. I will not be humiliated. I will accept no opera tickets. I will wear my baldness like the pink (God, will it be pink?) badge of courage, like Yul Brynner, like Kojak, like an eagle.

Of course, I could always get myself a wig. I could go to Mr. Ray's Hair Weave, and wind up looking like that couple on television, on whose rejuvenated heads Mr. Ray seems to have draped two muskrats.

Or I could try one of those expensive mystery techniques developed in France and administered in California, where I imagine they saw off the top of your head, and push mink through like pasta.

Or I could go the route of Sen. William Proxmire, and have someone pluck the hairs from the back of my head, and sew them into the front. Yet people would then say, "Oh, you and Bill Proxmire, huh?"—suggesting a companionship neither of us seeks. And how long can such a treatment go on before one is as bald in back as one was once up front? Besides, I do not wish to look like a bald man with hair. I would rather look like a hairy man going bald.

Which (I'll say it now) is exactly as I do look.

Well, I will neither change nor cover up. I will go forth and be brave, and I won't be patronized. Those same people who remarked upon my emerging scalp, will now tell me baldness is a sign of virility. I know better. Nor will I sashay through life like Bette Davis in *Mr. Skeffington,* as if my affliction did not exist. Instead, I will turn east, and develop a Zenlike serenity on the subject, concentrating not on the baldness that is present but rather on the hair that is gone, caressing with my mind, as I did with my forefinger, a lost horizon.

For, as no portion of physical matter ever totally disappears, so must there be a world to which all lost hairs go. And I know that somewhere among the inexplicable stars all my dear, departed hairs stand suspended—no longer drooped and weak, but vital, strong, and proud, waiting for me to rejoin them, to be rejoined to them, in the territory of goodness and mercy where all heads are equal.

January 22, 1979

The Fat
in the
Fire

❧❀❧

A CLERGYMAN GROWN FAT is a clerical error, for fatness is a
sure sign of dissipation, whereas being a clergyman leaves a
modicum of doubt. I know very little about the clergy, but I'm an
expert in fatness—the lesson for today—having been fat for at least
one third of my life, although the third, as I, was spread around. I've
gone for five and six years at a clip thin as a rail, as they say. Now
I'm fat as a pig, as they say, though I'm about to slim down again,
much to my disgust.

Well, not really fat as a pig. If you saw me walking down the block,
coming out of the International House of Pancakes, for instance, you
wouldn't say to yourself: There goes a pig. You would say: There
goes a man who injured his back a year ago, and who, in spite of
unimaginable bravery in the presence of excruciating pain—pain that
he never allowed his family or friends to see, his being that sort of
fellow—still was never able to take the proper exercise, and so,
through no fault of his own, put on twenty extra pounds. That is
what you would say, and you would be wrong. True, I did hurt my
back, and I haven't been able to work out much. But as for putting
on twenty pounds against my will, fat chance.

You see, I kind of like being fat, at least being as fat as I am. I don't think I'd like to be as fat as Orson Welles, because I wouldn't know where to buy those odd black shirts, and I don't have the rich, fat voice. Yet clearly Mr. Welles is content as he is, or he'd be back doing the Charlie Kane dance in the newsroom, instead of filling the TV screen like the wave in *The Poseidon Adventure,* recollecting the maxims of Paul Masson. At some point in his young, sprightly life, Mr. Welles simply said, "All right, I'll go to hell," just like Huck Finn. I've said so too, plenty of times, and I'd say so now if it weren't for the heat.

But with summer coming on, I'll have to shed my pounds, which will be all too easy, and all too dull. It isn't that I mind the idea of health. What hurts is the self-righteousness I'm bound to acquire, and worse, the loss of sin. I will deeply miss my twenty. For the past year I have nurtured them like orchids, thanks to a brilliant diet of my own invention; and I will hate to see them go.

The diet, by the way, is clean and simple, like the Scarsdale, and I commend it to anyone who wishes to remain exactly twenty pounds overweight:

Monday. Breakfast: two orange slices.
Lunch: one grape (seedless).
Dinner: three glasses, water. A carrot.

Tuesday. Breakfast: one okra.
Lunch: one endive (or celery stalk).
Dinner: nothing.

Wednesday Breakfast: four glasses, water.
Lunch: a cucumber.
Dinner: fruit cup with extra sherbet; two sirloin steaks; sweet potatoes with marshmallows; mashed potatoes with butter or margarine; bread, rolls; Stove Top stuffing; pizza (anchovy); milk shake (chocolate); Häagen-Dazs vanilla; two Twinkies; plus a late-night snack of tapioca pudding; two more Twinkies; and a peanut butter and banana sandwich, with brown sugar, on English muffins.

Which is to say, it takes monumental perseverance to stay fat, just as it does to stay evil. And while I would not deny that it also takes monumental perseverance to stay thin, and thus virtuous, still the preservation of virtue is not as valuable as the preservation of vice, primarily because virtue knows no moral restraints.

Need I draw the example of Jerry Brown? Not an ounce of fat on him; and so, unencumbered by any outward sign of mortality, he traipses about the globe in dead earnest rectitude, telling everyone where to get off—something he certainly wouldn't do if gadding about took more effort. Ditto for slim Jane Fonda. Ditto twice for Dick Gregory, whose virtuousness increases in direct proportion to his fasts. On the other hand, take William Howard Taft or Boss Tweed, both big as blimps. One look at a picture of the casual, carefree Tweed, as opposed to a picture of, say, Sen. Carl Schurz, who cleaned up the Grant administration by standing for the straight and narrow—being straight and narrow himself—and there can be no doubt who was the happier man.

I don't want to belabor the point, but I firmly believe that one's stomach is like one's conscience. And a conscience is good for nothing unless it is in a state of constant violation. The peasantry of Western Europe could pay no higher compliment than to tell someone: "You've greatly fallen into meat"; and *fallen* is the word. I cannot know what Adam and Eve looked like in Eden, but I'll bet they blew up like balloons once outside the gate, and not on apples, either. The burden of virtue lifted, they became—what?—human. And this is the great solace of fatness, the gift of twenty pounds of flesh.

Yet mine will go. I'll run and starve and do all the necessary humiliating things so as to be able to fit into the old, thin clothes, having worn out my fat pants and jackets. That is the principal reason for this reformation—not discomfort, and not vanity either, which is a pale vice compared with gluttony. But if I had the choice right now of meeting my maker by becoming so thin as to disappear, or eating so much as to explode, I'd make for the kitchen on all fours; there to eat Twinkies until everything snapped, and I dwelt among the fat, white stars.

May 14, 1979

Maggie
and Wilbur

T HE NAMES OF Margaret Trudeau and Wilbur Mills have not before been linked in public, and doing so here does not mean that there has been any canoodling, hi-jinks, jim-jamming or hanky-panky between them, or even that the two have actually met. But as notorious celebrants they do have a few things in common which raise a couple of questions about our lust for swingers: (1) Why do we enjoy reading of the escapades of the mighty? (2) Do the mighty swing as freely as they used to?

Taking the second question first, along with Wilbur, before he passes from memory: What precisely did Wilbur do to set tongues wagging and the mysterious corps of Washington gag writers at work on Wilbur jokes? In October 1974 he cavorted with Fanne Foxe the stripper; they guzzled champagne in a nightclub; Wilbur was sozzled; he and Fanne danced the fandango in the Tidal Basin. After which, "the powerful Ways and Means Committee" had its "even more powerful" chairman no longer. Wilbur reeled from disgrace to thin air, stopping off in Boston to emcee Fanne.

And Maggie? This March she checked into Mick Jagger's hotel in Toronto, then followed the Rolling Stones to New York, afterwards protesting "there was no mucking with Mick." Soon she announced she was taking her own apartment in the big city in order to work as a photographer for *People,* and that she would see her children and the prime minister on weekends. She knew this decision would "blow minds," but she is "a free spirit in a free world." Alone in a Manhattan bar she wrote in her diary: "Maggie is a lady who insists on freedom."

As far as we know, Wilbur did not insist on freedom when he went on his binge; he was just having—in the words of Thurber's butler—a bit of a time below stairs. But Maggie is a modern girl, and as everybody knows, nothing is more important to modern people than asserting their self-estimated value, even if it blows minds or careers. To be fair to Maggie, however, she is hardly the first first lady to jiggle a ministry for a spree. In fiction Glencora Palliser did it to her own *prime minister;* and in rumor Eleanor of Aquitaine strayed a long way from Saint Louis on the Second Crusade because the king was a bore.

By all accounts, Maggie's most avidly, Pierre Trudeau is not a bore, nor a geezer either—"he has the body of a twenty-five-year-old"— and unlike King Louis he takes to Disneyland at Easter. About Mrs. Mills, all we know is that she had her ankle in a cast at the time of Wilbur's romp, and some stiff words for Wilbur. There is nothing yet to connect Mrs. Mills and Mr. Trudeau, but there is this odd connection between Wilbur and Maggie: Both of them had escapades befitting their respective generations, and both of their escapades were very dull.

Wilbur, in fact, may go down as having flung the least inventive fling on record. Whom did he fancy? A floozy. Where did they go? A speak. What did they drink? Bubbly. What did they then? Jump in a pool.

Whom did Maggie fancy? A rock star. Where did they fly? The Big Apple. What does Maggie seek? Her own pad. What will become of her? A "photojournalist."

No two escapees could be more like caricatures, yet their adventures seem, or are made to seem, infinitely intriguing, which returns us to the question of why. Maggie presses her nose on John Warner's front gate in order to get a shot of Elizabeth Taylor, and this is fascinating. Is it all yet another sign of the expanded American middle? Have the mighty fallen to middle-class sprees? Or has the middle class grown so rich as to afford everything upper crust—first tennis, then horses, now whoopee? And are we enchanted by these tales because with a little luck and moxie they could be ours—a wave at the door, an ish kabibble, MasterCharge, and off to Bali?

How exciting, how possible—to shuck the Unbearable Frustrations, *volare,* and solve everything by cutting a rug or doing the hustle. That *(isn't she something?)* is what Maggie is doing. Even with Pierre fit as a fiddle, "working as a prime minister's wife is so boring" *(compared to Mick and Liz),* which is undoubtedly true, as it is undoubtedly boring to bear three kids in four years, and to be upbraided for a short skirt in the White House; as it is yet more undoubtedly boring to head the Ways and Means Committee or to grow old and wrinkled and ever "more powerful," on the prowl for some hot patootie who laughs at you. What we see in these two are not just the clichés of effect, but the clichés of cause *(I know how they feel).*

Extremism in defense of liberty is not as expensive as it used to be, but it's just as costly, perhaps more so. Wilbur lost his Ways and Means, and Maggie's madcap monkey business will not do much for Mr. Trudeau with his dour Canadian voters, to whom a handshake with Mickey Mouse is small recompense for an errant wife. (Canadian novelist Robertson Davies recently characterized Canada as "The Daughter Who Stayed at Home.") In a way our swingers die that we may live, going the distance in the open. Maybe we're grateful to them for their foolishness, for their easy or desperate self-assertions.

Surely we don't resent them, not in the way Auberon Waugh suggests in his painfully funny slap at Maggie in last month's *Spectator,* reprinted in the *Washington Star*—resents her for being crazy *and* selfish (an unfair conjunction), and for not living up to the responsibilities of State. Middle-classedness invades all institutions when it invades one; and if Mr. Trudeau loses his job Canada will not totter, any more than Congress suffered anything worse than titillations and a pay raise after Wilbur got his, and Wayne Hays his. When the middle class mounts the governments, it brings the accoutrements of the middle class along, including talaria (Adidas), and the governments adjust, are prepared for the drabbest whimsy, the commonest flights. If we resent our swingers at all it is *for* their commonness, for showing how puny our extravagances are.

Wilbur and Maggie will probably never meet, and if they should, will probably never fall in love, which is a pity because as cultural figures they were made for each other. Paul Williams could have written a major contemporary ballad to them, and Sammy Davis, Jr., could have sung it, and the flags of two nations could have flown atop their combination penthouse-motel room.

As it is, Wilbur is nearly forgotten, and Maggie soon will be, and shortly we'll be scanning the papers again, like the stars, for another glimpse of the good life.

May 7, 1977

Five Minutes, Miss Lenska

QUESTION NO. 2: Why is it that of all the people on earth the only ones who continually have to be reminded what time it is are actors and actresses? That is not my main question of the day, but it was brought to mind recently by a TV ad for Alberto VO-5 hair spray with Miral 80, in which an actress by the name of Rula Lenska is sitting in her dressing room, chatting about hair spray, when an off–dressing room voice calls: "Five minutes, Miss Lenska." It is always thus. All the actors in history have had to be told by some unseen stagehand the amount of time remaining before their entrances. That these people cannot keep track of the time themselves is mysterious to me, so I asked the drama critic of *The Post* why it is so. Barely raising his head, he made with some gibberish about the time warning being a subtle device used to ascertain if the performer was drunk or asleep—in effect, telling me to take a walk.

He was not so cavalier about Question No. 1, which I had deliberately held back to lull him off his guard: All right, then, who *is* Rula Lenska?

She appears in not one, but several, ads for Alberto VO-5 with Miral 80. I'm not sure if there are three separate ads, but there are at least three separate scenes: Rula Lenska alighting from a small plane;

Rula Lenska showing friends around London; and the dressing room scene. In each her role is a star's. Her voice is a star's—something Czech or Russian scumbled over with British, the kind of voice Anastasia would have had, had she been played by Rula Lenska. Her poses are a star's poses, as are her words, which, when they are not devoted to Alberto VO-5 with Miral 80, concern themselves breathlessly with the hectic life of a great and famous actress. And, of course, her hair is a star's, a field of auburn heather that swishes when she swishes, and fairly hums as she stands under a marquee beside an enlarged theater notice on a poster, bearing the single word BRILLIANT—a reference, no doubt, to a performance of hers.

So I should have known who she was. And at first I chalked up solely to my bottomless ignorance the fact that I recognized neither the face nor the name of an out-and-out star, who surely would not be endorsing Alberto VO-5 with Miral 80 were she not an out-and-out star. Yet I did not recognize her, which brought me to question my friend the drama critic, who that time said: "Beats me."

Cleared. If the drama critic of *The Post* did not know who Rula Lenska was, she had to be a nobody. And if she was a nobody, what was she doing sashaying about like a somebody? (Question No. 3.)

Because—it occurred sadly—she very much wanted to be recognized as a great and famous actress, or at any rate, someone in the upper reaches of the Alberto VO-5 with Miral 80 company wanted that for her. Therefore the elaborate pretense—the theatrical chitchat, the notice poster, the "Five minutes, Miss Lenska." Cheaper than hiring a bona fide star, to be sure. But how does Miss Lenska feel once the ad is shot, and five minutes have passed and all she has is her hair in perfect shape?

I remember seeing an ad like Miss Lenska's once before, twenty years ago. It was for a different kind of hair spray, and in it a movie director used a light meter to read the sheen reflected in the hair of a young and pretty woman. The woman was one Olga Nicholas, referred to in the ad as "rising starlet, Olga Nicholas." I never saw Miss Nicholas rise anywhere but in that ad, eventually concluding that a rising starlet could only rise to the rank of starlet anyway, and not to a full-fledged star. If Miss Nicholas has risen at last, she must be forty now, and she must also have changed her name.

In fact, it may be that her new name is Rula Lenska, who looks to be about forty. If that is so, so much the worse, as it would mean that Miss Nicholas or Miss Lenska or whoever has led an entire life of star playing, when the bitter truth is that her hair, not she, is the star, her lustrous eye-catching hair that must seem to her now as Lassie and Trigger must have seemed to their owners—a beautifully trained animal whose glory reflects everything save the soul of its trainer. Imagine the petty ignominies:

I'm Rula Lenska, Mr. Coppola.

Julia who?

Rula Lenska. Remember . . .

Oh sure. The girl in the ad for Alberto VO-5 with Miral 80. How ya doin'?

And so on. No blown-up word of praise. No voice calling out, "Five minutes." Nothing but a stylish woman, whose performance in its way is more demanding than anything ever tried by Sarah Bernhardt.

For it is no great trick for a star who actually is a star to play a star selling hair spray. But for a star who is not a star, although she would like with all her heart to be a star—for her to play a star selling hair spray is something else. And if I could, I would give Miss Lenska five minutes—not of preparation, but of life—five minutes in which the unrecognizing world would come to a stop and point as she passed by, saying: There goes Rula Lenska. *The* Rula Lenska. How dazzling. How brilliant. And will you look at that hair.

August 6, 1979

Ashley Montana
Goes Ashore
in the Caicos

From "Free Speech in America," a monologue performed at New York's American Place Theatre in fall–winter, 1991–92.

STROLL INTO THE HEART of the Republic. Eavesdrop on the chatter in the diners, the Sizzlers, the Bob's Big Boys, the Le Cirques, the Four Seasonses, the International Houses of Pancakes. Pick up the discussions in the schoolrooms. Absorb the prayers in the churches or in the synagogues of your choice. Listen to everything said. The compliments! The insults! The anecdotes! Things so amazing—said in all seriousness—they would bring your eyes to tears! A treasure trove, I tell you. A horn of plenty. I do not exaggerate. Free speech in America! It is an embarrassment of riches. An embarrassment *and* riches.

Where else but in this blessed land may one pick up a copy of *Sports Illustrated* and, merely because some caption writer exercised his or her right of free speech, be transported to a world of inexpressible splendor?

I refer to the *Sports Illustrated* swimsuit issue, celebrated nationally for its annual devotion to swimsuits.

On the cover of this year's swimsuit issue stands a large, tanned, gorgeous young woman in a white straw hat and a white bathing suit with a large gap in the back. Her lips are pink and puckered. Pink and puckered in a petulant yet perky pout. Her blond hair, like strands of fine hay, falls at a sharp angle across the bridge of her nose as if it were glued to it. Her arms are extended straight behind her. She appears to be shooing away a mob in pursuit.

And the caption to all this, written on the cover of *Sports Illustrated* in white type against the blues of the sea and sky, reads: ASHLEY MONTANA GOES ASHORE IN THE CAICOS.

Ashley Montana Goes Ashore in the Caicos! It may seem odd that in spite of the fact that Miss Montana is said to be going ashore, having emerged from the sea, the picture shows her to be nearly bone dry. Yet that is how it is.

Ashley Montana Goes Ashore in the Caicos! From seven little words, freely conceived and conveyed, the reader is borne to the center of the American Dream.

I come to the final wonder of free speech: that free speech allows us to *dream*. Free speech as an instrument of revelation. It reveals us through our dreams.

We have so far discovered how free speech shapes our culture, informs our politics, encourages our development of character, arouses our capacity for fun. Now with this caption, "Ashley Montana Goes Ashore in the Caicos," free speech carries us to a higher plane.

How might that wonderful caption be made sensible? What story can I write to bring those words to life?

We are aboard my sailing yacht, Ashley Montana and I. I too am named Ashley Montana, as is the boat. We are all three called Ashley Montana. Ashley and I have just made love four times in the past fifteen minutes. She is pooped. *I* am full of pep and vim. She stretches out on the poop deck and veils her vague, blue eyes behind the lenses of her oversize Porsche sunglasses.

"Pooped?" I ask.

"Bored," she barely says.

The word terrifies me. If Ashley is bored, she is bored with *me*. I know it's true.

It was not so in the beginning, when love was young. Or as she put it, "relationship" was young. In those days, Ashley and I were *new*, everything *new*. We were modern life itself! How the time flew by! We would lunch alfresco at those cramped, tiny restaurants on Madison Avenue with the little tables spilling out onto the middle of the sidewalk. We stared past each other and ordered water. How gaunt we looked! How pained!

We read *Vanity Fair* magazine from cover to cover. Often it took days. Yet we knew everything one could possibly know about Princess Di and Fergie and Jeremy Irons. Our heads swam with knowledge.

We took up ceramics. We bought each other stuffed animals. We gave them names! We called them both Ashley. We were invited to benefits for serious diseases. We went! How we laughed!

We threw each other surprise birthday parties, where everyone brought hilarious gifts and everyone made hilarious toasts, and weren't we both surprised! Guests came dressed as their favorite form of aerobic exercise. Such fun guessing.

We attended the lectures of John Bradshaw on PBS. We discovered the child within us. We killed it.

We watched *Masterpiece Theatre*. We saw another thirty-part series on the collapse of the British Empire. Britain had to give India back to India. We wept for weeks.

We talked about our latest projects with other people. We talked about *their* projects. So many screenplays, so many movies of the week, docudramas, miniseries, so many first novels. (We had always wanted to write one.) We redid the kitchen. (We could not use the apartment for a year!) We bought land in Wyoming. We renounced drugs—though neither of us had ever taken any. Nonetheless, we admitted ourselves to the Betty Ford clinic. Everyone said it was a beautiful gesture. It made the columns.

We *found* ourselves. We *lost* ourselves. We *found* ourselves again. We *lost* ourselves again. Someone found ourselves *for* us, and returned them, but demanded a reward. We learned how to *be* ourselves. We learned how to be *other people*. Other people learned how to be *us*. It was confusing.

We had breakthroughs and breakdowns and breakfast and peaks. We cleaned up our act. We were in a time warp. We were burned out. We reached critical mass. We experienced éclaircissements, and rapprochements and *Schadenfreude* and vertigo and *Fahrvergnügen*. And déjàs vu. We had the flu. We decided to go somewhere completely different for the summer, at first, but in the end, well, when would we see our friends? We kissed everybody and everybody kissed us.

We came on to each other. We had it all together. We got on with our lives. We told each other: "Go for it!" *It!* We were there for each other. *There!* We refused to learn from history and thus we were bound to repeat it.

We were state of the art. We were on the cutting edge. We had our priorities straight. We had our heads on straight. We were superpersons: We were bank presidents in the morning, coached Little League in the afternoon, and cooked coq au vin at night. I don't know *how* we did it.

We were caring persons. We cared for *us*.

We *saw* Penn and Teller. We *shopped* at Dean and DeLuca. We *called* Jacoby & Meyers. We *knew* Crabtree & Evelyn. Well, we knew Evelyn. We knew *Sy Syms*. We were educated consumers. We were his best customers.

We had liposuction. We had hipposuction. We had rhinoplasty. We had elephantiasis.

We lost thirty pounds with Ultra Slim-Fast. We got gravely ill.

We woke up and smelled the coffee. It was Folger's. Mountain grown.

We were laid back. We were uptight. We were ripped off. We were on a roll. We were in a rut. We were boss! We were fly! We were bitchin'! We were fabulous! Didn't you just love us? We got *every* joke that David Letterman made. We mastered *every* arm gesture on Arsenio. We knew the names of *every* rock band on *Saturday Night Live*. We liked the way they *dressed*.

We had brunch!

We ate shiitake mushrooms and Buffalo wings and a terrine of carpaccio with a paillard of chicken.

We fought for animal rights. We opposed capital punishment. We opposed capital punishmnent for animals. A pussy cat was electrocuted in Texas. A serial killer. Mice, mostly. We held a vigil.

We were *above* the law. We were *below* the fold. We were *beyond* the pale. We were *under* a great deal of pressure. We were *around* the block. We were *over* the hill. We were *beside* ourselves. We were *beneath* contempt.

We were into yoga. We were into health foods. We were into feelings. We were into prepositions.

We were Eurocentric. We were Eurotrash. We interfaced. We faded in. We faded out. We cut to the chase. They picked up our option.

We did construction work. We did *de*construction work.

Our phone answering machine left exceptionally clever messages. The phone never stopped ringing. We received calls from cars, from planes, from briefcases. We received a "Life Call" from Mrs. Fletcher: "I've fallen, and I can't get up." We let her lie there.

We had eyeglasses made in one hour.

We lost contact. We began to bicker.

I wanted to switch to MCI, she wanted to stay with AT&T. I said Certs was a candy mint. *She* said it was a breath mint. I said her shoes looked like a pump. *She* said they felt like a sneaker. I said: "Tastes great." *She* said: "Less filling."

We fought over *Ed McMahon*. We argued whether Ed was a slave to Johnny or a star in his own right.

Could we both be right? We made up. We vowed to have no more big dinner parties. We did the right thing. We had a nice day. We had a good one.

And then, suddenly, it was all gone. Gone. And now . . .

Lately, I have tried without success to attract Ashley's interest. She says everything is boring. I attempt to engage her enthusiasm about politics. Boring, she says. I show her a photograph of Treasury Secretary Nicholas Brady. Boring, she says.

The world of current events, which enchants me completely, sets her to yawning. Nuances of language, which have me mesmerized, hold her not. Books, movies, the antics of public figures, all of which make me leap for joy, are as nothing to Ashley. I try to bring back the old days. I sing her "Macho Man." She looks away. I sing "Kumbaya." She says she never heard of it. Still I worship the sea she sails on.

Now, on our boat, the *Ashley Montana,* I plead with her, Ashley Montana: "Don't be bored, darling." I say to her: "Let's find an island. A place for us. Somewhere." We had already visited ten such islands. One was on the Perillo Tours. Yet none of the islands had truly seized Ashley's imagination—an illusive thing, to be sure. Nonetheless, the idea perks her up.

"Aruba?" I suggest. She shakes her head no. "Anguilla?" I offer. She rolls her eyes skyward. "St. Bart's? St. Kitts? St. Croix?" Not a nod.

Ashley asks, "How about Portosan?"

I explain to her that Portosan is not an island.

"How about the Caicos?" she says.

"Never heard of them," I retort.

She sits bolt upright. "Never *heard* of them? Never heard of the *Caicos?*" She explodes in laughter so shrill it scatters the fish.

"Ashley, Ashley," she sighs woefully. "*Everybody* knows the Caicos. The Caicos are *it*! Jerry Zipkin goes there. Oscar de la Renta is there right *now*. Claus von Bülow, Imelda Marcos, Norman Mailer. *All* the best people. Look, I'm sorry. But if you've never heard of the *Caicos,* what's the point, I'd like to know, of us going on?"

It was the moment I had dreaded. Shamelessly I beg her to stay with me. But I can see that she's ready to jump ship. It was plain from the start: She has her world, I mine.

"Go," I tell her. "But stay dry."

"Good-bye, Ashley," she says, and jumps overboard.

For a minute or so I watch her swim toward shore, the water beading—and immediately evaporating—on her swimsuit as she glides through the sea. Soon she is far away. I turn my yacht about and sail north.

Putting on my tape of Zamfir, I console myself by listening to the unbeatable pan flutist as he plays "I Dreamed a Dream." Images rush to me that fortify my life. Everyone is present: David Brinkley and Ronald Reagan; George Wallace and Jimmy Carter; Alexander Haig and Zbig and Ivana and Al Sharpton; Nixon and George Bush; Cher and Nancy and Dave Del Dotto and Dan Quayle; and Gerry Ford; Strom Thurmond and Bill Bennett; and Norman Mailer and Madonna; and Pat Buchanan and John Sununu; and the Christian Children's Fund; school boards and war criminals; mayors and movie stars; old ladies and great writers and journalists and tycoons; all "releasing" perfumes and having "fun."

I embrace every one of them in my heart, which is brimming over with love and melancholy and gratitude. Especially that. Boundless gratitude . . .

While in the distance, with the sun full upon the sea, and the air as free as you and I, as free as speech itself, Ashley Montana goes ashore in the Caicos.

November 1991

Like a
Natural
Woman

O N   A   S T I L L, hot Saturday afternoon in late September [1992],
Candice Bergen sits in her child's garden of a yard in the Los
Angeles hills, and spins an answer to a single question: Why has
Murphy Brown become a model for American women? Tomorrow
she will devote the day to posing for a national-magazine cover on a
beach near Malibu. The following morning she will be up at three to
appear on *CBS This Morning* to discuss the much-publicized season's
first episode of *Murphy Brown,* to be aired that night. The show will
be watched by nearly 50 million people—more than the total number
who viewed any hour on any night of either the Democratic or
Republican convention last summer on ABC, CBS, NBC, and PBS
combined. Included among the viewers will be Vice President Dan
Quayle, who will gather a group of viewers, including black single
parents, in Washington, D.C., for the occasion. By Tuesday morning,
Quayle will have responded to Murphy's defense of her single-moth-
erhood, which he had attacked last spring as contrary to "family
values."

The atmosphere of surrealism will have been abetted by the show
itself. On the *Murphy Brown* opener—a work of fictional television,
one must remind oneself—Dan Quayle will appear, on television,

attacking Murphy Brown. Ms. Brown, the television celebrity anchor, will then counterattack Dan Quayle on her television news
show on the television sitcom. The vice president, like the rest of the
country, treating all this as real, will have seen to it that his *Murphy*-
watching support group will be televised watching television. He will
have sent a toy elephant with an accompanying note to Murphy's
television baby, and, to demonstrate good-naturedness, has already
filmed a commercial for *Murphy Brown,* declaring the show his
favorite . . . *"not"*—a joke popularized by television. The morning
after, there will be television reports on the Murphy-Quayle clash.

To add a surrealistic footnote: On the final episode of *Murphy* last
season, when she gave television birth to her television baby, the
unifying device for the episode was a camcorder tape on which the
show's characters delivered welcoming messages to the television
newborn for television posterity. In short, the device made a television show within a television show for a television child whose
television birth had been attacked by the vice president of the United
States, who had, in effect, joined the cast.

Atop these gyres of fantasy sits a real woman who, prodded, is
attempting to account for Murphy Brown's astonishing popularity
and influence. Bergen contends that while she admires Murphy, she
is not the same person. Her front-yard surroundings confirm this.
Murphy would never live in such well-tended disorder: the cat Furball doing standing high jumps onto chairs and laps; the dog Lois
waddling about in a shocking-pink collar and kissing as many humans as are available; the less demonstrative, waist-high plastic cow
with a lavender ribbon about its neck; the His Master's Voice dog,
also plastic; the stone rabbit; the pig made of something; the couch
whose legs are logs; the faded yellow store sign that reads, NOVA
SCOTIA FERTILIZER CO.—AGENTS TO THE CELEBRATED; the round
green table umbrellaed by a Japanese parasol of white, pink, and
blue, where Bergen sits, looking out over the amply housed hills.

These furnishings are set within a small space of red brick paths,
flowerpots, a kumquat tree, a Brazilian peppertree, greenery, and
murmurs of color. Impatiens with lavender and orange blossoms
hang below the wood-shingled roof. A couple of tall sycamores rise
in a fenced-in garden, called "the pasture" because of the cow and
pig. The one-story house is splendid-modest. The swimming pool,
out of sight of the yard, is of modest size, too. The woman who lives
here chooses comfort over grandeur, but the comfort is at once rich
and protective—a wealthy child's design.

To be sure, a real child lives here. In the yard there are a pint-size table and chairs for Chloe, the blond, seven-year-old daughter of Bergen and her husband, the French movie director Louis Malle. But the mother clearly delights in the mixture of delicacy, self-mockery, fancy, and surprise. So this is not Murphy Brown's home. And Bergen is herself.

Yet there is a good deal of Murphy Brown in Candice Bergen, and, as the show's top-five ranking would attest, in millions of American women. This is what Bergen is attempting to get at, sitting at her green table, discussing Murphy's appeal:

"First of all she's a great character, a sort of female W. C. Fields. She crosses gender lines. And she's at the top of a man's world. She lives her life like a man, a take-no-prisoners journalist. Women like that about her. I think women also like the fact that she's a professional woman in her forties. She's going to be dealing with that soon, dealing with the sacrifices that she had to make, the sacrifice of a personal life. I think women respect the honesty of it.

"And she's endearingly cantankerous, and opinionated. So many of us are constrained by rules of good behavior most of the time. Murphy has never been confined by that. I think that a lot of us who chafe under those kinds of constrictions find it incredibly refreshing to have a woman or a man like that. I think the fact that Murphy is a woman just makes it gravy for people because there's never been a woman character quite like this before. And she is really indifferent to people's opinions of her. She doesn't care if she's liked or not. And she is literally fearless. And she's always ready. She's got her hand on the gun in her holster. She can really take care of herself. She can drink men under the table. She can take the pot at poker."

"But," I suggest, "if I were to say to you that every Monday night America would be enthralled by a woman who takes no prisoners, who conducts herself like a man, who is not affected by other people's opinions . . ."

"Or their feelings . . ."

"Or their feelings. Who makes men into mice, and so forth, you'd say this was crazy."

"In real life, you know, women like Murphy consume a lot of oxygen," Bergen says. "In real life I've rarely found them to be as likable. . . . That sort of person is exhausting. *Murphy's* exhausting, though I try not to let her get meanspirited. Yet she *is* alone. The only true relationship she has is with her housepainter. That is reflective of a lot of women I know at this age who can't find relationships anywhere, but who are incredibly skilled at what they do, and yet have a desolate personal life to come home to. Still, you see her punctured and deflated constantly. I think that saves it for people. . . . And there is something to the fact that she doesn't get her way all the time, and that everybody sees her for what she is. . . . She's a secret fantasy for a lot of women."

"What exactly is the fantasy?"

"I think that people identify with Murphy the way people identified with the movie *Network*—where people lean out their windows and say they're mad as hell and they're not going to take it anymore. They identify with her anger, her righteous rage. It helps that she expresses rage in a way that's likable. It's sympathetic because she's funny, and smart. And she's careful who she picks on. But I think people are generally pissed off. And all of us squelch it. And we're all going to get cancer. But Murphy isn't. She has no patience. There is no membrane of censorship between Murphy's mind and what comes out of her mouth. Inside all of us is somebody who is pissed off, and we're not going to take it anymore. Except that we *do* take it. And none of us finally crosses the line where we lean out the windows and yell into the night. But Murphy does. . . . And then there's her self-absorption. I always have such admiration for someone who dares to be unlikable, who flies in the face of public opinion and public sympathy just to be one's own person."

"You can be your own person and run roughshod over others."

"Yes. I know someone who is vulgar and offensive. He's been vulgar and offensive to heads of state. He's been vulgar to his wife. He's insulted all of us. And the fact that he's so democratic in his vile behavior has always earned him a place of respect with me, has always impressed me."

"Impressed you, but he hasn't won your heart."

"No."

"Yet Murphy has."

"Yes."

Stars, when they are interviewed, tend to say that their current stage of life is their best and happiest yet. Never before have they understood themselves so deeply, never did they have greater command of their temperaments, and so forth. Bergen talked that way in an interview ten years ago, and she talks that way today. But today the terms of her self-scrutiny seem more secure, so when she says that her life is better than ever (the name of the song she hilariously brays in the movie *Starting Over,* her comic debut), it sounds like neither a boast nor a brave lie. She simply means that while the life within and outside her front yard still has some ghosts and sudden noises, it has better, surer components than it has had before—husband, child, a career that fits.

In her much-chronicled forty-six years she has been seen and heard in public as the daughter of Frances Westerman, who modeled for billboards as the Chesterfield Girl and in magazines as the Ipana Girl, and the beloved ventriloquist Edgar Bergen; as a child performer on Bergen's radio show, a tot on the playing fields of Hollywood, a Swiss-boarding-school rebel, a homecoming queen, a college flunk-out, a premier fashion model, a celebrity photographer, an intrepid traveler, a *Today*-show commentator, a movie actress, a reluctant preppy, a reluctant hippie, a loner, a lover (or seeker of love), a writer, a salon figure, a wife, a mother, and always a beauty.

She has led what is called a charmed life, with all the wonder and pathos the term entails. Her playmates were the children of the Dick Powells, the Ray Millands, the Jimmy Stewarts, the Arthur Rubinsteins, the Ronald Reagans. It was ordinary to see Fred Astaire and Cary Grant as guests in the house, to ride on the miniature train on the property of "Uncle Walt" (Disney), to have David Niven play Santa Claus at Christmas. The gifts dispensed were Georgian silver, ivory animals, mechanical birds in gilded cages—toys for the progeny of the czar. If they wanted a white Christmas, the limbs of the tree would be shagged with artificial snow.

All the Red Seas parted for her. When Bergen wanted to be a photographer, Charlie Chaplin was ready to pose. She did not even have to seek a career as a movie actress: the movies went after *her*. As for men, she always seemed to be drawn to those guaranteed to self-destruct. One was Terry Melcher, a record producer, the son of Doris Day, and a golden boy who increasingly swallowed his life with booze and pills. When Melcher's stepfather died, $20 million was discovered missing from the family fortune.

At about the same time, Melcher had been smitten with Charles Manson and his acolytes, but had grown leery after Manson kept badgering him to sign him to a recording contract. With his mother in financial trouble, Melcher left the big house in which he and Bergen had been living together and Roman Polanski and Sharon Tate moved in. Manson let it be known he was looking for Melcher.

"But it could have been *me*!" Bergen, shaken and terrified, shouted at him. "I could have been killed!" Melcher asked, "Why don't you say *we*?"

After Melcher there was the producer Bert Schneider (*Easy Rider, Five Easy Pieces*), who brought with him the world of '60s radicalism—"open relationships," Abbie Hoffman, the Black Panthers—but little else. For years, there was a "love life," but neither element was entirely authentic. Her beauty alone shaped her life, drove and contained it, like a classic car with the doors soldered.

At one time the beauty was confounding. Bergen was twice blessed, thus once cursed, with being born both beautiful and smart. So extraordinary was her face, whole rooms of glittering people would come to a standstill when she walked in. But Bergen, because she was smart too, had the wit to understand that her beauty gave her a free pass in life—thus her early feelings of unworthiness. Thus, too, her demanding concentration on herself. She was rescued from being alone with herself by marriage and child. Now she has other people to pay attention to.

She pays very careful attention to her twelve-year marriage to Louis Malle, which, in spite of its odd schedule, seems to work quite well. "Each is the only person the other could have married," says Alice Arlen, who wrote the filmscript for Malle's *Alamo Bay*. Arlen observes how remarkable the two of them are, how quick-minded and quick-witted, how unimpressed by money and flashy displays. It would take extraordinary people to survive, much less flourish in, a marriage that has Malle living in Paris most of the year, with a few brief conjugal visits to L.A., until the summer, when Bergen's *Murphy* takes a rest. Malle detests L.A., and as a practical matter the writer-director of *Au Revoir les Enfants* could never do the kind of movies in Hollywood he does in France. For her part, Bergen would not have him functioning as a sidecar to her career.

But the marriage may actually thrive because of its separations. Bergen is suffused with common sense. Malle, born to French upper-middle-classness verging on aristocracy, lives in perpetual motion, the way that spoiled and gifted children sometimes do. He darts from idea to idea, project to project—"LouisLouisLouis!"—like a wren. The pace has its costs. In early October, Malle had surgery to replace a valve in his heart. The operation, successful, was performed in L.A. and Bergen was with him.

One reason the marriage succeeds is that it does not require high maintenance, perhaps because as individuals they don't either. Another is that they fit together well. "They have a deep respect for each other," says the literary agent Ed Victor. "No one is according the other anything automatically." Another friend notes, "Louis is a romantic masquerading as a cynic. Candy is the reverse."

She also pays very careful attention to Chloe. In the morning Chloe will bounce about the yard, instructing Furball on a number of points, transferring the plastic cow's lavender ribbon to Lois, and asking a flood of questions about the day's activities, along with everything else that strikes her agile, souped-up mind. Bergen, meanwhile, will be trying to get herself ready to be photographed and seen by millions once again. Even for her, after hundreds of similar experiences, this is a nerve-racking business. Yet none of Chloe's questions will go unanswered, and Chloe's welfare will be the main thing she attends to. Bergen's television schedule, and all that goes with it, would excuse her delivering her daughter into the hands of a dozen caretakers, but she does not do that. The result is a normal, laughing child, and, not incidentally, a normal mother.

Yet, the knowledge that her beauty has always come first to people's minds has left a residue of mistrust. Bergen, while gracious, can be exceedingly cautious. She is cooler, deeper, sharper, funnier, and more considerate than most extraordinarily beautiful people, but sitting in her yard, answering a stranger's questions, she still shows the capacity to open and close at will, like one of e. e. cummings's roses.

She actually is more beautiful today than when she began to model for Revlon Tawny lipstick ads, and when she played her first movie role, in *The Group,* in her late teens. In those years the face appeared to be a collection of features, like butterflies in a glass case, each lovely yet unrelated to any other. She resembled a police composite drawing of a beautiful suspect. On *Vogue*'s February 1969 cover, she is only technically beautiful—the way Mariel Hemingway looked until recently, when mature thought, seriousness, and perhaps grief infiltrated the perfect eyes, nose, and lips, and gave them coherence. So it is for Bergen, who is now more comfortable with herself and celebrates the fact that it is possible to "survive without the camera capturing your soul." The gold hair still flies in remarkable spiky patterns, but the eyes are a little tired and the smile is brilliant or sexy only when the inspiration is internal.

It is easier to think of this woman as comic now, not only because she is playing a comic character, but also because she is fluid and coordinated, thus a greater setup for humiliations. Henri Bergson, the author of the only theory of comedy that does not lead to depression, said that people laugh when momentum is suddenly broken; one expects things (words, actions, faces) to go one way, but then all at once they go another. The reason that beautiful comediennes of the movies like Carole Lombard or Myrna Loy are funny is that they allow, even encourage, the momentum of their beauty to be broken, as with a pratfall—the contrast between laughter and sublimity makes both more intense.

Beauty can be funny on its own, for its effect on others. When one sees a face so much more beautiful than the average, there is an impulse to laugh because the face, too, thwarts expectations. In an October 1971 piece Bergen wrote and photographed for *Vogue*, she said of Paul Newman, "His face is so handsome you almost start to laugh."

Bergen as Murphy is following a tradition of beautiful funny women on television. Lucille Ball was stunning, as was Mary Tyler Moore, except for a frightened rigidity, which actually aided the character Moore portrayed. Like Ball, Bergen plays her show at a very loud volume, which also undercuts her looks. Bergen herself does not speak loudly, but she does create deliberate bubble-shaped tones in her speech, which can have comic effect when the content is funny.

A certain masculinity has crept in as well, perhaps as a result of playing a character who can do any man in—a character who is, in fact, the only real man on the show. Murphy is not merely essential to her show; she *is* her show. This is what makes *Murphy Brown* different from, and less complete than, other enduring sitcoms. Great series like *Cheers, M*A*S*H, The Dick Van Dyke Show,* or *The Mary Tyler Moore Show* were true ensemble efforts. In *Murphy,* if the star is absent from a scene, the scene wobbles and flounders. The program is much closer to sitcoms like *Sergeant Bilko* and *Roseanne,* where the central character comes on like a human stampede. *Murphy*'s main weakness, besides an irritating strain of political correctness, is that Murphy is so dominant both the humanity of the enterprise and the range of humor are limited.

Bergen is, as others have noted, smaller and more fragile in person than she appears on the TV screen, where Murphy swaggers and breaks china. But she is demonstrably strong and in control of her complicated life. In the hired car on the way to the beach tomorrow she will make a point of learning the driver's name right away, not only to be pleasant with him, though she is that, but also to be able to direct him more effectively. On the camcorder tape made for her television baby, Murphy sings lines from "A Natural Woman," but she is not really a natural woman. She is more "*like* a natural woman," one who has seized male prerogatives and male attitudes but has sensed a reawakening of her femininity.

Fear, rage, and loneliness. These are not elements one would ordinarily associate with a sitcom, but Bergen seems to be right in identifying them as central to Murphy's appeal to women. That she focuses on these three particular elements also says something about Bergen.

Murphy Brown may be fearless, but Candice Bergen is full of fears. In two days' conversation the subject of death keeps rising to the surface—perhaps partly because she was brooding about her husband's impending surgery. At lunch in a Los Angeles restaurant, she brought up out-of-body experiences, the testimonies of people who had come close to death and reported on it, and spoke of Elisabeth Kübler-Ross's book *On Death and Dying*. The following day, on the road to the cover shoot, the driver will make a sudden stop. Bergen will predict grimly, "We're going to be rear-ended." In the front yard she laments that one cannot speak of deep, personal things to one's closest friends: "You don't talk about the fear of death." Bergen speaks of the proximity of death when one goes to a doctor for a checkup. "A casual visit to a gynecologist is like 'Eeeeah!' It's not so casual anymore. Death just seems to be lurking. But let's not get on *that* subject." Yet she does. She mentions a summer camp with which she has worked. She says at first that it is a camp for "terminally ill" children, then quickly changes the term to "chronically ill," as if it were a jinx to say the other.

Knock Wood, the first-rate autobiography she wrote in 1984, takes its title from fear. It, too, has death on its mind, beginning with the description of two funerals—one for her turtle, one for her father. The book is forthright about Bergen's fear of self-expression, probably caused by and certainly intensified by her cool and distant father, and in its account of the strange, competitive relationship she had with Edgar Bergen's "firstborn," his dummy Charlie McCarthy. By now Bergen has told the story of that relationship so often there is something false about its significance, perhaps to her as well.

But the disturbing thing about *Knock Wood* is the fear that remains within it, in spite of her candor and various exorcisms. As much as she explains her feelings about her father, she holds back too. There are things that Edgar Bergen said and did to his daughter in the name of standards and discipline that were harsh, almost cruel. Bergen's way of recounting these incidents is always the same. She tells of some painful thing her father did, then she defends and justifies it, in the process blaming herself.

When Bergen turned twenty-one, her father moved the date of her inheritance up to twenty-five, citing her financial irresponsibility.

Then, for the same reason, the date was moved to thirty. There was very little justification for these decisions, which hardly disabled his successful model-actress daughter, but they were his way of withholding approval, and, beneath that, love. Later, when Bergen had turned thirty, she gave an interview to *McCall's* in which she spoke of the postponement of her inheritance, and of the distance between her father and herself. Her father was now quite old. She took him out to dinner, alone. In *Knock Wood* she writes:

"My voice jumping to the octave level of Bambi's, I tried, once again, to apologize, to tell him I loved him, to make certain he understood. I explained that my regrettable mention of money in that interview was not about money at all but about what I saw as the long-postponed promise of his approval. Nothing more. Nothing less. How was he to know? Anointing me was hardly his job, of course. He had enough to do without dispensing paternal seals of approval. If I believed life began with his benediction, that was *my* problem." Of course, it was *his* problem.

Bergen's fearfulness is in part the fear of someone who has lived well for a very long time, and now, suddenly, realizes how blessed she has been, how much she has to cherish, and to lose. Used to walking jauntily along the roof's edge, she is for the first time in her life glancing down.

The fear is connected to the passage of time. "As I grow up," she says, "I find that not only does gravity start to pull at you physically, it starts to weigh on you emotionally. The gravity of our situation, the gravity of the situations of the people not lucky enough. You lose the buoyancy, and you also, you hope, become more aware of people's feelings. The wiseass remarks you once would have made that would have hurt someone do not get past your tongue, because you know that there are risks involved, and life is cruel enough to people."

The thought comes full circle to death: "Freud says it's sex— everything, sex. For me it's death. Death. Ever since I was fourteen. It gives my life a certain richness, because I'm very reluctant to squander my time."

Like fear, the element of rage, admired in Murphy Brown, is submerged in Bergen—though not as completely as it once was. She speaks of it openly. She has a way of speaking of things openly while keeping them partly hidden. There was certainly as much rage as fear behind her apology habit as a child and young woman. No sooner had she appeared in *The Group,* at nineteen, than Pauline Kael pounced on her performance: "As an actress her only flair is in her nostrils." Bergen later wrote that Kael's criticism was "on the nose." But real anger at a distinguished critic's bullying of a novice actress would have seemed a more appropriate, and more genuine, response than her lame-joke concession. Now, at least, she seems more aware of the presence of anger:

"I know any number of long-suffering wives whose husbands have either philandered on them or abused them in some way, constantly. And these women felt powerless to fight back, or chose not to fight back, because of the alternative, which was solitude. . . . It's homicide turned inward. It's when they can't murder their husbands, because they're too well mannered. But really what they want to do is push them down the stairs, or strangle them in their sleep, or put something in their vodka. And when they can't do that, it's this kind of unbearable rage turned inward. It metastasizes. It turns to cancer."

Rage may be the one factor that distinguishes Murphy Brown from the TV comic queens before her. Lucy had no rage, but then, there was nothing on the show to incite it. There was lots of rage to incite the Mary Tyler Moore character, who, like Murphy, worked in television journalism, but behind the cameras, and always under the thumb of Ed Asner's Mr. Grant. Mary's theme-song line was "You're going to make it after all"—quite a different line from "You make me feel like a natural woman." One is built on ambition, from the viewpoint of surprise, the other on nostalgia, from the viewpoint of earned power. Yet if Mary was angry with her lot, it showed only in comic spurts. She had made it, after all, as far as she felt she could go.

Murphy, on the other hand, has made it all the way, and she has done it largely on rage. Her way of dealing with impediments is not to sweet-talk but to rail at them. When she was extravagantly pregnant last season she wielded her stomach like a battering ram. In one hilarious moment she exploded off the elevator bellowing at some guy who had pushed the wrong button and delayed her: "I don't care if you did push the fourteenth floor by mistake; if we stopped there, you should've gotten off—push and off." But Murphy's rage goes to the heart of the character, because it is connected not only to work but also to the absences in her life—home, hearth, husband. For her, having a child is not just an assertion of life over loneliness; it, too, is an expression of rage, which is unlikely to be tempered this season by the child himself.

In fact, Murphy will probably use her baby as a battering ram as well. The child will serve her rage the way long hair and beards served the rage of young people in the '60—as a way of saying "Fuck you" to the world. One of the interesting and perhaps representative things about Murphy is how awkward her rage often makes her seem. Like most American women until recently, she is a stranger to what are literally the corridors of power. She careers down them showing none of the caution or oppressive politeness of men, who are more used to the rules of the game. And she gets away with conduct no man would allow in another man.

This blustery quality, more than her decision to be a single parent, may have caused some people to side with Dan Quayle against Murphy. The character is a loose, if highly principled, cannon in a world of corked cannons. Funny as she is, she may be resented, or envied, for that.

Happily equipped with home, hearth, and husband, Bergen feels rage that is not the same as Murphy's, even though the long separations from Louis Malle effectively make Bergen a single mother, too. But she has a different source of rage—two sources, in fact. One, which relates to her childhood, she will not talk about. "I had enormous rage as a child." What was it about? "Who knows?" Tomorrow, when asked again if she knows what that rage was about, she will say, "Yeah." Then she will add, not altogether persuasively, "But I don't see any point in looking back on that. I'm so glad to be at an age when I don't care where the anger came from."

The rage she will talk about is directed outward, at cruelty and violence in the country. "We're not only talking about sexual harassment [referring to the navy's Tailhook incident]. Look at the racial homicide, the racial beatings that are going on. The last one I read about . . . this Vietnamese student [in Florida]. It's, it's some pack mentality. It's . . ." Her voice trails off into helplessness.

And there's the rage that comes from high-level work and a high-wire life, both hers and Murphy's. "I'm talking about well-heeled rage, of course, not about the rage of the inner cities. . . . Everybody is living under tremendous pressure these days. . . . Murphy is a woman in her forties living alone. Now a single mother. Probably soon facing competitiveness in her market. In a society that's collapsing. And a system that's no longer working." Bergen, evidently feeling her own pressure, will speak the next day of lifting *Murphy* from the top five to number 1 or 2.

The elements of fear and rage lead to and from a well of loneliness, which is palpable in Murphy and occasionally noticeable in Bergen.

In the process of answering the question about Murphy's attractiveness to women, Bergen identified Murphy's desolation, the flip side of her brash independence. Bergen, independent without being brash, has something of that desolation in her. In *Knock Wood* she described her younger brother, Kris, as a "child of light" and herself as a "child of shadows." Most of her movie roles were women who were alone or who wound up alone. While she acknowledges and celebrates her own good fortune today, something inside is still isolated.

Part of the loneliness has to come simply from being a public person, a walking event. Celebrities are alone almost by definition because their social status sets them apart from others, and because the motives of those who seek their company are always suspect.

The loneliness also has to come from being funny. Bergen took to the Murphy role, indeed strove to get it, because she knew that her talent, like her father's, lay in comedy. In the movie *Rich and Famous,* Bergen is a scream as a shrewish trash novelist, and she accomplishes the seemingly impossible feat of making audiences forget her looks. The basis of her success here, and on *Murphy Brown,* is that her comedy keeps people at arm's length. It is essentially an isolating device. People who are funny by nature know that comedy can distance them from others. Often they enjoy being funny for that reason. In Murphy's hands particularly, a joke becomes an assault weapon that happens to cause the reaction of laughter but could just as easily kill.

One may only guess how much Bergen enjoys being alone, but she has hinted at it, and the structure of her surroundings hints at it now. In a June 1971 article for *Vogue,* she gloried in her first house. It was originally built by John Barrymore as a kind of medieval castle. The estate had heated kennels and an aviary. Bergen had played there as a kid. She christened her bedroom "The Rainbow Room" because of the Frank Stella–like rainbow she had painted above her headboard, and she described it as "the perfect child's room"—for someone in her midtwenties. In *Knock Wood* she writes of this room, "If evenings were idyllic [with parties and men], mornings found me, alone, under the rainbow, fighting a slight case of what the decade identified as 'anomie.' There was an emptiness in my life that slept fitfully and woke way before I did—a little furry ball of foreboding that made me vaguely afraid to face the day alone."

There is clearly less emptiness in her life today. Yet the front yard, with its artificial animals, seems an outdoor version of the Rainbow

Room. The child—not Chloe—is somewhere around still. "How did I happen, the solitary, introspective child, afraid of feelings, who preferred to play alone?" she asked at Kris's birth. Perhaps she had answered the question earlier when describing her father's rebuffing of her mother's exuberant displays of affection toward him. "She learned . . . to swallow 'I love you's.' And that is how loneliness grows."

"Don't shut me out, Bergen!" That is what she remembers a former lover shouting at her years ago, and that is what one is tempted to say, if not shout, even on short acquaintance. Often her shuttings-out may simply be discretion—she does have to be discreet. But her isolation seems a habit of mind as well. She is alert to it in others:

"There's a crushing sense of loneliness out there," she will say tomorrow looking out the car window. "I always wonder if people in Israel are lonely. I think that's why a lot of Americans go to Israel, because they're longing to live in a country where there's a higher sense of purpose."

"Do you think that America is a lonely country?"

"I do. But I don't want to live anywhere else. I never found our capacity for friendship in any other country. It comes from the loneliness we have, the needfulness. In other countries they still have religion to hold on to, which is the psychiatry of the ancients. In America I'm always so amazed that there are people whose loneliness is so undisguised, so unmasked."

Then, too, there is the loneliness of the necessary artifice of her life. The photo shoot will begin early in the morning, in a haze that will never burn off, in spite of predictions to the contrary. She will alight from the car, and spend three hours being dressed, having her hair scooped and tousled, her face colored and pointed like bricks. Outside her trailer will stand a huge open tent which will contain four racks of dresses, a rack of sweaters and bathrobes, three tables of hats, a table with nine or ten boxes of jewelry, another with two boxes of sunglasses, a third piled with at least thirty pairs of shoes. Thirty or forty people in tattered beachy wear will mill about, snacking near the other trailer, where the caterers have cooked a smoked turkey. Soon the horses will arrive. On the beach a great white sheet will billow like the sail of a boat in the America's Cup. And a white platform, like a stage, will await her.

Finally, from her trailer she will emerge, a work of creams and sprays, wrapped in translucent veils of pink and green. Down she will go to the beach, where the photographer will crouch and urge, a big box will blare music, and she will assume shapes and poses unknown to woman or man. The second number to rise from the box will be Aretha Franklin singing "A Natural Woman"—while Bergen continues to look about as natural as an automatic teller machine, and she knows it.

Within or in spite of the fear, rage, and loneliness—within or in spite of the child's yard and the child's world of celebrity—Bergen is very much a grown-up. So is Murphy, and that may be the overarching factor in her popularity. Murphy has the advantage over Bergen of existing in half-hour segments, and her lines are written for her, so her maturity lies mainly in her forcefulness. Yet she has been through a lot, has lost a lot, has paid a price, and has done considerably more than survive. Bergen admires Murphy for the same reason most women do: Murphy laughs and triumphs while bulling her way through a state of pain. She lives a tragedy inside a comedy. And she is not a whiner. That may be what women, and men, like most about her.

What Bergen seeks from life nowadays is order, which is probably the general middle-age dream. She concedes that her "marriage by commute" is not ideal. "But I don't know too many ideal marriages, period . . . although it certainly did come back into fashion, didn't it?"

"Do you think people are happier in families these days?"

"I don't know if it's just a natural reaction to everything. The atoms that were spun apart, the way people were spinning out in the 1970s. I knew so many marriages that broke up in the '70s that should never have broken up. Today they would just be going through a difficult moment. I think people realize now how very threatening the world is . . . and how we're all responsible for each other.

"I want to find a way to give back something to the system. The people I respect are the ones who put something back. Even if it doesn't amount to much, the effort counts. . . . It's just . . . you know . . . family values!"

"Are you religious?"

"If I were, I'd be more of a pantheist than anything else. I do pray. A very close friend of mine who is in A.A. does what they call the gratitude prayer all the time. I went with her to an A.A. meeting a long time ago, and what stuck with me was the sense of gratitude. So I say prayers of gratitude. . . . And I pray the way they do in A.A. They say, 'God, take my fear,' or 'take my anger,' or 'take my loneliness.'

"But my life is incredibly full, so I'm really . . . praying with a full deck." Then, like Murphy: "Instead of playing with a full deck."

At the end of the afternoon, the sky darkening even in Los Angeles, the phone rings inside the house. The answering machine picks up, and Chloe's voice breezes out into the yard. Chloe is on her first sleep-away at a friend's house, and her mother has been anxious to hear how she is doing. At the sound of her child's voice, Bergen cocks her head like a terrier's. She stops talking, and smiles as if in her sleep. She has never looked lovelier.

December 1992

Residuals on
An American
Family

A LITTLE OVER A YEAR AGO the William C. Louds of Santa Barbara, California, were the most widely discussed and written about family in the United States. They were the stars and subjects of *An American Family,* an experimental exercise in television verité, invented and undertaken by a director, Craig Gilbert. For thirteen straight weeks the lives and characters of each member of this family were made plain to us. We responded by analyzing what we saw, and by inspecting our own feelings. In the very short time since, the Louds have been nearly forgotten.

This is confusing to the Louds, who regarded their initial stardom as merely the beginning of future risings. Only a few months ago they reconvened on *The Dick Cavett Show,* where they had also appeared in their heyday, before Bill and Pat Loud got their divorce. On the second appearance Pat was unsuccessfully promoting her book, *Pat Loud: A Woman's Story,* and the children, all five, were frantically promoting themselves as a hard rock group. They performed a song written by Lance Loud called "Muscle Boys," but again, no sale. The Louds talked with Cavett about their enormous disappointment in not being able to sustain their renown.

An American Family was, I think, one of the most significant events of our recent popular culture. The Louds would have a right to be surprised at their fading, were it not for the fact that all events in popular culture, no matter how big and brassy, are ephemeral. It is a tenet of popular culture that things come and go. The disappearance of an item is as essential as its rise and prominence.

But the disappearance of the Louds presents a special problem. The family's prominence did not merely wane; it was obliterated, as if by popular demand. There were those who simply disliked the show or found it boring. There were more who deeply hated the show and the idea of the show as well. *An American Family* has not been rerun. It flourished within popular culture, but it also did something to popular culture, something that even popular culture, which accepts all things, could not abide.

At a time when questions of censorship were being put so ardently in the press, it is interesting how smoothly the Louds passed by. People who debated *Deep Throat* and *Last Tango in Paris* did not include *An American Family* in their conception of debilitating and tasteless influences. The reason may be that the Louds were not naked in their episodes, not naked in the sense of performing without clothing. Their intimacies, where they occurred, were merely verbal, thus evidently more tolerable, despite the fact that once a week we all sat down to watch an organization of human beings deliberately set out to psychologically murder one another. Despite the accuracies achieved by television verité, we started out viewing most aspects of the Louds' behavior as the antics of a family of some other country. However as the show progressed public criticism of *An American Family* became quite personal. One judged the success of each episode, and the whole series, by deciding whether one liked the Louds, a decision that hinged on our surface identifications with, and correspondences to, the family, and gradually became refined to the point where we declared some Louds better than other Louds—healthier, more honest, more entertaining. Eventually we began to root for our favorite Loud.

This is a procedure with which we are quite familiar, and it is accomplished almost by reflex. Every radio and television show, movie and comic strip built on the family format has required of us the same superficial discriminations. Even as the Louds were asserting their presence in their medium, they were in direct competition with shows of the sort that continue to succeed today: *The Brady Bunch, All in the Family, Family Affair, My Three Sons, The Partridge Family,* and more. It may be argued that *An American Family* was real-life drama and ought not to be yoked with *The Brady Bunch,* but theoretically a semblance of reality is the aspiration of *The Brady Bunch,* and of the other shows as well. The questions of propriety raised by *An American Family* were no different in kind from those raised by the Bunker family, which has been both hailed and scorned solely because of its proximity to reality.

It is far less interesting that the Louds were real than that we reacted to them as if they were not. Because they came to us on a regular schedule each week—the same cast, the same setting—because they engaged in a new and complete adventure every episode, edited largely in the same patterns, and because our appreciation and apprehension of them increased according to the sequence of the performances, we reasonably took the Louds to be fictitious. If they had been on radio, they would have brought to mind *One Man's Family.* On television they became the new Ozzie and Harriet Nelson, a notable American family of another age, whose appeal, like the Louds', derived from their being the same family offstage and on. Like the Louds, Ozzie and Harriet had teenage children, and a nice house, and confusions and misunderstandings. Ozzie did something for a living—it was never clear what—but his family, like the Louds, never wanted. Ozzie was a "good guy," just like Bill. Ricky was a rock 'n' roll star, just as Grant and Kevin hoped to be (Delilah sought to become a tap dancer).

We focused mainly on Mrs. Loud because, like Harriet, she ran her show. She answered everybody's questions, and solved all problems. She arranged airplane tickets, reminded the children of their school calendar, reinforced various routines. She insisted on the role of stabilizer and organizer—"I've got enough mutinous troops around here"—and the others conceded her that role eagerly. In fact, they made her assumption of it necessary, a fine courtesy, by affecting chaos and disorder at every opportunity. Even when the Louds simply walked together, they loped distractedly like water birds in an open zoo.

The principal difference between the two women was that Harriet used to urge on the maturity of her boys to the point of the show's survival through David's and Ricky's marriages. Harriet had the advantage over Pat of being confined by her director to the business of making peanut butter and jelly sandwiches, so her benign toleration of everybody else's changes was born partly of circumstance. Mrs. Loud quite openly did not wish her family to change. When Kevin returned from overseas, he showed signs of independence that

Pat resented, and tried to tease him out of. She much preferred her neurotic Lance, who was down and out in Europe. On the phone one time Pat told Bill to wire Lance another fifty dollars, and when Bill protested, "He's got to do it for himself," she treated his comment as an aphorism.

This difference aside, Pat and Harriet could have played each other. More than any superficial similarity, they shared the fundamental condition of being simultaneously the firm foundations of their families and the romantic idols in which great dreams had been invested. Each was her Juno, of O'Casey's play, married to a dreamer and bungler whose wildest dream (and biggest bungle?) was she herself. Eventually the object of the dream had to become the solidifying agent because the dreamer wished to go on dreaming. The stability of the family came to depend entirely on her. She initially had been the end of romance, and now encouraged romance in others (the tap dancers, the rock 'n' roll stars) in order to hold on to her power. In Harriet this was theater, in Pat, life, but it was the same part played.

To parallel real and fictitious characters in this way should be an offensive idea. The suggestion it carries is that the real person is diminished by the comparison, her complexities and variations, which are the human signs, reduced to the simplifying elements of melodrama. Yet Pat was not diminished in the slightest by her identification with fiction. Indeed her complexity was enhanced by it, because she seemed purposefully to cultivate the trappings of simplemindedness, as if she sought to be fictitious herself.

She came on from the start as a woman who had absorbed all the components of attractiveness without permitting herself to become attractive. Always informal—her white slacks were startling—she gave the impression of having studied long and hard to look so smart. By now her appearance came automatically, and the outfits that were supposed to be casual were worn like a kind of uniform. She descended to breakfast each morning like a piece of machinery, yet it was clear that she was aware of her rigidity. Instead of working counter to it, she elaborated on it, just as the children elaborated on their own loose-jointedness.

Her props were her glasses—oversized, stylish, worn like a visor. Her voice, like Harriet's, had the tone of instructions piped through earphones on a museum tour. Neither warm nor cold, it sustained rather than created conversation, a family trait. Mrs. Loud has thick dark hair, which she tied back like a young girl's, but she did not look young because of it. Nor did she look old, nor old trying to look young. She looked as if she were frozen at thirty-five, though at the time of the show she had reached forty-six, yet the question of age did not really crop up. The control she exerted over herself, her body and gestures, so dominated the impression we took of her that in a sense the force of that control, which ordinarily should have been repellent for its dehumanizing effect, was her most attractive feature.

But Mrs. Loud would not allow even that attraction. She had mastered the craft of withholding herself: from her clothing, her voice, her homosexual son with whom she played a perpetual Venus and Adonis. On her visit to Lance in New York, she lolled about his pad like the siren of a world that might have been. Then she was off again, to a Baltimore shipping depot, or to a shoe store to buy taps for Delilah, or to a bookstore. When she called her husband long-distance, even before they officially became estranged, she sounded as if it were she who had answered the phone. He tried to pump up their talk, as if with an organ bellows. She gave him the time and the weather.

The terrible thing, or what ought to have been the terrible thing, was, as we learned in one of the later episodes, that Mrs. Loud knew what we thought of her. Deciding after twenty years that she would divorce her husband because of his countless infidelities, she brought her case to her brother and sister-in-law. They discussed divorce over a barbecue. Pat said that the pain Bill had put her through caused her to become "unlovable." The word was not only exactly right, but brought Bill to mind; Bill who was constitutionally lovable, who did not withhold himself, who was born with a face that takes everything (nothing) seriously, and bears the expression of a man eternally in line for something, like a TV taping. Bill always gave his all, which was also all surface and aboveboard; yet Pat was leaving him for his dishonesty, his disingenuousness, which she said made her unlovable.

She told her in-laws that her husband had made his philanderings so obvious to her that she could only suppose he meant them to be discovered. What she did not say directly is that when she made the discoveries, she had reacted to them on her own terms. She had ordered Bill from the house on those earlier occasions, and would do so this time as well. She would make a "scene," even though it is not certain that a scene is what Bill was seeking when he so obviously planted the evidence of his guilt. But it is a scene he would get, nevertheless, because a showdown, for all its stomping and screaming, would still be in Pat's control. It would require no thinking of anybody, no revelations and no changes. Just like Ozzie caught dancing too close to his old flame at the class reunion, Bill Loud was in the doghouse.

The divorce of the Louds, the central action of the series, was a great sadness. Why were we so unmoved? Strangely, we would have been more disturbed by the sight of Harriet going through the same experience, sitting down collectedly with Thorny the neighbor, and painfully unburdening herself of her contempt for the simpleton Ozzie, the tedium of his golf playing and boyish fakery, for David the straight, Wheaties-grown dullard, for Ricky with his narcotized eyes, for her own infernal sandwiches, and their whole vacant, sun-drenched life. Done right, that scene would have stunned us power-fully. But not Pat Loud. When she laid bare her life, it seemed as if she were talking about someone else.

Her evasion was well suited to television. In television's terms it was realism at its best. The main reason television is so offensive an instrument is that it attempts to create its own brand of realism, and to destroy our idea of reality in the process. Ordinarily this effort might not be deemed offensive because in one way or another every-thing that pretends to realism attempts to destroy our idea of reality, and does so, as television does, by substituting its own. What is called "realistic" in literature is always much harsher and tougher than what we recognize as real life, and the "realistic" decisions we are occasionally asked to make are inevitably the ones that disfavor us or belittle our very real imaginations. In television, however, realism represents neither the excessively harsh nor excessively practical. It is our crises, the points of highest intensity, that television calls real, and it seeks to obliterate our own sense of what is real by bombarding us with continuous and undiscriminated excitements until we are unable to tell the exciting from the tedious, the important from the trivial, and ultimately until we are unable to tell what is happening at all.

The Louds' divorce was a real event; it actually occurred. Never was there greater realism on television except in the murders of Oswald and Robert Kennedy. Nevertheless the event seemed staged because it took place within a context in which almost every event was treated with equal fervor. There is no question that the Louds and their children were upset over this business, but in fact appeared no more upset than they had been elated about Deliah's tap dancing solo in school. Nor did the family seem any more or less excited by that than by their casual breakfast conversation that inaugurated the series. Everything the Louds did and apparently felt was always at the same pitch, always an extravaganza. When it came to divorce, therefore, nothing was left to heighten the situation or make it seem that it was anything but another adventure dictated by the script.

This pervasive and predominant sense of melodrama was the heart of the Louds' troubles. The reason each member of the family was interchangeable with some stock counterpart is that the Louds were playing *American Family,* not living it, just as they had played *American Family* long before Craig Gilbert hit upon his brainstorm. I do not mean that the editing of the series produced an artificial dramatization. I mean that the Louds did so themselves, that they created and managed an imitation of life passing for the real thing because it was a careful imitation, accurate to the letter. The Louds were born a TV program waiting to be discovered. They had always thought of themselves as a family show.

The show they finally became was both production and reproduction, the fact and the copy. The desire to reproduce life and art accurately has become vitally important to us in the past few years. In many obvious ways we have substituted reproduction for invention, our lives made plentiful through Xerox. Photographic equipment, particularly the close-up lens, is enormously expensive, yet people buy it up eagerly. The standard for excellence in phonograph recording is "high fidelity," the precise recapturing of sound. Prints and lithographs have become very special and valuable works of art. Tape and cassette recorders are commonplace. Even videotape machines do well—all such mechanisms made and distributed in the interests of the detailed replay of our existence.

An American Family was a very high fidelity recording: as precise and complete a record as one could make of experience. Yet our sense of the product in this instance was that it was not true to life, that it was in fact terribly and infuriatingly false. There is a curious correspondence here with Richard Nixon, who was the real Nixon on tape, and the fake, the liar, when not on tape. This is one reason we sought those tapes so avidly: to see the real person in the nation's trust. The Louds, however, had more integrity than Nixon. They were equally unreal on and off camera, so infinite reproductions of their lives would never produce a variant. Nor were they more or less attractive or successful as reproductions of themselves than they were in the first edition. We could not see the difference; there was no difference to see.

At the first installment of the series Craig Gilbert was careful to point out that he was about to present us with *an,* not *the,* American family. His caveat was both unnecessary and untrue. Nothing could be clearer than that the Louds were chosen for presentation because of their seeming typicality, because they had teenagers, a suburban life, multiple cars, a swimming pool, because they photographed well, and because they were Californians. They were meant to be identifiable as types, and were so. No one knew this better than the Louds. Yet precisely because the externalities of their lives declared them to be *the* American family, they did not know what it is to be *an* American family, or any kind of family for that matter. They knew they were typical, all right, but believed that people are supposed to be typical. Their pathos was not that they resembled the Nelsons, but that they were pursuing the Nelsons' reality.

Where did they get such an idea? From popular culture itself, the culture in which they thrived and by which they were supported. Like the Louds, popular culture carries the illusion of intensity, but allows for no genuine tragedy, heroism, or stature. Like *An American Family*, too, it is to be taken seriously, but is not serious itself. At base it is the culture of the critical mind, the culture by which, if we care to, we may see most clearly our frailties and self-deceptions. High culture demonstrates someone else's nobility. Popular culture plays to our own weaknesses.

The false typicality of the Louds was the cause of their downfall both as family and show. Yet in the framework of our intellectual history the Louds were indeed typically American, heirs in their way to Franklin and Whitman, a landmark in the progress of democracy. The most noticeable feature of the Loud family was their freedom. Bill was the model of free enterprise in his strip-mining equipment business. The children were children of nature, free to do almost anything. Lance was free to choose the clownish and miserable character of his life. Pat was free to let it happen. The Louds were also free to destroy: the land and eventually themselves. Their ultimate exercise of freedom was to be free of each other, yet clearly before their separation was made legal, they had been free of each other, of responsibility, of feeling, consecutive thought, and especially of history.

The Louds were in fact so free that they seemed constitutionally unable to make connections with any things or people. Ironically *An American Family* put a temporary end to that. Here was a context, a work of art, in which such connections could be made possible and with a vengeance. When the Louds finally became the event toward which they had been tending, they did at last reach others, ourselves, which is the function of art, popular and otherwise. What they reached us with, however, was the truth of their falsity, which was a perversion of the democratic ideal in cultural, historical, and personal terms. The Louds were intensely free. Their last great freedom was the freedom to disintegrate, which we wished on them because of their falsity and because of our potential for a similar falsity, of which they served as repugnant and glittering examples.

Robert Warshow asked, what use can we make of our experience in a world of mass culture? The answer, as he knew, is that mass culture produces the art of mass experience, individual experience distended into types and categories that spread over the land confusing and distorting our taste, and threatening our need for authenticity. The striving toward fictional normality shaped the Louds, tore them asunder, and left them naked before us. Their unconscious pretense was what we felt close to, and could not bear.

November 23, 1974

Fathers'
Days

~~~~~~~

THE FIRST TIME I swam—I mean, all by myself, feeling only
Long Island Sound beneath me, and moving, actually moving in
that fearful, unnatural element that could take my five-year-old life
away if I stopped moving—that very first time I did it, my father was
not with me. Yet he had taught me to swim. Day after day at Compo
Beach in Westport, Connecticut, he had stood waist high in the
low-tide kiddy ocean, holding me about the middle like a magician
proving there was no possible way his assistant could be supported,
but supporting me surely, only relaxing his grip by the smallest
degrees as he waited for the moment I would flip off like a tadpole on
my own. As long as he was there, however, that moment never came.
Feeling his support disappear, I would mount an inversely propor-
tional panic, and by the time I was free I was lost.

But when he was away in New York one day, I swam, and immediately hollered to my mother to see what I could do. It was worth a
holler. My parents had had a time with me that summer, especially
after I'd acquired the inner tube, which, while it was no father, could
still support me very well, thanks, way past the teenagers on the dock,
and out toward Spain. Every day at least once, one of my parents
would turn to the other with an implicit "Where is he?" and immedi-

ately look due west for a bump on the horizon. Then up would spring my father, who in those days had plenty of spring. And I would be saved. I loved to watch him come for me, chugging like a sub, I seeing as much pleasure as disapproval in his eyes as he towed me home.

He would have liked to see me take my first swim, I know, and I also know that I never could have swum with him close by, and worse, that I probably unconsciously timed my big moment deliberately to disappoint him, or to show him up—to confound his pride and love. That is the odd way of fathers and sons, a continuous wrestling match in which arms and legs, and victories and defeats are indistinguishable.

Such as the time eight years later, when we were on a short family holiday on Cape Cod, and my father and I agreed to swim out to a float, and back. Being thirteen, I had so much strength, I never thought about it. Yet my father kept up, his dignified crawl beside my splashy riot. When we reached the float, however, his chest was heaving as if in sobs, and so he rested on the float for a while like a beached fish, before very cautiously dog-paddling back, holding on to the rope that led from the shore to the float, and sometimes holding on to me. Mortality, he explained—that being the last thing I wanted to hear.

Or such as the time seven years ago, when I accompanied my eldest son, then six, to a playground. While he shot baskets, I sat reading on a bench at a distance great enough that an outsider might not see the connection between us. So when a couple of big boys came over, they thought my son was unprotected, and took his ball away to play a game on their own. My son did not protest, merely taking his shots whenever the ball rolled his way. And when I called him to me to ask, discreetly, if he wanted me to intervene and get his ball back, he said, "No, Dad, I can handle it"—that also being the last thing I wanted to hear.

But you've got to hear it. Freud said it is a complicated business, the relationship of son to father. And I'm sure it is, since every father's son is different. Yet most of the time it seems a terribly simple thing: The father sees his past and present in the son; the son, his present and future in the old man; and both resent and celebrate their fate.

"You want to be free, don't you, boy. Well, who's free?"

"I am." (Insistently, followed by a million hours of shouting and needling, until the wrestlers, out of breath, slow down at last, and the match, while never totally finished, becomes careful and stately as if the combatants were wrestling in water, or in that dense blue fluid in the jar where the answers float to the top.)

After I was grown, so to speak, and had children of my own, and my father and I had worked out our SALT XXXV, and would meet in the summers, as world powers meet, to discuss this and that—then we were friends. At night, with everyone else asleep, we would sit together in the kitchen of some country house he rented, talking about the past and future, even talking politics, which took a long time to learn to do without explosions, and hearing the Atlantic in the long pauses. When we were ready to turn in, I would put away the glasses, but it was always he who locked the doors.

And when he died a few years ago, and I realized that from then on it would be up to me to lock the doors, I wanted to say: Look, Dad, it was *you* who taught me to swim.

June 11, 1979

Speech for a High School Graduate

YOUR OFFICIAL commencement speaker tackles the big themes, tells you to abjure greed, to play fair, to serve your community, to know thyself. Your more personally devoted commencement speaker agrees with all that.

But he has special wishes for you too—idiosyncratic, of course, what an educated daughter may have come to expect from an oddball. People always said that you resemble him.

What he wishes you first is a love of travel. Travel will hold you back from doting on your troubles, and once you've seen something of the world, you will recognize foreign places as instances of human range. The logic of Athens, the fortitude of London, the grace of Paris—a city for every facet of the mind. He would have you connect travel with an appreciation of the past as well. In Jerusalem recently, he walked the Old City, brushing thousands of years of faith and murder. He would like you to see yourself as history, to wonder what you would have shouted, or at whom, as Jesus struggled up the Via Dolorosa. He hopes that you will husband your own past too. The past means possibility.

He also wishes you a love of animals, which you feel strongly already; he hopes that tenderness lasts and grows. Animals, too, draw people out of excessive self-interest, their existence a statement of need. A dog's eyes search your face for a mystery as deep as God, asking nothing and everything, the way that music operates. He hopes that you always love music, even the noisy boredom you clamp to your ears these days, while he harbors the prayer that in later years will follow Vivaldi and Bix Beiderbecke. If you learn to love jazz, you will have a perpetual source of joy at the ready. Jazz is *serious* joy, much like yourself.

For some reason, he has always favored culs-de-sac, so he hopes you live on one, someday, a neat little cutoff that surprises the city's motions with a pause. Trees on the street; he would like that for you, and low, modest houses so the sky is evident. He hopes that your mornings are absolutely still except for birds, but that the evenings bulge with human outcry, families calling to one another in the darkening hours. He wishes you small particulars: a letter received indicating sudden affection, an exchange of wit with a total stranger, a moment of helpless hilarity, a flash of clarity, the anticipation of reading a detective thriller on a late afternoon in an electric storm.

He hopes that you learn to love work for its own sake. You have to be lucky for that (of course, he wishes you luck), and find a job that grows out of dreams. Something to do with helping others in your case, he should think, since he has seen your natural sympathy at work ever since your smallest childhood and has watched you reach toward your friends with straightforward kindness. Friends, he knows, you will have in abundance. He wishes them *you.*

He hopes that you will always play sports, just as ruthlessly as you play sports now. He hopes that you will always seek the company of books, including the trashy romances; that you will always be curious about the news, as long as you do not mistake the news for life. Believe it or not, he even hopes that you will always be crazy about clothes, particularly once you establish your own source of income—fashion plate, charge plate. You seem to know the difference between vanity and style. On you high style looks good, kid.

Eccentrics: he hopes that you always have plenty of them about you, and few, if any, sound thinkers. Sound thinkers appear on television; sycophants award them prizes for sound thinking. Eccentrics have a sound of their own, like the wild Englishman Lord Berner, who invited a horse to tea, or less extravagantly, Bill Russell, who played basketball to meet only his own standards of excellence. Russell told *his* daughter that he never heard the boos of the crowd because he never heard the cheers—no easy feat in an age pumped up by windbags. Your commencement speaker hopes that you will turn a deaf ear to empty praise as much as to careless blame, that you will scare yourself with your own severity.

Solitude he wishes you as well, but not solitude without a frame. Choose creative times and places to be by yourself. In museums, for instance, where you may confront Vermeer or Velázquez eye to eye. On summer Sundays, too, when you may be alone with the city in its most clear and wistful light: the mirrored buildings angled like kitchen knives, the Hopper stores dead quiet, the city's poor dazed like laundry hung out to dry on their fire escapes. For contrast, seek real country roads, tire-track roads straddling islands of weeds and rolling out into white haze. Such roads are not easy to find these days, but they exist, waiting to trace your solitude back into your memories, your dreams.

You never back down from a fight. Your commencement speaker cheers you for that, and hopes you do not weaken or think safe. Still, it helps to learn that some fights are too small for kindling, and if you must fight out of your weight class, always fight up. Hatred without a fight is self-consuming, and fighting without hatred is purposeless, so regretfully he wishes you some hatred too. But not much, and not to hold too long. There is always more cheapness in the world than you suspect, but less than you believe at the time it touches you. Just don't let the trash build up. And there is much to praise.

Such as your country, which, odd to admit, he hopes that you will always cherish, that you will acknowledge the immeasurable good in the place as well as the stupidities and wrongs. If public indignation over the scandals in Washington proves anything, it is that Americans remain innocent enough to believe in government by laws, and to be angered by deceit in power. He hopes that you retain and nurture that innocence, which is your country's saving grace.

In general, he wishes that you see the world generously, that you take note of and rail against all the Lebanons of violence, the Africas of want, but that you also rear back and bless the whole. This is not as hard to do as it may seem. Concentrate on details, and embrace what you fear. The trick is to love the world as it is, the way a father loves a daughter, helpless and attached as he watches her stretch, bloom, rise past his tutelage to her independent, miraculous ascendancy. But you must never let go entirely, as he will never let you go. You gave birth to each other, and you commence together. Good-bye, my girl.

June 29, 1987

The Aged Mother

A NOTHER MOTHER'S DAY down, the awkward ceremony
survived. Loaded like a German fruitcake, you smiled wide as
a freeway, wobbled under tulips, chocolates, a witty card, wished her
all the happiness in the world and told all the old stories. Wasn't it
fun? Wasn't she pleased, the ancient matriarch who, in a time so
distant that it seems made up, slid you out soaked, milky, blind into
the sheets? On her designated "day," that same panting, sweating girl
sat dry as a museum bone, a china plate receiving alms.

You remember her as reckless, consenting to squat to catch what
you called your Feller fastball: clumsy, imperiled dame. Young mothers have the constitutions of gaming stewards, the organizational
ferocity of sergeants, show an abundance of guts and style. (Didn't
she look the bee's knees in those swishy navy blue dresses of the
1940s?) Want to go to the park, Mom? Yes. Want to watch me do a
jackknife dive? Yes. Sure. Can do. Can read *Tom Sawyer* aloud at
bedside. Can tie sneakers. Can poach an egg, hold a job, do long
division, mend porcelain, ride bikes, chase dogs, go.

But these days the eyes water like a weak opinion, and the skin on
her hand feels like pie dough rolled on an enamel tabletop. (Let me
give you a hand, Mom.) A Whistler pose, she is content to sit staring
outward much of the time, as if on the deck of a Cunard liner, or to

dip into that biography of Abigail Adams you gave her (a lady for a lady), at manageable intervals. Television interests her not, except occasionally the nature shows that PBS specializes in. Motionless before the mating eland. The memory clicks on and off. The older the anecdote, the clearer in detail. Typical of her much analyzed years, she will forget the sentence before last but in the next will come up with a name from 1923 and a Gershwin lyric that, once sung, swims her back into a world she really occupied.

In the world as it is, she seems only to have the place of a designation. The Aged Mother. Like a painting of the aged mother, or a play called *The Aged Mother,* or an essay in a magazine. Swathed in the shapeless dress, the indefinite hairdo, she has become something to be noticed and attended, as if she were forever on the verge of vanishing lest one remind oneself to look in on Mother. "And how's your mother?"

Is the woman still a mother? Impertinent question. You dared not ask it on Mother's Day pumped up with bonhomie, but now a few weeks afterward, in the cooler hours, the problem takes a tomblike shape. In terms of technical, logical definition, can a mother be a mother without doing a mother's things? At her advanced stage of life is she supposed to function institutionally, monumentally, like mother nature, mother wit? Mother Russia: perhaps she is to be seen as Yeats's country for old men. Mother earth: big as all outdoors. Not her, the featherweight fossil in your arms, as you help her up a step. Who, what, does she mother these days?

You could say she mothers the past, not yours alone, but a whole world gone. She superintends Coolidge, Chaplin, the Charleston. (She danced the Charleston.) Or that she mothers the future, herself the future to which you begin to resign yourself as your own eyes blear a bit and breaks in the bones take eternity to heal. There she sits in old age ahead of you, still mothering experience, if only by example. Can do.

But the fact is that the problem is not hers, it's yours, the designation yours: the aged mother. To the person in question, she is the aged woman, the aged teacher, the aged Charleston dancer. Motherhood was merely part of a swooping, long, and complicated ride that included a sizable fraction of American history, with vast tracts of Europe tossed in. She reads her category in your attentiveness, but privately she has other fish to fry. Who, what, does she mother now? Your attentiveness. Still the center of your universe, you assume that the only thing she really wanted out of life was to play catch in the park with you.

There comes a time when one learns to recognize that the people to whom one is related are not usefully defined by that relationship and are actually diminished by the act. One learns this with children first. Something said by the child offhand, an unusual gesture, an unfamiliar fact, and suddenly you recognize that the creature you cuddled seemingly a moment ago has been off on a life of its own. It achieved its education elsewhere. It has some weird ideas about social justice. The transformation is alarming. The favorite son, the my-little-girl is a stranger, an impostor in the house, until you pipe down, readjust your vision and see that a different sort of relationship is possible, one that requires of you real imagination, a true athlete's reflexes; you have to start listening to what the creature says. Gradually, it comes to you that the mind, even one as heavily padlocked as yours, is capable of affection and judgment all at once, though you look as if you've seen a ghost.

With parents that process of recognition seems more difficult, perhaps because as parents grow older, they need you more, and more basically, and need reinforces the sense of family. Or one may simply wish to retain a parent to retain one's childhood, to establish a comforting mythology in which, however dignified and responsible one feels, still there is the illusion that somewhere the elder presides, like a god. As long as she is enthroned as Mother, you do not have to ascend the genealogy and command the family line.

But see how huge she stands on her own two feet: a colossus, Queen Lear exulting in a private language about ripeness being all. Motherhood was an achievement, but so is age. Is it not time to look at the woman squarely for the life she led outside you? Before her inaccessibility gets out of hand, is it not time to celebrate her other days?

The tulips you brought her have a capacity to curl and lose their body after a while. You may not approve of their progress, but change is not in your control. The aged mother might like you to know that, might wish to teach you to love things as they are, but sometimes she forgets what she means to say, and besides, it is impossible to be severe with a child who means so well, and who will weep like a baby at her death. She smiles instead. Her day gone once again (thank God), she returns to her evening and to the image of that night she glowed like a plum and swept your father in her arms.

June 1, 1987

Introduction
to the
Reader

MY FATHER AND I were seated next to each other in identical red chairs, watching the seven o'clock news, when George Wallace came on. This was in 1968, before Wallace became a man-to-be-reckoned-with in the Democratic Party. In those days he was simply a fear monger with sweet talk. When he addressed the nation, as he did for a full three minutes that night, you knew that you were getting pure hate and death, unsullied by platform politics. My father, not taking his eyes from the screen, thought for a while, and said, "Good. A few years ago that man would not have been allowed out of his state. Now, thanks to you liberals, he's a television star."

When my father said things like that he sounded exactly like Edward G. Robinson. Until his last years he looked and carried himself like Edward G. Robinson as well—not Little Ricco, but a cross between Dr. Clitterhouse and the criminology professor of *The Woman in the Window*. He was small and stately. For most of the year he wore three-piece suits with triangular handkerchiefs and black oxfords from Brooks Brothers with no tooling on the leather. He wore gray felt hats from Cavanagh's, until they went out of business, and complained that he didn't know where he would get hats as good in the future. For a few summers he sported a straw "skimmer," but eventually gave it up as impractical. My father believed in hats as signs of civilization.

The sight of him sitting at the television set was at first preposterous, then commonplace. He had never wanted a set in our house, and resentfully accepted our hulking Motorola from a grateful patient when I was thirteen. He started out not watching at all, strictly limiting the viewing hours of my brother and me. Later he would emerge from his reading or writing to watch the late-night talk shows: Jerry Lester, Steve Allen, and Jack Paar. Sometimes we would watch the Knicks together, *Playhouse 90, Studio One,* and *Your Show of Shows.* By the time I was seventeen and he, fifty, he had narrowed his viewing to *Perry Mason,* which remained his favorite long after it, too, went out of business.

On Saturday nights, while my father watched *Perry Mason,* I was usually at the bathroom mirror making an exquisite study of my face. The fact that the part in my hair, which took fifteen minutes to find, might have been mislocated after all, troubled me. I wondered if my eyes were indeed blue, as I always believed, or did I not detect the finest sliver of green radiating from the pupils? I had no worry about the proportions of my face; the distances from the hairline to the top of the nose, from the top of the nose to the upper lip, and from the upper lip to the bottom of the chin were equal. Yet there was an undoubted bend in the nose. In a smile my lips appeared asymmetrical.

I was perversely happy to see my father enjoy *Perry Mason* because it established my critical faculties as superior to his. The gargantuan figures of Mason, his assistant Paul Drake, Lieutenant Tragg, Della Street, Mason's secretary, and the district attorney, Hamilton Burger (a name from heaven), were ridiculous to me. The format, trivial. The fact that Mason could guess and intuit things for which we had no evidence, that he could point to the murderer like a compass needle at the last minute every week, that apparent guilt was always innocence and apparent innocence, always guilt—these things, I told my father, proved the show boring and inaccurate. My father ignored my analyses the way in later years he ignored my children's television-inspired harassments against his smoking.

No one was more immovable than my father when he concentrated. One evening he yelled at my mother because she had said "Of course" to cousins of his from Buffalo who had phoned to ask if they could drop over. Except for his parents, my father did not admit the existence of his relatives. Moreover nobody ever dropped over on my father. He vowed not to speak a word the entire evening, a vow he kept by sitting on a bench in the living room and whistling show tunes to himself in low and ghostly tones. My father's cousin, his wife, and two daughters sat like dolls on the couch, staring forward. My mother fluttered in an occasional question between the vast silences. My mind straddled embarrassment and hilarity. My father whistled "Embraceable You."

The world of my father extended from Ninth Street and Second Avenue, where he was born, on November 29, 1907, to our home in Gramercy Park between Twentieth and Twenty-first streets, to Doctors Hospital, on Eighty-first Street and East End Avenue, where he was president of the Medical Board, to his office on Eighty-fifth Street and Fifth Avenue. He taught at New York Medical College; did clinical work at Metropolitan Hospital and before that at City Hospital. I believe that he did his residency at Montefiore Hospital in the Bronx. Except for summers he never lived outside New York City. Except for Bruce Catton, Gibbon, and *The New York Times,* which he despised, he read nothing unconnected with medicine. The few social events he attended were professional meetings or events. The few guests he and my mother entertained were doctors.

With all this he never liked the practice of medicine very much. He had a bent for research and wrote a good deal, including two books, on diseases of the chest. He preferred doing pieces that involved the history of medicine because they allowed more rhetorical flourishes. He would have preferred to become a journalist. As a kid he had been a copy boy on *The New York Herald Tribune* (at night; in the daytime he sold hot dogs in the Polo Grounds), but knew that there would be no money or safety in writing. Either he knew or his parents told him.

My father's father had been a professor of romance languages in Heidelberg and continued as a teacher at Columbia when he came from Germany in the 1890s. Grandpa had an unusual mind. Because he was suited only for contemplation, he decided to become a businessman, first founding a school for secretaries and, when that failed, turning the rooms he held into meeting places for various and curious clubs. My first summer job was working for Grandpa, where nothing ever happened. I killed time by writing poems, doing the *Times* crossword puzzle, and shooting chalk out the fifth-story window. My grandfather would spend the day going from borough to borough to interview candidates for janitorial positions, and would phone me at two- or three-hour intervals. "Hello, Rog. Anything new?" "No, Grandpa. Nothing new." Then he would hang up without saying good-bye; too busy.

My father said little when his father died. He attended to everything, as he always did, including the sixteen years back taxes that Grandpa had neglected to pay. Then he seemed merely to let his father pass into inconsequential history, just as he had let pass his childhood, poverty, the old neighborhood, Judaism, and most things. For God-knows-what reason I used to loiter in his old neighborhood and insisted on a bar mitzvah in the oldest orthodox synagogue in New York. I laid tefillin, tying the little black boxes to my arm and my forehead with straps that traversed my body like black snakes. But formal religion was insincere on my part. My father knew it was insincere and let it pass as well.

He made no sudden moves, my father; his intimacies, because infrequent, were surprising. There was the time he and I were lolling on one side of a swimming pool watching my mother read story after story to my four-year-old brother on the opposite side of the pool. "She has remarkable patience," my father said with sudden tenderness and admiration. There was the time we were riding in his car together a few months after his first heart attack, when he confided to me that he was afraid of physical pain.

But most of his thoughts were not shared with anybody. He was in no way taciturn and often talked a blue streak, particularly on his pet hates of Mayor Lindsay, Ramsey Clark, and medicare; yet I rarely believed that he was thinking seriously about these things as he talked. At the same time I never knew anyone more precise with details. When my wife and I were planning to visit one of the summer homes he rented on Long Island, my father called three or four times with explicit driving directions. He mailed us a map. Even so when we drove down from Cambridge at dusk he was standing in the driveway with a flashlight to make sure that we had the right house.

Here are some aphorisms and habitual phrases associated with my father:

1. Never go out with anyone from the Bronx. (This became Brooklyn if I was considering taking out a Brooklyn girl, and, in that variant, was originally and most heatedly applied to my father's brother's wife.)
2. If you lie down with dogs, you get up with fleas. (Used usually

as a forewarning concerning other kids, but occasionally as a maxim after the fact.)

3. The person who knows what he wants is way ahead of all others.
4. Never trust a Hungarian. (A reference to the Gabor sisters.)
5. I will, in a pig's eye. (Or, "you will, in a pig's eye." Said with more finality than nightfall.)
6. Now you're cooking with gas. (An exhortation used not to indicate that I had actually achieved something, but that I had rounded the bend, was at long last headed in the right direction.)
7. Nothing good ever came out of New Jersey. (Different from number 1 by degree; there were no exceptions.)

Were it not for one boy, who almost never came to school, I would have ranked dead last in each of my high school classes. My father concealed his rage in disgust, or sometimes vice versa. Because of indolence, a word I learned from my report cards, television periodically was forbidden me. Pretending to study, I spent most nights playing silent basketball in my room or kneeling on the window seat, staring at the lights in other buildings. On Sundays I walked the city. Sundays were terrible for television, anyway. I could not bear the politeness of Alistair Cooke and his *Omnibus*: the Rodeo ballets, dramatic readings in tuxedos, and other chitchat of the dead.

On Sundays when I was very young my father would take me up to the hospital with him in his Lincoln Zephyr. I would sit idly in the hospital waiting room, furnished by Sloane's, for over an hour (although in the joke between us, my father always promised twenty minutes at the outs). Afterwards we would go to a drugstore uptown and have sandwiches at the counter. Once on the way home we stopped at Grand Central Station—it must have been 1944—to watch the troop trains. I confuse that day with the movie *Grand Central Station,* its swirling crowds and missed appointments.

Sometimes on those early Sundays we all would go to movies in the afternoon. *The Maltese Falcon* (re-released). *The Asphalt Jungle.* My father liked mysteries, but he loved musicals and musical comedy. These later became the bases of his singing and dancing spasms, which could be triggered by anything by Cole Porter. One year he got hold of a Lester Lanin record of Cole Porter favorites, which he foisted on the phonograph nearly every night. To "Night and Day" or "Silk Stockings" or "You're the Top" my father would dance like a basketball center pivoting, occasionally do an arm-flap at some private signal, and, since he knew no lyrics beyond the first three words of any song, sang da da da to everything.

Family reaction to the singing and dancing spasms poised between delight (shown by expressions of dismay) and impatience, the latter increasing as my father would insist on completing every number. What was funny for ten or fifteen seconds became outrageously tedious at the end of four minutes, but no amount of disapproval would stop him. Puffing and wheezing my father would finish his last da, bow, and turn off the machine to an assault of booing and razzberries.

The Gramercy Park Association plants tulips in hedge squares every April. The old park trees, in their deliberate variety, bloom like huge broccoli. The birdhouses are repainted. The aged scions of the neighborhood take walks again and comment loudly on the pleasantness of the air. Here my parents settled thirty-five years ago. My father had his first office here, and his first patient, an Indian with a stomachache who happened to notice my father's shingle.

Neighborhood merchants treated my father reverently. His manner with them, a mixture of the officious and confidential, seemed to encourage a military attitude toward him. They mentioned him to me as if he were of another age, as if we all were discussing the master of the house. My father's sense of privacy was the key; deeply uninterested in most of the life about him, he walked and spoke as if he had been authorized to run that life. He berated traffic cops with such ferocity that they apologized to him for tie-ups.

Seeking total privacy in the summers, my father rented Southampton "cottages" for family vacations. These cottages, on three or four acres, had twenty bedrooms, forty rooms in all, and backed on the Atlantic. The cost of the rentals was astounding, but worth it to him; both the quiet and absurdity were worth it. He spent the days sitting on vast lawns, reading and dozing, or arranging a project such as getting the car washed. In the past few years my children provided the whoops and giggles which my brother and I had supplied in earlier summers. From a distance we looked like the Roosevelts at play: the stately fun of great, rich families.

My father never was rich, yet never conveyed the impression of being anything else. I once overheard him complain to my mother that he had been forced to sell a movie camera given him in order to pay the cleaning lady. His extravagances were masterfully well-timed. Hired chauffeurs drove my parents to us on visits to Massachusetts and Washington. Occasionally hired chauffeurs were also used to transport my father's luggage. Yet these were not extravagances in the gaudy sense. My father knew the exact limits of his energy, as if by land survey, and knew that a livelihood depended on his energy. He saw to it that this was so.

He was a genius at the art of leverage. As I grew to be a bigger and stronger kid, I kept wanting to test my physical strength against his. His one expressed concern was how long he could afford to be hospitalized if I hit him with my full weight; so when I lunged at him, he simply grabbed my fingers and bent them back. He got so good at this eventually that he didn't have to stir from his chair to bring me to my knees.

My son takes great pleasure in this story. He likes the image of me brought to my knees and the image of my father triumphant. My father could not stop doing things for my son and daughter. Last year he arranged a trade of baseball cards between my son and the son of one of his colleagues. For my daughter he bought a gold bracelet when she was three, a nightgown from Dior when she was five. He talked to them both for long periods. When we visited New York, he fixed toast for them.

I have a photograph of my father as a new father holding me, two weeks old, on a level with his eyes. His face is serious and scientific, the stare of a man trying to read the watermark in a stamp. They named me Roger, but my father never sounded comfortable with that name, and, like his father, called me Rog. Although I never would have addressed him by it, his name, Milton, made me uncomfortable as well. These were not the names of people, but of eras.

I have a photograph of my mother and father on their honeymoon in December 1932. They are standing on the Atlantic City boardwalk, my mother smiling, dressed in a slim sable coat and a close-fitting cloth hat, arm in arm with my father, not smiling, in a dark overcoat, gloves, and a derby. I have a later photograph of my father in whites, holding a tennis racket, again not smiling. I have one with him smiling: on a fishing trip off Stonybrook, Long Island, with his doctor cronies, in 1948. The last photo of him I have has him standing in his dining room between the television set and my daughter's toy rabbit. The rabbit has on a green tam-o'-shanter, and my father is not smiling.

That photograph was taken this past Christmas, one month before he died. I see in it now the deep creases of his face, sunken and pulled

424 ❦ ROGER ROSENBLATT

down, no longer the face of Edward G. Robinson. I see in it, too, or read into it, the toll of his fear. He himself pointed out to me the diseases of the aged one can spot in Rembrandt's paintings. Shortly after New Year's he was hospitalized for congestive heart failure, the third attack in eight years. We talked long distance in the evenings once he was out of the intensive care unit, about the advisability of his retirement and a book he might do on the history of medicine.

The fourth heart attack, which killed him, happened a few days after he had been released from the hospital and was on his way to his cardiologist. His heart stopped as he entered the hired car. My mother and the chauffeur brought him to the nearest hospital, where he lived, technically, for another fifty hours. His tie, suit, and all his clothes were cut from his body. Tubes arced from his arms and mouth. Only his eyes moved, from corner to corner.

July 19, 1975

ABOUT THE AUTHOR

ROGER ROSENBLATT is a contributing editor and essayist for *Vanity Fair, The New Republic, Family Circle,* and *Men's Journal,* and is a regular essayist on *The MacNeil/Lehrer NewsHour* on PBS. Mr. Rosenblatt holds a Ph.D. in English and American Literature from Harvard University, where he taught literature and creative writing from 1963–1973.

He has written four books: *Black Fiction* (Harvard University Press, 1974); *Children of War* (Anchor Press/Doubleday, 1983); *Witness: The World Since Hiroshima* (Little, Brown, 1985), and *Life Itself: Abortion in the American Mind* (Random House, 1992).

Mr. Rosenblatt lives in New York City with his wife, Ginny, their daughter, Amy, and son, John. Their oldest son, Carl, is married and lives in Washington, D.C.

ABOUT THE TYPE

This book was set in Sabon, a typeface designed by the well-known German typographer Jan Tschichold (1902–74). Sabon's design is based on the original letterforms of Claude Garamond and was created specifically to be used for three sources: foundry type for hand composition, Linotype, and Monotype. Tschichold named his typeface for the famous Frankfurt typefounder Jacques Sabon, who died in 1580.